Running

Microsoft®
Office:mac
2001

**Steven Schwartz
and Robert Correll**

PUBLISHED BY
Microsoft Press
A Division of Microsoft Corporation
One Microsoft Way
Redmond, Washington 98052-6399

Library of Congress Cataloging-in-Publication Data
Schwartz, Steven.
    Running Microsoft Office 2001 for Mac / Steven Schwartz, Robert Correll.
       p. cm.
    Includes index.
    ISBN 0-7356-0971-3
    1. Microsoft Office. 2. Business--Computer programs. I. Correll, Robert. II. Title.

  HF5548.4.M525 S383 2001
  005.369--dc21

                                                  00-053303

Printed and bound in the United States of America.

1 2 3 4 5 6 7 8 9   QWE   6 5 4 3 2 1

Distributed in Canada by Penguin Books Canada Limited.

A CIP catalogue record for this book is available from the British Library.

Microsoft Press books are available through booksellers and distributors worldwide. For further information about international editions, contact your local Microsoft Corporation office or contact Microsoft Press International directly at fax (425) 936-7329. Visit our Web site at mspress.microsoft.com. Send comments to *mspinput@microsoft.com*.

Acquisitions Editors: Christey Bahn, Alex Blanton
Project Editor: Wendy Zucker
Technical Editor: Jim Fuchs

To Sheri, my sorority girl
—*Steve Schwartz*

For Anne, my wonderful wife
In remembrance of Beetlejuice, our faithful cat
—*Bob Correll*

Acknowledgments

We would like to gratefully acknowledge the assistance provided us by the following individuals:

- David Fugate and Matt Wagner of Waterside Productions, Inc., for their efforts as our literary agents

- Irving Kwong of Microsoft for his valuable insight as the Office 2001 for Mac Product Manager

- Wendy Zucker, Christey Bahn, Kristen Weatherby, Sandra Haynes, Shannon Leuma, and Alex Blanton of Microsoft Press for their tireless work and publishing expertise

- Nancy Wagner and Jim Fuchs for their excellent technical editing skills

- The Macintosh Business Unit at Microsoft for their input

Bob would also like to express the following personal acknowledgements:

I continually thank God for all things. He steadfastly loves, supports, protects, and strengthens my wife and me. Anne, my partner in life, is a talented, beautiful, funny, and caring woman. She picks me up when I feel down and helps me get back on track when I need a little correction. I also want to express my special thanks and warm regards to Keri Walker of Apple Computer, Inc., for her valuable assistance. Without her kind help and special expertise, I couldn't have written this book.

Chapters at a Glance

Table of Contents

Introduction

Welcome to *Running Microsoft Office 2001 for Mac*, the official guide to Microsoft Office 2001. Here you'll find the information you need to run all the programs in the Microsoft Office 2001 suite: Microsoft Word, Microsoft Excel, Microsoft PowerPoint, and Microsoft Entourage.

How This Book Is Organized

Running Microsoft Office 2001 for Mac is divided into seven parts. Each part is devoted to a specific Office application (such as Microsoft Word) or how the applications relate to one another. Every part has several chapters, each devoted to a discrete topic.

The parts cover the following material:

- **Part I: Microsoft Office 2001 Essentials** Chapters 1 through 3 introduce you to Office, tell you about the new features introduced in Office 2001, and explain basic operating procedures (such as creating and saving files, using the toolbars, and getting help). Chapter 4 shows you how to get the most from the new centralized Address Book in Office.

> **NOTE**
>
> *Running Microsoft Office 2001 for Mac* was written as a reference book. As such, you can skip around in it as much as you want. However, we strongly recommend that you read or at least glance through the material in Part I. To avoid repetition, common procedures—such as printing and using the toolbars—are covered only in Part I.

- **Part II: Microsoft Word** Word is unquestionably the most well-known and frequently used application in the Office suite. Using Word, you can create impressive memos, letters, and reports. Because Word shares many features with desktop publishing programs, you can use its advanced formatting features to add tables, graphics, and movies to your documents.

- **Part III: Microsoft Excel** In Part III, you'll learn how to use Excel, a spreadsheet application that supports multiple worksheets (organized in workbooks), charting, databases, and list management.

- **Part IV: Microsoft Entourage** Entourage is a new addition to the Office suite. It's based on Microsoft Outlook Express for the Macintosh and Microsoft Outlook for Microsoft Windows, so it's a powerful e-mail application and newsgroup reader.

- **Part V: Microsoft PowerPoint** You can use PowerPoint to create business and education presentations and slide shows—complete with notes, special effects, animations, and transitions between slides.

- **Part VI: Mastering Microsoft Office 2001** After you've had some time to master the basics of the core applications in Office, you'll want to turn here. The chapters in Part VI explain how to set up Office in a multi-user environment, create links between information in the applications, use the Office Internet and Web features, and exchange data between other programs and Office.

Who This Book Is For

Running Microsoft Office 2001 for Mac is for anyone who wants to learn the essentials of using Microsoft Office 2001.

It doesn't matter whether you're new to Office or a veteran user, or whether this is your first Mac or your seventh. All that's assumed is that you are familiar with the basics of operating a Macintosh—that is, you know how to use a mouse, how to choose commands from menus, and so on. And if you've used other versions of Office or any of its applications (Word, Excel, PowerPoint, Internet Explorer, or Outlook Express), you'll find that our step-by-step explanations of using the new features in Office 2001 will help you get up to speed quickly.

Conventions Used in This Book

The following sections explain the few important conventions you should understand when reading this book.

Menu Commands and Keyboard Shortcuts

To choose a command from a menu (in Office, the Finder, or in any other application), you click the menu name (such as Edit) to open it, drag down to select the desired command, and release the mouse button to select the command.

Many Office 2001 commands also have keyboard shortcuts that you can press, rather than choose the command from a menu. A *keyboard shortcut* is a combination of keys that you press together—normally, a character key (a letter, number, or symbol) in combination with one or more modifier keys (Shift, Option, Command, or Control). To type a keyboard shortcut, you press and hold down the modifier key (or keys) and then—while still holding down the modifier keys—type the character key. The table below shows the modifier keys as they appear in text, on your keyboard, and in menus.

Key Representations.

In Text	On Keyboard	In Menu
Shift	Shift	⇧
Command	⌘	⌘
Option	Option	⌥
Control	Control	Used in combination with mouse clicks, rather than menus

When discussing menu commands, we list the related keyboard shortcuts such as ⌘-P, where holding down the ⌘ key while pressing P is the equivalent of choosing the Print command from the File menu.

Web Page Addresses

Web page addresses are displayed in the form *www.microsoft.com* or *macconnection.com*—that is, only the characters that you must type into your Web browser's Address box are listed. (Since you'll probably be using Microsoft Internet Explorer 5 as your browser, you never have to type the *http:* prefix. If you omit it, the program will fill it in for you.)

More About Office 2001 for Mac

For product updates, important virus information, support for Office 2001 (and for previous versions), and free downloads of Microsoft Internet Explorer 5 and Microsoft Outlook Express 5, visit the MacTopia Web site at *www.microsoft.com/mac*. You'll also find a calendar of events, including seminars and expos devoted to Macintosh users of Microsoft products.

Contacting Us

Every effort has been made to ensure the accuracy of this book. If you have comments or questions, you can contact the authors via e-mail at *MSOff2001@hotmail.com*.

- For questions/comments concerning our coverage of Entourage or Internet Explorer, include *Attn: Steve* in the Subject line.

- For questions/comments concerning our coverage of Word, Excel, or PowerPoint, include *Attn: Bob* in the Subject line.

- To contact Microsoft Press concerning this book, send e-mail to *MSInput@Microsoft.com* or a letter to Microsoft Press, Attn: Running Series Editor, One Microsoft Way, Redmond, WA 98052-6399.

- For product-related questions and support, open the Help menu in any Office program and choose Help On The Web.

Please note that product support isn't offered through the above addresses.

PART I

Microsoft Office 2001 Essentials

CHAPTER 1

Introducing
Microsoft Office 2001

Since you have this book, it's safe to assume that you also have your own copy of Microsoft Office 2001. In this introductory chapter, you'll learn a bit about the tasks you can accomplish with each Office application. And if you're already familiar with a previous version of Office, you'll want to read about the new features that are introduced in Office 2001.

The Office Applications: Picking the Right Tool for the Job

Office 2001 is a suite of five interrelated Macintosh applications: Microsoft Word, Excel, PowerPoint, Entourage, and Internet Explorer. If you're unfamiliar with them, here are the types of tasks you can perform with each Office application:

? SEE ALSO

Word is discussed in Part II, "Microsoft Word."

- **Word** is an advanced word processing program that you can use to create impressive, formatted documents of any length—from brief memos to complete books.

? SEE ALSO

Excel is discussed in Part III, "Microsoft Excel."

- **Excel** is a spreadsheet application. (The documents that you create with Excel and other spreadsheet programs are referred to as *workbooks*.) You can use Excel to make complex calculations, manage lists, and chart data.

? SEE ALSO

Entourage is discussed in Part IV, "Microsoft Entourage."

- **Entourage** is an application for sending and receiving electronic mail (commonly called *e-mail*), as well as for reading messages from and posting to newsgroups. Combining the best elements of Microsoft Outlook and Outlook Express, Entourage is a powerful Internet application that adds a few new wrinkles of its own, such as task linking and an integrated Calendar and Address Book.

? SEE ALSO

PowerPoint is discussed in Part V, "Microsoft PowerPoint."

- **PowerPoint** allows you to create presentations (in the form of slide shows, for example) that contain advanced features such as within-slide animations, between-slide transitions, speaker notes, and audio narration.

- **Internet Explorer 5** is an application known as a *Web browser* that you can use to view and download information from the Internet or company intranet.

New Features in Office 2001

While Office 2001 offers many new features, the following are some of the most important ones. To help you get quickly up to speed with the changes introduced in Office 2001, each new feature includes a cross-reference to the chapters in which it is discussed.

New General Features

The following features and enhancements can be found in all Office applications—that is, they aren't specific to a single program.

- The Project Gallery (see Chapter 2, "Microsoft Office Basics") serves as a general interface for opening new and existing documents and templates in Word, Excel, PowerPoint, and Entourage. Unless disabled, the Project Gallery window appears whenever you launch an Office application by double-clicking its icon or an alias of its icon.

- If you routinely (or occasionally) share your files with Windows users, a simple click on the Append File Extension check box in the Save dialog box (see Chapter 2) will ensure that the file is recognizable on a PC and can be opened by Office 2000 users.

- You can use the floating Formatting Palette to apply formatting to text or objects in Word, Excel, or PowerPoint. By combining the most popular formatting commands in a single palette (see Figure 1-1), Office 2001 saves you innumerable trips to the toolbars and menus.

FIGURE 1-1.

The Formatting Palette contains all the major formatting options in one convenient window

- Office 2001 provides extensive support for drag-and-drop (see Chapter 2), a Macintosh system software feature that enables you to drag text or objects from one point in a document to another, from one Office document to another, between open documents in different drag-and-drop enabled applications, and between the desktop and Office documents.

■ Office 2001 also provides support for several key Apple technologies (available in OS 8.5 and higher), such as Navigation Services (improved dialog boxes for opening and saving files), QuickTime transitions and import file filters, and Color Picker.

■ Although the Address Book (see Chapter 4, "Using the Address Book") and the new Calendar (see Chapter 18, "The Calendar and Information Management Features") are parts of Entourage, all Office applications can access them. You can quickly add names and addresses from the Address Book to letters in Word, for example. You can also flag any Office file for follow-up on a later date, linking it to the Calendar.

■ When you install Office, one step is to create an "identity" for yourself (see Chapter 4)—providing information, such as your name, work and home addresses, phone numbers, and e-mail addresses. Office applications can automatically use your identity information for tasks such as filling out forms and templates.

■ The Clip Gallery is accessible from any Office application, enabling you to drag images into your documents easily. You can add your own images to the Clip Gallery, create categories to organize them, and assign keywords to the images (enabling you to find them quickly). The Clip Gallery is also linked to Microsoft's Clip Gallery Live at *cgl.microsoft.com/clipgallerylive/ default.asp?nEULA=1&nInterface=0* (see Figure 1-2), from which you can download additional free images to use in your documents.

FIGURE 1-2.

In addition to the Clip Art that was copied to your hard disk during the installation of Office 2001 and the Value Pack, you can download additional images from Microsoft's Web site

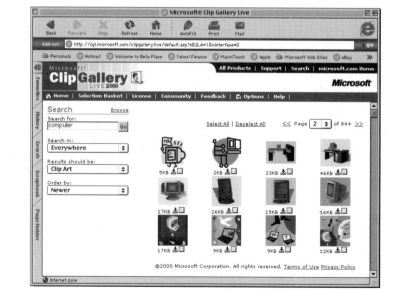

■ Because images are so frequently included in documents, Office 2001 now provides support for connected digital cameras and scanners, enabling you to transfer or scan an image directly into a document. Office also provides image editing tools, as well as support for any installed Adobe Photoshop plug-ins.

■ The Office Clipboard—a feature found in Office 2000—is now available for the Macintosh (see Chapter 3, "Understanding the Office Interface"). Each time you cut or copy an item in an Office document, the cut/copied item is added to the Clipboard and is made available for pasting into any open Office document. Items can be pasted individually or all at once.

■ The Encarta World English Dictionary can be used to look up the definitions of words. The dictionary is accessed from the Tools menu or by Control-clicking a word in your document and choosing Define.

■ Office applications make it simple to create Web pages from documents via the Save As Web Page command (see Chapter 30, "Office 2001 and the Web"). You can also preview the Web pages onscreen prior to saving. In Excel, you can export specific worksheet ranges or charts as Web pages, as well as automate the exporting process. Entourage users can publish their calendar as a Web page. And PowerPoint presentations can be exported and viewed in a Web browser.

New Features in Word

Word 2001 contains the following new features and enhancements:

■ Word has several new and improved Internet features (see Chapter 29, "Linking Environments via Linking and Embedding"). You can create a Web (HTML) page from any Word document, enabling you to publish it on the World Wide Web or a company intranet. Pages can incorporate hyperlinks and *Web objects*, such as check boxes and scrolling text. Using the Web Page Preview command, you can see what the current document would look like as a Web page without leaving Word (eliminating the need to jump back and forth between Word and a browser).

■ In order to make Word easier for new users, you can now click *anywhere* on a page that you wish to type, so long as you're in Page Layout view. For example, if you want to type something in the middle of a blank page, simply double-click the spot where you want to position the next bit of text. Word automatically inserts the blank lines and tabs needed for you to reach that part of the page. Similarly, you can create a header or footer by clicking in the header or footer area of the page—without having to choose the Headers and Footers command.

■ Formerly known as Mail Merge, the new Data Merge Manager simplifies the task of creating a mail or e-mail merge (see Chapter 9, "Special Tasks in Word," and Chapter 31, "Configuring Office in a Multi-User Setting").

■ Tables in Word 2001 (see Chapter 8, "Adding Tables, Columns, and Graphics") are more flexible than in previous releases. Support is provided for *nested tables* (tables within tables), and there are additional table border options.

■ The current word count for every document is now displayed in the status bar at the bottom of the document window.

■ AutoCorrect works more intelligently, automatically fixing more common typing errors.

■ Word 2001 now supports *picture bullets* (bullet symbols that are actual pictures, rather than typed characters). Bullets such as marbles and planets are often used in Web pages. Now you can use picture bullets in the same manner in your Word documents (see Chapter 7, "Formatting Text and Documents").

New Features in Excel

Excel 2001 contains the following new features and enhancements:

■ While Excel is an outstanding program for handling complex formulas and calculations, many people routinely use it to manage simple lists that require few—if any—calculations. Recognizing this, Microsoft has added new features that enhance Excel's list management capabilities. The new List Manager (see Chapter 13, "Selecting, Moving, Finding, and Sorting Information") automatically recognizes when you are attempting to create a list and then offers to let you use List Manager, which creates a table with persistent headers and pop-up menus that enable you to quickly enter previously entered data and sort the list by a chosen column, as shown in Figure 1-3.

FIGURE 1-3.

When you define a range as a list, you can sort the list by clicking the appropriate column header

- When typing in a cell, Excel uses an improved AutoComplete feature (see Chapter 12, "Entering and Formatting Data") to list items that match the current input. If you see a choice that matches what you're typing, you can pick it from the list.

- A new calculator (see Chapter 12 and Chapter 14, "Creating Charts and Using Functions") is provided that assists users in creating and editing formulas.

- Excel 2001 supports the Euro currency.

New Features in Entourage

Entourage is a new addition to the Office suite. Based on a combination of Outlook Express and Microsoft Outlook, this is the first time that an e-mail/newsgroup/personal information management application has been a part of the Macintosh version of Office. Unlike Outlook Express, which has always been a free application, Entourage will only be available to Office users.

The following Entourage features will be new to Outlook Express 5 users:

- In addition to the e-mail and newsgroup features formerly provided in Outlook Express 5, Entourage adds an integrated calendar with reminders (see Chapter 18), an Address Book that is available from other Office applications (see Chapter 4), and the ability to link tasks, e-mail messages, and documents (see Chapter 29).

- Like Outlook Express 5, Entourage provides support for multiple users (see Chapter 31). Each person can keep his or her Entourage e-mail, Calendar, Address Book, tasks, and notes separate on the same computer.

■ When addressing an e-mail message, Entourage uses Address AutoComplete (see Chapter 19, "Writing and Sending E-mail") to present a pop-up list of potential recipients based on what you are typing—regardless of whether it's the recipient's name or e-mail address. Entourage also remembers the names of the last 150 hand-addressed messages and includes them in the list. To further simplify things, Entourage tracks the frequency with which you e-mail people. For example, if you frequently e-mail a person named Sheri, when you start an address with *S*, Entourage automatically selects Sheri's address for you.

■ Any message can be flagged for follow-up at a later date (see Chapter 20, "Reading and Managing E-mail"). An automated reminder will appear at the appropriate time.

■ Sending e-mail attachments is handled simply and sensibly (see Chapter 19). By default, Entourage encodes attachments using AppleDouble, enabling them to be received on either a Mac or PC. To ensure that all attachments are readable under Windows, you can optionally instruct Entourage to add the appropriate three-character extension to each attached file.

■ A summary of the important information in a contact record can be viewed in the Preview Pane, as shown in Figure 1-4. In addition to addresses, phone numbers, and e-mail addresses, each summary also shows the date of the last message sent to and received from the person.

FIGURE 1-4.

Rather than opening the Address Book, you can view summary information for any contact in the Preview Pane

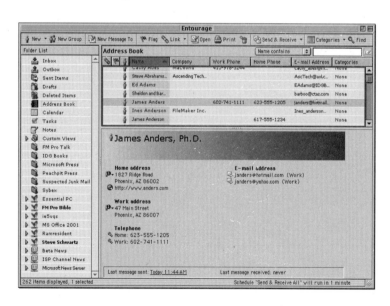

■ To help organize your e-mail, you can create custom views (see Chapter 20). A custom view can present related information, such as all e-mail sent or received from one person. You can also create and assign color-coded categories to messages, contacts, appointments, and tasks.

■ Following the capability introduced in Microsoft Outlook, Entourage includes the ability to create, send, and receive *vCards* (a format for exchanging contact information) as explained in Chapter 4. Similarly, Entourage uses the iCalendar format for exchanging meeting requests (see Chapter 8, "The Calendar and Information Management Features").

New Features in PowerPoint

PowerPoint contains the following new features and enhancements:

■ A new tri-pane view enables you to view your slides, notes, and outline all at the same time (see Chapter 24, "Introducing Microsoft PowerPoint").

■ In order to support presentations with distinct sections, you can now create multiple masters for a single presentation (see Chapter 24).

■ PowerPoint now has its own table feature (see Chapter 25, "Creating Slides"), enabling you to create tables without having to move them in from Word or Excel.

■ Within-slide movement is available through PowerPoint's support of animated GIFs, entry animations, and exit animations (see Chapter 25).

■ By using the new Make Movie command (see Chapter 26, "Using Colors, Drawings, and Animations"), you can turn the current presentation into a QuickTime movie—complete with QuickTime between-slide transitions and an MP3 sound track.

■ When saving a presentation as a Web page, PowerPoint is able to generate HTML that automatically scales for different screen sizes and resolutions (see Chapter 26).

New Features in Internet Explorer

If you are currently using Internet Explorer 4.5 or earlier, you should note the following new features that were introduced in Internet Explorer 5:

- The Auction Manager, shown in Figure 1-5, was one of the most attention-grabbing features introduced in Internet Explorer 5. If you participate as a buyer or seller in Internet auctions at eBay, Yahoo Auctions, or Amazon.com Auctions, you can use the Auction Manager to track the progress of selected auction items and have it notify you when you've been outbid.

FIGURE 1-5.

When tracking an auction, you can tell the Auction Manager the events on which you wish to be notified, the frequency with which it should check for changes in the auction status, and the manner in which you should be notified

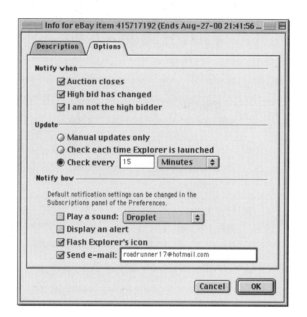

- The Explorer Bar has been expanded by adding two new tabs: Internet Scrapbook and Page Holder. You can use the Internet Scrapbook to make permanent records of pages, such as advertisements and online purchases. If you find a Web page that contains many links you'd like to explore, you can add the page to the Page Holder, display a list of all the links contained in the page, and visit as many as you like without having to click the Back button (as you normally would).

 NOTE

Internet Explorer 5 was introduced months before Office 2001 and has always been available as a separate, free download from the Microsoft Web site. The version of Internet Explorer included with Office 2001 is identical to the older, free version. Thus, if you already have Internet Explorer 5 installed, there is no need to install the one that's on the Office 2001 CD.

CHAPTER 2

Microsoft Office Basics

In this chapter, you'll learn the basics of working with Microsoft Office. The procedures discussed here are relevant to every Office application. (If there are important differences between how a procedure works in one application and how it works in another, we'll point them out to you.)

Running an Office Program

There are many ways you can start (or *launch*) an Office application. The method you choose depends on how you've configured Office and your system software, as well as whether you want to create a new document or open an existing one. To launch an Office application, do any of the following:

- Double-click the application's icon (or its alias).

- Select the application's icon (or its alias), open the File menu, and choose Open (or press ⌘-O).

> **NOTE**
> An *alias* is a special icon that serves as a shortcut to a program, document file, folder, or disk (as explained in "Creating Aliases and Favorites," later in this chapter). When you double-click an alias, the original program, document, folder, or disk opens.

- Control-click the application's icon (or an alias for the application), and choose Open from the contextual menu that appears. (See Figure 2-1.)

> **NOTE**
> To *Control-click* means to hold down the Control key as you click the mouse button, which will activate the contextual menu.

FIGURE 2-1.

When you Control-click desktop icons, contextual icons will pop up

- If you've saved the application as a Favorite (as explained in "Creating Aliases and Favorites," later in this chapter), you can choose it by opening the Apple menu and then opening the Favorites submenu, as shown in Figure 2-2.

FIGURE 2-2.

You can add frequently used programs and documents to the Favorites menu, making it easy to launch them

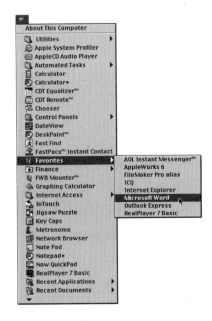

Microsoft Office 2001 Essentials

- If you've recently run the application, you can choose it by opening the Apple menu and then opening the Recent Applications submenu.

- If you use the Launcher control panel and have dragged icons of the Office programs into the Launcher window (see Figure 2-3), you can click an Office icon to launch the selected program.

FIGURE 2-3.

If you've enabled the Launcher control panel on your Mac, you can drag aliases for favorite programs and documents into the Launcher window

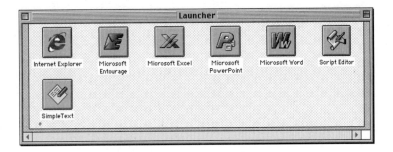

- If you launch an Office application and have the Project Gallery enabled, the Project Gallery dialog box appears, as shown in Figure 2-4. A document or task that's relevant to the chosen application is highlighted. Click OK to open the application or execute the task. Alternatively, you can click another icon to open a different Office application or perform a different task.

- If you've disabled the Project Gallery, on the other hand, the chosen application launches immediately. If the application is Microsoft Word, Excel, or PowerPoint, a new, blank document is automatically created. When you launch Entourage in this manner, it opens to the view that was active when you last ran it.

Creating Aliases and Favorites

To make it more convenient for you to launch the Office applications, Office documents, or any of your other favorite programs or documents, you can create aliases for them or store them as Favorites. An *alias* is an icon that serves as a shortcut to the original program, document, folder, or disk. You can move an alias to any drive and folder or add it to the Apple menu. When you double-click a program alias, the program launches. When you double-click a document alias, the appropriate program launches and opens the document.

To create an alias, select the original program or document icon, open the File menu, and choose Make Alias (or press ⌘-M). Then drag the alias icon to the drive or folder of your choice. In older versions of the software, you can add an alias to the Apple menu by selecting the original program or document icon, opening the Apple menu, opening the Automated Tasks submenu, and then choosing Add Alias To Apple Menu.

The Apple menu contains a folder named Favorites in which you can store links to your most frequently used programs and documents. To create a new Favorite, click to select a document or program icon, open the File menu, and then choose Add To Favorites. You can then launch the document or program whenever you like by choosing Favorites from the Apple menu, as shown previously in Figure 2-2.

TIP

You can also make aliases of folders or disks. For example, if you make an alias of your hard disk and put it in the Apple menu, you can open any program or document contained on the hard disk by choosing it from the Apple menu.

FIGURE 2-4.

From the Project Gallery dialog box, you can launch any Office application, as well as create documents from templates and wizards

Select a category

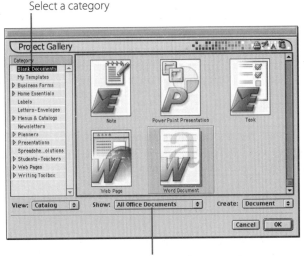

Restrict document list
to those of one application

The Project Gallery

The Project Gallery dialog box serves as the start-up window for all Office applications, except Microsoft Internet Explorer. Regardless of which application you launch, the Project Gallery dialog box appears. In addition to using the Project Gallery to launch any Office application, you can open templates, wizards, and existing documents with it. To disable the Project Gallery (preventing it from appearing whenever you start an Office application), you can set a General Preferences option. If you later want to re-enable the Project Gallery, launch Word, Excel, or PowerPoint, open the Edit menu, choose Preferences, click the General tab (or the View tab in PowerPoint), as shown in Figure 2-5, and then check the Show Project Gallery At Startup option.

FIGURE 2-5.

You can enable or disable the Project Gallery in the General tab of the Preferences dialog box

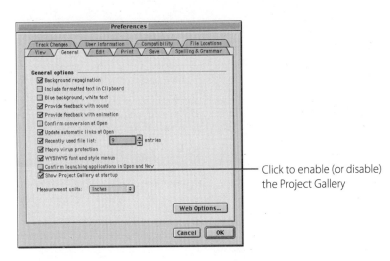

Click to enable (or disable)
the Project Gallery

While running any Office application (except Internet Explorer), you can use the Project Gallery to launch a *different* Office application. From the File menu, choose Project Gallery (or press Shift-⌘-P).

To launch an Office application while simultaneously opening one or more existing documents, do any of the following:

■ Double-click an Office document icon (or its alias).

■ Return to the Finder desktop, Shift-click several Office document icons (or drag a selection rectangle around them), open the File menu, and choose Open (or press ⌘-O).

■ If you have the Project Gallery enabled, you can double-click an Office application icon (or its alias). When the Project Gallery appears, click the Open button to select the document you want to open.

■ If you've recently worked on the document, you can choose it by selecting Recent Documents from the Apple menu.

■ If you've saved the document as a Favorite, you can choose it by selecting Favorites from the Apple menu.

TIP

The number of recently opened documents and applications that are recorded in the Recent Documents and Recent Applications folders are determined by settings in the Apple Menu Options control panel, as shown in Figure 2-6.

FIGURE 2-6.

To set the number of recent documents and applications that the Mac OS tracks, open the Apple menu, choose Apple Menu Options, and enter new numbers

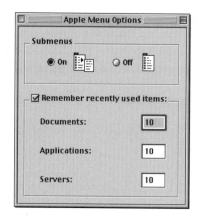

TIP

You can also open some non-Office documents by dragging their document icons onto the Office application in which you want them to open. For example, you can open many text and word processing files in Microsoft Word. This is referred to as *drag-and-drop*.

Creating New Documents

As mentioned earlier in this chapter, when you launch Excel, Word, or PowerPoint without simultaneously opening an existing document, a new document is automatically created for you. Once the program is running, you can create additional new documents in any of these programs by opening the File menu and choosing New in Excel, New Presentation in PowerPoint, or New Blank Document in Word. You can also press ⌘-N or click the New, New Presentation, or New Blank Document button in the toolbar.

You can also create a new document that is based on a template. A *template* is a reusable formatted Word, Excel, or PowerPoint document that comes with Office, or that you create. Examples might include a fax form, a memo or form letter layout, a departmental presentation layout, or a monthly budget worksheet. Unlike opening a normal document, when you open a template, you are merely opening a *copy* of the document—not the original.

> **NOTE**
>
> Macintosh templates were formerly referred to as *stationery documents*.

To create a new document based on a template, follow these steps:

1 From the File menu, choose Project Gallery or press Shift-⌘-P. The Project Gallery window appears, as shown earlier in Figure 2-4.

2 In the Category list on the left side of the window, click a template category (such as Letters-Envelopes) to view templates provided by Office, or click My Templates to view your own templates. (Note that if you haven't created any of your own templates, the My Templates list will be empty.)

3 *Optional:* To restrict the visible templates to those for a particular Office application, choose a document type from the Show pop-up menu.

4 Click to select the template that interests you, and then click OK (or simply double-click the template).

When saving a document that is based on a template, be sure either to name it something different from the original template or to save it in a different folder. Doing so will ensure that you don't overwrite the template by mistake. (Note that when saving a document that is based on a template, Office automatically assumes you wish to save it as a normal document rather than as a template—which is generally correct.

All you need to do is name the new document and choose a location on disk in which to save it.)

To save one of your own documents as a template (see Figure 2-7), open the File menu and choose Save As, enter a file name in the Name text box, choose Document Template from the Format pop-up list, and then click Save. By default, all templates are saved in the My Templates folder.

FIGURE 2-7.

Save templates in the My Templates folder

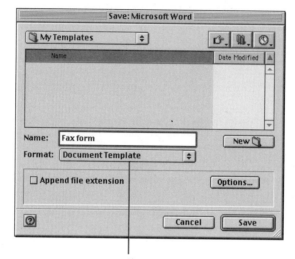

Choose Document Template from the Format pop-up menu

Opening, Closing, and Saving Documents

Once you've launched an Office application, you can open, close, and save documents—just as you do in most other applications.

Opening Additional Documents

When an Office application is already running, you can use any of the following techniques to open additional documents:

- From the File menu, choose Open, press ⌘-O, or click the Open button in the toolbar. In the Open dialog box shown in Figure 2-8, navigate to the drive and folder in which the document is stored, select the document's filename, and then click Open.

> NOTE

In the Open dialog box, you can make it simpler to find a desired document by clicking the Show pop-up menu and selecting one type of file to list, such as All Word Documents. By choosing an option from the Open pop-up menu, you can either open the original document (Original), an unnamed copy of the document—treating the document as though it were a template (Copy)—or specify that you can read but not edit the opened document (Read-Only).

FIGURE 2-8.

The Open dialog box

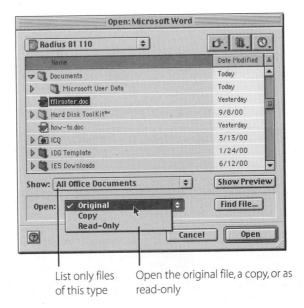

List only files of this type

Open the original file, a copy, or as read-only

- To open a document that you recently created, modified, or viewed, choose its name from the bottom of the File menu.

- From the desktop, double-click a Word, Excel, or PowerPoint document icon (when its creating program is already running).

- From the desktop, drag a document icon onto the related program icon. (You could drag a SimpleText document icon onto the Word icon, for example.)

** TIP**

The only restriction on the number of Office documents you can simultaneously have open is the amount of memory that is allocated to the program. To increase a program's memory allocation, quit the program, select its icon in the Finder and, from the File menu, select Get Info, and then select Memory. Increase the number for the Preferred Size, and then click the window's close box.

To return to the desktop, you can choose Finder from the Application menu (in the right-hand corner of the menu bar), click any empty area of the desktop, or—on most Macs—press ⌘-Tab one or more times to toggle through the active programs until you reach the Finder.

Finding Files

If you can't remember the name of a particular Office file or where it's saved on disk, click the Find File button in the Open dialog box (refer to Figure 2-8). The Search dialog box appears, as shown in Figure 2-9.

FIGURE 2-9.

The Search dialog box

Repeat a saved search

Enter all or part of a filename

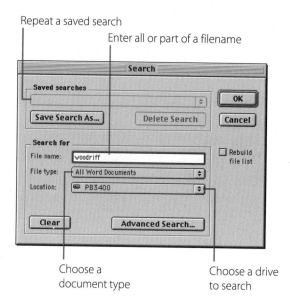

Choose a document type

Choose a drive to search

You can perform a simple search by entering criteria in this screen. Choose a document type from the File Type pop-up menu and a local or network drive to search from the Location pop-up menu. (Listed network drives will be limited to those for which file sharing is enabled and to which you have access.) Enter all or part of the document name. Click OK to begin the search.

To find *all* documents of a particular type, choose the type from the File Type pop-up menu, leave the File Name box blank, and then click OK.

If you've previously conducted this search and saved it by clicking Save Search As, you can conduct it again by selecting the search name from the Saved searches pop-up menu at the top of the dialog box.

Click the Advanced Search button if you want to simultaneously search multiple drives or particular folders, search for text entered in the Summary section of the document's Properties settings, or search for files created or last saved within a specific date range. For instance, if you can't recall what you named or where you saved a recent file, you could perform an advanced search and specify a date range in the Timestamp tab of the Advanced Search dialog box. To search for all files created or modified after a particular date, enter only a From date, leaving the To date blank. Possible matches are listed in the Find File dialog box. Select Preview from the View pop-up menu and highlight a possible match, and a preview of the file appears in the right pane of the dialog box. If it's the desired file, click the Open button.

 NOTE

> Can't remember where you saved the found file? Check the left-hand pane of the Find File dialog box. It's organized to show drives and folders.

Closing Documents

To close an Office document, select it—which makes it an *active document*—and then do one of the following:

- Click the close box.

- From the File menu, choose Close.

- Press ⌘-W.

If the document has never been saved or has been modified since the last save, you will be given an opportunity to save it. (See Figure 2-10.) If the document has never been saved, a normal Save dialog box will appear after you click the Save button.

FIGURE 2-10.

Click Save to save the document, Don't Save to discard changes to the document, or Cancel to return to the application with the document still open

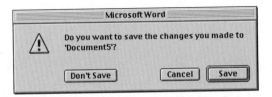

Saving Documents

The documents that you create in Office and the changes that you make to them are permanent only if you save them to disk. Whenever you make important changes, remember to save the document.

To save a newly created document, follow these steps:

1 From the File menu, choose Save, press ⌘-S, or click the Save button in the toolbar. The Save dialog box appears, as shown in Figure 2-11.

FIGURE 2-11.

The Save dialog box

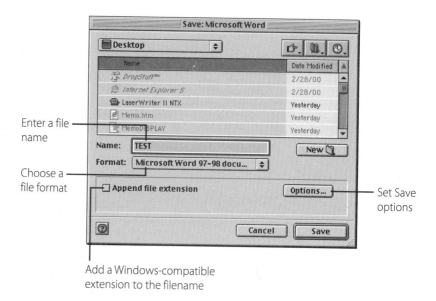

Enter a file name

Choose a file format

Set Save options

Add a Windows-compatible extension to the filename

2 Navigate to the drive and folder where you want to save the file.

3 Accept or replace the default filename.

4 If desired, select a different file format from the Format pop-up menu and set options (such as saving autorecovery information) by clicking the Options button.

5 Click Save.

Every Office application offers different Save options. Although the default settings will suffice for most documents, you should familiarize yourself with the available settings. Just click the Options button to do so.

When you use the Save command to save an edited version of an existing document (as opposed to a new one), the new version automatically replaces the old one on disk—the Save dialog box doesn't appear. If you want to keep multiple copies of the document, open the File menu and choose the Save As command instead. This activates the Save dialog box, giving you the chance to rename the new version or save it to a different disk or folder. In either case, the original file is preserved. And if you decide that you want to replace the original file, simply click Save and then click Replace in the confirmation dialog box that appears. (See Figure 2-12.)

FIGURE 2-12.

Click Replace to overwrite the original document, or click Cancel to save the file with a different filename or to a different location

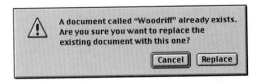

A document called "Woodriff" already exists. Are you sure you want to replace the existing document with this one?

Cancel   Replace

Saving in Different File Formats

Normally, you'll save all Office documents in the default format presented to you in the Save dialog box. However, if you need to share the file with others, it's also important to save a second copy of the document in a format that they can use. This comes up frequently when friends or colleagues use an earlier version of Office or a different application entirely.

If possible, save a copy in the recipient's version of the application (Word 6, for example). Alternatively, you can save the file in another format that the recipients application can read. While other word processing programs may not be able to open Word documents, for instance, they may be able to read Rich Text Format documents and can certainly read Text Only documents. Note, however, that if you want to preserve as much of your original formatting as possible (such as fonts, type treatment, and alignment), you should use Text Only format as a last resort.

⭐ **TIP**

If you intend to use the document on a PC as well as a Mac, click the Append File Extension option in the Save dialog box (shown previously in Figure 2-11). Windows determines a file's type by the three-character extension that ends the filename (such as .doc for a Word document).

> Word, Excel, and PowerPoint documents can be saved as HTML (Web page) files, suitable for viewing in a Web browser on the Internet or a company intranet. To learn about this feature, see "Saving a Document as a Web Page," in Chapter 30, "Microsoft Office 2001 and the Web."

Using QuickTime

Office 2001 provides full support for QuickTime, a feature of the OS that enables your Mac to play video and audio clips. The QuickTime software is included free with the Mac OS. You can create livelier memos, presentations, worksheets, and e-mail by adding QuickTime clips to them. And any QuickTime-compatible video or audio files found on Web pages can be played within Internet Explorer.

> At a minimum, you must install and enable the QuickTime extensions and control panel. QuickTime 4 or later is recommended. Go to *www.apple.com/ quicktime/download/support/* to download the latest version of QuickTime.

Configuring QuickTime

While the default QuickTime settings will suffice for most users, you may want to examine the options that are available—particularly if you want to be able to use Internet Explorer to view movie clips, streaming video, audio clips, and streaming audio. To configure QuickTime, open the Apple menu, choose Control Panels, and then choose QuickTime Settings. The QuickTime Settings control panel appears. Within the control panel, you can do the following:

- To see which version of QuickTime is installed, choose About QuickTime from the pop-up menu at the top of the control panel. (See Figure 2-13.)

- Choose Browser Plug-In from the pop-up menu. (See Figure 2-14.) Unless you prefer to start movies manually by clicking the play button, leave the Play Movies Automatically option checked. If you want to be able to replay movies without having to download them again, check the Save Movies In Disk Cache option. To view the types of files that the QuickTime plug-in will play, click the MIME Settings button. (See Figure 2-15.)

FIGURE 2-13.

The About QuickTime section of the QuickTime Settings control panel

Choose the settings to view

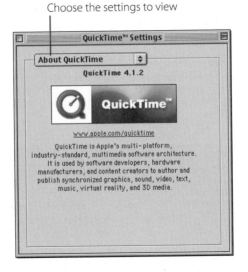

FIGURE 2-14.

Browser plug-in settings

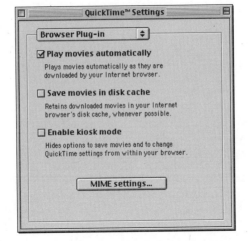

FIGURE 2-15.

MIME settings

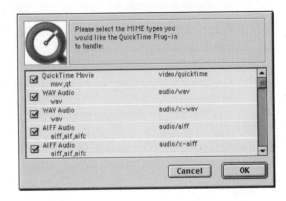

■ Choose Connection Speed from the pop-up menu (see Figure 2-16), and click the radio button for the speed of your modem and Internet connection.

FIGURE 2-16.

Connection Speed settings

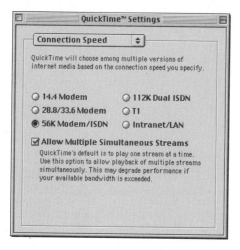

■ If your Internet connection requires that you use proxy servers, choose Streaming Proxy from the pop-up menu and enter the information provided by your ISP or network administrator.

If you download and save video or audio clips from the Internet, you can open them directly with QuickTime Player or Movie Player, free viewers that are included with the QuickTime software. You can also use Windows Media Player from Microsoft to play many types of video and audio. Go to *www.microsoft.com/windows/mediaplayer/en/download/Macintosh.asp* to download the Windows Media Player.

Adding a QuickTime Clip to a Document

Now that you've enabled and configured QuickTime, you can start inserting movie clips into your documents. To add a QuickTime clip to a Word document or Excel worksheet, open the Insert menu, choose Movie, select the movie from the dialog box that appears (see Figure 2-17), and then click Open. The movie clip is inserted into the document as a floating object, as shown in Figure 2-18.

FIGURE 2-17.

Selecting a movie clip
to insert

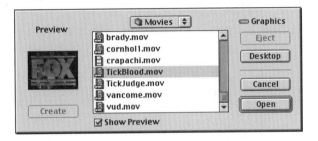

FIGURE 2-18.

Playable movie clips
can be inserted into
Word documents

Movie toolbar

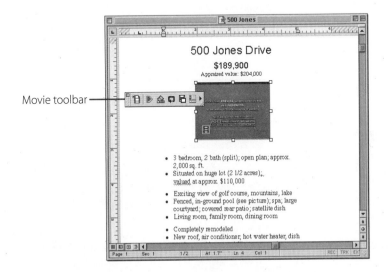

To add a QuickTime clip to a PowerPoint slide, follow these steps:

1 Switch to or create the slide in which you wish to add the movie clip.

2 Choose an appropriate slide layout from the Formatting palette, such as Media Clip & Text, or Text & Media Clip. (You can also choose a slide layout from the New Slide dialog box when you create the slide.)

3 On the slide, double-click the media clip icon, as shown in Figure 2-19. The dialog box for choosing a movie appears, as shown previously in Figure 2-17.

FIGURE 2-19.

FIGURE 2-19.

Both the Media Clip & Text and Text & Media Clip slide layouts contain a placeholder for a movie clip

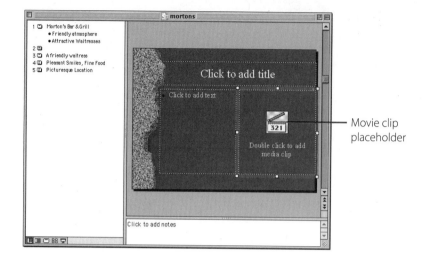

Movie clip placeholder

4 Select a movie, and click the Open button. The opening shot of the movie clip appears in the area reserved for the media clip.

5 If the Assistant is enabled (see the "Getting Help" section later in this chapter), you will be asked whether the movie should play automatically when the slide is viewed. Click Yes or No.

E-mailing Movie Clips to Others

A QuickTime movie is a file just like any other file, meaning you can use Entourage to e-mail your clips to friends and business associates. To include a QuickTime clip as an e-mail attachment, follow these steps:

1 Create a new message by opening the File menu, choosing New, and then choosing Mail Message (or press ⌘-N).

2 Address the message, enter a Subject, and then compose the message.

3 Click the triangle button to the left of Attachments. (See Figure 2-20.)

FIGURE 2-20.

Click the triangle button to reveal the attachment commands

View/hide attachment list

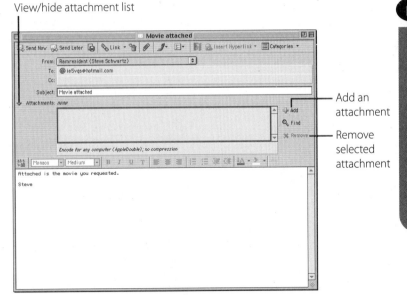

Add an attachment

Remove selected attachment

4 Click the Add button. The Choose Attachment dialog box appears, as shown in Figure 2-21.

FIGURE 2-21.

The Choose Attachment dialog box

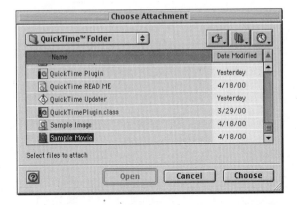

5 Select the movie file, and click Choose.

Movie clips that you receive in Entourage can be viewed in the Preview Pane or when you open the message in its own window. Whether recipients of *your* clips can view them without leaving their e-mail program depends on the program they use. For example, Microsoft Outlook Express 5 has this capability; others may not.

Actually, there is one difference between QuickTime clips and other document files. Movies that are more than a few seconds in length can be extremely large files. Before e-mailing a clip as an attachment, you should check to see whether your outgoing mail server or the recipient's incoming mail server has a limit on attachment size. Then check the size of the clip by going to the desktop, selecting its icon, and pressing ⌘-I. Note, too, that when an attachment is converted by Entourage (or any other e-mail program) for transmission over the Internet, it tends to get larger. Leave yourself some leeway.

Playing a QuickTime Clip in a Document

A QuickTime clip embedded in an Office document shows a single frame of the movie and a film strip symbol, indicating that it is a movie.

To play an embedded clip, you can do any of the following:

- Double-click the clip.

- Click the Play button in the floating Movie toolbar, as shown in Figure 2-22. (If the Movie toolbar isn't visible, open the View menu, choose Toolbars, and then choose Movie.)

- Single-click the clip to select it. Click the Play button in the controller beneath the movie. (If the controller isn't visible, click the Show Controller button in the Movie toolbar.)

FIGURE 2-22.

When selected, a movie can be played and controlled by clicking buttons in its controller, or buttons in the Movie toolbar

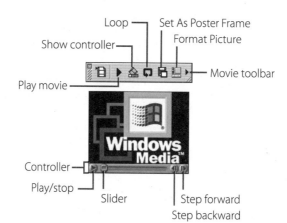

To pause or stop playback, click the clip once, click the Play button again, or press the spacebar. Repeat any of these actions to continue the playback. To go directly to any scene, drag the slider to the

desired position. Use the Step Backward or Step Forward buttons to move one frame in the appropriate direction for each click. To make the movie repeat endlessly, click the Loop button in the Movie toolbar.

> **NOTE**
>
> When recipients of your documents attempt to play an embedded QuickTime clip, the movie file must be accessible to them. Thus, when transferring such a document to others, you must be sure to transfer a copy of the movie, too. (However, if you and the person are on the same network and the movie is a shared file, transferring the movie won't be necessary.)

Changing a Clip's Attributes

Like other objects in Office documents, you can modify many of the attributes of a movie. To change the size of a movie frame, for example, you can either click and drag one of its handles or enter new height and width settings in the Formatting Palette. (See Figure 2-23.) (If the Formatting Palette isn't visible, open the View menu and choose Formatting Palette.) You can also choose a wrapping style in the Formatting Palette by clicking the current choices for Style and Wrap To.

FIGURE 2-23.

In this floating window, you can change the formatting for a movie

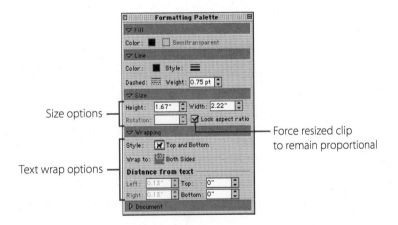

Size options

Text wrap options

Force resized clip to remain proportional

> **TIP**
>
> If you'd like the opportunity to modify *all* of the movie's attributes in a single dialog box, open the Format menu and choose Picture or click the Format Picture button in the Movie toolbar. You can also use the Format Picture dialog box (see Figure 2-24) to set other attributes, such as cropping, brightness, and contrast.

FIGURE 2-24.

The Format Picture dialog box

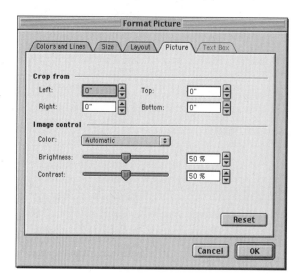

Printing

Although the basic process of printing in Office 2001 is identical to that of printing from any other application, Office adds many Print and Page Setup options that are not found elsewhere. In addition, each application—except PowerPoint and Entourage—offers a Print Preview function, enabling you to see what each page of the printout will look like without actually printing.

> Because each Office application has different print options, this section discusses only the common elements of printing from Office. For information on printing from a particular application, see the application-specific chapters of this book.

Using the Chooser to Select a Printer

Before you can print anything, you must use the Chooser desk accessory to select a printer to use. Unless you later select a different printer, all print jobs—from every application—will automatically be sent to the chosen printer. To select a printer, follow these steps:

1 Make sure that the printer you want to use is turned on. You can print to any printer that is connected to your Macintosh or that is available on your network—assuming you're on a network.

2 Choose the Chooser desk accessory from the Apple menu. The Chooser window appears. (See Figure 2-25.)

FIGURE 2-25.

The Chooser desk accessory (after selecting a print driver)

Print drivers

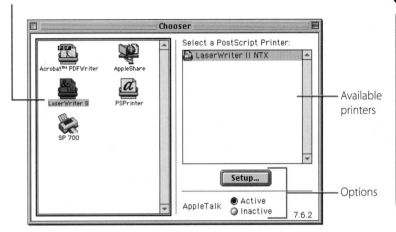

Available printers

Options

3   In the left side of the window, click to select the print driver for the device you want to use.

4   The available printers that can use the chosen print driver will appear in the right side of the window. Click to select the printer you want to use. (Note that only printers that are on line will be listed.)

5   Set options by clicking buttons or icons, such as choosing a printer port, enabling/disabling background printing, and activating/deactivating AppleTalk. (Note that options vary considerably and depend on the chosen print driver. For additional information, refer to your printer manual or—if you have an Apple printer—to your system software documentation and Help.)

6   Close the Chooser window by clicking its close box. All changes are automatically saved.

7   If you've switched from one print driver to another, you will be prompted to use Page Setup to check your settings. To do so, open the File menu and choose Page Setup from the Finder or from within any application.

NOTE

If you have only one printer, this is a one-time setup procedure. If you sometimes switch among printers (or devices that are treated as printers, such as fax modems or print-to-disk software), you must revisit the Chooser each time you change devices. The only other time you are required to respecify a printer is after installing or updating your system software.

Microsoft Office 2001 Essentials

Printing a Document

After selecting a printer with the Chooser, you can print the current document by following these steps:

1 *Optional:* If you want to print in landscape mode or to a different size or type of paper than the standard 8.5 x 11", open the File menu and choose Page Setup. Select options in the Page Setup dialog box that appears, as shown in Figure 2-26. Click OK when finished.

 NOTE

> Page Setup settings are document-specific; that is, if you specify Page Setup options for a document and then save it, the settings are saved, too. The next time you print the document, the saved settings will automatically be used.

FIGURE 2-26.

The appearance and options presented in the Page Setup dialog box will vary from printer to printer

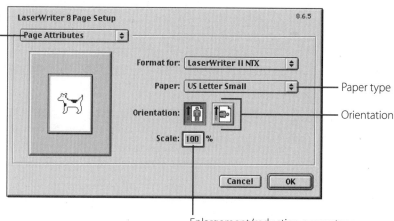

2 *Optional:* To see what the printout will look like before committing it to paper (as shown in Figure 2-27), choose Print Preview from the File menu or click the Print Preview button in the toolbar.

FIGURE 2-27.

A Word document in
Print Preview mode

Print preview button   Magnification cursor

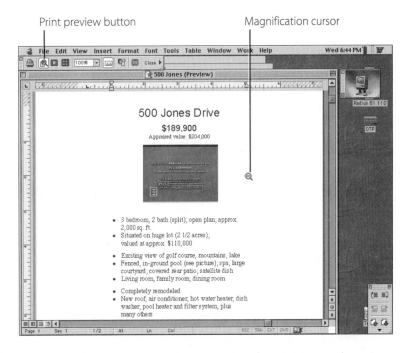

Microsoft Office 2001 Essentials

3 From the File menu, choose Print or press ⌘-P. The Print dialog
box appears, as shown in Figure 2-28.

4 Set options (such as the number of copies and the page range to
be printed), make sure the printer is on, and click Print.

FIGURE 2-28.

The appearance and
options presented in
the Print dialog box
will vary from printer
to printer

Additional options   Number of copies   Page range

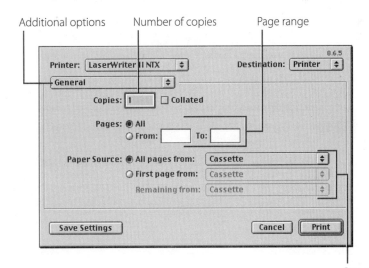

Paper source

To print a document on the default printer using the current Print and Page Setup settings, click the Print button in the toolbar. No dialog boxes will appear.

Faxing from Office 2001

If your Mac has a modem with fax capabilities, you can transmit Office documents as faxes to any fax machine or fax modem. In general, the way faxing works is that your fax software provides a special print driver that, when chosen, intercepts the current print job, converts it into fax data, and then transmits it over your modem. (Note that your fax software—not Office—determines the manner in which this is accomplished. See the fax software's manual for instructions.)

In general, faxing from Office (or any other application on your Mac) is done as follows:

1 In Office, open the document you want to fax.

2 Issue your fax software's fax command.

   If you use GlobalFax software, for example, hold down the Option key while opening the File menu. The Print command is replaced by the Fax command. In other programs, you may have to open the Chooser desk accessory in the Apple menu, select your fax modem driver, and then simply print the document.

3 Set fax options, such as the number of pages to include, whether to use a cover page, and the recipient's phone number.

4 Turn on your modem (disconnecting from the Internet, if necessary) and issue the software's command to convert and transmit the fax.

If you want to create a standard fax rather than faxing an Office document, a variety of fax form templates are provided with Office.

Getting Help

Office 2001 provides several types of help for problems you may be having and procedures you don't fully understand, as well as explanations of the purpose of program elements (such as toolbar components).

Office applications include animated characters called *Assistants* that offer to help you perform common tasks, display alert messages, and provide tips. See the section, "More Assistance with Office Assistants" in this chapter for additional information.

You can get extra help with some Office tasks by choosing a tool from the Tools menu or the Project Gallery. These tools, or *wizards,* as they're referred to in Office, help you create some types of documents, calculations, and the like by presenting a dialog box in which you enter information. In Word, for example, you can use the Letter Wizard (see Figure 2-29) to format and enter the basic data for a personal or business letter.

FIGURE 2-29.

Wizards can walk you through the process of formatting a letter or creating a formula

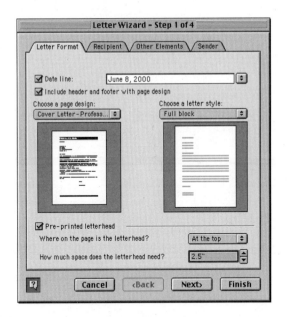

⭐ **TIP**

A wizard dialog box may contain multiple tabs, indicating additional sections where you can enter information. Be sure to examine each tab before clicking OK. (Some wizards automatically move you from tab to tab when you click a Next button; others merely present the tabs.)

To summon the main help system for an application (see Figure 2-30), open the Help menu, choose *Program name* Help or Contents and Index. To jump to a different or related topic, click the underlined text.

FIGURE 2-30.

Select a category on the left side of the application's Help window

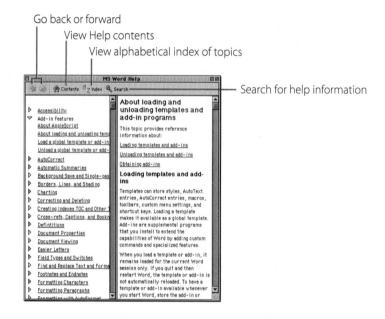

Go back or forward

View Help contents

View alphabetical index of topics

Search for help information

To learn the names of toolbar components, rest the cursor over the component for a few seconds. This pop-up help (see Figure 2-31) is referred to as a *ToolTip*.

FIGURE 2-31.

When the cursor rests on a toolbar element, the element's name appears

To request more elaborate pop-up help than the ToolTips provide, open the Help menu, choose Show Balloons, and then rest the cursor over a toolbar, window element, or dialog box item, as shown in Figure 2-32. Note that Balloon Help is a system-wide help facility. It simultaneously affects the Finder and *all* running applications. To turn off Balloon Help, choose Hide Balloons from the Help menu.

FIGURE 2-32.

Balloon Help provides detailed explanations of the purpose of toolbar buttons and system software components, such as window parts

You can summon up-to-date Office help information by opening the Help menu and choosing Help on the Web from within any Office application. Assuming that your computer is configured to use the Internet, your default Web browser launches and displays a Web page (see Figure 2-33) with links to areas on the Microsoft Web site.

FIGURE 2-33.

Help on the Web

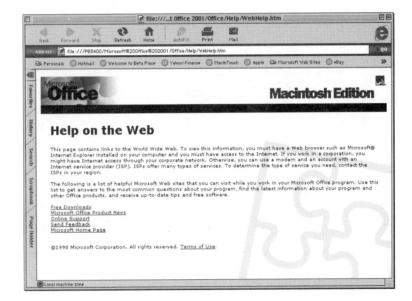

If you need help from Microsoft Technical Support, you can obtain the necessary contact information by opening the Apple menu, choosing About *Office application*, and then clicking the Tech Support button in the dialog box that appears.

More Assistance with Office Assistants

The Office Assistant watches as you work. When you perform a procedure or activity for which the Assistant has help information, a balloon pops up, such as the one shown in Figure 2-34. Click a radio button to make your choice. If the Office Assistant has a useful tip to offer about the current task, it displays a yellow light bulb. Click the bulb to view the tip.

FIGURE 2-34.

The Office Assistant believes you're writing a letter

You can also request help by clicking the Office Assistant. It presents a balloon in which you can type a help request (see Figure 2-35) and then click the Search button, click the Options button to set Office Assistant preferences, or click the Cancel button to dismiss it.

FIGURE 2-35.

When you click the Office Assistant, you can type a statement or question that describes the type of help you need

Unless you instruct it otherwise, the Office Assistant automatically intercepts all requests for application help. If you wish, you can bypass the Office Assistant for certain types of help requests (that is, summoning help for a wizard or pressing the Help key—if your keyboard has one—to open Help for the current application). To set these options, click the Office Assistant, click the Options button, enter or remove checkmarks in the Options tab of the Office Assistant dialog box (see Figure 2-36), and then click OK.

FIGURE 2-36.

The Options tab of the Office Assistant dialog box

Office Assistant
Gallery \ Options
Assistant capabilities
☑ Respond to Help key   ☑ Move when in the way
☑ Help with wizards   ☐ Guess Help topics
☑ Display alerts   ☑ Make sounds
☐ Include product help in Visual Basic Editor   ☐ Speak alert text
Show tips about
☑ Using features more effectively   ☐ Keyboard shortcuts
☑ Using the mouse more effectively
Other tip options
☐ Show the Tip of the Day at startup   [Reset My Tips]
[Cancel] [OK]

Office includes many different Office Assistants, which can be added by installing the Value Pack software (included on the Microsoft Office CD). The other Assistants work in the same manner. However, their appearances and personalities vary considerably.

To change to a different Assistant, follow these steps:

1 Click the Assistant.

2 Click the Options button in the pop-up balloon that appears. The Office Assistant dialog box appears.

3 Click the Gallery tab.

4 Click the Next and Back buttons to view all installed Assistants, as shown in Figure 2-37. When you see one you like, click OK.

FIGURE 2-37.

You can pick a new assistant in the Gallery section of the Office Assistant dialog box

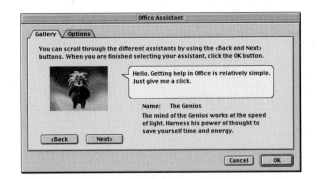

The state of the Office Assistant feature is either on or off for *all* installed Office applications. To turn the Office Assistant on or off, open the Help menu and choose Turn Assistant Off or Turn Assistant On. (You can also turn off an Assistant by clicking its Close box.)

Quitting an Office Application

To quit any Office application, open the File menu and choose Quit (or press ⌘-Q). If documents are open that contain changes you haven't saved, you'll be given an opportunity to save them. Otherwise, the application quits immediately.

CHAPTER 3

Understanding the Microsoft Office Interface

In this chapter, you'll learn about the Microsoft Office 2001 interface—using the menus and toolbars, working with dialog boxes, and working with and managing document windows. The chapter concludes with a series of shortcuts that will help improve your productivity when using Office.

If you're a long-time Macintosh user or have used previous versions of Office, much of the material in this chapter will be old hat to you. Nevertheless, it's a good idea to at least skim through it, read the tips, and acquaint yourself with the new features. Otherwise, you might miss some information that will save you time and improve your productivity.

Using the Menus and Toolbars

The menus and toolbars in Office are unquestionably the most important parts of the user interface. By interacting with the menus and toolbars, you can perform a wide array of tasks, such as choosing and executing program commands, setting formatting options, and modifying the document display.

Using Menus

Menus in Office 2001 work as they do in other Mac programs. Click any menu title in the menu bar to expose the menu. (See Figures 3-1 and 3-2.) Drag down with the mouse to choose a command from the menu, and then release the mouse button.

FIGURE 3-1.

The menu bar in Microsoft Entourage

When examining the Office menus, you'll note that many commands are followed by unusual symbols. These symbols represent keys on your keyboard that, when pressed in combination, execute the menu command without you having to choose it from the menu. These key combinations are referred to as *keyboard shortcuts* and can be tremendous time-savers.

FIGURE 3-2.

Clicking a menu title causes the menu to drop down

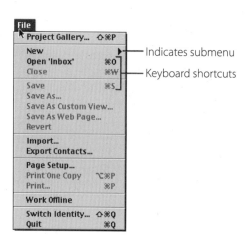

A *grayed out* menu title or command cannot be chosen. Office watches what you're doing in the current document and automatically grays out commands that are not applicable. For instance, unless you have a text string or object selected, you cannot choose the Cut command.

Keyboard shortcuts consist of a letter, number, or character key in combination with one or more modifier keys (Shift, Option, and ⌘). To execute any keyboard shortcut, hold down the modifier key or keys and then tap the letter, number, or character key. Refer to Table 3-1 to see how the modifier keys are displayed in the menus.

Table 3-1.   Keyboard Shortcuts.

Appearance on Keyboard	Appearance in Menu
⌘	⌘
Shift	⇧
Option	⌥

The Control (or Ctrl) key is a special modifier key. Although it could be used by some programs as a keyboard shortcut, the more common use of this key is as a mouse-click modifier. When you hold down the Control key and press the mouse button, a contextual menu appears. See "Control-Clicking," later in this chapter for more information.

Using Toolbars

To put an application's most common commands at your fingertips, Office provides an array of toolbars. Toolbars can contain buttons, menus, and text boxes. To avoid hunting for commands in the menus, you can often click a button that will perform the same action for you, such as saving the current file, adding formatting to a selected object or text string, and so on. To execute additional commands that aren't shown on a toolbar, click the arrow at the end (or bottom) of the toolbar, as shown in Figure 3-3.

FIGURE 3-3.
Microsoft Word toolbars

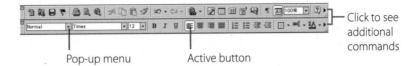

Click to see additional commands

Pop-up menu   Active button

Office manages toolbar elements in the same manner that it does menu commands. If a command is currently not applicable to what you are doing, Office grays it out, making it temporarily unusable.

When running Microsoft Word, Excel, or PowerPoint, you can choose which toolbars you want to display at any given moment, as well as those that are displayed by default when you launch the application. To display a toolbar, from the View menu choose the toolbar name from the Toolbars submenu. (See Figure 3-4.) To remove a toolbar, click its close box or choose its name from the Toolbars submenu (removing its check mark). To specify the toolbars that appear at program launch, see "Customizing Menus and Toolbars" in the following section.

FIGURE 3-4.

From the View menu, open the Toolbars submenu to enable or disable particular toolbars

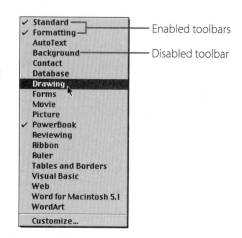

Since toolbars take up room onscreen, you'll normally want to keep their number small. Another way to reclaim the space used by a toolbar is to move it to an unused area onscreen. Normally, toolbars are displayed above the document window at the top of the screen. You can drag a toolbar by its title bar to any other screen position—including allowing it to float mid-screen. If you drag a toolbar to a screen edge, it automatically locks in place. You can also resize a toolbar or change it from horizontal to vertical by clicking and dragging its lower-right corner (just as you can with most document windows).

TIP

Office applications have built-in help for elements on their toolbars. Depending on the application, this help is referred to as *ToolTips* or *ScreenTips*. To display an element's name, rest the cursor over it for a moment, as shown in Figure 3-5. For more extensive help with toolbar elements (see Figure 3-6), open the Help menu and choose Show Balloons.

FIGURE 3-5.

Rest the cursor over any toolbar element to view its name

FIGURE 3-6.

When Show Balloons is enabled, ToolTips provide more information

Customizing Menus and Toolbars

Like its previous incarnations, Office 2001 can be customized to suit the way you work. In Word, Excel, and PowerPoint, you can add or remove menu commands and toolbar elements, as well as specify the default toolbars that will be displayed each time you launch the application. To customize the menus or toolbars in any of these three programs, choose Customize from the Tools menu. The dialog box shown in Figure 3-7 appears.

FIGURE 3-7.

The Customize dialog box

To change the default toolbars, click the Toolbars tab (refer to Figure 3-7) and add or remove check marks, as desired.

To modify any of the application's menus or change elements on a toolbar, click the Commands tab. To add a toolbar element or menu command, drag it from the Customize dialog box into a toolbar or the temporary menu bar. (See Figure 3-8.) To remove a toolbar element or menu command, drag it off the toolbar or out of the menu. Click OK when you are done making changes.

FIGURE 3-8.

To add a command, you can drag it from the Commands box into a menu or a toolbar

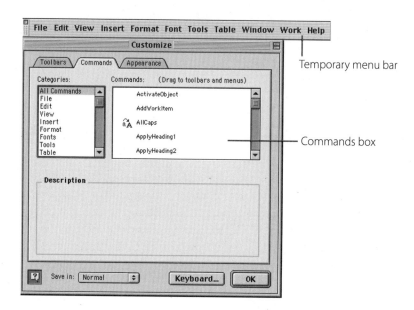

Temporary menu bar

Commands box

You can also rearrange elements on any toolbar. Hold down the ⌘ key as you click a toolbar element, and then drag it to a new position.

NOTE

The toolbars in Entourage are fixed. Although different toolbars appear in the various Entourage components, you cannot modify them or display additional ones. However, you can hide the toolbars by opening the View menu and choosing the Toolbars command, removing its check mark. Like Entourage, Microsoft Internet Explorer contains a single toolbar, displayed at the top of the document window. You can add or remove icons from the Internet Explorer toolbar by opening the View menu and choosing Customize Toolbars.

About Dialog Boxes

Whenever you have to set options—particularly several related options, such as those found in Preferences or the Font dialog box in Word (see Figure 3-9)—Office displays a dialog box. Dialog boxes are *modal*; that is, you cannot continue working on your documents until you dismiss the dialog box. To close a dialog box, click OK, Cancel, or a similar button. (Certain dialog boxes, such as the Find And Replace and the Spelling and Grammar dialog boxes in Word, can—or *must*—be dismissed by clicking their close box; otherwise they will remain open.)

FIGURE 3-9.

The Font dialog box, like other modal dialog boxes, must be dealt with before you can continue working

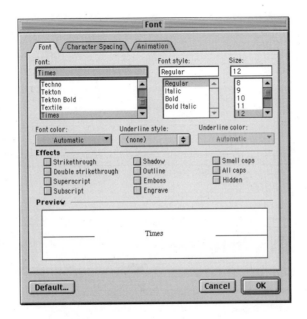

NOTE

An *alert box* is a special kind of dialog box that appears as a warning, caution, or notification of a problem. (See Figure 3-10.)

FIGURE 3-10.

Warnings and cautions are displayed as alert boxes, denoted by an exclamation point in a yellow triangle

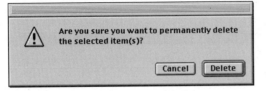

Microsoft Office 2001 Essentials

Setting options in Office dialog boxes is accomplished in the same manner as it is in other Mac programs. You can type in text boxes, click check boxes and radio buttons, and choose from pop-up menus.

> Whenever you choose a menu command that is followed by an ellipsis (…), a dialog box appears.

Dialog Box Shortcuts

Although you can click in dialog boxes to set most options, select text boxes, and switch to different sections, there are many keyboard shortcuts you can use, too. If a dialog box contains text boxes, you can switch among them by clicking a specific text box or by pressing Tab/Shift-Tab. If a dialog box has tabs at the top, you can switch to a different tab by clicking it or move through them by pressing Option-Tab/Shift-Option-Tab. (If this doesn't work, try Control-Tab/ Shift-Control-Tab. These commands enable you to navigate the tabs in the Word and Entourage Preferences dialog boxes, for example.)

You can even click most buttons by pressing keys on your keyboard. To click the currently highlighted button, press Return or Enter. To click the Cancel button, press ⌘-(period). To click most other buttons, press ⌘ and the first letter of the button name.

Working with Windows

As in other Mac applications, Office 2001 uses windows to display documents and palettes. This section explains the sorts of things you can do when working with windows.

> Not all window commands and procedures discussed in this section, such as splitting windows or cycling through open windows, are available in all Office 2001 applications.

Switching Between Windows

To work in an open window, it must be *active*; that is, it must be the currently selected window. Only one document window can be active at a time—even though several may be onscreen—and you can only work in the active window. An active window is distinguished from all other document windows by the presence of horizontal lines in its title bar. (See Figure 3-11.) To make a window active, you can either click in it or choose its name from the bottom of the application's Window menu.

FIGURE 3-11.
A window's title bar shows whether it is active or inactive

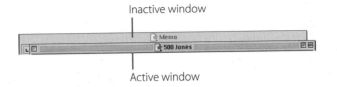

Inactive window

Active window

 NOTE

Entourage and Internet Explorer have a special command to help move through any currently open windows. From the Window menu, choose Cycle Through Windows (or press ⌘-~) to switch from one open window to the next. You can also display important Entourage and Internet Explorer windows by typing their ⌘-key equivalents, as listed in the Window menu. (See Figure 3-12:)

FIGURE 3-12.
You can display any Entourage window by choosing its name from the Window menu or by pressing its ⌘-key equivalent

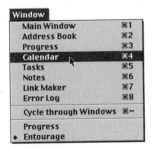

Moving Windows and Changing Their Sizes

While Office will automatically position and size new windows as it sees fit, you're free to move them around, change their size, collapse them, or even hide them completely. When working with a single document window, this usually isn't necessary. As you work with more and more windows (or if your Mac has a small monitor), window manipulation takes on greater importance.

To move any window from its current screen position to another, click and drag in the title bar or any of the window's edges, as shown in Figure 3-13. To change a window's size, click and drag in its lower-right corner. After manually resizing a window (or using one of the Window commands to automatically size it), you can zoom the window between the two sizes by clicking its zoom box. To reduce a window so that it shows only its title bar, click the expand/collapse box. Click the box a second time to restore the window to its normal appearance.

FIGURE 3-13.

Most Office windows can be repositioned by dragging their title bars or any edge

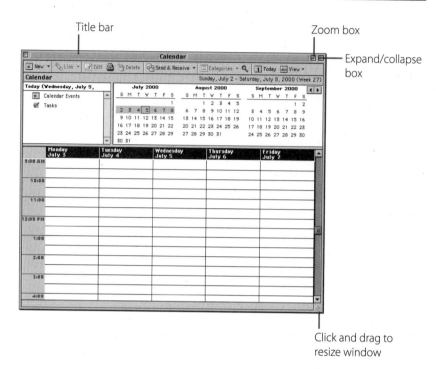

Title bar

Zoom box

Expand/collapse box

Click and drag to resize window

> **TIP**
>
> If you set an option in the Appearance control panel (as shown in Figure 3-14), you can also expand or collapse any window by double-clicking its title bar.

FIGURE 3-14.

Enable this option in the Appearance control panel so you can expand or collapse any window by double-clicking in its title bar

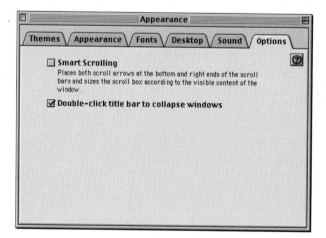

Unlike the other Office applications, Excel has a special command that you can use to completely hide a workbook. You might, for example, wish to hide a workbook on which the current one depends. Click to

make it active (or choose its name from the Window menu), and then—from the Window menu—choose Hide. To reveal a hidden window, open the Window menu, choose Unhide, choose the window from the Unhide dialog box that appears (see Figure 3-15), and click OK.

FIGURE 3-15.
Select a workbook to unhide and click OK

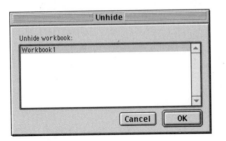

> **NOTE** Palettes, such as the Formatting Palette, cannot be resized or zoomed. All you can do with a palette is move, collapse/expand, and close it.

Window Arrangement Commands

If you occasionally work with multiple documents in Word, PowerPoint, or Excel, each application provides Window commands with which you can automatically arrange all documents onscreen. Depending on the application, the documents can be displayed side-by-side, one above the other (see Figure 3-16), tiled, or cascading from upper left to lower right.

FIGURE 3-16.
In Word, from the Window menu, choose Arrange All to arrange all open documents in a vertical stack

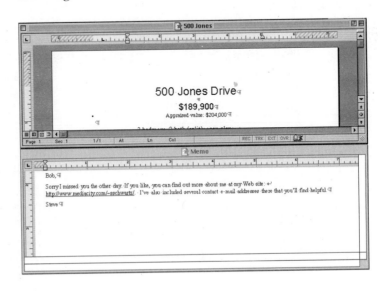

Microsoft Office 2001 Essentials

To arrange document windows, from the Window menu choose Arrange All (Word and PowerPoint) or Arrange (Excel). If you're working in Word or PowerPoint, the documents are immediately rearranged for you. If you're using Excel, the Arrange Windows dialog box appears as shown in Figure 3-17. Click a radio button to register your choice and click OK.

FIGURE 3-17.

When arranging windows in Excel, you can choose any of these arrangement options

When working with arranged windows, you can click any document's zoom box to enable its window to take over the screen. When you're ready to work with a different document, click the zoom box again to restore its "arranged" size and onscreen position.

Creating Multiple Views of a Window

Depending on the Office application, you can create additional views of the same window in one or two ways: by creating a new window or by splitting the window (in Excel and Word only). Why create additional views at all? Because it can be useful to work in one part of a document (such as a worksheet or a word processing document) and be able to refer to a different section of the same document without having to scroll back and forth. You can also instantly see how changes in one part of a worksheet affect calculations in another part. To create a new view of the current window, open the Window menu and choose New Window.

When you split a window into two or more parts (rather than creating a new one), the parts scroll independently of each other. There are two ways to split a window. First, from the Window menu, you can choose the Split command. In Word, the document is vertically split into two parts. In Excel, the document is split horizontally and vertically into four parts. Second, you can drag the split box in Word or Excel to determine manually how the page is divided. (See Figure 3-18.)

FIGURE 3-18.

You can split a document by dragging the split box to any position in the document window

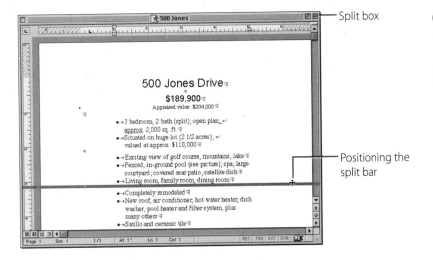

Split box

Positioning the split bar

After a document has been split—whether manually or automatically—you can change the percentage of the screen available to each part by simply dragging the split dividing line to a new spot. To remove a split, choose Remove Split from the Window menu, double-click the split bar, or drag the split bar off the edge of the document.

 NOTE

> Excel has a related command that is often used with splits: Freeze Panes. Choose this command from the Window menu to lock the dividers in their current location. Choose Unfreeze Panes if you need to reposition one or more of the dividers.

Closing Windows

You can close any document window by clicking its close box or by making the window active, opening the File menu, and choosing Close (⌘-W). If you've made changes to the document, Office will give you an opportunity to save them.

Productivity Shortcuts

In addition to using the obvious Office tools to accomplish your tasks, Office 2001 provides several less obvious procedures and new tools to help improve your productivity.

Control-Clicking

All of the Office applications support Control-clicking. That is, you can hold down the Control key as you click objects, selected text, worksheet cells, message headers, toolbars, and so on. When you Control-click, an appropriate pop-up menu appears, enabling you to apply formatting to text or an object, switch to another part of the application, customize the application in some way, and so on. (These pop-up menus are known as *contextual menus*.) The point of Control-clicking is to save you time, preventing unnecessary trips to the toolbars and menus. In Word, for example, you can Control-click to select a synonym for a word, as shown in Figure 3-19.

FIGURE 3-19.

Try Control-clicking everywhere in Office

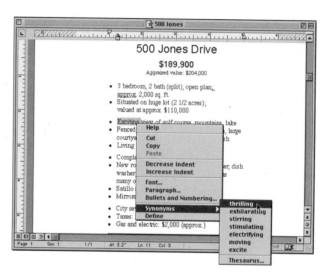

> **NOTE**
>
> If you are a Windows user, you should note that Control-clicking on a Macintosh is the equivalent of right-clicking on a Windows PC. Since Macintosh mice typically have only one button, Mac application developers support Control-clicking instead.

Where should you Control-click? Click everywhere and everything in each application. If it makes sense to support Control-clicking in a particular spot, it's probably there. Here are some of the most useful Control-clicks we've found:

Toolbars (Word, Excel, and PowerPoint)

- Control-click a blank spot in a toolbar to add or remove toolbars.

- Control-click a button or element in a toolbar and choose Properties to get a detailed explanation of how the button or element works.

Word

- Control-click a selected word to apply word or paragraph formatting, choose a synonym, or look up the word's definition.

Excel

- Control-click a cell or range, to apply formatting, summon the calculator, or insert a comment.

- Control-click a cell or range, and then drag to another location. The pop-up menu lists all of the move, copy, and shift options you can apply.

- Control-click a row or column heading to set an exact height or width, insert or remove rows or columns, and hide/or unhide the row or column.

- Control-click a sheet title (at the bottom of the worksheet window) to add, delete, rename, move, or copy sheets.

PowerPoint

- Control-click a slide to turn rulers or guides on/off. You can also choose another layout, background, or color scheme for the slide.

- Control-click selected text strings or text boxes to apply formatting commands.

- Control-click objects to send them backward/forward and to group/ungroup them.

Entourage

- Control-click a message header to mark it as read or unread, assign categories, apply rules, set a priority, flag/unflag it, move it to a different folder, or add the sender to your address book.

- Control-click a folder in the Folder List to create a new folder or subfolder.

- Control-click a name in the Address Book to address a new message or assign categories to the person.

- Control-click the headings above the Tasks window to add or remove headings.

- Control-click a date in the Calendar to add a new event or switch the display to show a day, week, workweek, or month.

- Control-click a selected word in a note or message to look up the word's definition.

- Control-click a selected text string to apply an Auto Text Cleanup procedure to it.

- Control-click a blank area in the toolbar to switch among the Entourage component windows.

 TIP

> It's sometimes possible to select multiple objects or items and then Control-click to apply the same command to them all. This is particularly useful when formatting objects and when dealing with multiple e-mail messages.

Internet Explorer

- Control-click a blank spot in the toolbar to customize it or change the color scheme.

- Control-click a link in a Web page or in the Explorer Bar to copy it to the clipboard, open it in a new window, or add it as a Favorite.

- Control-click a button in the Favorites bar to delete, rename, or open it in a new window.

- Control-click a graphic on a Web page to copy it, open it in a separate window, or download the image to disk.

- Control-click a blank spot on a Web page to add it as a Favorite, add it to the Favorites bar, set it as your home page, track it with the Auction Manager, or refresh the page.

Using Drag-and-Drop

If you've had your Mac for awhile, you're probably familiar with using the copy-and-paste or cut-and-paste commands to copy and move text and objects from one place in a document to another, between different documents, or even between applications. *Drag-and-drop* is a Macintosh system software feature that enables you to do the equivalent of a cut-and-paste or copy-and-paste by merely dragging the text or object to where you want it to go and then releasing the mouse button.

Office 2001 provides extensive support for drag-and-drop. For instance, you can use drag-and-drop in Word, PowerPoint, or Entourage to rearrange paragraphs or bullet points. You can drag edited text from a Word document onto a PowerPoint text slide or the Notes section. You can also use it to move cells in an Excel worksheet.

When dragging text or objects within an Office document, the dragged items are *moved* to the new location. When dragging text or objects between documents or applications, the dragged items are *copied* to the new location—leaving the original material intact in its original location.

 TIP

As mentioned previously, drag-and-drop is a system software feature rather than an Office feature. As such, you can drag-and-drop between many different types of software—not just Office applications.

You can also use drag-and-drop to create *clippings files*. Just drag a text selection or object from a document onto the Macintosh desktop. A clippings file appears on the desktop, as shown in Figure 3-20. (Note that creating a clipping leaves the original text or graphic intact; that is, it is a copy procedure rather than a move.) Double-click the file icon to view the clipping. (See Figure 3-21.) You can drag a clipping back into the same or a different document, if you want.

FIGURE 3-20.

A clippings file

FIGURE 3-21.

You can double-click any clippings file to view its contents

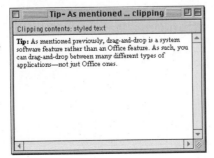

You can drag a contact card from your Address Book onto the desktop to create a *vCard* (.vcf) file, as shown in Figure 3-22. If you're tired of retyping your contact information every time someone requests it, you can e-mail your own vCard to anyone who uses Office 2001 or Microsoft Outlook. They can then easily add it to their address book.

FIGURE 3-22.
A vCard file contains most of the contact information entered for an individual

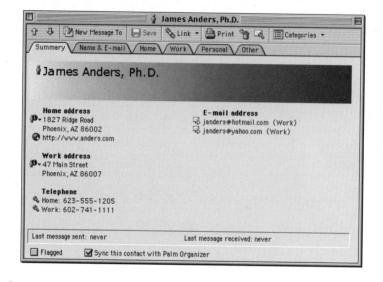

 ## Using the Formatting Palette

When you tire of making trips to the menus and toolbars, you'll really appreciate the new Formatting Palette (available in Word, Excel, and PowerPoint). By clicking check boxes and options and choosing from menus in the Formatting Palette, you can apply all major formatting options to the current text or object. Click the triangles to expand or collapse sections of the palette. (If the Formatting Palette isn't visible, open the View menu and choose Formatting Palette.)

The contents of the Formatting Palette automatically change, depending on what you're doing. As shown in Figure 3-23, for example, when working with numbers or text in Excel, the Formatting Palette options are very different from when you're working with draw objects.

FIGURE 3-23.

The Formatting Palette in Excel when working with cells (left) and draw objects (right)

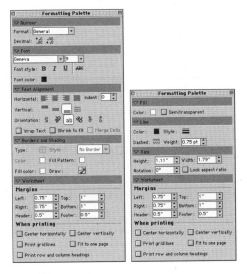

 TIP

Some sections of the Formatting Palette (such as color selections) can be torn off and become separate palettes, as shown in Figure 3-24.

FIGURE 3-24.

You can tear off some palette sections, such as this Font Color palette

Using the Office Clipboard

The Macintosh system software provides an area in memory called the *Clipboard* in which copied or cut text and objects are temporarily stored. When you copy or cut an item (using the Copy or Cut commands from the Edit menu), it is stored in the Clipboard and is available for pasting into the same document, another document, or another program. The contents of the Clipboard remain intact until you copy or cut something else or until you turn off the Mac.

Office improves on the Clipboard by providing an advanced version of it that's available when you're using or exchanging data between Excel, Word, and PowerPoint. Rather than restricting the contents of the Clipboard to a single item, the Office 2001 Clipboard can store up to 60 items (or 16MB of data). When you elect to paste in any of these programs, you can paste any stored item or simultaneously paste them all. And unlike the Mac Clipboard, the contents of the Office Clipboard remain intact until you specifically clear it—even when you turn off your computer.

 TIP

Although the Office Clipboard isn't available in Entourage, text that you copy or cut from Entourage documents *is* added to the Office Clipboard—enabling you to paste them into documents in other Office applications.

Here are different ways to use the Office Clipboard:

■ In Excel, Word, or PowerPoint, choose Office Clipboard from the View menu. The Clipboard window appears, as shown in Figure 3-25. (Items are copied to the Office Clipboard only when it is open.)

FIGURE 3-25.

The Clipboard palette shows all items that you've copied to the Office Clipboard

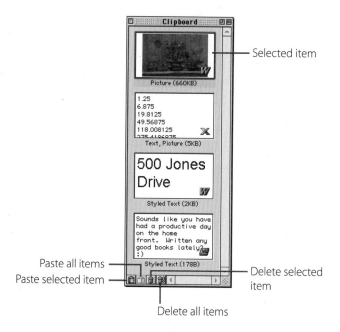

■ Select text or objects to copy or cut. From the Edit menu, choose Copy (⌘-C) or Cut (⌘-X), or drag the item(s) onto the Clipboard.

- To paste a single item into the current document, position the cursor where you want to paste, select an item in the Clipboard, and then—from the Edit menu—choose Paste, press ⌘-V, double-click the item, or click the Paste Selected button at the bottom of the Clipboard. (You can also drag the item from the Clipboard onto the document.)

 TIP

> You can simultaneously paste or delete multiple items from the Office Clipboard. Shift-click to select additional items, and then click the appropriate button at the bottom of the Office Clipboard—either Paste Selected or Clear Selected.

- To remove an item from the Clipboard, select it and click the Clear Selected button at the bottom of the Clipboard window. To delete *all* items, click the Clear All button.

CHAPTER 4

Using the Address Book

Microsoft Outlook Express—Microsoft's free e-mail program—has an Address Book in which you can store contact names and e-mail addresses, as well as home and work mailing addresses, phone numbers, and similar information. Now, however, Entourage is an Office component, and it—and its Address Book—will replace Outlook Express for Office users. Unlike the Address Book in Outlook Express, the Entourage Address Book is accessible from Microsoft Word. If you're addressing a letter, you can use the Address Book to insert the recipient's name and mailing address.

This chapter will explain how to accomplish the following tasks with the Address Book:

- Import your existing contact information into the Address Book

- Add and edit contacts in the Address Book

- Create contact groups

- Access your address data from Word

- Search for contact records

- Customize the Address Book

- Synchronize records in the Address Book with a Palm or Handspring Personal Digital Assistant (PDA)

Importing Address Data

While the Address Book can be accessed from Word, the first place you'll encounter it will be in Entourage. When you first run Entourage, you'll be given an opportunity to import your current Address Book from Outlook Express, Eudora, Netscape Communicator, or several other popular e-mail and contact programs. If your program isn't one of the supported ones, you can often export your contacts to a tab-delimited text file and then import them into Entourage.

If you neglected to import your existing contacts when you set up Entourage, you can do so now by following one of the processes outlined here.

To import your contacts from another program, follow these steps:

1 Launch Entourage.

2 From the File menu, choose Import. The Begin Import screen of the Import wizard appears, as shown in Figure 4-1.

3 Click the top radio button (Import Information From One Of These Programs), and click the radio button for the program from which you want to import your contacts.

FIGURE 4-1.

Using the Import wizard, you can import contacts from many e-mail programs, Address Book utilities, and databases

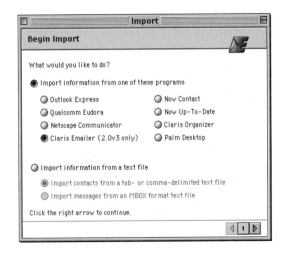

4 Click the right arrow button to continue. The Ready To Import screen of the Import wizard appears, as shown in Figure 4-2.

FIGURE 4-2.

Select the items you want to import

5 Click check boxes to indicate the data you want to import. (The specific check boxes listed will vary from program to program.)

6 Click the right arrow button to continue. Entourage searches your hard disk for the appropriate data file. If it is found, the data is imported into Entourage.

NOTE

> When you choose to import contacts, all contacts are added as new records in the Address Book. Any existing Address Book records remain intact. However, if importing contacts creates *duplicate* records, you will have to remove them manually.

To import your contacts from a tab-delimited text file, follow these steps:

1 In your Address Book program or e-mail program, export or save your Address Book as a tab-delimited text file. (See the application's documentation or Help if you need assistance doing this. Note, however, that while widely available, this capability is not found in all programs.)

2 Launch Entourage.

3 From the File menu, choose Import. The Begin Import screen of the Import wizard appears (as shown in Figure 4-1).

4 Click the second radio button (Import Information From A Text File), and click the radio button for the type of file from which you want to import your contacts. In most cases, this will be the first one (Import Contacts From A Tab- Or Comma-Delimited Text File).

5 Click the right arrow button to continue. The Import Text File dialog box appears, as shown in Figure 4-3.

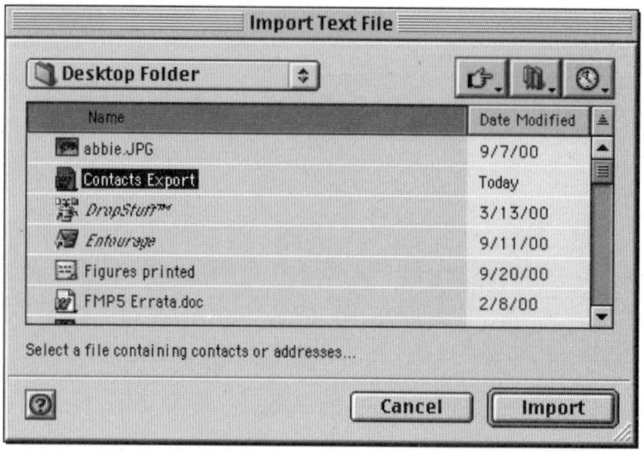

FIGURE 4-3.

Select a text file to import from the Import Text File dialog box

Import Text File	
Desktop Folder ⬍	📂 📖 🕐
Name	**Date Modified** ▲
🖼 abbie.JPG	9/7/00
Contacts Export	Today
🗜 DropStuff™	3/13/00
🗂 Entourage	9/11/00
📇 Figures printed	9/20/00
📄 FMP5 Errata.doc	2/8/00 ▼
Select a file containing contacts or addresses...	
?	Cancel Import

6 Select the text file, and click Import. The Import Contacts dialog box appears, as shown in Figure 4-4. Here you will match up the imported fields to Entourage fields.

FIGURE 4-4.

Before importing contact data, you must specify how the fields in the two databases are to be matched

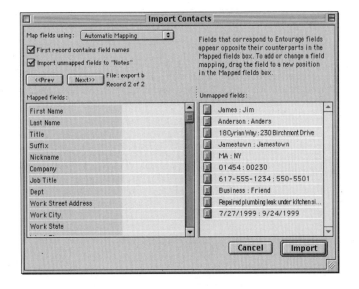

7 By default, Entourage automatically attempts to match fields based on the names of the imported field (if the first record contains a list of the field names). To complete the field matching (see Figure 4-5), do as follows:

- If the first record does *not* contain a list of the field names in the export file, clear the first check box.

- If any imported field in the Mapped Fields list is incorrectly mapped, drag it up or down so that it is beside the appropriate Entourage field. Similarly, any fields in the Unmapped Fields list can be dragged into the Mapped Fields list and placed beside the matching Entourage field.

- Depending on the state of the second check box, any fields remaining in the Unmapped Fields list will either be discarded or copied into the Notes field.

- Click the Prev and Next buttons to scroll through the records that you are about to import. As a sanity check, make sure the data for several records is being mapped correctly.

FIGURE 4-5.

This is the Import Contacts window after fields in the two files have been matched

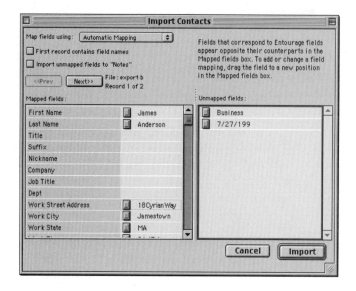

8 Click the Import button.

9 If you've modified the automatic field matching, you will be given an opportunity to save the mapping, as shown in Figure 4-6, in case you will be repeatedly importing data from the same program. If you want to save the mapping, click Save and then enter a mapping name when prompted to do so. (The saved mapping name will be added to the Map Fields Using pop-up menu in the Import Contacts dialog box.) The new records are imported into the Address Book. While Entourage is incapable of importing Address Books from Windows programs, you may be able to export such an Address Book as a tab-delimited text file and then use the preceding procedure to import it into Entourage.

FIGURE 4-6.

If you want to save the mapping for this export file so it can be reused, click Save

Adding New Contacts

There are three main ways that you can create a new contact card:

■ Manually enter the contact in the Address Book.

■ Create a new contact based on the e-mail address in a received message.

■ Create a new contact from a *vCard file* (a file containing a person's contact information) received as an e-mail attachment.

Manually Creating a Contact Card

As you make new contacts in your business, education, or personal life, you'll want to add them to your Address Book. If the address information isn't based on a received e-mail message (as explained in the next section), you can manually create a new contact record by following these steps in Entourage:

1 Issue the command to create a new contact.

- Click the down arrow beside the New toolbar button, and choose Contact.

- From the File menu, choose New and then Contact.

  or

- If the Address Book window is open, you can press ⌘-N. (To open the Address Book, you can click or double-click the Address Book icon in the Folder List, choose Address Book from the Window menu, or press ⌘-2).

A Create Contact dialog box opens, as shown in Figure 4-7.

FIGURE 4-7.

Enter information for the person, company, or organization in the Create Contact dialog box

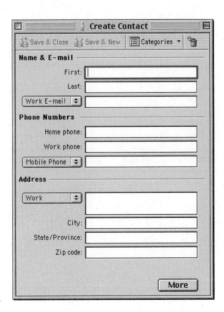

2 Fill in as much of the contact information as you want. You can also assign a category to the contact by selecting one from the Categories pop-up menu.

3 To save the contact record, click Save & Close. To save this record and create additional records, click Save & New.

> **NOTE**
>
> If you'd like to enter additional information (such as the person's birth date, children, or a photo), click the More button after step 2. Complete the record by clicking the Save button.

If you're in Word, follow this procedure instead:

1 If the Contact toolbar isn't visible, display it by opening the View menu, choosing Toolbars, and then choosing Contact.

2 Click the right arrow at the end of the Contact toolbar, and choose Address Book.

3 When the Address Book opens, click the New button. A Create Contact dialog box opens, as shown in Figure 4-7.

4 Perform steps 2 through 3 from the previous step list. Click the magnifying glass icon beside the number to enlarge it, as shown in Figure 4-8.

FIGURE 4-8.

To see information more clearly, click the magnifying glass icon beside the number in the contact summary

Magnified number

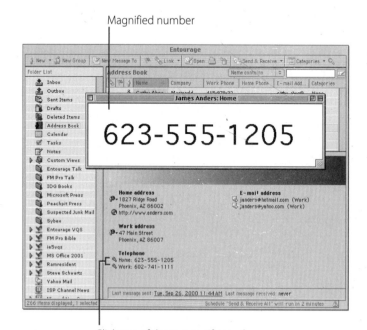

Click one of these magnifying glasses

If you're entering several contacts at the same address or company, you can save yourself a lot of typing by selecting one of the contacts, opening the Edit menu, and choosing Duplicate Contact. Then edit the duplicate record's name and other information as needed.

If you're trying to phone a contact and are having difficulty seeing the person's number, click the magnifying glass icon beside the number in the contact summary. (See Figure 4-8.)

Creating a Contact Based on a Received Mail Message

If you receive e-mail from a person, company, or organization that you think you'll want to contact again, you can save their e-mail address information as a contact card by following these steps:

1 Control-click the message header in the message list, and choose Add Sender To Address Book from the pop-up menu that appears.

   If a contact record for this e-mail address doesn't exist, a new one is created and opens.

   or

   If a contact record for this e-mail address already exists, a dialog box will ask if you want to open the record, as shown in Figure 4-9. To review and/or change the existing record, click Open. Otherwise, click Cancel.

2 Make any necessary changes, and click the Save button. (If you've made no changes, the Save button will be grayed out. In that case, just click the record's close box.)

FIGURE 4-9.

This dialog box appears if you try to add an existing contact to the Address Book

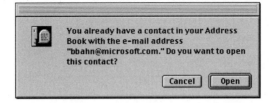

You already have a contact in your Address Book with the e-mail address "bbahn@microsoft.com." Do you want to open this contact?

Cancel   Open

> If you follow this procedure by Control-clicking a header in the message list, the Add Sender To Address Book command will always present itself, even if a record for the person is already in the Address Book. On the other hand, if you open a message in its own window and Control-click the sender's e-mail address, the Add To Address Book command will only appear if there isn't already a contact record for the person.

Creating, Sending, and Receiving vCards

One contact card is more important than all the others. It's the one that identifies *you* and provides your contact information. The information for this card was collected when you installed Office. If you open the Address Book or view it in the main window, you'll note that your card is marked with an *i* icon.

To make it easy to exchange contact information with others, you can forward your card (or anyone else's card) as an e-mail attachment in vCard format. If the recipient has Entourage or Microsoft Outlook, he or she can open the vCard and optionally save it as a new contact record. If the person has a different e-mail program—one that doesn't support vCards—he or she can open the file in any text editor or word processing program. And, of course, the reverse is also true. When you receive a vCard as an e-mail attachment, you can save it as a new Address Book record, if you want.

Sending a vCard

To e-mail your vCard (or anyone else's contact information from your Address Book), follow these simple steps:

1 Open the Address Book.

2 Select the contact record that you want to e-mail or double-click it to open the card in its own window.

3 From the Contact menu, choose Forward As vCard. A new message window appears. The person's name is used as the Subject (FW: Rebecca Theim, for example), and the vCard is automatically inserted as an attachment.

4 Compose the message (see Figure 4-10), and send it.

FIGURE 4-10.

You can e-mail a vCard as a file attachment

vCard attachment

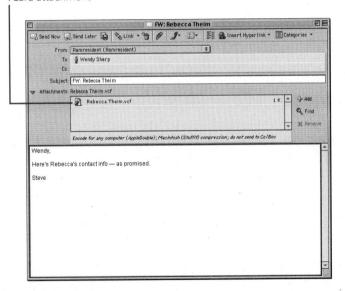

> **NOTE**

Entourage vCards have fields that aren't available in Outlook 2000 vCards. If you send a vCard from Entourage to an Outlook 2000 user, the additional fields will be ignored.

Receiving a vCard

Saving a received vCard as a new contact record is the simplest way to add detailed contact information to your Address Book. When you receive a vCard from someone, it will appear in the message's Attachments window as a file name ending with *.vcf*. To add the vCard as a new Address Book record, select the attachment and click the Open button. The card opens in its own window. Click the Save button in the toolbar to save it as a new record.

> **NOTE**

Saving a received vCard will *always* create a new record—even if a record for the person already exists. Be sure to check for and delete any duplicates.

Changing Your Personal vCard

There are two ways to change your vCard. First, you can open it in the Address Book, edit it as you like, and then click the Save button to save your changes. Second, you can substitute a *different* contact card for the existing one by selecting that card in the Address Book window, opening the Contact menu, and choosing This Contact Is Me.

TIP

> While one Address Book record will always represent your identity, there's nothing stopping you from creating additional records for yourself. For example, you might want a contact record that shows your mailing address but not your phone number or other personal information—such as the names of your children and your age. You can create a second record for yourself with the sensitive information stripped out and e-mail *that* one as your vCard.

Editing Contact Records

Of course, contacts in your Address Book will change over time. People move, change jobs, change e-mail addresses, get cell phones, and sometimes cease to be important to you.

To modify a contact's information, begin by opening the contact record. You can accomplish this by double-clicking a name in the Address Book, Control-clicking a name and choosing Open Contact, or selecting a name in the Address Book and doing one of the following:

- From the File menu, choose Open Contact.
- Press ⌘-O.
- Click the Open button in the Address Book's toolbar.

Make the necessary edits to the person's contact record, and then click the Save button to record the changes.

 TIP

> One way to help you identify a contact is by adding his or her picture to the record. In the record, click the Personal tab and then drag a picture file into the box on the right, as shown in Figure 4-11.

Microsoft Office 2001 Essentials

FIGURE 4-11.

You can drag a picture into a contact record

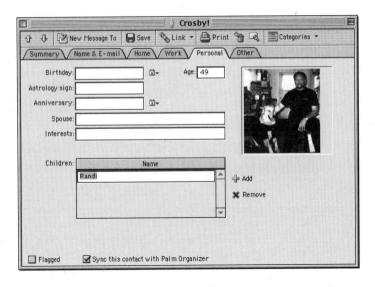

You can also delete records that are no longer necessary. Select the record in the Address Book, and do one of the following:

- From the Edit menu, choose Delete Contact.

- Press ⌘-Delete or Delete.

- Click the Trash button in the Address Book's toolbar.

- Control-click the record, and choose Delete Contact.

- Drag the record onto the Trash icon on your Mac's desktop.

Ⓧ CAUTION

You cannot undo a contact record deletion, and the deleted record is not transferred to the Deleted Items folder. (And if you've disabled the Notification preference to Require Confirmation When Deleting, no warning dialog box appears when you delete a record.) Be careful not to accidentally delete contacts.

Never Get Lost Again

In conjunction with Expedia.com, you can request maps and driving directions for any person or company in your Address Book—as long as you've entered an address for the contact and have an Internet account. Launch Entourage, select or open the contact record, open the Contact menu, and choose Map Address, Driving Directions From Home, or Driving Directions From Work. Your default Web browser launches and fetches the requested information from Expedia.com.

Creating Contact Groups

If you routinely send the same messages to a particular set of people, you can simplify the task of addressing the messages by defining groups. A *group* is any hand-chosen set of individuals who have something in common with each other. For example, back when I was writing Nintendo books, it would have been extremely helpful to have a group that consisted of game publishers.

To create a group, follow these steps:

1 Open the Address Book, or select it in the Folder List.

2 Click the New Group button (or open the File menu, choose New, and then choose Group). An Untitled Group dialog box appears, as shown in Figure 4-12.

> If one or more names were highlighted in the Address Book when you issued the New Group command, those contacts are automatically included in the group list. If you like, you can pre-select group members in this way. ⌘-click to select multiple, non-contiguous records; Shift-click to select contiguous records.

FIGURE 4-12.

The Untitled Group dialog box appears when you issue the New Group command

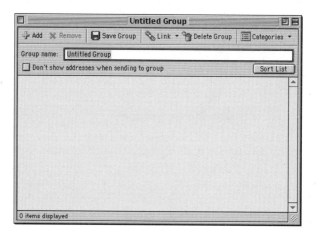

3 Enter a name for the group.

4 Add group members by clicking the Add button, typing part of the person or company's name, and selecting it from the list that appears. To remove a member, select his or her name and click Remove.

★ TIP

You can also add members by dragging their names from the Address Book into the Group window.

5   Unless you want group members to see the names and e-mail addresses of every other group member, click the Don't Show Addresses When Sending To Group check box.

6   Save the group by clicking the Save Group button. A completed group definition is shown in Figure 4-13.

FIGURE 4-13.

The completed group definition includes a group name and a list of group members

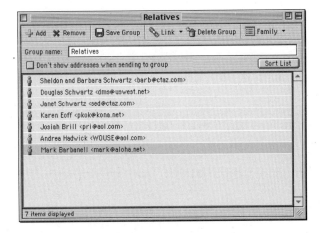

To send an e-mail message to a group, use the same procedure as when sending a message to an individual. However, instead of putting a person's contact name in the To box, you choose the group name.

⊗ CAUTION

Like record deletions, you cannot undo a group deletion. It happens instantly; no warning dialog box appears

To delete a group you no longer need, begin by selecting it in the Address Book list. Then Control-click the group name and choose Delete Group, choose Delete Group from the Edit menu, press ⌘-Delete, or press Delete. Note that deleting a group does *not* delete the records of the group members; it merely deletes the group definition.

Accessing the Address Book from Word

Accessing Entourage from Word enables you to use address information in your documents, as well as to create and edit contact records. To make Address Book data available in Word, choose items from the Contact toolbar. To display the Contact toolbar, shown in Figure 4-14, choose Toolbars from the View menu and then choose Contact.

FIGURE 4-14.

You can access your contact records from Word by displaying the Contact toolbar

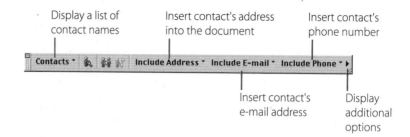

Display a list of contact names

Insert contact's address into the document

Insert contact's phone number

Insert contact's e-mail address

Display additional options

Here's how you use the Contact toolbar:

- To insert a contact person's name in the current document, position the cursor where you want the name to appear and then select a contact from the Contacts list.

- To insert additional information for the same contact, select his or her name in your document. Address information that's available is represented by the active buttons in the Contact toolbar (Include Address, Include E-mail, and Include Phone). Click any active button to insert the selected information.

- To open and work with the Address Book (adding, editing, or deleting contact records), click the right arrow at the end of the Contact toolbar and choose Address Book.

Searching for Contact Records

If your Address Book has many entries and you want to search for a contact without scrolling through the list, there are two options available to you:

- For a simple search, you can *filter* the list.

- For more advanced searches, you can conduct a Find or an Advanced Find.

Filtering the List

Most searches in a typical Address Book can be accomplished by filtering the list—based on the person's name, company, or e-mail address. Beneath the Address Book toolbar, choose a filtering option from the pop-up menu (Name Contains, Company Contains, or Category) and then type all or part of a keyword in the text box. (If you've chosen Category, you must choose a category from the new pop-up menu that appears.) Entourage automatically displays all matching records, as shown in Figure 4-15. To revert to the full list, delete whatever is in the text box by clicking the Eraser button, or set the Category to All.

⭐ TIP

When filtering by Name Contains, you can either type in part of the person's name or part of their e-mail address. If you know that a friend uses America Online but don't remember her name, you could enter *@aol. com* to view a list of AOL users only.

FIGURE 4-15.

You can view a subset of your contact records by filtering the address list

Filter pop-up menu   Filter text   Erase button

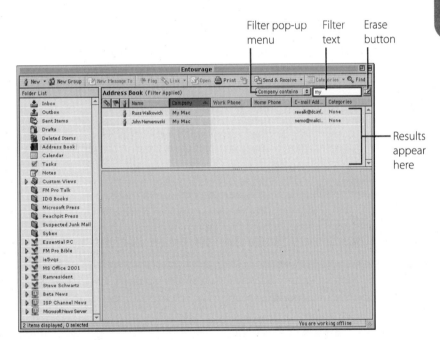

Results appear here

Conducting a Find or Advanced Find

If you need to search more than just the Company, Name, or Category field, you can perform a Find or an Advanced Find. A simple Find can simultaneously search all fields in the Address Book. An Advanced Find is useful when you want to restrict the search to one or more specific fields or if you need to combine conditions, such as searching for all contacts from Wisconsin over the age of 35.

To perform a simple Find:

1 Open the Address Book, or select it in the Folder List.

2 From the Edit menu, choose Find (or press ⌘-F). The Find dialog box appears.

3 Enter a search string in the text box, as shown in Figure 4-16.

FIGURE 4-16.

In this example, the search will display all records in which you recorded a Federal Express shipper ID somewhere within the record

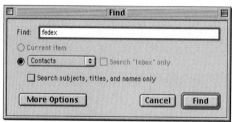

4 *Optional:* To search all fields in the Address Book, remove the check mark from Search Subjects, Titles, And Names Only.

5 Click the Find button. The matching contact records are displayed in a new window named Search Results.

> **NOTE**
>
> You can switch between a Find and an Advanced Find by clicking the More Options or Fewer Options buttons in the Find dialog box.

To perform an Advanced Find, follow these steps:

1 Open the Address Book, or select it in the Folder List.

2 From the Edit menu, choose Advanced Find (or press Option-⌘-F). An expanded version of the Find dialog box appears as shown in Figure 4-17.

3 Make sure that the Contacts check box is checked.

4 Specify search criteria by choosing from pop-up menus and typing in the text boxes. To specify additional criteria, click the Add Criterion button.

FIGURE 4-17.

The dialog box for an Advanced Find lets you specify multiple criteria, as well as do more than simply search for a text string

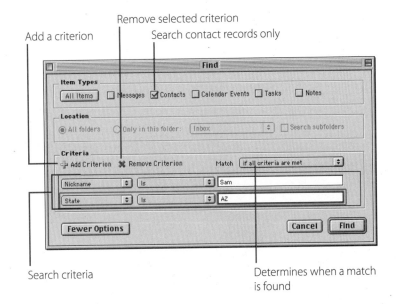

Add a criterion

Remove selected criterion

Search contact records only

Search criteria

Determines when a match is found

5 Choose an option from the Match pop-up menu.

6 Click the Find button. The matching contact records are displayed in a new window named Search Results.

 **TIP**

Entourage introduces an *extremely* useful e-mail command: Find Related Items. Using this command, you can ask Entourage to display all correspondence from and to any contact in your Address Book. Select the contact in your Address Book, and then choose Find Related Items from the Edit menu.

Customizing the Address Book

To make the Address Book better suit your needs, you can customize it as described in the following sections.

Adding, Removing, Resizing, and Moving Columns

If the Address Book display isn't exactly as you want it, you can add and remove columns, change the size of any column, or alter the order in which the columns are presented.

■ To add or remove an Address Book column, open the View menu, click Columns, and select a column to add or remove, as shown in Figure 4-18. Checked columns will be displayed in the Address Book; unchecked columns will not be displayed.

■ To change a column's size, move the cursor to the right edge of the column's head. It will change to a double-headed arrow. Drag to the left to reduce the column's width or to the right to increase its width.

■ To change the order in which the columns are displayed, click a column head and drag it to the desired position.

FIGURE 4-18.

You can choose column heads to display from this menu

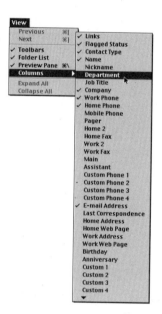

Sorting the Address Book

You can sort the Address Book by the contents of any displayed field (as represented by the column heads). To sort by a column head, just click the head. The direction the triangle beside the head points shows whether it is an ascending (pointing up) or descending (pointing down) sort. To reverse the sort order, click the same column head again.

Defining Custom Fields

If you open any contact record and flip through the tabs at the top, you'll notice several fields that are labeled "Custom." You can use these fields to gather any type of contact data that you like. To make it easier to use these fields, open any contact record, click a Custom field label, enter a new label for the field (as shown in Figure 4-19), and click OK. The new field label will now appear in every contact record in the database.

FIGURE 4-19.
You can rename any Custom field to indicate the type of data you intend to collect in it

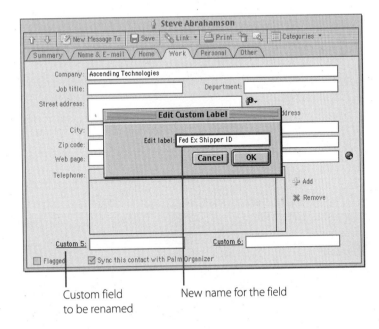

Custom field to be renamed

New name for the field

Setting a Default Format for Phone Numbers

Although it's a minor thing, Entourage lets you specify a default format to be used for newly entered phone numbers, providing consistency in the way they're displayed. To choose a format, open the Edit menu, choose Preferences, and then choose General. Click the Address Book tab, make sure that Format Phone Numbers is checked, and choose a format from the Format pop-up menu, as shown in Figure 4-20. You can also specify a default area code, if you want. Any seven-digit telephone number that you later enter will be assumed to be from the default area code. (Leave this blank if you don't want an area code automatically added to numbers.)

FIGURE 4-20.

To ensure consistency in newly entered phone numbers, you can specify a standard format to be applied to them, as well as specify a default area code to use when one isn't entered

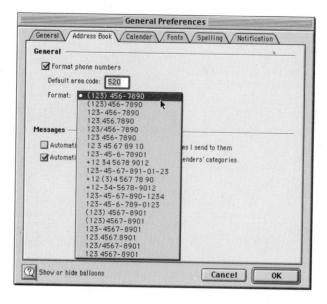

NOTE

The default formatting is only applied to numbers that you enter starting now. Phone numbers in previously entered or imported contact records will *not* be reformatted for you. To correct the formatting in previously entered phone numbers, you'll have to re-enter them.

Synching Contacts with a Palm Handheld

As was the case with Outlook Express 5, if you have a Palm or Handspring Visor Personal Digital Assistant (PDA), you can *synchronize* your Address Book contacts with those on your PDA—that is, whether you make changes in Entourage or on your PDA, you can make the two sets of information match, thereby *synchronizing* them. In addition to this capability, Entourage enables you to synchronize tasks, notes, and calendar events. You must have Palm OS 2.0 or higher installed in your PDA and Palm Desktop 2.6.1 or higher installed on your Mac. You must also install the Entourage Conduit that's included in the Office 2001 Value Pack. Installing the conduit instructs Palm Desktop to synchronize with Entourage rather than with the Palm Desktop data. To synchronize the PDA and Entourage data, insert your PDA into its cradle and press the HotSync button.

Microsoft Office 2001 Essentials

> **NOTE**
>
> Unless your handheld user name and your Entourage identity match, no synchronization will take place. If necessary, rename your Entourage identity by choosing Switch Identity from the File menu, selecting the identity, clicking the Rename button, and then entering the new name.

You can optionally specify which Entourage contact records will be synchronized and which ones will be ignored. Open a contact and—at the bottom of any page of the record (as shown in Figure 4-21)—you'll see a checkbox marked Sync This Contact With Palm Organizer.

FIGURE 4-21.

The state of the check box determines whether this contact record will or won't be synchronized

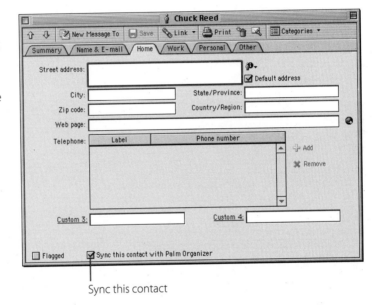

Sync this contact

CHAPTER 5

Introducing Microsoft Word

Microsoft Word, or more simply, Word, is a word processing application. As such, it has been created to "process" words. This basically means that you enter text and graphics into Word documents with your keyboard and mouse, format the contents of the document to suit your aesthetic tastes and functional needs, and then print the document or publish it electronically for people to read. Word will help you at every step along the way as you perform these tasks, except that it obviously won't create the content of your documents for you.

As you'll learn from this and other chapters, Word is a powerful yet easy-to-use application. It is full of features that will enable you to produce functional and professional-looking documents. You can take advantage of as many or as few of these features as you want. If you want to type a short, informal letter to a friend, you can do that, or if you need to create a lengthy, professional report you can do that, too. In order to provide this kind of flexibility, Word is a complex application. But don't let that scare you. You may never need all the features Word has, but if you do, you won't have to run out and buy another software package. This chapter will introduce you to Word and get you started creating documents. Later chapters will cover in more detail the topics of entering text and graphics, formatting, and publishing.

Running Word

? SEE ALSO

You can find more information about running the Office applications in Chapter 2.

As you learned in Chapter 2, "Microsoft Office Basics," there are many ways to launch a Microsoft Office application. Rather than duplicate that discussion here, the following lists the most popular methods you can use to launch Word:

- Open the Microsoft Office 2001 folder in your hard drive, and double-click the Microsoft Word icon.

- From the Apple menu, select Recent Applications to launch Word. (This technique works best if you use Word often.)

- Create a Word alias on your desktop, and double-click the alias to launch Word.

- Find a Word document you want to edit, and double-click its icon.

- From the Apple menu, select Recent Documents to launch an existing Word document.

★ TIP

The last two methods, finding and opening Word documents rather than launching Word itself, bypass the Project Gallery that pops up when you launch an Office application. Word starts without any intervening screens and displays your document. This saves you a bit of time and keeps you from having to click excessively to open an existing document.

Getting to Know the Interface

As powerful as Word is, you'll never comprehend its full potential if you don't understand the interface. An *interface* is simply how a program looks, feels, and works; it's what is staring you in the face when you run the program.

When you first run Word, you are presented with a daunting array of windows and toolbars, each of which can be customized to suit your tastes and needs. Figure 5-1 provides you with an annotated illustration to follow along with as we explain the different parts of the interface in the subsequent sections.

FIGURE 5-1.

The Word interface in its default state

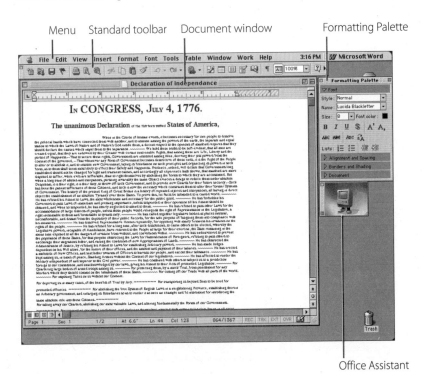

Menu Standard toolbar Document window Formatting Palette

Office Assistant

The Document Window

The majority of your screen is taken up by the main document window, as shown in Figure 5-2. At first, it's just a blank page. You can move the window by clicking the title bar or one of the other three window borders and dragging it to a new position on your screen. Resize the window by clicking on the lower-right corner and dragging the corner to a new position.

FIGURE 5-2.

The document window is where you'll create your documents

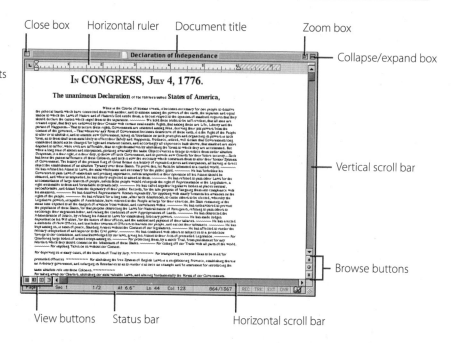

Close box Horizontal ruler Document title Zoom box

Collapse/expand box

Vertical scroll bar

Browse buttons

View buttons Status bar Horizontal scroll bar

Along the top and left sides are rulers that show the page boundaries as well as tab and indent positions (on the top ruler only). Areas in the ruler with a light gray diagonal stripe are outside your page setup area.

NOTE

The top ruler changes significantly when you use more than one column or insert tables in your document.

To the right and bottom of the main document window are scrollbars and arrows you can use to move the document around within the main window. In the lower-right corner of the window, where the horizontal and vertical scrollbars meet, are a few special buttons. The double arrows are called browse arrows. By default, they jump one page ahead or back from where you are currently in your document. You can change this behavior (paging up or down when you click the double arrows) by selecting the round button, which allows you to select a different browse object, such as graphics. For example, changing the browsing behavior to graphics will cause your document to jump to each graphic in succession when you click one of the double arrows rather than when you page up or down.

To the left of the horizontal scrollbar are a series of buttons that allow you to change the view of the document. Clicking on one of these buttons (Normal View, Online Layout View, Page Layout View, or Outline View) will change how Word displays your document.

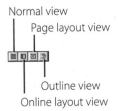

The views you can choose from are:

- **Normal View** This view is the default view that you can use to enter, edit, and format text.

- **Online Layout View** This view is best used when you are creating a Web page or a document that will be presented onscreen.

- **Page Layout View** Think of this view as the "Print View." You can see (and modify) how all of your text, graphics, and other elements are arranged on your page from this view.

- **Outline View** This view arranges your document to make it look like an outline.

You can also select these view options from the View menu.

At the bottom of the window is the status bar, which displays useful information about your document and Word. You may have to enlarge your document window to see the entire status bar. If the window isn't wide enough to display all of its features, they are hidden from your view.

The Standard Toolbar (and More)

One of the most important toolbars you encounter when using Word is the Standard toolbar, which is above the document window by default when you launch Word for the first time. In this toolbar, you'll find all sorts of buttons that perform a variety of tasks.

 **TIP**

> Most buttons on the toolbars duplicate menu choices that are also available. The method you prefer to use is up to you, although using the buttons on the toolbar can be quicker than accessing the various menu choices.

Because one toolbar just isn't enough, there are several others you can view onscreen. Select the View menu and choose Toolbars (see Figure 5-3) to see the other toolbars that are available. When you select one, it is displayed, and a checkmark appears by its name in the Toolbars menu.

FIGURE 5-3.

Show or hide any of the numerous toolbars from the Toolbars menu

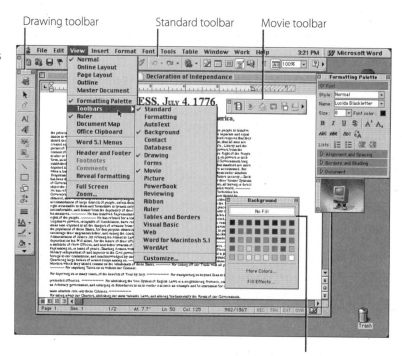

You can close toolbars by clicking the close box in the upper-left corner of the toolbar. If you don't like where your toolbar is, you can move it around by clicking (carefully, you don't want to select a button) and dragging it to a new position.

NOTE

The Word menu appears at the top of the screen and has virtually every command available to Word within it. It is important to think logically when you're trying to find something in the menus. If you need to insert something in your document, try the Insert menu. Quite often, if you talk yourself through the menus, you can find what you need in no time at all.

 # The Formatting Palette

The Formatting Palette, shown in Figure 5-4, is new to Word 2001, and takes the place of the Formatting toolbar found in previous versions. You use the Formatting Palette to format text in your document.

 TIP

You can still use the Formatting toolbar if you don't like the Formatting Palette. To do this, close the Formatting Palette, choose the View menu, select Toolbars, and then choose Formatting to open the Formatting toolbar.

FIGURE 5-4.

The Formatting Palette is new to Word 2001 and replaces the Formatting toolbar from previous versions

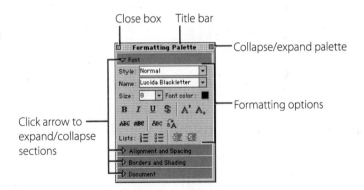

 SEE ALSO

The Formatting Palette is also discussed in Chapter 3, "Understanding the Microsoft Office Interface."

The Formatting Palette is divided into four sections (click the arrow next to the name to expand or collapse the section):

■ **Font** This section enables you to modify the style, font, size, color, and other text attributes. Numbered lists, bulleted lists, and indentation are also found here.

■ **Alignment And Spacing** This section contains options that control horizontal and vertical alignment, spacing, orientation, paragraph spacing, and indentation.

II

Microsoft Word

SEE ALSO

Document formatting and the Formatting Palette are covered in greater detail in Chapter 7, "Formatting Text and Documents."

- **Borders And Shading** This section enables you to create borders of various types, thicknesses, and colors, as well as shading effects, in your document.

- **Document** This section contains document-wide formatting options, such as the print margins, theme, and viewing options.

The Office Assistant

 SEE ALSO

More information on the Office Assistant can be found in Chapter 3.

The Office Assistant is a visually interesting portal to the large amount of helpful information about Word and the other Office programs. Click on the Office Assistant to ask it a question.

Click to ask a question

Creating Documents

 SEE ALSO

Opening, saving, closing, and printing Office documents is also described in Chapter 2.

Now that you've taken a tour of the Word interface, it's time to create a few documents. To do so, you can either start with a blank page and perform all the work yourself, or you can choose a template from the Project Gallery. Templates are "prefab" documents of various types that are formatted and ready for you to customize to the precise task at hand.

Do It Yourself

The prime benefit of starting with a blank page and creating everything yourself is that you have total control over your document from start to finish. The disadvantage is that you have to do all the work, from entering text, graphics, and other elements, to laying out your pages and formatting your content. In this section we'll cover the basic steps for creating a document yourself.

1 Launch Word using one of the techniques previously described.

2 When the Project Gallery opens, make sure that Blank Documents from the Category list on the left and Word Document in the main window are both selected and click OK, as shown in Figure 5-5. Word appears and displays a blank document entitled "Document1" in the document window.

FIGURE 5-5.

A blank document is one of many types of documents you can create from the Project Gallery

Document categories   Preview area

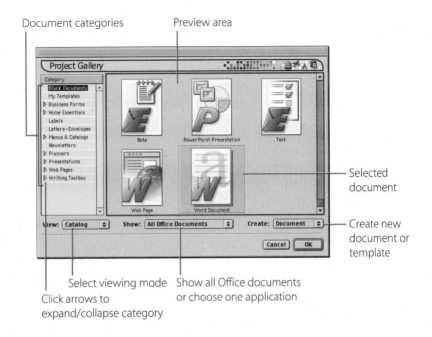

Selected document

Create new document or template

Select viewing mode   Show all Office documents or choose one application
Click arrows to expand/collapse category

3 Within the document window you should see a flashing vertical line. This identifies the "insertion point," or more plainly, where text will appear if you start typing. If you type enough, you'll see that the words run to the right margin and then automatically wrap around and create a new line. This is an important feature that many novices to word processing forget. The only time you need to press Return or Enter is to create a new paragraph. Finish your first paragraph, and then press Return to start another and continue typing.

4 Now play with the document on your own for a while. Try selecting letters, words, and paragraphs and change their formatting by using the Formatting Palette. If you make a mistake, click the Undo button on the toolbar.

> **NOTE**
>
> Undo (⌘-Z) and Redo (⌘-Y) are two of the most useful tools on the Standard toolbar. The great thing about Undo (and Redo, which "undoes" your undos) is that you can go back several steps to undo something you entered some time ago. The bad thing is that you can't selectively undo an action ten steps back: You have to undo everything to that point.

II

Microsoft Word

When you're finished, you should save your work. To do so, follow these steps:

1   Click the Save button on the Standard toolbar, or select the File menu and choose either Save or Save As. The first time you save a document, regardless of which method you choose, Word will ask you what you want to name it and where you want the file to be stored.

2   Choose a location on your hard drive or network to save the file.

3   Enter a name for your file in the Name text box. (See Figure 5-6.)

4   Select Save.

FIGURE 5-6.

Saving a Word document the first time involves choosing a file name and location

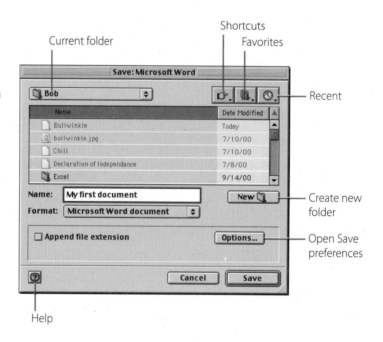

NOTE

Remember to save early and often when you are working in Word! There is nothing more frustrating than to be working on a lengthy project, letter, or report only to lose everything when you experience computer or power problems and haven't saved your changes.

When you're finished with your document, you can close it by selecting the File menu and choosing Close (⌘-W) or by clicking the close box.

If you want to return to your document to work on it some more, you can use the File menu to open it again. If your document was one of the last four you worked on, it will be visible in the File menu. Simply select the File menu, and then choose *your document* to open it. If it's not there, select the File menu, choose Open, and select your file from the Open dialog box, as shown in Figure 5-7. The Open dialog box displays all your Office 2001 documents by default, but you can select Word documents from the Show pop-up menu to show only Word documents.

FIGURE 5-7.

Opening documents requires that you find the document on your hard drive, select it, and then choose Open

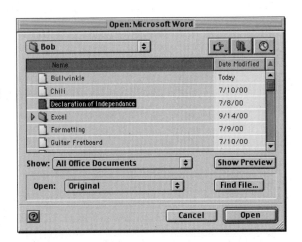

Using Templates

Templates are a different sort of beast altogether. Rather than designing a document on your own, Word has a host of prefabricated document templates that you can choose to start with. Once you open one, all you need to do is enter your own content. Table 5-1 summarizes the different document templates available in Word.

Table 5-1. Word Document Templates Available in the Project Gallery.

Category	Effect
Blank Documents	Allows you to create a blank Web page or Word document
My Templates	Templates that you have created are available here
Business Forms	Brochures, Fax Covers, Invoices, and Letterheads are found here
Home Essentials	Family Medical, Home Budget, and Resumes are found here
Labels	Launches the Mailing Label Wizard
Letters-Envelopes	Several types of letters and envelopes are found here, as is the Envelope and LetterWizard
Menus & Catalogs	Generic catalogs and different menus are found here
Newsletters	A Business Newsletter is found here
Planners	Checklists, Meals-Diets, Shopping Lists, and To Do Lists are found here
Web Pages	Two main designs, Cypress and Zero, with several different types of pages, are found here
Writing Toolbox	Journals and Reports are found here

The following steps show you how to create a document using Word's templates.

1 Launch Word.

2 When the Project Gallery opens, select Word Documents from the Show pop-up menu, as shown in Figure 5-8 on the following page.

3 Browse through the categories and choose one that looks interesting. If there is a Word template available, you'll see it previewed in the main window.

FIGURE 5-8.

Simplify your options by showing only Word documents that you can create

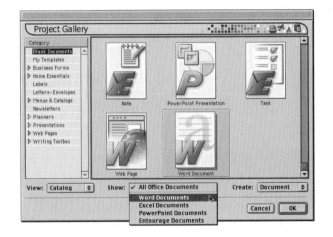

TIP

Categories that can be expanded in the Project Gallery are shown with an arrow beside them. Click the arrow to reveal subcategory templates.

4 Click OK when you've selected the type of document you want to create. In Figure 5-9, we've chosen the Resumes category to create a new resume with a modern appearance.

FIGURE 5-9.

Document templates are previewed in the main window

Expanded category   Selected template

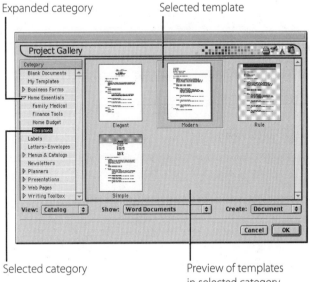

Selected category   Preview of templates
                           in selected category

5 Word then opens the template in the main document window, as shown in Figure 5-10. Now you're ready to start customizing it.

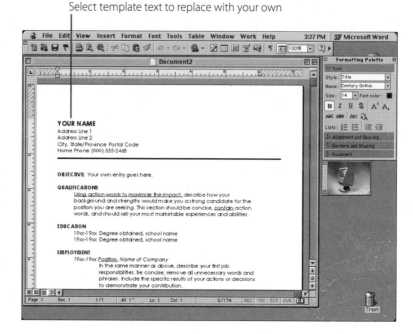

Select template text to replace with your own

6 All you need to do now is select the different parts of the resume, such as YOUR NAME, and enter your own information. Use your mouse to highlight the word, line, or paragraph that you want to change and start typing.

Getting Help

 SEE ALSO

More information on the Office 2001 for Mac Help system can be found in Chapter 2.

Word has several methods for accessing its extensive Help library. The most obvious is the Office Assistant, which we have already discussed in Chapter 2. All you have to do is click the Office Assistant to ask it a question, as shown in Figure 5-11.

To banish the Office Assistant, choose Turn The Assistant Off from the Help menu.

FIGURE 5-11.

Enter the key words you want to search for, and click Search to find help

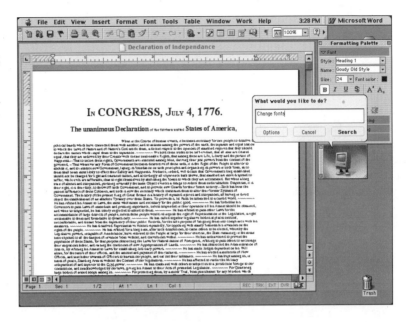

In addition, Word pops up ToolTips (see Figure 5-12) when you let your mouse rest over an interface element such as a button. If you forget the name of a button, just wait for the ToolTip to pop up and tell you.

FIGURE 5-12.

Let your cursor hover over a button, and watch for the ToolTip to pop up

Cursor over button   Tool tip

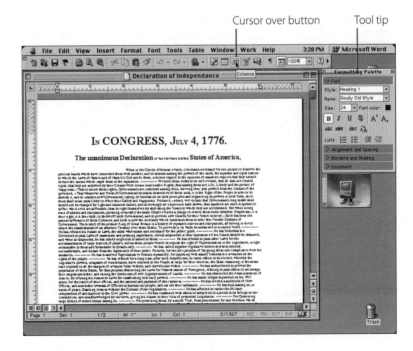

The Help menu offers other tools as well, such as:

- **Show Balloons** With this feature turned on, balloons pop up when your mouse hovers over many of the features in Word, as shown in Figure 5-13.

Cursor over object

FIGURE 5-13.

Balloon Help pops up when your cursor hovers over an object

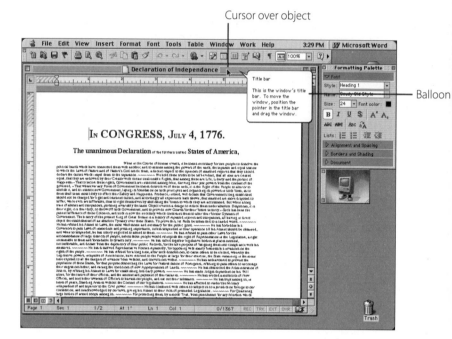

Balloon

- **Microsoft Word Help** This feature offers you another way to ask the Office Assistant a question.

- **Contents And Index** This feature opens the actual Help file, where you can browse through the contents or look up a word in the index. Click on a subject in the left-hand pane and it will expand to give you more choices. Click on an entry that you think will answer your question and help will appear in the right-hand page. (See Figure 5-14.) Click the Index tab to see the index.

FIGURE 5-14.

The Contents And
Index pane

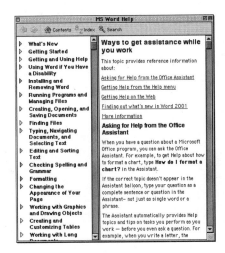

■ **Help On The Web** This feature opens your Web browser and
displays several links for you to visit on Microsoft's Web site that
offer downloads, support, and other information.

Typing and Editing Text

For some people, typing is a chore they would rather leave to the experts. If you fall into this category, you most likely use the "hunt-and-peck" technique while typing. If that's true, Microsoft Word 2001 offers some great features that will enable you to successfully enter text and spell words correctly, among other things. On the other hand, if you're a skilled typist, you don't need to learn how to type, but you do need to learn how to type in Word.

Whether you are a novice or a typing guru, Word accommodates your needs. This chapter will show you how to enter, select, cut, copy, paste, and move text, as well as perform spelling and grammar checks.

Entering Text

Entering text is fairly straightforward. You need an open Word document to begin. If you are starting from scratch, the document will be blank. Otherwise, you can add material or change it as you enter text.

Entering Text and Creating Paragraphs

If your document is blank, you have little choice about what to do next. Make sure you can see the insertion point (the blinking vertical bar) in your active document, and begin typing.

> **NOTE**
>
> If you want to type something in the middle of a blank page, switch to the Page Layout view and double-click the spot where you want to position your text. Word automatically inserts the blank lines and tabs needed for you to reach that part of the page.

You will probably also see the mouse cursor floating around your screen. It may be in the form of an I-beam or an arrow, depending on where it's located. Don't worry about the position just yet, as it doesn't affect the text until you click somewhere in your document.

> **NOTE**
>
> When you start typing, the cursor should disappear. To get it back, just wiggle your mouse a bit and it will reappear.

When you want to start a new paragraph, press the Enter or Return key. This inserts a carriage return and starts a new paragraph, as shown in Figure 6-1.

> **NOTE**
>
> A *carriage return* is a term used to indicate a hard return in a document that either starts a new paragraph or inserts extra lines. A *soft return*, by comparison, occurs when the lines wrap across the screen automatically as you type.

SEE ALSO

To learn more about tabs, indenting, and line spacing, see Chapter 7, "Formatting Text and Documents."

Unless you indent your paragraphs or have extra space between them, it can be hard to tell where one paragraph ends and another begins. For now, you can differentiate between them by looking at how Word wraps lines. Normally, lines wrap to the edge of the document and then automatically continue on the following lines.

Most people don't sit down and type a letter or other document from start to finish without going back and changing something. To make changes, move the cursor to the point where you want to "jump into" your document and press the mouse button. This moves the text insertion point to where you just clicked.

FIGURE 6-1.

Type text and press Return to start a new paragraph

First line of each paragraph is indented

Text is automatically wrapped to the next line within paragraphs

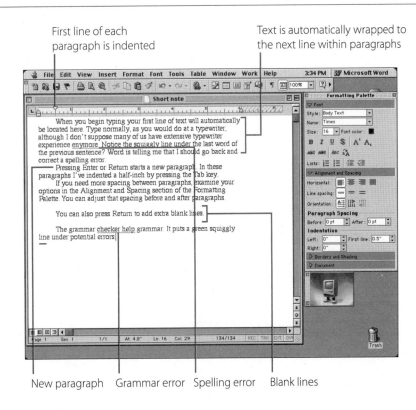

New paragraph   Grammar error   Spelling error   Blank lines

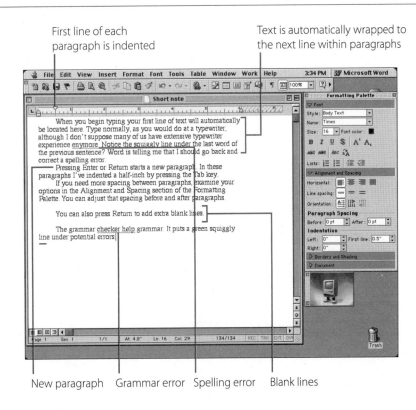
TIP

If you miss your target by a space or two, use the arrow keys (left, right, down, and up) to move the cursor to the exact location.

When you're happy with the new location, start typing again. If you make a mistake and want to correct it right away, you can either click the Undo button on the Standard toolbar (or press ⌘-Z) or delete the text you just entered. Press the Delete key to delete one character (or space) backwards from the text insertion point.

The Tab Key

You can use the Tab key to indent paragraphs or align text on your page. The default tab stops are every half-inch. Press Tab each time you want to jump to the next tab stop and continue typing. Selecting the Formatting menu and choosing Tabs opens the Tab dialog box so you can add or remove tabs, change the default tab stop length, and change the type of tab leader, which fills the space between tabs with dashes, dots, or a line.

Microsoft Word

Entering Special Characters

In your document, you may at times need to use special characters—such as degree symbols or copyright symbols—that aren't on your keyboard. Follow these steps to insert special characters into your document:

1   Move your cursor, and click in the document where you want to insert the special character or symbol.

2   Select the Insert menu and choose Symbol. This opens the Symbol dialog box, as shown in Figure 6-2. Symbols are shown by default, but you can switch to another font by selecting it from the drop-down Font menu, or you can insert special characters by selecting the Special Characters tab.

FIGURE 6-2.

Choose a symbol from this extensive list and click Insert to enter it into your document

Select to see special characters

Select to choose different font

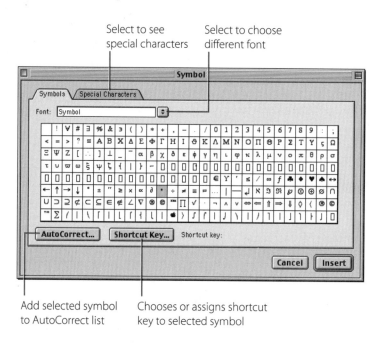

Add selected symbol to AutoCorrect list

Chooses or assigns shortcut key to selected symbol

3   Next find the symbol or character you want to insert and select it by clicking it.

4   Click Insert.

 TIP

If you frequently use one or more symbols or special characters in the Symbol dialog box, assign a shortcut key to it by clicking the Shortcut Key button, or place the symbol or special character in the AutoCorrect list by clicking the AutoCorrect button. Either method speeds up the process of inserting a symbol or special character.

Creating Headers and Footers

Not all the text you enter has to be in the main document. In fact, some information, such as the page number or date, is best left out of the main body of text. Headers and footers are special text areas that are applied to every page of your document (should you want) and aren't moved around by other text you enter in the body of the document. Follow these steps to create a header or footer:

1 Select the View menu and choose Header And Footer. (You can also double-click the header or footer area of the page if you are in Page Layout view.) This reveals the header and footer of your document, as shown in Figure 6-3. Headers and footers have a dashed line around them to signify that they are a special region of text. Notice that the text in the main portion of your document has changed to gray. This means that you can't enter or edit text in that area until you finish working with your header and footer. In addition, a new toolbar appears, which includes tools that allow you to insert special information automatically in your header or footer.

FIGURE 6-3.

Selecting the View menu and choosing Header And Footer enables you to enter headers and footers

Header area

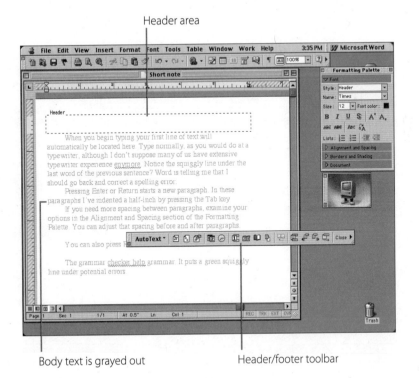

Body text is grayed out

Header/footer toolbar

2 Click in either the header or footer (if you can't see the footer, scroll down in the main document window), and enter the text that you want. The process of entering text is identical to how you enter text in the body of your document. You can increase the size of the header or footer by pressing Return or Enter.

3 Should you want to include information such as the page number, select that button from the Header/Footer toolbar; its buttons are summarized in Table 6-1.

TABLE 6-1. Available Buttons On The Header/Footer Toolbar.

Button	Description	Button	Description
AutoText	This is a list of already formatted information, such as the author, creation date, file name, and the page number	Insert Page Number	Inserts the page number
Insert Number Of Pages	Inserts the total number of pages that the document has	Format Page Number	Opens the Page Number Format dialog box, which allows you to modify how the page numbers are displayed, such as changing them from Arabic to Roman numerals
Insert Date	Inserts the current date	Insert Time	Inserts the current time
Different First Page	Allows you to have a different first page header and footer	Different Odd And Even Pages	Allows you to create different headers and footers for odd and even pages
Document Layout	Opens the Document dialog box, where you can modify the page layout	Show/Hide Document Text	Shows or hides the document text while editing the header and footer
Same As Previous	Allows you to make the current header or footer identical to the previous page	Switch Between Header And Footer	Switches the view between the header or footer
Show Previous	Shows the previous header or footer	Show Next	Shows the next header or footer
Goto	Allows you to select a header or footer to jump to from a list	Close	Closes the Header/Footer toolbar and takes you back to your main document

4 Click Close when you are finished entering text and information. Figure 6-4 shows a typical header.

FIGURE 6-4.

In this case, the header in light gray text is a combination of automatically generated information and material the user supplied

Header appears as light gray

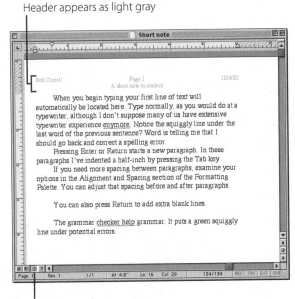

Header and footer visible only in Page Layout view

After you finish entering your header and/or footer, Word will return you to your main document so that you can continue writing or editing. You won't see the header and footer information while in Normal view mode; you must switch to Page Layout view to see your document header and footer.

 NOTE

> You can't edit headers or footers in the Page Layout view. You can only edit the header and footer by selecting the View menu and choosing Header And Footer.

Using AutoText

AutoText (previously referred to as Glossary entries) is a feature that actually does the writing for you. AutoText allows you to put a word or a lengthy phrase in storage and use it over and over. For example, if you work in a company whose name is lengthy, you may want to create an AutoText entry for that company so that you don't have to type the entire name out every time.

Several predefined entries exist. To use them, choose the Insert menu and select AutoText. Within the AutoText menu there are seven broad categories of phrases, which are summarized in Table 6-2.

TABLE 6-2.   AutoText Categories.

AutoText Category	Entries	AutoText Category	Entries
Attention Line	Attention: ATTN:	Closing	Best regards, Best wishes, Cordially, Love, Regards, Respectfully yours, Respectfully, Sincerely yours, Sincerely, Take care, Thank you, Thanks, Yours truly
Header/ Footer	- PAGE -; Author, Page #, Date; Confidential, Page #, Date Created by; Created on; Filename; Filename and path; Last printed; Last saved by; Page X of Y;	Mailing Instructions	CERTIFIED MAIL, CONFIDENTIAL, PERSONAL, REGISTERED MAIL, SPECIAL DELIVERY, VIA AIRMAIL, VIA FACSIMILE, VIA OVERNIGHT MAIL
Reference Line	In reply to:, RE:, Reference:	Salutation	Dear Mom and Dad:, Dear Sir or Madam:, Ladies and Gentlemen:, To Whom It May Concern:
Subject Line	Subject:		

You can also create new AutoText entries by following these steps:

1 Select a word or phrase you wish to add to the list.

2 Select the Insert menu and choose AutoText, followed by New.

3 When the Create AutoText dialog box appears, enter a name for your entry and click OK. (See Figure 6-5.)

The AutoText name doesn't have to be the same as the entry itself. In fact, if the entry is large, it helps to have a shorter name. Then, when you are typing along and Word sees the first few letters or words and recognizes them as a potential AutoText entry, it will prompt you with a yellow highlight box with your AutoText entry. (The name must be at least four characters long to use AutoComplete.) Press Return to accept the entry.

FIGURE 6-5.

Enter a word or phrase in the Create AutoText dialog box

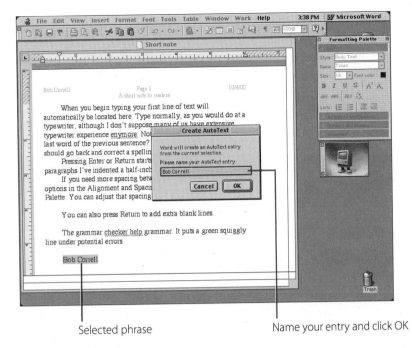

Selected phrase   Name your entry and click OK

Selecting Text

Selecting text is an invaluable tool as you edit your document, but it's an intermediate step. In other words, selecting text, just to select it, does nothing by itself. The larger aim of selecting text is to perform another action on it. After you select text, you might:

- Format the text differently

- Cut, copy, or delete the selection

- Move the selection

Fortunately, you're not limited to how much you can select. You can select as little or as much as you desire, from individual letters to words, sentences, paragraphs, and the entire document.

Selecting text sometimes involves dragging your mouse. Follow these steps to select text:

1 Move your cursor to the position where you want to start the selection.

2 Press and hold the mouse button down.

3 Move (drag) your mouse in the direction you want to select text. If you clicked at the beginning of a word and you want to select the entire word, for example, you should drag the mouse to the right until the entire word is highlighted. Figure 6-6 shows this procedure.

FIGURE 6-6.

Select text by clicking at the beginning of the selection, holding your mouse button down, and highlighting the rest of the selection

Click here to start selection

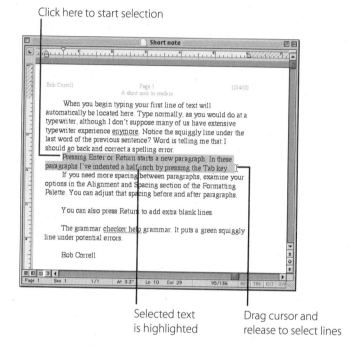

Selected text is highlighted

Drag cursor and release to select lines

4 Release the mouse button.

Other selecting methods allow you to move your cursor outside of the writing area (but remain within the main document window). You should look for the position and the shape of the cursor. When you want to select a line, for example, move your cursor to the left side of the line you want to select. The cursor should change to a right arrow, as shown in Figure 6-7. When you click with the cursor at that position, the entire line to the right of the cursor is selected, as shown in Figure 6-8.

FIGURE 6-7.

When you select a line of text, the cursor should change to a right arrow

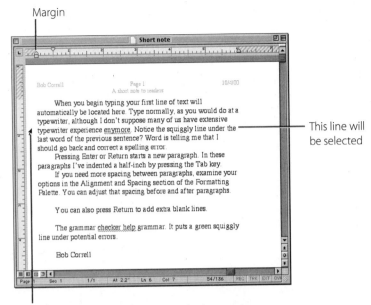

Margin

This line will be selected

Cursor changes to an arrow outside the margin

FIGURE 6-8.

Material that is selected is highlighted

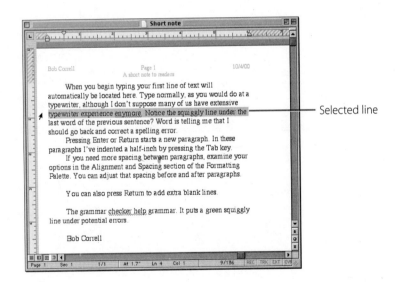

Selected line

You can also use your keyboard to select text. This requires you to enter a keyboard shortcut or use your arrow keys. Table 6-3 summarizes how to select text in Word 2001.

TABLE 6-3. Selecting Text.

Selection	Action
Any text, from letters to the entire document	Use your mouse to click at the beginning of the selection, drag to the end, and release the mouse button.
One word	Double-click the word.
A line	Move your cursor to the left of the line until it changes to an arrow, and then click. You can also press Shift-down arrow.
Multiple lines	Select a line and drag upwards or downwards. You can also press Shift-down arrow-down arrow.
One sentence	Press ⌘, and then click in the sentence.
A paragraph	Move your cursor to the left of the paragraph, as you would select a line, and double-click. You can also triple-click in the paragraph.
More than one paragraph	Move your cursor to the left of the paragraph, as you would select a line, and double-click. When the first paragraph is selected, drag up or down to add other paragraphs. You can also press Shift-Alt-down arrow-down arrow.
A large block of text	Move to the beginning of the text you want to select, click, and then scroll to the end of the selection. Press Shift, and click at the end to select everything between the two clicks.
The entire document	Move your cursor to the left of the document, and triple-click or press ⌘-A.

Cutting, Deleting, Copying, Pasting, and Moving Text

These tasks all involve first selecting the desired text—be it a letter, word, paragraph, or block of text—and then performing the desired operation on the selection, using your mouse or keyboard. Table 6-4 summarizes how to perform each operation (once you've selected the text) except for moving text, which is described immediately following the table.

TABLE 6-4. Cutting, Deleting, Copying, and Pasting Text.

Operation	Description	Button Used	Keyboard Shortcut
Cut	Removes text from your document; somewhat similar to deleting, but it saves it in your Clipboard so you can paste it	Cut	⌘-X
Delete	Deletes a block of text and doesn't save it to the Clipboard	None, but you can choose to cut the text and it will be removed. If you use the Cut command (⌘-X), the text will be stored in the Clipboard.	Delete
Copy	Copies a block of text to the Clipboard, without removing it from the document, so you can paste it in another location	Copy	⌘-C
Paste	Inserts a previously copied block of text into your document at the insertion point	Paste	⌘-V

Moving text is a drag-and-drop operation. Follow these steps to move text:

1 With your mouse, select the text you want to move.

2 Click on the selected text, and hold your mouse button down.

3 Drag the text to a new location in your document, as shown in Figure 6-9.

II

Microsoft Word

FIGURE 6-9.

You can move text by selecting and dragging it to a new location in your document

Text will be placed at insertion point when dropped

Selected text has a border to reflect its size when dragged

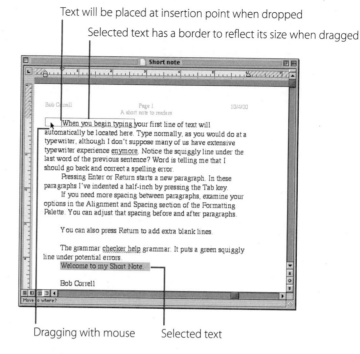

Dragging with mouse   Selected text

4 Release your mouse button.

Finding and Replacing Text

Part of the "fun" of editing a document can be trying to find something inside it. This can be especially problematic if the document is large. The solution is to use the Find (⌘-F) or Replace (⌘-H) tools in Word. Find allows you to search your document for a word or phrase, while Replace uses the results of Find to replace the text you just found with something else.

Launching Find or Replace is quite easy. Simply select the Edit menu and choose Find or Replace. Once there, you can switch between the two by selecting the Find or Replace tab. (See Figure 6-10.)

FIGURE 6-10.

You can find or re-place text with the same dialog box

Enter text to find

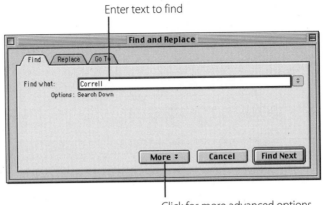

Click for more advanced options

Enter a word or phrase in the Find What field of the Find And Replace dialog box, and click Find Next to start your search. Word will find the first occurrence of the word from the point of the cursor, if present, and highlight it for you while keeping the dialog box open. Keep clicking on Find Next to find all occurrences of the word.

Click the More button in the Find And Replace dialog box to make advanced find options available. You can change the direction of the search from down to up, select matching case, find words by their formatting, and find special characters.

Wildcards are character placeholders you can use if you don't know the exact spelling of a word or want to catch all instances of words that begin with or contain certain character sequences.

Click the Replace tab to enter Replace mode, and enter the word you want to find in the Find What field, only this time enter text to replace that word in the Replace field. Clicking Find Next searches through your document for the search text but doesn't replace it right away. Click Replace to perform that operation.

If you're sure you want to replace every instance of the word in your docu-ment, go ahead and click Replace All. Be careful, though: if the text you are replacing is sufficiently broad, you might end up replacing text that you don't want to replace.

II

Microsoft Word

If you want to copy and paste a word into the Find And Replace dialog box, you must use the keyboard shortcut to paste your selection (⌘-V) because the Paste menu is not available when the Find And Replace dialog box opens.

Using the Proofing Tools

Using Word's proofing tools is like having your own English teacher by your side as you create documents. Word offers several proofing features:

- Real-time spelling and grammar checking
- Spell-checking on demand
- Grammar checking on demand
- AutoCorrect as you type
- A customizable dictionary

Despite their power, these tools are not perfect. You should recognize their limitations and be prepared to proofread your important documents manually in addition to using the proofing tools.

Using the Spell Checker

As you type, Word actually checks your spelling and displays reminders for you. If it sees a potentially misspelled word that it can't automatically correct, it draws a red, squiggly line underneath it. This draws your attention to the fact that you should double-check the word. Control-click the offending word, and Word will open a context-sensitive menu that allows you to choose a possibly correct spelling, ignore every instance of the word, add it to your custom dictionary, or open the Spelling window. (See Figure 6-11.)

 NOTE

> Word also displays a Spelling And Grammar Status icon (which looks like a small book) in the status bar of the main document window. If the icon has a red X in it, there is an error in your document; otherwise, a red check mark indicates there are no problems. Double-clicking the Spelling And Grammar Status icon causes Word to jump to potentially misspelled words and offer a corrected spelling for you.

If you want to conduct a complete spell check, select the Tools menu and choose Spelling And Grammar. This opens the Spelling And Grammar dialog box, shown in Figure 6-12.

FIGURE 6-11.

When you Control-click a misspelled word, Word will open a context-sensitive menu that allows you to choose from a number of options

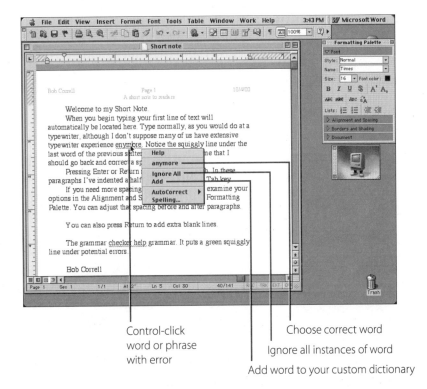

Control-click word or phrase with error

Choose correct word

Ignore all instances of word

Add word to your custom dictionary

FIGURE 6-12.

The Spelling And Grammar dialog box gives you total control over the process

Context of potential error

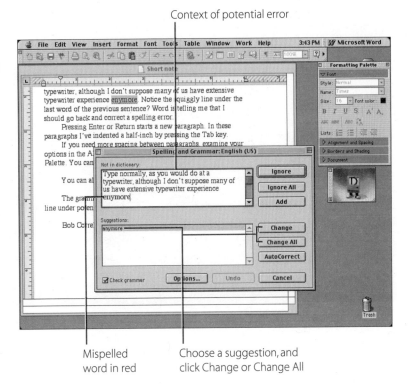

Mispelled word in red

Choose a suggestion, and click Change or Change All

II

Microsoft Word

Word will scan your entire document and find all the words it thinks are misspelled, highlight them one at a time, and prompt you for action. You can ignore the word, ignore all instances of it, add it to your dictionary, choose a suggested spelling and change it, choose a suggested spelling and change all instances of it, or cancel the operation.

NOTE

> If you choose to ignore a misspelled word, Word will not consider it misspelled, even if it is. Therefore, be careful when you choose to ignore potentially misspelled words.

Using the Grammar Checker

Word checks your grammar as you type, and if you make obvious mistakes, it will put a green, squiggly line under the offending material. Again, you can Control-click the sentence (or whatever is causing the problem) and select Grammar from the context-sensitive menu to open the Grammar dialog box. (See Figure 6-13.)

FIGURE 6-13.

When you Control-click a word or phrase that Word has marked as grammatically incorrect, Word will open a context-sensitive menu that allows you to choose from a number of options

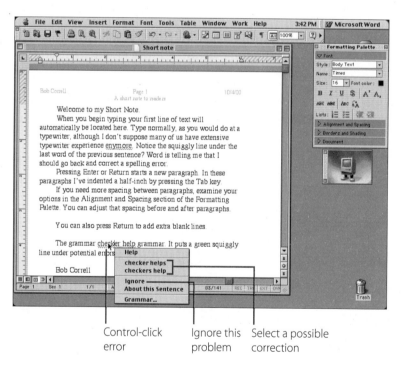

Control-click error

Ignore this problem

Select a possible correction

When you conduct a spell check through the Spelling And Grammar menu, Word checks the grammar at the same time, so long as you have the Check Grammar While You Type option enabled. Spacing problems, passive voice, usage, tense, and other grammatical rules are all checked, and Word may offer several solutions.

 NOTE

> The grammar checker may incorrectly identify problems or offer incorrect solutions, especially with lengthy sentences or in sentences with proper nouns that Word doesn't recognize.

Using AutoCorrect

AutoCorrect is a feature that corrects your spelling as you type. To customize its operation, follow these steps:

1 Select the Tools menu and choose AutoCorrect to open the AutoCorrect dialog box, shown in Figure 6-14.

FIGURE 6-14

AutoCorrect fixes errors as you type

Click to enable AutoCorrect as you type

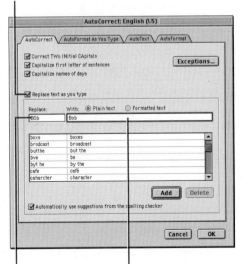

Enter mispelled word or abbreviation

Enter correctly spelled word or expanded phrase

2 The top area of the AutoCorrect dialog box allows you to enable or disable various AutoCorrect options. These are common mistakes that many of us make when we type, such as accidentally

II

Microsoft Word

capitalizing the first two letters of a word. The most powerful option replaces text as you type (which is how Word corrects misspelled words automatically), although this can be frustrating. For example, if you want to enter the letter c in parentheses, (c), because you are working on an outline or a list of options, Word will automatically replace that with the copyright symbol ©. Uncheck any options you want to disable.

3 Click OK to close the AutoCorrect dialog box.

If Word makes a correction that you don't want, immediately click the Undo button (or press ⌘-Z) to cause the word to revert back to its original form.

Although Microsoft has entered many of the most commonly misspelled words and the derivative misspellings for you, you can also add or delete AutoCorrect entries. This feature allows you to enter the words you misspell the most. Follow these steps to add AutoCorrect entries:

1 Select the Tools menu, and choose AutoCorrect to open the AutoCorrect dialog box.

2 Ensure that the Replace Text As You Type option is checked.

3 To add a new entry, enter the word or phrase you want to replace in the Replace field, and enter the corrected word or phrase in the With field.

4 Click Add to add the entry.

5 Click OK to close the AutoCorrect dialog box.

CHAPTER 7

Formatting Text and Documents

Formatting is an important component to word processing. Although you create documents to convey information through the content they contain, the manner in which you present your material can have a critical impact on your audience. Microsoft Word has a plethora of formatting tools that allow you to create many different types of looks for your documents. These formatting options include changing fonts, increasing or decreasing text size, adding color, and setting different page margins. This chapter will first introduce you to the broader concepts of formatting, then show you how to use the Formatting Palette and toolbar, and conclude with a look at how you can apply special types of formatting to your document.

What Is Formatting?

Formatting is both a process and a result. You format documents (the process) so that they convey information with a functional or aesthetic emphasis (the result). The process involves understanding the mechanics of Microsoft Word and employing the formatting tools that it provides. When you make a word bold, you format that word. The result is a word that stands out from its neighbors, which causes it to be emphasized. The ultimate meaning behind the emphasis you add can vary and relies on common conventions as well as your own personal style.

Another aspect of formatting intends to create a larger, or even global, change to the appearance of your document. Changing the font is one such example. If you don't like the default font (Times) and choose to change it in the entire document, you're certainly not emphasizing everything at once. You're changing the entire look of the document for a different reason.

Format changes may be made for aesthetic reasons, such as a certain color preference, or for functional reasons, such as changing the page margins to accommodate a required number of pages.

> **NOTE**
>
> You may have to change your approach when using emphasis in more extravagant documents. In those cases, think of how to make a word or phrase *different* from the rest, not necessarily larger or bolder. For example, in a document with lots of italics (or maybe the font is a script that looks italicized), italics won't stand out, but bold or underlining will.

The Process of Formatting

You'll primarily use the Formatting Palette (new in Office 2001) or the Formatting toolbar to change the appearance and alignment of text on the page. We will discuss this process in the following sections.

Achieving the Results You Want

If you know how to format but not why you should or should not do so, you can ruin an otherwise fine document. Some of this knowledge comes from practice and experience. How do *you* like to see a document formatted? Examine what works and what doesn't in the documents you see, and copy the best examples you find. Look at how the pages are laid out, the use of fonts in titles and body text, the sizes and colors of text, and the use of emphasis.

When Is Enough Enough?

Have you ever read a book, perhaps a text used in a class for school, and high-lighted important words or phrases? This is one of the fundamental reasons you format documents—in order to *emphasize* words, phrases, or concepts. However, if you highlight the entire book, it will all look the same. This results in nothing standing out from the context, and the point of emphasizing is lost. Thus, when you choose to emphasize, do so prudently. Remember, you're trying to draw attention to a relatively small bit of information, not the entire document.

Using the Formatting Palette

 As we mentioned in Chapter 5, "Introducing Microsoft Word," the Formatting Palette is new to Word. When you launch Word, the Formatting Palette sits to the right of your main document window.

The Formatting Palette, shown fully expanded in Figure 7-1 (click the arrows to expand or contract the individual section), allows you to control virtually every aspect of formatting in your document. It is separated into functional areas that correspond to the types of formatting you'll be applying. The following section discusses the elements of the Formatting Palette, roughly mirroring how it is arranged.

FIGURE 7-1.

The Formatting Palette

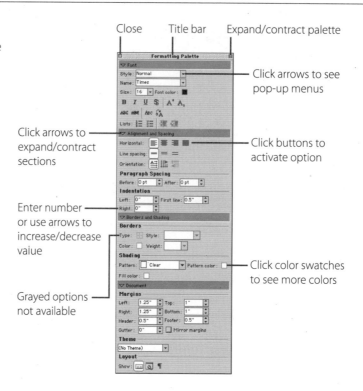

Close   Title bar   Expand/contract palette

Click arrows to see pop-up menus

Click arrows to expand/contract sections

Click buttons to activate option

Enter number or use arrows to increase/decrease value

Click color swatches to see more colors

Grayed options not available

> **NOTE**
>
> The Formatting Palette is a common tool throughout the Office 2001 applications. Learn how to use it once, and that knowledge will go a long way. Because space limitations don't allow us to cover each feature on the Formatting Palette in exhaustive detail, this section gives you the basic information you'll need to use the Formatting Palette. Most of the time that involves selecting text, choosing a formatting feature, and then clicking a button, selecting a menu choice, or entering a value in the Formatting Palette.

Formatting Words and Characters

The formatting tools change the way words and letters look in your document. The font style, name, size, color, and other font formatting options are all applied using the Font section of the Formatting Palette, shown in Figure 7-2.

FIGURE 7-2.

Change the appear-
ance of text in the
Font section

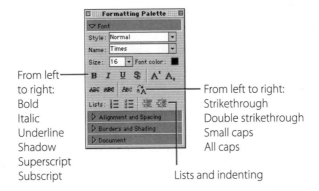

From left
to right:
Bold
Italic
Underline
Shadow
Superscript
Subscript

From left to right:
Strikethrough
Double strikethrough
Small caps
All caps

Lists and indenting

Applying any of these formatting choices is easy, but how you do it
depends on whether you are turning the option on or formatting existing text. If you want to enter bold text, for example, follow these steps:

1 Position your cursor at the location you want to begin typing,
and click to place the text insertion point at that location.

2 Select the Bold button (which is a bold *B*) from the Formatting
Palette. This toggles bold text on.

3 Enter the text you want to make bold. (See Figure 7-3.)

FIGURE 7-3.

Clicking the Bold but-
ton toggles bold text
on and off

Bold text

4 Select the Bold button again from the Formatting Palette. This
turns bold text off.

Should you need to go back and format text, say to change the color,
follow these steps:

1 Select the text you want to change.

2 Click the Color box on the Formatting Palette.

3 Select a new color, as shown in Figure 7-4.

FIGURE 7-4.

Select text and then choose a formatting option from the Formatting Palette

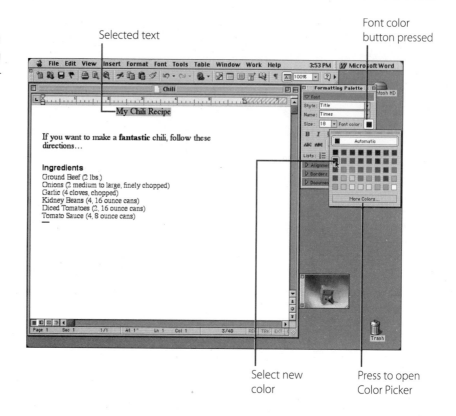

Selected text

Font color button pressed

Select new color

Press to open Color Picker

Continue with other formatting choices or more typing. You'll notice that this time, the formatting you chose didn't stay on. You applied it once, and anything else you type will revert to the default formatting choices.

Lists and Indenting

Lists are useful if you want to organize information, and they come in two varieties: numbered and bulleted. Both types of lists are sprinkled liberally throughout this book so that you can see how they are used. Figure 7-5 shows the Lists And Indent toolbar.

FIGURE 7-5.

The Lists And Indent toolbar

Numbered list

Bulleted list

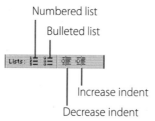

Increase indent

Decrease indent

To create a list from scratch, press either the Numbering or Bullets button and type your list, as shown in Figure 7-6. When you press Return, Word automatically continues your list. When you are finished, press Return once more (this will create a number or bullet with no entry) and then press the Numbering or Bullets button again to turn the list off.

FIGURE 7-6.

Create lists to organize information

Press the Bullets button to end list and start new line without bullets

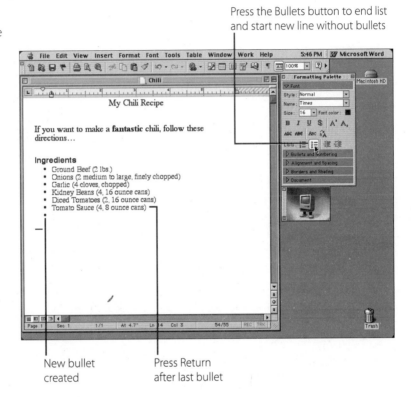

New bullet created

Press Return after last bullet

 TIP

> Pressing Return after you have completed your last list item is important. If your cursor is on a line that contains information you want in the list, when you turn the list formatting off, it will revert to the normal (non-list) style.

When you press the Numbering or Bullets button, you'll notice that the Formatting Palette activates the Bullets And Numbering section, shown in Figure 7-7. You can change the properties of your list here, from the number it starts at, to the type of bullet, to spacing between lines.

FIGURE 7-7.

Bullets And Number-
ing portion of the
Formatting Palette

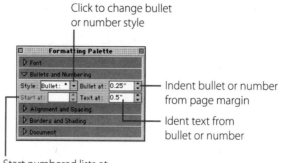

Click to change bullet
or number style

Indent bullet or number
from page margin

Ident text from
bullet or number

Start numbered lists at
any number or continue
from previous

There are several list styles to choose from. Select the Style pop-up
menu, and choose one of the following options to change the type
of list:

- 1, 2, 3 (a normal numbered list)

- I, II, III (a numbered list using capitalized Roman numerals)

- i, ii, iii (a numbered list using small Roman numerals)

- A, B, C (a numbered list using capitalized letters)

- a, b, c (a numbered list using lowercase letters)

- 1st, 2nd, 3rd (a numbered list that refers to each item by 1st, 2nd,
  and so forth)

- One, Two, Three (a numbered list that spells the numbers out)

- First, Second, Third (a numbered list that spells out first, second,
  and so forth)

- 01, 02, 03 (a numbered list that contains zeros before single-digit
  numbers so they contain two characters)

- Bullets of various types (bulleted lists with different types of
  bullets)

Word also creates both kinds of lists as you type. If you enter a number or a dash and then type your list item followed by Enter or Return,
Word identifies your content as a list and changes its formatting
immediately—without any intervention by you. Continue entering list
items until you are finished, and then turn the list off as discussed above.

Lists in Word are dynamic in that when you press the Tab key to increase the indentation of a list item (other than the first), that item is demoted so that it falls under the item above it. For example, pressing Tab in front of the second numbered list item (number 2) increases the indent of the second item and changes its list number from *2* to *a*. Using this feature, you can create nested numbered or bulleted lists.

The Decrease Indent and Increase Indent buttons each move an *entire paragraph* to the right or left each time you press the button, as shown in Figure 7-8. You'll even see the ruler change at the top of your document to reflect the new margins for the section you've modified.

FIGURE 7-8.

The Increase Indent button causes the entire paragraph to be indented; in this example, the Note paragraph has been moved over

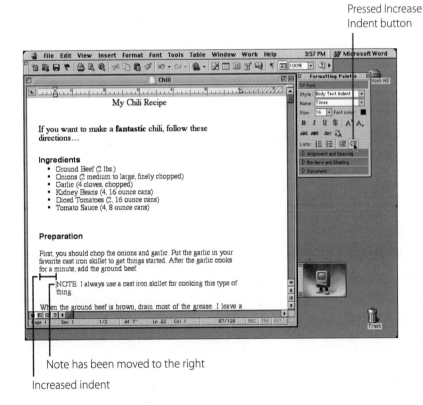

Pressed Increase Indent button

Note has been moved to the right

Increased indent

Alignment and Spacing

Alignment affects how your text (or other objects) is placed horizontally in your document.

You can choose from the alignment and spacing options by placing your cursor in the paragraph of text you want to change and pressing one of the buttons listed on the following page. (See Figure 7-9.)

FIGURE 7-9.

The Alignment And Spacing portion of the Formatting Palette

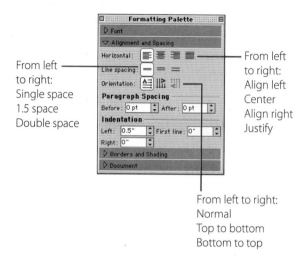

From left to right:
Single space
1.5 space
Double space

From left to right:
Align left
Center
Align right
Justify

From left to right:
Normal
Top to bottom
Bottom to top

- **Align Left** This is the default alignment, which aligns the text with the left margin but leaves the right margin "ragged."

- **Center** This option centers the paragraph within the page margins.

- **Align Right** This option is the opposite of Align Left. Align Right creates a flush-right margin but leaves a ragged-left margin.

- **Justify** This option makes your document look like a book or magazine, with flush-left and flush-right margins.

Figure 7-10 shows examples of each type of alignment.

FIGURE 7-10.

Each type of alignment has a distinct look and purpose

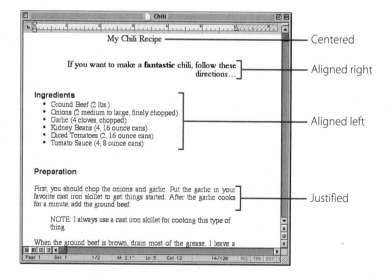

Centered

Aligned right

Aligned left

Justified

> In order to justify text and have both margins be flush, you must have a certain amount of text to work with. When you justify text, Word inserts extra spacing (in the program, not by adding spaces) so that words are spaced out evenly.

Line spacing changes the amount of space between lines in your document, which changes the vertical appearance of your text. You can select a style of spacing and start typing or select a block of text to modify it. Your options are:

- Single space

- 1.5 space

- Double space

Figure 7-11 shows examples of each type of spacing.

FIGURE 7-11.

Examples of the three different styles of line spacing

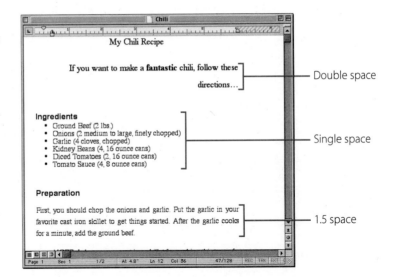

Single spacing is the default, and, as opposed to single spacing on a typewriter, is quite readable. Extra spacing isn't really required in Word unless you want more room to make comments on printed copies. Try different options, and use the one you like best.

Changing text orientation alters the direction text is displayed (and printed). Normally, you won't need this unless you like to type with your head bent over sideways. However, it does come in handy if you want to format the text in table cells or text boxes. Ensure that your cursor is in the table cell or text box you want to modify, and select a new text orientation (either top-down or bottom-up).

Microsoft Word

Indentation is used to change how far in from the left or right margin a paragraph is placed. Set the indentation by placing your cursor in the paragraph you want to change and either entering a new numerical value (in inches, with hundredths of an inch precision) in the Left or Right indent field, or using the small arrows to increase or decrease the values, which default to half an inch. You can also set the first line of a paragraph to be indented more or less than the other lines of the paragraph. Use the First line field to change this setting.

Borders and Shading

Borders allow you to create boxes of various types around text, whether the text is a character, a word, or a more lengthy selection. Figure 7-12 shows the Borders And Shading section you'll use to create borders.

FIGURE 7-12.

The Borders And Shading section of the Formatting Palette

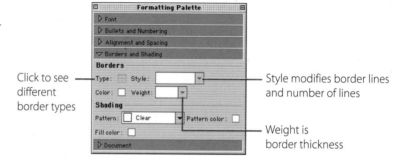

Click to see different border types

Style modifies border lines and number of lines

Weight is border thickness

Follow these steps to create a border:

1 Select the amount of text you want to create a border around.

2 Press the Type button in the Borders And Shading section of the Formatting Palette.

3 Select a border type from those shown.

Figure 7-13 shows an example of a border placed around the Note paragraph.

FIGURE 7-13.

Borders create an obvious emphasis for portions of text in your document

A single border surrounds this paragraph

You can then proceed to change the border's style, color, and weight (or line thickness). Select any of these options from the Formatting Palette, and choose a new setting.

Shading applies shading to either a selection of text or within a border. In other words, you can have a background color or pattern "behind" your text. Select the text you want to shade, and press one (or more) of the following options:

- **Pattern** This option allows you to set the "density" of the pattern, which is reflected by a percentage.

- **Pattern Color** This option modifies the pattern color, which are the dots you see if you have selected a pattern.

- **Fill Color** This option modifies the background of the shaded area.

Figure 7-14 shows an example of shading.

FIGURE 7-14.

Shading sets material
off from the rest of
the text

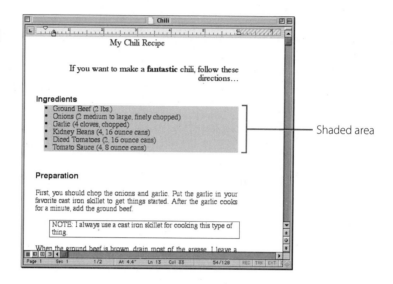

FIGURE 7-14.

Shading sets material
off from the rest of
the text

Document Formatting Options

The Document section of the Formatting Palette (shown in Figure 7-15)
enables you to change several document-wide properties, the most obvious formatting option being the page margins of your document.

FIGURE 7-15.

The Document
section of the
Formatting Palette

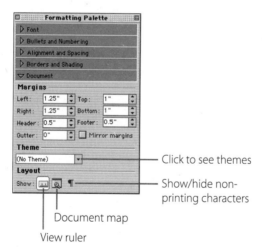

You can enter a numerical value (usually in inches) in any of the Margin fields, or you can use the spin-boxes to increase or decrease the
values. The margins you can change are:

- **Left, Right, Top, Bottom** These fields change the amount of space between your text and the edge of your document.

- **Header** Although a bit counter-intuitive, increasing the header margin will at first shrink the header (a special text area that is applied at the top of every page in your document) and then move it down the page. Decreasing the value makes the header take up more space on the top of the page.

- **Footer** In this field, increase the value to enlarge the footer (a special text area that is applied at the bottom of every page in your document) and decrease the value to make it smaller.

- **Gutter** This field is used to create extra space on the left margin for binding purposes. For example, if you are printing a report that you will bind into a notebook, you'll need extra space on the left side of the paper to account for the holes you will punch or other binding process you may use.

> **NOTE**
>
> If you are going to print your document, ensure that you set margins that are inside the printable area of your page. Typically, these do not extend less than one-quarter of an inch from any page border.

- **Mirror Margins** You can also select Mirror Margins. At first glance, you might think this option sets the left and right margins, or top and bottom margins, to the same value. However, it instead creates margins that simulate a printed book, with the inside margin (running along the book's spine) being one value and the outside margin being another.

> **NOTE**
>
> You can also access the page margins and layout by double-clicking the ruler. Double-click in the gray area if you don't want to accidentally set a tab stop.

The Theme menu enables you to instantly apply a predesigned color and graphical theme to your document, as shown in Figure 7-16. Word will then format your document with the styles inherent in the theme. You can choose from dozens of themes, ranging from Blueprint to Fiesta to Postmodern. Each one has a distinctive look and feel. To see some of the Theme effects (for example, background), you need to be in Online View.

FIGURE 7-16.

Choose a theme to give your document a makeover

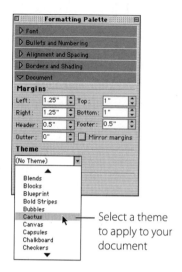

Select a theme to apply to your document

Below the Theme area is the final set of document-wide options you can modify. The Layout options allow you to show or hide the ruler, a document map, or paragraph (carriage return) symbols. Document maps are like the table of contents in a book. (See Figure 7-17.) They appear in a new pane in the document window and show the headings of your document. (You can select headings as styles within the Formatting Palette.) Clicking on the headings in the document maps takes you directly to that section in the document.

FIGURE 7-17.

The document map

Document map headings correspond to headings in document

Drag border left or right to resize document map and panes

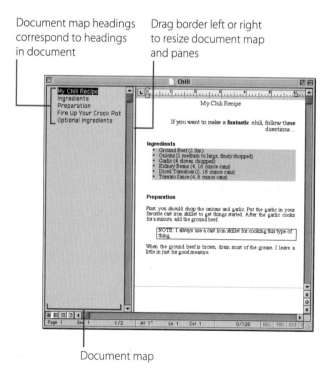

Document map

Now that you know the mechanics of using the Formatting Palette to apply formatting to your documents, let's take a brief look at the other ways you can accomplish the same tasks.

Using the Formatting Toolbar

The Formatting toolbar is a holdover from earlier versions of Word. If you don't like the Formatting Palette, by all means close it and use the Formatting toolbar. The functions of the buttons are the same as those you see in the Formatting Palette, except for Highlight, which is found only on the Formatting toolbar.

> **NOTE**
>
> Although Fill Color is in the Shading section of the Formatting Palette, it isn't the same as highlighting. The result looks the same at first glance, but highlighting can be applied over shading, while shading is not visible when applied over a highlighted section.

To view the Formatting toolbar, select the View menu and choose Toolbars, and then choose Formatting. Figure 7-18 shows the toolbar and lists its buttons.

FIGURE 7-18.

The Formatting toolbar has many of the same features as the Formatting Palette

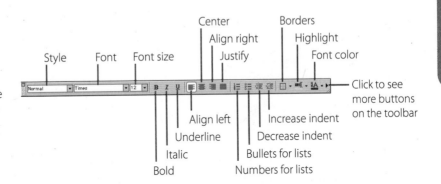

Other Formatting Options

? SEE ALSO

For information on how to create columns in your document, see Chapter 8, "Adding Tables, Columns, and Graphics."

Although it might seem like it, not everything is packed into the Formatting toolbar. The following formatting options are available only through the Format menu:

- **Columns** This option allows you to add, delete, or change the number of columns in your document.

- **Tabs** This option enables you to set, change, and clear tab stops.

- **Drop Cap** This option creates a drop cap, which is when the first letter of a paragraph is formatted larger than the rest of the letters and extends to the lines below it.

- **Change Case** This option enables you to quickly change the capitalization of a selected portion of text. Available options are Sentence case, lowercase, UPPERCASE, Title Case, and tOGGLE cASE.

- **AutoFormat** This option analyzes and formats your document according to preset styles.

- **Background** This option enables you to select a background color and fill for your entire document.

Using the Ruler

You can get by without ever messing with the horizontal ruler in Word (see Figure 7-19), although it can make your life easier if you know how to use it. Not only that, it is likely that you'll accidentally click in the ruler at some point and have to undo what you just did.

FIGURE 7-19.

The horizontal ruler in Word

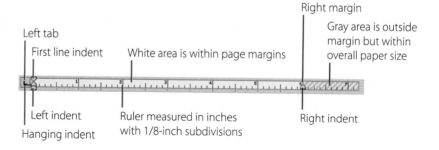

Right margin

Left tab

Gray area is outside margin but within overall paper size

First line indent

White area is within page margins

Left indent

Ruler measured in inches with 1/8-inch subdivisions

Right indent

Hanging indent

NOTE

There is also a vertical ruler that is visible in the Print Preview or Page Layout modes, although you can't set tab stops and other options with it.

The ruler, which appears at the top of your document, gives you a visual representation of the left and right page margin (top and bottom as well if you are in the Page Layout view), paragraph indentation, tab stops, and column widths. It also allows you to modify the settings associated with each property. Each one of these items appears differently on the ruler. The area of your page in which you can enter text or other objects is shown in white on the ruler. The area outside of your page borders is gray. You can change the page margins from the ruler as well. Move your mouse to the margin border within the ruler, click the border, and drag it in either direction to a new position (left/ right if you are changing the horizontal page margins using the ruler at the top of the document window or up/down if you are changing the vertical page margins using the ruler to the left of the main document).

> If you don't see a ruler in your Word document, select the View menu and choose Ruler to turn it on. The vertical ruler that runs along the left-hand side of the page appears only if you are in Page Layout view.

You can change paragraph indentation by dragging the gray arrows that appear in the top ruler in either direction. From top to bottom (as they appear on the horizontal ruler), the symbols are:

- First Line Indent

- Hanging Indent

- Left Indent

Tab stops appear as little black markers on the ruler. Clicking in the ruler in an open area sets a tab stop. There are five types of tab stops:

SEE ALSO

Using the Tab key is discussed in Chapter 6, "Typing and Editing Text."

- **Left Tab** The text aligns and therefore starts at the tab and extends to the right.

- **Center Tab** The text is centered on the tab.

- **Right Tab** The text aligns to the tab and extends to the left.

- **Decimal Tab** Decimal points align.

- **Bar Tab** No, this isn't what you owe after you have dinner or drinks at a bar. Use this option if you need vertical lines running down your page to separate information. Unlike the other tabs, text doesn't align to a bar tab. Setting a bar tab simply displays a vertical line at the point of the tab.

NOTE

> Word has default tabs built in at half-inch increments.

Microsoft Word

CHAPTER 8

Adding Tables, Columns, and Graphics

This chapter covers some of the structural and visual elements you can add to your documents, either to organize them or liven them up. Columns allow you to create a document that looks like a newspaper or brochure. Tables enable you to structure information in an easily understandable format. Graphics allow you to illustrate concepts or information that might be hard to explain with words. (The old adage about a picture being worth a thousand words is very often true—if only we could convince our editors of this fact and get paid a thousand times more for figures!) You can also use graphics to spruce up your document.

Adding Multiple Columns

There are two methods for adding columns. One is pretty simple and uses the Columns button on the Standard toolbar, and the other, more complicated (yet more powerful) method uses the Columns submenu of the Formats menu.

Inserting Columns the Easy Way

To create columns in a simple manner, follow these steps:

1 Click the Columns button on the Standard toolbar. (See Figure 8-1.) This is where you will select the number of columns to create.

FIGURE 8-1.

Click the Columns button to create quick and easy columns

Click the Columns button to add columns

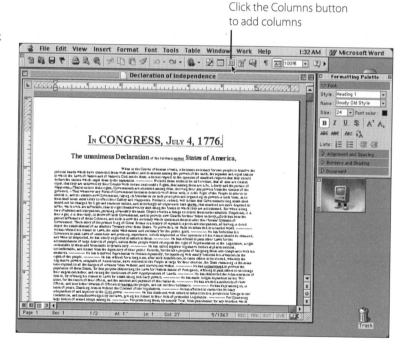

⭐ **TIP**

Although you don't need to hold your mouse button down for the next step, doing this allows you to create more than four columns. Holding your mouse button down allows you to drag over and extend the column selection area.

2 You should see four columns and a cancel area in the pop-up column area. Drag your mouse over the number of columns you want to create, from one to six. (Although four columns are shown by default, if you keep dragging to the right, the number will increase to six.) The columns you have currently selected are shaded, as shown in Figure 8-2. In this example, we have chosen to create two columns.

FIGURE 8-2.

Highlight the number of columns you want to create

Drag to highlight number of columns   Columns pop-up menu

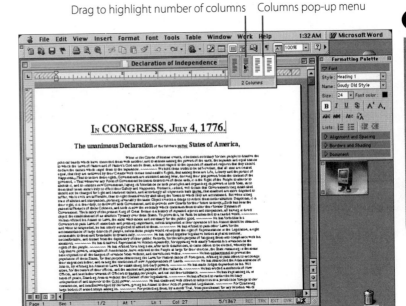

3 Release your mouse button (or click on the number of columns you want) to complete the process.

Microsoft Word

Microsoft Word will immediately change the number of columns in your document to the number you specified. Take a look at the ruler to make sure. You should be able to count the columns by the number of white areas in the ruler, as shown in Figure 8-3.

FIGURE 8-3.

A Word document with two columns

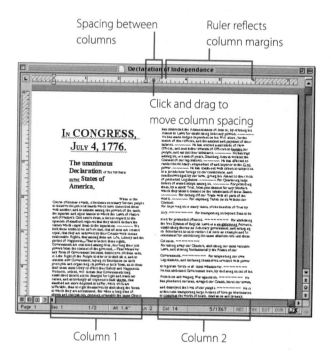

Although this is the easiest way to create columns, you don't have any control over the process other than to determine the total number of columns. If you want to change the width of the columns, drag the column margins in the ruler, or select Columns from the Format menu and change the width and spacing there.

Creating More Powerful Columns

It's possible to specify more conditions at the outset of creating columns. To do this, follow these steps:

1 Select Columns from the Format menu to open the Columns dialog box, shown in Figure 8-4.

FIGURE 8-4.

The Columns dialog box offers you more power and flexibility as you create columns

Click Presets to select column layout

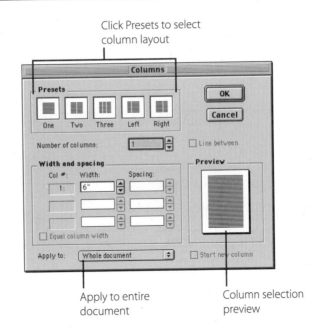

Apply to entire document

Column selection preview

2 You can choose from one of five preset column formats:

- **One** Reverts back to one column.

- **Two** Creates two columns.

- **Three** Creates three columns.

- **Left** Creates two columns, with the left being about a third the size of the right. You can also increase the number of columns (see Step 3) and Word will keep the left-most column smaller than the rest, which will all be the same size.

- **Right** Creates two columns, with the right being about a third the size of the left. You can also increase the number of columns (see Step 3) and Word will keep the right-most column smaller than the rest, which will all be the same size.

3 If you don't want to choose from a preset column format, enter the number of columns you want to create (up to six) in the Number Of Columns field. You can also use the small scroll arrows to increase or decrease the number.

NOTE

> Notice that the Preview window in the Columns dialog box dynamically updates based on the parameters you supply. This enables you to visualize what you're doing, albeit on a small scale.

4 Enter a new "standard" column width, if desired, for your columns in the Width field. By default, all your columns will be equal width. If you want to make some larger or smaller than others, clear the Equal Column Width check box.

5 Alter spacing by changing the Spacing number. This is the "dead space" between each column. As with column widths, you can only apply different values to columns if you clear the Equal Column Width check box. Otherwise, all your spacing will be the same.

NOTE

> If you try to create columns whose width (and the spacing between them) adds up to more space than your page margins allow, you won't be allowed to further increase either the width or spacing. You might have to juggle your column widths and spacing to get them to fit, or cancel the Columns dialog box and reset your page margins.

6 Select how you want Word to apply the columns. You can choose to apply your changes to this section (if you have multiple sections in your document), this point forward, or the whole document.

7 Next, check the Line Between check box if you would like Word to separate each column with a vertical line.

8 Click OK to close the dialog box. Word will create your columns.

Using Section Breaks

The most practical way to fashion a document that has areas with differing numbers of columns is to break your document into one or more sections. This can be an effective way of formatting a document, as you can have a single-column introduction followed by a multi-column layout, for example. The four types of section breaks are as follows:

■ **Next Page** Creates a section break and starts the next section on a new page.

■ **Continuous** Creates a new section but doesn't break the page.

- **Odd Page** Inserts a section break and starts the new section on the next odd-numbered page.

- **Even Page** Inserts a section break and starts the new section on the next even-numbered page.

Insert section breaks by selecting Break from the Insert menu, as shown in Figure 8-5, and by selecting the correct type of section break from the list. Once you've sectioned off your document, you can apply columns to the different sections without affecting the entire document.

FIGURE 8-5.

Insert breaks to have sections of your document contain different numbers of columns

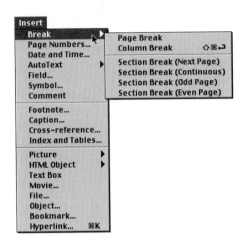

Creating Tables

Tables are powerful organizational tools that enable you to present text and graphics in a clean, useful way. In addition, tables are "smarter" than normal text, because you can sort and perform calculations on data in tables, which you can't do when you have numbers in a normal paragraph or list.

There are a few different ways to create tables. Which one you decide to use in a given situation will depend on how much control you need over the initial table layout.

Inserting Tables

The easiest way to create a table is to use the Insert Table button, located on the Standard toolbar. To create a table, follow these steps:

1 Click the Insert Table button on the Standard toolbar. You should see a grid five columns wide and four rows high below

the button, as shown in Figure 8-6. This is where you will select the size of the table you are going to create.

FIGURE 8-6.

The Insert Table button offers a quick way to create tables

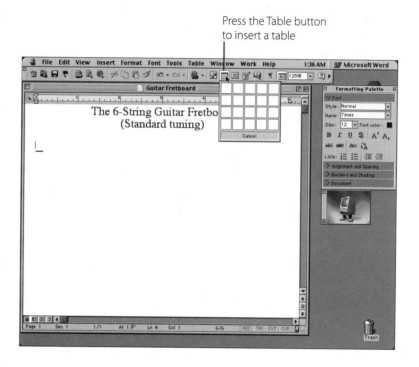

Press the Table button
to insert a table

 **TIP**

As with the Columns button, you don't *need* to hold your mouse button down for the next step, although this is useful if you want to create a large table. Holding the mouse button down allows you to extend the number of rows and columns.

2 Drag your mouse down and to the right to add rows and columns to the table, as shown in Figure 8-7. If you keep dragging down or to the right, the table will increase in size (that is, add more rows and columns) to the limit of your monitor size. The size of the table you have currently selected, measured in rows and columns, is shaded and the display changes to provide additional feedback.

3 Release your mouse button (or click at the location you want) to complete the process.

FIGURE 8-7.

Drag your mouse over
the number of rows
and columns you
want your table to
have

Highlight number of rows and
columns you want in your table

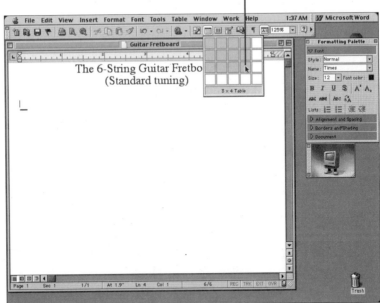

Word will create the table and insert it into your document. The cells
will be separated by lines. (See Figure 8-8.) When you print your
document, the lines in the table are printed in addition to any content the table contains.

Click a cell and type
to enter content

Press Tab to move
between cells

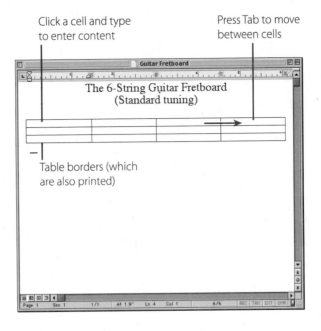

Table borders (which
are also printed)

At this point, your task is to enter information in the table cells. Click in a cell to make it active, and type the information you wish—or insert graphics or other objects. You can format information in a table cell just as you format text in other parts of your document. Figure 8-9 shows a completed table with formatting applied.

FIGURE 8-9.

A formatted table in Word

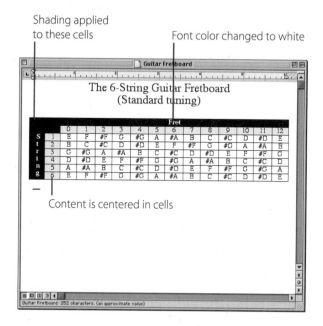

Shading applied to these cells

Font color changed to white

Content is centered in cells

You can also change the size of the cells by moving your mouse over a border, and when your cursor changes to a double vertical line with arrows, click and drag the border to a new location. Figure 8-10 shows this process in action.

FIGURE 8-10.

Drag a column border to change its size

Click and drag a table border to resize cells

Cursor becomes double vertical line with arrows

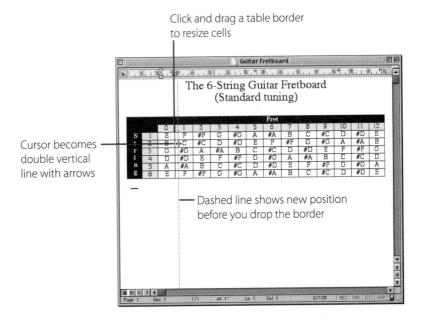

Dashed line shows new position before you drop the border

Choose Select from the Table menu to select the table or individual rows, columns, or cells. If you decide to add or remove tables, cells, rows, or columns, use the Table menu and subcommands from the Insert and Delete options.

Creating Tables from the Menu

If you want more initial control over the tables you create, use the Table menu and follow these steps:

1 Select Insert from the Table menu, and then select Table. This opens the Insert Table dialog box, shown in Figure 8-11.

FIGURE 8-11.

The Insert Table dialog box allows you more control over the tables you create

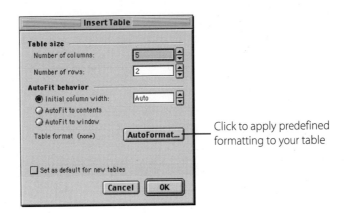

Click to apply predefined formatting to your table

2   Change the number of columns and rows to suit your needs.

3   Select an AutoFit behavior from the list:

- **Initial Column Width** This option sets the column widths of the table when it is created. You can choose Auto or enter a measurement in inches.

- **AutoFit To Contents** This option makes each table column fit the largest data in each column.

- **AutoFit To Window** This option helps you plan to publish your document on the Web. It makes the table fit the width of the page, no matter how the Web browser window is sized.

4   Next, select a table format. The default option creates a fairly plain-looking table. Click the AutoFormat button if you want to choose additional table formats.

5   If you want Word to use this table as the pattern for future tables, select the Set As Default For New Tables check box.

6   Click OK.

Using the Tables And Borders Button

The Tables And Borders button is a feature that enables you to create much more complex tables than the other two tools. Follow these steps to draw a table:

1   Click the Tables And Borders button on the Standard toolbar. This opens the Tables And Borders toolbar, shown in Figure 8-12.

FIGURE 8-12.
The Tables And
Borders toolbar

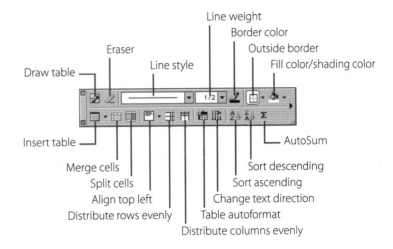

2 The Draw Table button is selected by default. Move your cursor over to your document at the point where you want to draw your table.

3 Next, create the overall table. Start at the top left of the table, click and hold your mouse button down, drag to the lower right corner of the table, and then release the mouse button. You'll see a box showing the dimensions of the table as you drag your mouse. (See Figure 8-13.)

FIGURE 8-13.
Drawing the
overall table

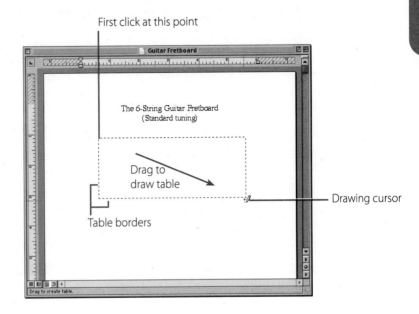

4 Next, create rows and columns. Create a row by moving your cursor to the left side of the table, clicking and holding your mouse button down, and dragging to the right side of the window. (See Figure 8-14.) When you release your mouse button, the row is created. Columns are created similarly, only you draw from the top down. You can also go from right to left and from bottom to top.

FIGURE 8-14.

Drawing a table row

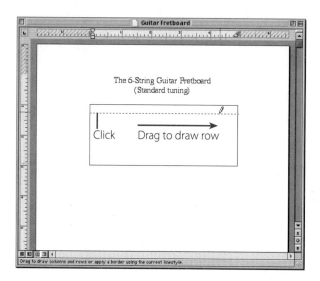

Inserting Graphics and Other Objects

⊗ **CAUTION**

If you insert a large number of graphics, especially movies, into your file, the file size can balloon into the megabyte range (or greater). If you plan to e-mail your document via a standard Internet connection (56 Kbps) you should be prepared to wait a few moments while your document is sent. You also might want to warn the recipient that you are sending a large file if he or she is also using a standard modem.

Inserting pictures and other graphics—such as movies, HTML objects, and hyperlinks—into Word documents has never been easier. The methods you use to insert each type of material are remarkably similar, and all use the Insert menu.

Inserting Pictures and Clip Art

Pictures are a nice addition to many Word documents, and they can easily be added. Of course, you'll have to have the pictures on your hard drive in order to send them. If you have a digital camera or scanner, and have taken pictures and uploaded them to your computer, you're in business. There are also many third-party software packages that contain licensed artwork for you to use.

Follow these steps to insert a picture in your document:

1 Place your cursor at the point you want to insert the picture.

2 From the Insert menu, select Picture and then From File to open the Choose A Picture dialog box, shown in Figure 8-15.

FIGURE 8-15.

Inserting a picture from a file requires that you find it first

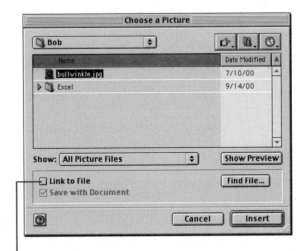

Click to link to picture instead of inserting the picture file in the Word document

3 Navigate to the location where your picture is stored and select it.

4 Click Insert.

Once your picture is present in your document, you might need to re-size it or alter its position. You can also add interesting effects to your pictures. Select the picture by clicking it. This opens the Picture toolbar, shown in Figure 8-16.

NOTE

You can also open the Picture toolbar by selecting Toolbars from the View menu and then select Picture.

CAUTION

Unless you are using your own artwork, pay special attention to any copyrights and abide by all the restrictions associated with the material you are using. The best way around this is to create all your own graphics, but even then, you might not legally be able to use pictures of trademarks in a commercial publication. Home use is another story. You can pretty much use whatever you want so long as your document is for personal use.

Microsoft Word

FIGURE 8-16.

The Picture toolbar enables you to change the properties of your picture

From left to right:
Image control
More contrast
Less contrast
More brightness
Less brightness

Free rotate

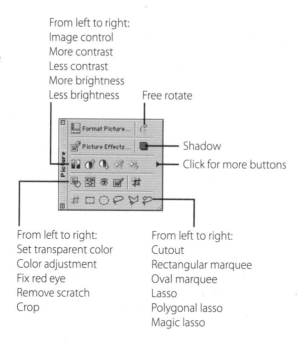

Shadow

Click for more buttons

From left to right:
Set transparent color
Color adjustment
Fix red eye
Remove scratch
Crop

From left to right:
Cutout
Rectangular marquee
Oval marquee
Lasso
Polygonal lasso
Magic lasso

As you can see, you have quite a few options available. Table 8-1 explains the use of the buttons on the Picture toolbar.

Table 8-1.   Buttons on the Picture Toolbar.

Button	Effect
Format Picture	Opens the Format Picture dialog box, which you can use to crop and resize; apply fills, lines, and arrows; and control text-wrapping around the picture
Picture Effects	Opens the Effects Gallery, which enables you to select and apply some amazing effects (such as Mosaic) to your pictures
Shadow	Enables you to create different types of drop shadows that are cast by your picture
Free Rotate	Enables you to rotate the picture
Image Control	Enables you to make your picture black and white, or various shades of gray
More Contrast	Increases the contrast in your picture

(continued)

Table 8-1. *continued*

Button	Effect
Less Contrast	Decreases the contrast in your picture
More Brightness	Increases the brightness of your picture
Less Brightness	Decreases the brightness of your picture
Button	Effect
Set Transparent Color	Enables you to set a color that will become transparent
Color Adjustment	Allows you to adjust the color balance of your picture
Fix Red Eye	Eliminates those pesky red eyes in pictures
Remove Scratch	Removes scratches from pictures
Crop	Allows you to cut out portions of your picture
Cutout	After you select a portion of your image, allows you to cut it out
Rectangular Marquee	Selects a rectangular area of your picture
Oval Marquee	Selects a circular area of your picture
Lasso	Selects a freehand area of your picture
Polygonal Lasso	Selects a polygonal area of your picture
Magic Lasso	Makes selections based on differences in contrast
Arrow	The small arrow on the right side of the Picture toolbar expands to give you more buttons and menu choices, such as Insert Picture, Line Style, Text Wrapping, and Reset Picture

II

Microsoft Word

Clip Art is handled differently than pictures. Microsoft has gone to great lengths to create, collect, and organize a large number of graphics that can be applied in hundreds of situations. Follow these steps to insert Clip Art:

1 Position your cursor where you want to insert the Clip Art.

2 From the Clip Art menu, select Insert and then Picture to open the Microsoft Clip Gallery, shown in Figure 8-17.

FIGURE 8-17.

The Microsoft Clip Gallery contains many clips you can use in your documents

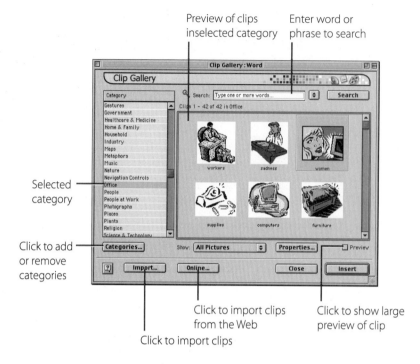

Preview of clips inselected category

Enter word or phrase to search

Selected category

Click to add or remove categories

Click to import clips from the Web

Click to import clips

Click to show large preview of clip

3 Select a category from the left window pane, and then browse through the images in the right window pane. Alternatively, you can enter one or more words in the Search field to find pictures suitable for your occasion.

4 Select the clip you want to insert.

5 Click Insert.

You can use the Picture toolbar to modify the clip just as you would another picture.

Embedding Movies in Your Document

You can insert, or *embed*, movies into your documents, just as you would pictures. To do so, follow these steps:

1 Place your cursor where you want to insert the movie.

2 From the Movie menu, select Insert.

3 Navigate to the movie on your hard disk, select it, and then press Open.

The movie will appear in your document, ready to play. Select it to open the Movie toolbar, which allows you to perform the following actions:

■ **Insert Movie** Inserts another movie into your document.

■ **Play** Plays the movie.

■ **Show Controller** Shows the movie controller (which allows you to play the movie, control the sound, and scroll through the movie frame by frame).

■ **Loop** Sets the movie to loop continuously.

■ **Set As Poster Frame** Sets the current frame as the frame to show in the document prior to playing the movie.

■ **Format Picture** Opens the Format Picture dialog box.

Using Other Graphical Objects

There are other graphical objects you can place in your document, all of which are available by selecting Picture from the Insert menu:

■ **Horizontal Line** Enables you to insert a fancy line (actually a picture) that runs horizontally across the screen.

■ **AutoShapes** Opens the AutoShapes toolbar, shown in Figure 8-18, which allows you to draw and create shapes in your document.

FIGURE 8-18.

The AutoShapes toolbar

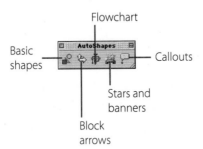

■ **WordArt** Opens the WordArt Gallery, shown in Figure 8-19, which is a selection of graphic effects you can use for text.

II

Microsoft Word

FIGURE 8-19.

The WordArt Gallery

Selected style

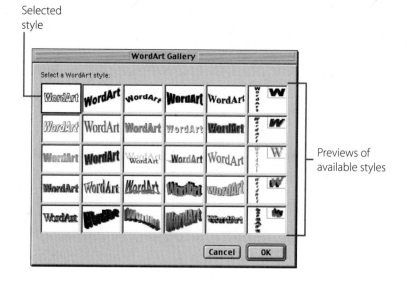

Previews of available styles

- **From Scanner Or Camera** Enables you to import pictures directly from your scanner or digital camera.

- **Chart** Opens Microsoft Graph, which enables you to create charts and embed them in your document.

And the Rest

There are even more objects you can insert into your Word document from the Insert menu. These include:

- HTML objects, such as background sounds, scrolling text, check boxes, option buttons, list boxes, text boxes, submit buttons, reset buttons, and hidden fields.

- Text boxes

- Files

- Objects

- Bookmarks

- Hyperlinks

CHAPTER 9

Special Tasks in Microsoft Word

Microsoft Word is such a versatile program that you're not limited to creating the standard fare of letters, notes, and the like. You can create other, powerful forms of documents that serve specific purposes. Outlines, labels, and Web pages are three types of documents we'll cover in this chapter.

Security is also an important topic that you should be aware of. Macro viruses have the power to infect your computer and Microsoft Office 2001 applications. We'll show you how to enable Word's built-in macro virus protection and offer some tips on how to stay virus-free.

Creating an Outline

If you need to create an outline for a report or project, Word has a complete set of tools that will enable you to create an exhaustive outline of many levels. You can also view and manage your outline in different ways as you create and use it.

As you create your outline, remember these concepts:

■ Outlines have different heading levels, from 1 to 7. Heading 1 is the highest level, and Heading 7 is the lowest. Body text can be used for the content of your outline, as opposed to the headings that make up the outline.

■ You can promote and demote headings easily. Promoting a heading raises its level, assuming it's not already a level 1 heading. Demoting a heading lowers its level.

■ Outlines are expandable and collapsible. You can choose to show an outline by levels; for example, you can see the outline and all the level 1 headings. In this view, Heading 2 and below are hidden. Conversely, you can choose to see level 3 headings. In this case, Heading 1, Heading 2, and Heading 3 are all shown, but those below Heading 3 are hidden.

Follow these steps to create an outline:

1 Create a new document by clicking the New Blank Document Button on the Standard Toolbar.

2 From the View menu, select Outline, or click the Outline View button at the bottom of the main document window. This opens the Outlining toolbar, as shown in Figure 9-1, and puts Word in outlining mode.

FIGURE 9-1.

Use the Outlining toolbar to create different levels in a Word document

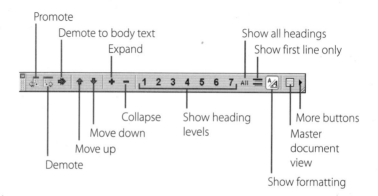

NOTE

You should be in outlining mode only when you're creating an outline. The functionality that allows you to create outlines quickly and easily isn't suited to creating a normal document.

3 Begin with the first line at Heading 1. Enter your first heading, and press Return or Enter.

NOTE

The following steps represent how we create outlines. You can choose to go through each heading in detail rather than taking the approach we do. The important thing is to find what works for you.

4 Continue entering your top-level headings.

5 Go back and flesh out each Heading 1. Place your cursor at the end of a Heading 1 line, and press Return. This creates another Heading 1. Immediately demote this blank heading by selecting the Demote button on the Outlining toolbar. This changes the heading to Heading 2.

6 Continue creating your second level of headings under each Heading 1.

7 Now go back and finish each Heading 1 by adding level 3 headings and below. Your outline should end up looking like the one shown in Figure 9-2.

II

Microsoft Word

FIGURE 9-2.

Outlines look much different than standard documents, and they organize thoughts effectively

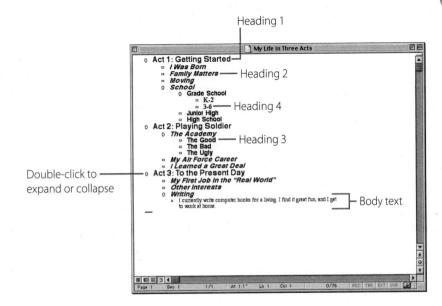

Performing a Data Merge

Data merge, also known as mail merge, is a way of combining a data source with a document that contains the format in which you want your information to be presented. In other words, Word uses two documents to make one document (or sends the information directly to a printer). You can create form letters, labels, envelopes, catalogs, and other unique documents by marrying the format necessary to print out the data with the data itself.

For example, a popular use of data merge is to create mailing labels. The structure of the labels (their size and the number you can fit on a piece of paper) doesn't change much over time and can be created and maintained in one document, called the main document. You create the information that you want printed on the labels in another document called the data source, which can be edited apart from the first. Sound complicated? It isn't really, so long as you understand the fundamental nature of data merge—that is, you are creating two separate documents, one with the page layout and another with the data, and then merging them together when you print.

Read through the following sections, and follow the steps to perform a data merge for the purpose of creating labels.

> **NOTE**
>
> Although we use labels to illustrate this process, you can create a wide variety of documents (different labels, form letters, envelopes, and catalogs) using data merge.

Creating the Main Document

The main document contains information specific to the type of label you are using and the type of information you want printed. For example, Word will format your main document to reflect the dimensions of a specific label, such as an Avery 5160 Address Label. You will also see placeholders for the category of information that will ultimately be shown, such as a title, first name, last name, address, and so on.

> **NOTE**
>
> It's important to remember that you don't actually enter data in the main document. Its purpose is solely to provide the structure you need to print out your labels. This way, you can create several main documents for different label types that use different types of information that all rely on the same or different data sources.

1 Create a new document by clicking the New Blank Document button on the Standard toolbar.

2 From the Tools menu, select Data Merge Manager. This opens the Data Merge Manager, shown in Figure 9-3.

FIGURE 9-3.

The Data Merge Manager contains the tools you'll need to perform data merges

Create main document

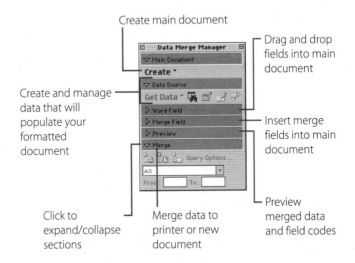

Drag and drop fields into main document

Create and manage data that will populate your formatted document

Insert merge fields into main document

Click to expand/collapse sections

Merge data to printer or new document

Preview merged data and field codes

3 Under Main Document, click Create, and then select Labels from the menu that appears. This opens the Label Options dialog box, shown in Figure 9-4.

FIGURE 9-4.

Make sure to select the exact label you have in the Labels Options dialog box

Select label manufacturer

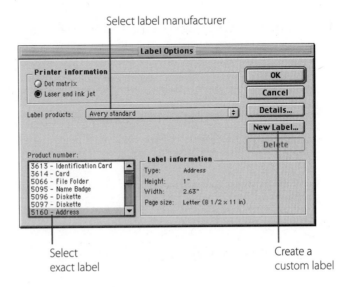

Select exact label

Create a custom label

4 Select the type of printer you have (dot matrix or laser/ink jet).

5 Select a label manufacturer from the Label Products pull-down menu.

6 Find and select the product number of your labels. The manufacturer's name is listed beside the product number for easy reference. You should notice that the information in the Label Information area of the dialog box updates to reflect the label you have chosen.

It's a good idea to double-check the label information presented in Word with the actual labels you have. Click the Details button for a graphical depiction of your label. You can also modify the dimensions in this area.

7 Click OK to close the Label Options dialog box. Word will format your blank document, and you will see placeholders for your labels.

8 Save your main document.

Creating the Data Source

The data source is a document that exists behind the scenes for the most part, although you can open it and edit it directly. Most of the time you'll find it more convenient to add and edit information through the Data Form dialog box. To do this, follow these steps:

1 To create the data source, click Get Data under the Data Source area of the Data Merge Manager and then select New Data Source. This opens the Create Data Source dialog box, shown in Figure 9-5.

FIGURE 9-5.

In the Create Data Source dialog box, add or remove header row fields so that you end up with only the ones you want

Enter new field names

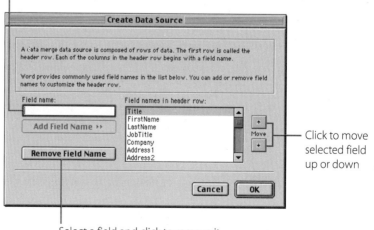

Click to move selected field up or down

Select a field and click to remove it

2 Review the names in the Field Names In Header Row list. Select those you don't want, and click Remove Field Name. You can also move the names up or down by selecting them and clicking the appropriate arrow button. If you need a field that isn't there, enter the name in the Field Name box and click Add Field Name. When you are finished, click OK.

3 Word will then ask you to save the data source file. Choose a file name and a location in the Save dialog box.

4 At this point, the Data Form dialog box appears, as shown in Figure 9-6. This is your opportunity to enter the data that will actually be printed on your labels. Enter information in each field, and press Return.

- Click Add New to add more records or Delete to delete the record that is visible.

- Use the arrows beside the record number to scroll through each record, which is just an individual label.

- If you want to search for a record, click Find.

- Click OK when you're done entering records.

FIGURE 9-6.

Entering the actual data occurs in the Data Form dialog box

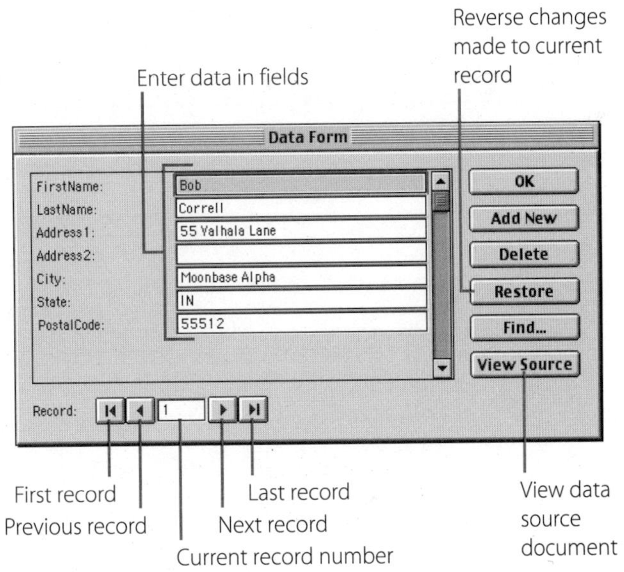

5 Now you have a chance to arrange the information on a sample label. Word opens the Edit Labels dialog box (see Figure 9-7) for this purpose. Choose Insert Merge Field, select each field, and then insert it into your sample label. You can place some fields on the same line or press Return to create multiple lines. You should also add spaces where appropriate, such as between first and last names. Conversely, add a comma if your order is last name and then first name. When finished, click OK. If your original blank document is still open, you should see the place-holders updated in the document.

FIGURE 9-7.
In the Edit Labels dia-log box, arrange the fields in the order and location you want them to appear in your printout

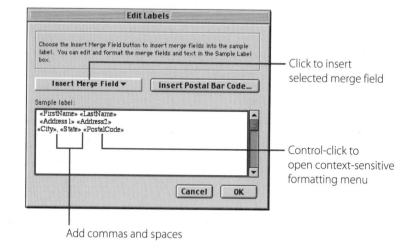

6 Now is a good time to save your main document again.

Previewing and Merging Your Data

This is the final set of steps you must complete to actually merge your main document with your data source.

1 Open you main document if you've closed (and saved) it.

> **NOTE**
>
> When you save your main document, Word will normally ask you to save the data source as well. Make sure you do—otherwise, the changes you make will be lost. Once you have associated a data source with a main document, you have to worry only about opening the main document. You'll see the name of the data source on the Data Merge Manager confirming the connection.

2 Select the View Merged Data button from the Preview section of the Data Merge Manager. Your main document will change to show you the actual label information, as shown in Figure 9-8.

FIGURE 9-8.
Previewing your labels

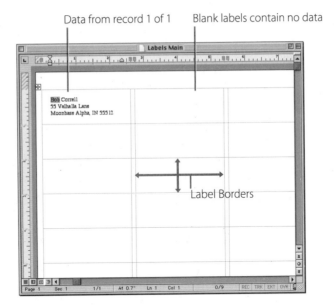

Data from record 1 of 1   Blank labels contain no data

Label Borders

3   Select the Merge To Printer or Merge To New Document button
    from the Merge section of the Data Merge Manager. Word will
    merge your label structure (the main document) with the data
    source and either print the result or create a new file that you
    can save and print (or e-mail) at a later date.

Using Word to Create Web Pages

Although Word excels as a traditional word processing application, it
has another forte as well: Web pages. Making Web pages with Word is
great if you don't know the technical nuts and bolts of creating Web
pages because all you need to know how to do is use Word.

Creating Web Pages with Word is about as easy as creating any other
type of document. Rather than selecting Word Document from the Project Gallery when you create a new file, select Web Page instead. Just
follow these steps:

1   Select Project Gallery from the File menu to open the Project
    Gallery.

Microsoft Word

2 Select the Web Page icon from the list of blank documents, as shown in Figure 9-9, and then click OK.

FIGURE 9-9.

Select Web Page to create a blank Web page

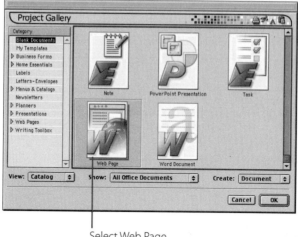

Select Web Page

> **NOTE**
>
> There are also Web page templates in the Project Gallery in the Web Pages category. Use these as you would any other type of Word template.

3 Word opens the blank document, and you're ready to create its content. Enter text, format it, draw tables, and do whatever else you need to create your page. You can also insert HTML objects such as check boxes and text fields by selecting HTML Object from the Insert menu and then selecting an object type.

> **NOTE**
>
> Because HTML is more limited than Word, you'll find that many of Word's formatting options aren't available when you create Web pages.

4 When you save your Web page, select Save As from the File menu. Word will prompt you to save your Web page, as shown in Figure 9-10. Don't change the extension following the name or the format. The three-letter extension, .htm, is necessary for your browser to recognize the file as a Web page.

FIGURE 9-10.

Save your Web pages in the Web Page format with the proper .htm extension

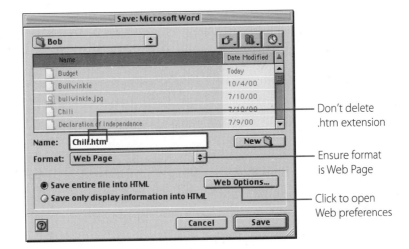

Don't delete .htm extension

Ensure format is Web Page

Click to open Web preferences

Protecting Yourself from Macro Viruses

Macro viruses are a serious threat to Microsoft Office users. They are created by malicious individuals intent on causing you and your computer harm. These viruses range from those that simply show themselves and say "Gotcha!" to those that can damage your computer or your data.

Ever since the Internet entered a large number of homes and offices around the world, e-mail has become the prime method of transmitting and receiving viruses. Before this explosion occurred, floppy disks were the prime medium of virus transmission. If you never share information electronically with friends, family, or coworkers, you are relatively safe, but viruses also have been known to be distributed on software CDs.

What is a Macro Virus?

Unlike other forms of computer viruses, macro viruses are aimed specifically at Office users. Although there are far more viruses that target Windows-based computers that run Office than those that run on the Macintosh platform, you still face a serious virus threat.

What makes a macro virus possible is the powerful programming language that programmers use to customize Office and automate tasks, Visual Basic for Applications. VBA, as it's known, is built right into the Office applications and can be accessed by opening the Tools menu, selecting Macro, and then selecting Visual Basic Editor In Word. Viruses often take advantage of e-mail programs, most notably Microsoft Outlook (a Windows application) or Outlook Express, to infect a computer and to propagate. However, as a Mac user, you still may receive an infected file and infect your machine when you open it. A virus that is intended to damage a person's Windows computer, and therefore targets specific Windows systems files, won't cause your computer any harm, but it may damage Word or your other Office programs.

The bottom line is to not become complacent. Although Mac users have been relatively unscathed, the newer, more powerful viruses are platform-independent and can infect Mac Office 2001.

Using Word's Built-In Protection

You can have Word help protect you from macro viruses by enabling an option in the Preferences dialog box. To do so, follow these steps:

1   From the Edit menu, select Preferences to open the Preferences dialog box.

2   Select the General tab.

3   Select (or confirm it is selected) the Macro Virus Protection option, as shown in Figure 9-11.

FIGURE 9-11.

Make sure Macro Virus Protection is enabled in the Preferences dialog box

Check to enable Macro Virus Protection

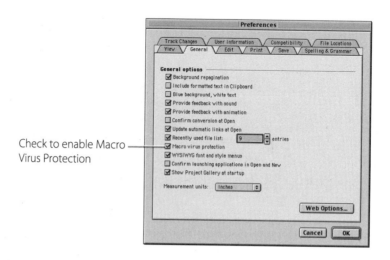

4   Click OK to close the dialog box.

Using Your Head

Viruses spread through ignorance and complacency. If you don't recognize the sender of an e-mail message, don't blindly open it—and try not to open any attachments from people you don't know. However, some viruses will be sent to you by people you know (such as the recent I Love You virus). This is why it is important to have a good anti-virus program that will scan e-mail attachments and external disks to protect you.

Disabling Word's macro virus protection isn't recommended. Although it doesn't scan e-mail attachments or files on disks, it is a crucial link in your virus protection chain.

CHAPTER 10

Customizing Microsoft Word

No application would be complete without offering you some way of modifying it to suit your needs. Rather than attempt to force you into one way of doing anything, Microsoft Word 2001 has a variety of customizable options.

Why should you care? After all, if you can use Word in its default state, never change a thing, and be perfectly happy, changing the way the program works doesn't seem to make sense. Well, if you are a first-time user of Word, chances are that after you use it for a while you'll find that some things just don't work for you. If you are asking how to get Word to work better for you, you need to look at its customization options. If you are a long-time user, you've probably got a good idea of what works for you and what doesn't. Gone are the days of being stuck with a program interface. If you don't like it, chances are you can change it and many other aspects of the program.

This chapter will help you find out which aspects of Word you can modify to suit your needs. Because there are so many ways to customize Word, we won't try to cover them all in exhaustive detail. We'll mainly concentrate on showing you where all the options are, and broadly explaining what you can accomplish.

> Most customizing options can be found in one of three places: Preferences on the Edit menu, Customize on the Tools menu (which is the same as selecting Toolbars, then Customize from the View menu), and other Tools menus.

Modifying Preferences

Word's preferences are the mother lode of customization. The preferences are organized into function areas and can be accessed by opening the Edit menu and selecting Preferences to open the Preferences dialog box, shown in Figure 10-1.

> If you have previously accessed Word's preferences and selected other tabs, the last one you viewed (which might not be the View tab) will appear when you open the Preferences dialog box again.

FIGURE 10-1.
The Preferences
dialog box

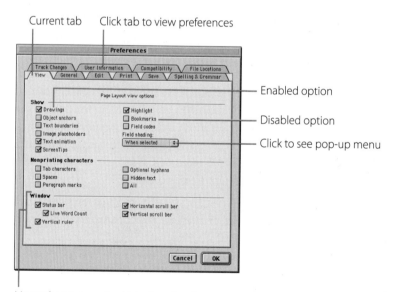

Current tab   Click tab to view preferences

Enabled option

Disabled option

Click to see pop-up menu

Most tabs are organized into functional areas

Notice each of the tabs running across the top of the dialog box. These are the functional areas that represent most of what you can change in Word. Click a tab to activate it and to see the preferences associated with it. Most of the time you can simply check a check box to change a preference. If a check box is checked, the option is enabled; if it is blank, the preference is currently disabled. In other cases, you select a choice from a pull-down menu.

⊘ NOTE

> If you make a mistake while changing preferences, click Cancel instead of OK. Word will disregard any changes made to the preferences since you brought up the Preferences dialog box.

For the remainder of this section, we'll show you each preference tab and briefly explain (if necessary) what each preference category does.

The View Tab

The View tab controls what you see onscreen and is dependent upon the current view you are in. You can change the way Word's interface looks, in addition to what the document window shows. In Figure 10-2, the dialog box indicates that these are the normal view options.

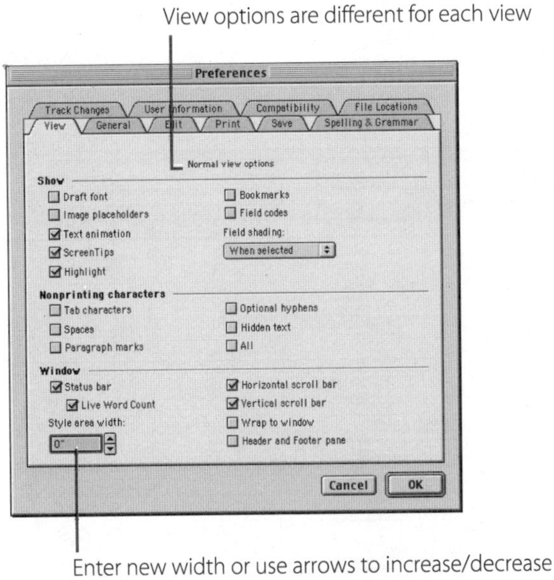

FIGURE 10-2.
The View tab

View options are different for each view

Enter new width or use arrows to increase/decrease

The View tab preferences are divided into three sections.

■ **Show** Controls items that are displayed onscreen, such as ScreenTips and Field codes.

- **Nonprinting Characters** Controls whether characters that don't print (such as tabs) are shown on screen.

- **Window** Shows or hides parts of the Word interface, such as the status bar or scrollbars.

If you work in a different view (such as the Page Layout view) most of the time, make sure you are currently in that view before opening the Preferences dialog box. The View tab preferences are uniquely targeted towards the view you are in at the time you open the Preferences dialog box. For example, the Show options for the Normal view contain Draft Font, Image Placeholders, Text Animation (checked by default), ScreenTips (checked by default), Highlight (checked by default), Bookmarks, Field Codes, and Field Shading. If you exit the Preferences dialog box, switch to the Page Layout view, and return to the Preferences dialog box (the View tab), the Show options have three additional preferences: Drawings (checked by default), Object Anchors, and Text Boundaries.

The General Tab

The General tab, shown in Figure 10-3, has only one section, called General Options. These options range from allowing Word to repaginate in the background to managing the recently used file list. The General tab is also where you can enable or disable macro virus protection and where you can decide whether the Project Gallery is shown when you launch Word.

FIGURE 10-3.

The General tab

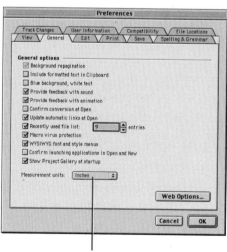

Click for different units

TIP

If you don't like sound or animated feedback from Word, you can turn it off in the General tab.

The Edit Tab

The Edit tab, shown in Figure 10-4, contains editing options, separated into two sections.

- **Editing Options** Enables you to modify how you edit text in Word, such as entering overtype mode, drag-and-drop support, and whether a tab or backspace sets the left indent.

- **Click And Type** Enables you to set the click and type options, which allow you to enter text and automatically apply different formatting.

FIGURE 10-4.
The Edit tab

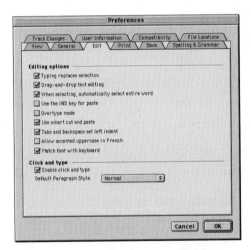

 TIP

If you find yourself making a lot of mistakes dragging and dropping text in your document, disable the Drag-And-Drop Text Editing option in the Edit tab.

The Print Tab

The Print tab, shown in Figure 10-5, allows you to set print options in Word. The Print tab is divided into three sections.

- **Printing Options** Two options involve updating fields and links before you print, and the third tells Word to print your document in reverse order.

II

Microsoft Word

- **Include With Document** These items, such as Drawing Objects, Hidden Text, or Comments, can be printed with your document.

- **Options For Current Document Only** These options apply only to the current document and allow you to print form data without the form, apply fractional width printing (which looks bad onscreen), and let you print PostScript code underneath text.

FIGURE 10-5.

The Print tab

 TIP

If you have a document with a number of comments, setting the Comments option in the Print tab is the only way to see your comments in a printout. Also, printing in reverse order can save you time collating a lengthy document. Normally, Word (and other programs) prints the first page first and continues to the last. You have to reverse the pages once they print out unless you request that the document be printed in reverse order in the Print tab.

The Save Tab

The Save tab, shown in Figure 10-6, offers options that can rescue your document if your computer (or Word program) crashes. The Save tab is divided into two sections.

- **Save Options** These options control how Word saves your document and how much protection you have in the form of backups.

- **File Sharing Options** These options control the security of your document. You can require that a password be entered to open the document or modify it, or have Word recommend that the document be opened in read-only mode. Enter a password in the field (to open or modify). If you check the Read-Only Recommended option, Word will suggest that this document be opened as read-only the next time it is opened.

FIGURE 10-6.

The Save tab

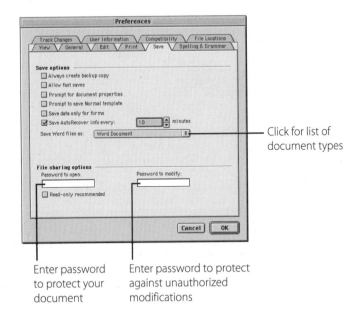

Click for list of document types

Enter password to protect your document

Enter password to protect against unauthorized modifications

⭐ **TIP**

Backups aren't always necessary, but we recommend that you enable AutoRecover options. If Word crashes, it uses AutoRecover information to recover the file you were just working on.

The Spelling & Grammar Tab

The Spelling & Grammar tab, shown in Figure 10-7, hosts the spelling and grammar preferences. The tab is divided into two sections.

■ **Spelling** These options, such as Always Suggest Corrections, affect how Word checks your document's spelling when you conduct a routine spell check and as you type (the Check Spelling As You Type option enables this feature). You can also add custom dictionaries here.

■ **Grammar** These options control Word's grammar checking, which can be disabled if you want.

II

Microsoft Word

FIGURE 10-7.

The Spelling & Grammar tab

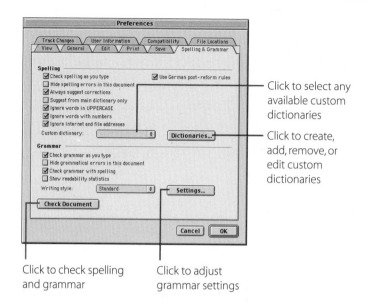

Click to select any available custom dictionaries

Click to create, add, remove, or edit custom dictionaries

Click to check spelling and grammar

Click to adjust grammar settings

Spell-checking is not foolproof. For example, one default preference tells Word to ignore uppercase words. This can be dangerous if you have words in upper-case and rely on the spell checker to correct them. Of course, dangerous is a relative term. If you're sending a personal letter, you probably won't endanger anyone's life with misspelled uppercase words, but if you're working at the CIA on a top secret document, that's exactly what could happen!

The Track Changes Tab

The Track Changes tab, shown in Figure 10-8, controls how Word tracks changes in your documents. This tab can be enabled by opening the Tools menu, selecting Track Changes, and then selecting Highlight Changes. These options are the same as those available if you press the Options button from the Highlight Changes dialog box. Each entry refers to a different operation that can occur to change your document.

The Track Changes tab is divided into four sections:

- **Inserted Text** This is text that has been inserted into the original (or subsequently revised) document.

- **Deleted Text** This is text that has been deleted from the original (or subsequently revised) document.

- **Changed Formatting** This is formatting, such as the font size, color, or style, that has been changed in the original (or subsequently revised) document.

■ **Changed Lines** This option causes vertical lines to appear next to lines that contain changes. Some changes, such as adding a space, are difficult to see. This option makes it easy to find small changes because the vertical lines direct your attention to any lines that have changed.

FIGURE 10-8.

The Track Changes tab

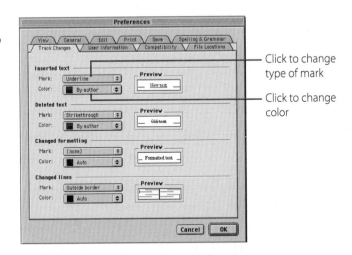

Click to change type of mark

Click to change color

The User Information Tab

The User Information tab, shown in Figure 10-9, contains personal information and is stored in your Address Book. Word uses it when you create documents from certain templates and wizards. If the fields are blank and you would like to personalize your copy of Word, fill it out.

FIGURE 10-9.

The User Information tab

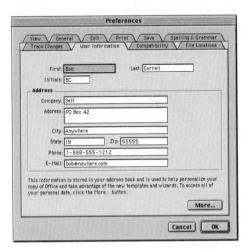

Microsoft Word

The Compatibility Tab

The Compatibility tab, shown in Figure 10-10, controls how compatible you want Word to be with other programs. The default setting is Microsoft Word 2000–2001. If you plan on sending documents created in Word 2001 to users who have an older version (or another application entirely), select a new preference from the pull-down list.

FIGURE 10-10.

The Compatibility tab

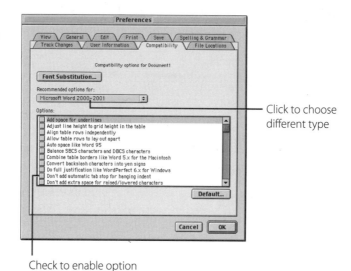

Click to choose different type

Check to enable option

The options you can choose are:

- Microsoft Word 2000–2001

- Microsoft Word 97–98

- Microsoft Word 6.0/95

- Word For Windows 1.0

- Word For Windows 2.0

- Word For Macintosh 5.*x*

- Word For MS-DOS

- WordPerfect 5.*x*

- WordPerfect 6.*x* For Windows

■ WordPerfect 6.0 For DOS

■ Custom

 NOTE

Selecting Custom allows you to create your own compatibility options set. If you select a program from the list and make any changes, the list changes to custom automatically.

The File Locations Tab

The File Locations tab, shown in Figure 10-11, tells Word where you want it to look first for files of various types. Setting these options can save you the time and trouble of having to click through endless dialog boxes as Word tries to find your files.

FIGURE 10-11.

The File Locations tab

Select file type

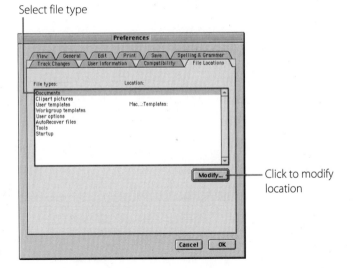

Click to modify location

The file types are:

■ Documents

■ Clipart Pictures

■ User Templates

■ Workgroup Templates

■ User Options

■ AutoRecover Files

■ Tools

■ Startup

Select a file type, and then press the Modify button to change its location preference.

 **TIP**

> If you save all of your documents in one folder (or in folders under a primary work folder), set the Documents option to that folder on your hard disk. This sets your work folder as Word's default storage and search location. Setting the Documents option to a commonly used folder will save you a significant amount of time opening and closing files because the Open and Save dialog boxes will use that folder (and not your Desktop or other location) when they prompt you to open or save files.

Customizing Toolbars, Commands, and Appearance

Aside from setting preferences, which modify how Word looks and works, you can modify Word's toolbars, commands, and other appearances. These options can be accessed by opening the View menu, selecting Toolbars, and then selecting Customize, or by opening the Tools menu and selecting Customize. When you select either menu, the Customize dialog box opens, as shown in Figure 10-12.

FIGURE 10-12.

The Customize dialog box

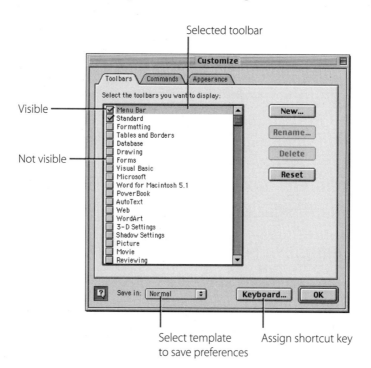

Notice the three tabs: Toolbars, Commands, and Appearance. Many people never realize that these options allow you to completely customize each and every toolbar and menu in Word. That's quite a bit of power, and the end result (should you choose to embark on this endeavor) is a program that truly fits your needs.

The Toolbars Tab

Selecting the Toolbars tab (see Figure 10-12) displays a list of toolbars you can show by checking the box beside their names. You can create new toolbars by pressing the New button. Word creates a blank toolbar to which you can drag buttons and menu commands so that it's customized. You can also rename and delete you own toolbars. Should you make changes to a built-in toolbar, you can select it and press Reset to cause it to revert to its default state. This is a very helpful feature, as it takes a lot of fear out of fiddling around with the toolbars. If you make a mistake (or just give up), open this dialog box and reset the toolbar.

The Commands Tab

The Commands tab (see Figure 10-13) enables you to add buttons to toolbars and menus—whether they're built-in or custom-created. Choose a category in the list on the left side of the dialog box if you want to narrow down the commands that appear in the window on the right side. When you select a command by clicking on it, a description appears in the Description portion of the dialog box. To add the selected command to a toolbar or menu, drag the command and drop it where you want it.

FIGURE 10-13.

Drag commands to toolbars and menus from the Commands tab

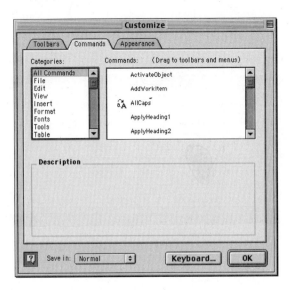

The Appearance Tab

The Appearance tab (see Figure 10-14) enables you to change Word's overall appearance.

FIGURE 10-14.

Change Word's appearance with the Appearance tab

> **NOTE**
>
> The settings in the Appearance tab affect all of your Office programs.

The Office 2001 Appearance and MacOS Theme Compliant choices change the background of toolbars and other items. Toolbars and other interface elements in the Office 2001 Appearance setting have a striped look, while the MacOS Theme Compliant setting reverts to a single shade of gray.

The four check boxes near the bottom of the dialog box enable you to change other appearances. You can choose to display large icons, ScreenTips, shortcut keys, and WYSIWYG font menus.

To conclude, remember that it may take you time working with Word to arrive at a point where you want or need to modify its preferences. Chances are, the first days you'll be more concerned about getting the basics down. With an understanding of how to modify Word's preferences, however, you can become more productive—whether at home, at school, or in the office—as you create your documents. You'll also be able to ensure, through Word's various preferences, that each document you present to the world meets the standards of quality you set.

Microsoft Excel

Introducing Microsoft Excel

Microsoft Excel, or just Excel, as it is most often called, is a worksheet application (some of you may be familiar with the term *spreadsheet,* which is used by other applications) that allows you to enter and, more important, manipulate data on worksheets. If you're not familiar with worksheets, the next few chapters will teach you how to create powerful worksheets (called workbooks) with Excel. If you're an experienced hand, you'll still benefit from reading through the chapters devoted to Excel to find out how it's different from other worksheet programs, as well as what's new in Excel 2001 for Mac.

This chapter will help you understand how worksheets are different from other document types and will take you on a tour of Excel's interface. In addition, you'll learn how to create new workbooks and get help from Excel.

Understanding Worksheets

A *worksheet* is not a word processing document or a slide show. Thus, your reasons for using Excel are fundamentally different from those you might have for using Microsoft Word, PowerPoint, or another application.

Excel is a much "smarter" application than the others included with Microsoft Office 2001 for Macintosh. Excel does much more than hold information, although it can serve that limited purpose. Excel offers you the ability to perform such tasks as:

- Calculating

- Comparing (both logical and mathematic)

- Sorting data based on varying conditions

- Charting and graphing data

- Analyzing information in different scenarios

- Analyzing statistics

In order to accomplish these and other tasks, Excel's nature is quite different from other programs you're probably used to using. Rather than present you with a blank piece of paper, as Word does, Excel uses *workbooks,* which are files that store your data. Workbooks contain worksheets, which are individual pages in which you enter data and functions, and create charts. Worksheets are divided into rows and columns. At the intersection of every row and column is a box called a *cell.* Cells hold information that is distinct and separate from the information in every other cell in the worksheet.

Because each cell is unique, each has its own address, so to speak. Columns are labeled with letters, and run from A to IV (the letters I and V, not to be confused with Roman numerals). Rows are labeled with numbers and go from 1 to 65,536. The first cell in a worksheet is called cell A1, and each worksheet has 16,777,216 cells. Excel creates three worksheets by default in a blank workbook, and you can add (or delete) worksheets up to a figure limited only by your available memory.

Because it's so powerful, Excel requires that you come to it with a modicum of knowledge in order to use it effectively. In other words, if you need to perform calculations on data, you have to know not only what to do but also how to do it. For example, Excel will calculate the mean and standard deviation from a given sample of numerical data.

However, if you don't know what a mean or a standard deviation is in the first place, or why you might need it, Excel will not really help you out much.

Running Excel

As you learned in Chapter 2, "Microsoft Office Basics," there are many ways to launch an Office application. The most popular methods you can use to launch Excel are as follows.

- If working in another Office application, select Project Gallery from the File menu and create a new Excel workbook.

- Open the Microsoft Office 2001 folder in your hard drive, and double-click the Microsoft Excel icon.

- Use the Apple menu to select Recent Applications. This technique works well if you use Excel often.

- Create an alias for Excel on your desktop, and double-click the alias.

- Find an Excel workbook you want to edit, and double-click its icon.

- From the Apple menu, select Recent Documents, and choose an existing Excel workbook to open it.

 TIP

> The last two methods bypass the Project Gallery that pops up when you launch an Office application, allowing Excel to start up more quickly.

The Excel Interface

It helps to know your way around the interface of a program if you're going to use it. Excel has the same major interface components as the other Office applications (with one exception: the Formula bar), each of which are discussed in detail in this section.

The Workbook Window

The workbook window, shown in Figure 11-1, is where you will enter all of your data and create charts, pivot tables, and other items. This window is analogous to the main document window in Word.

III

Microsoft Excel

FIGURE 11-1.

The main Excel window, which looks different from windows in other Office applications

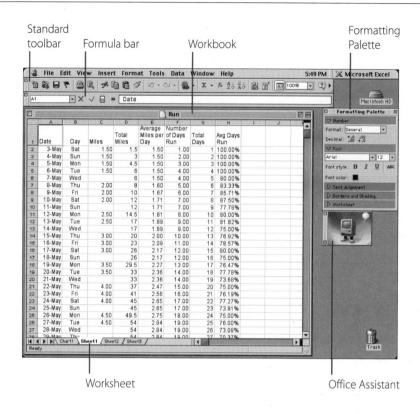

Standard toolbar
Formula bar
Workbook
Formatting Palette

Worksheet
Office Assistant

? SEE ALSO

For more information on managing worksheets (such as renaming them), see the Managing Worksheets section in Chapter 15, "Working with Worksheets and Workbooks."

The workbook window shows the cells that make up each worksheet, organized into rows and columns. Clicking in a cell makes it active and allows you to enter text, numbers, and other information. You can select the row or column header (the number or letter that identifies a row or column, respectively) to select all the cells in that row or column.

At the bottom of the workbook window (see Figure 11-2) are buttons that allow you to navigate between the different worksheets in your workbook and the sheet tabs themselves. Each sheet in a workbook has a name, which, in a default workbook, are Sheet1, Sheet2, and Sheet3. The workbook window also contains horizontal and vertical scrollbars as well as a status bar at the very bottom of the window.

FIGURE 11-2.

Buttons on the workbook window

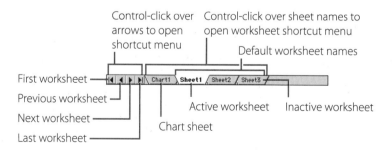

Control-click over arrows to open shortcut menu
Control-click over sheet names to open worksheet shortcut menu
Default worksheet names

First worksheet
Previous worksheet
Next worksheet
Last worksheet
Chart sheet
Active worksheet
Inactive worksheet

The Standard Toolbar (and More)

The Standard toolbar, an ever-present feature in Office applications, has the most commonly used tools you'll need when you work in Excel. Figure 11-3 shows the wide range of commands available.

FIGURE 11-3.

The Standard toolbar, which contains several buttons unique to Excel

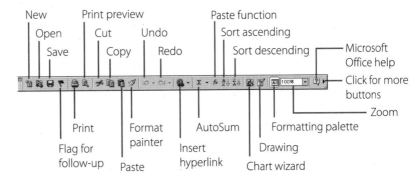

More toolbars are available; you can view them by selecting Toolbars in the View menu and choosing a specific toolbar. You can close toolbars by clicking the close box in the upper-left corner of the toolbar. If you don't like where your toolbar is, you can move it around by clicking (carefully—you don't want to select a button) on its left border and dragging it to a new position.

The Formula Bar

The Formula bar, shown in Figure 11-4, is unique to Excel and is a critical component of the application.

FIGURE 11-4.

The Formula bar, which displays formulas and functions and allows you to enter them

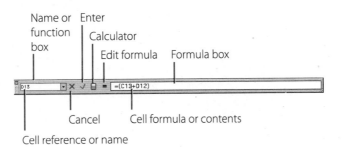

The Name Box displays the cell reference or name of the currently active cell. Skipping over the buttons that appear to the right of the Name Box you can see a long, white box. This is where Excel displays the contents of a cell, whether it's a formula or other type of data. You can also enter data in this area, although we don't recommend entering anything but a formula here because you can enter other data much more quickly in the cells themselves. A Calculator is also available. (See Figure 11-5.) You can enter any of Excel's available functions in a cell from the Calculator.

FIGURE 11-5.

The Calculator, your entry point to more advanced functions

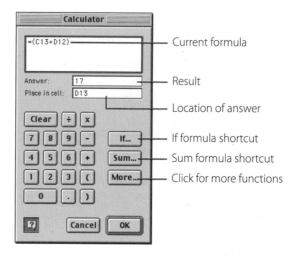

Clicking the More button opens the Paste Function dialog box, shown in Figure 11-6.

FIGURE 11-6.

Functions built into Excel so that you don't have to create them yourself

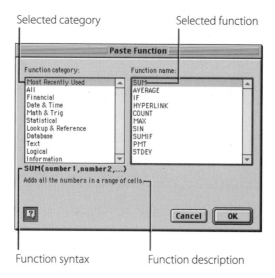

The Menu

Excel's menu has many of the same types of commands as the other Office applications, but also contains some unique commands. Study the menus carefully, and over time you'll know just where to look to find a particular feature. In general, the menus offer the following possibilities:

SEE ALSO

For more information on these menu items, see Chapter 13, "Selecting, Moving, Finding, and Sorting Information."

- **File** The File menu contains file commands that you use to open, close, save, and print files.

- **Edit** The Edit menu allows you to cut, copy, paste, delete, move, find, and replace information. Excel's preferences are located under the Edit menu.

- **View** The View menu controls what is seen onscreen, from toolbars to the Formula bar and Formatting Palette.

- **Insert** The Insert menu inserts various items into your worksheet and workbook.

- **Format** The Format menu formats the contents of cells and allows you to change the size of rows and columns.

SEE ALSO

For more information on the tools, see Chapter 12, "Entering and Formatting Data," and Chapter 15.

- **Tools** The Tools menu contains tools ranging from all-purpose tools like the spell checker to more unique items like Goal Seek and Cell Auditing.

- **Data** The Data menu contains tools to sort, filter, rearrange, and obtain external data.

- **Window** The Window menu gives you access to commands that you can use to alter Excel's windows.

- **Help** The Help menu gives you access to the Help system.

The Formatting Palette

The Formatting Palette, new to Office 2001, is shown in Figure 11-7 and is visible by default. (Click the arrows to expand or contract sections of the Palette.) You can format the contents of cells, change the format of numbers, control text alignment within cells, apply borders and shading, and change your print margins and options.

FIGURE 11-7.

The Formatting Palette, which changes not only the appearance, but also the numerical format, of your data

Click arrows to expand/collapse section

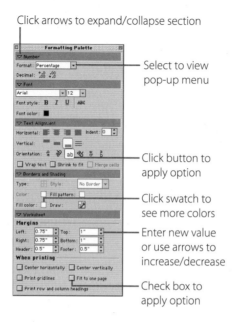

Select to view pop-up menu

Click button to apply option

Click swatch to see more colors

Enter new value or use arrows to increase/decrease

Check box to apply option

The Office Assistant

The Office Assistant, shown in Figure 11-8, is also shown by default. This is the easiest way to get help in Excel. Just click the Office Assistant and enter a question.

FIGURE 11-8.

Clicking the Office Assistant gets you help in Excel

Click to ask a question

Creating Workbooks

As with Word and PowerPoint, Excel offers two ways to create documents: either from scratch or by using the built-in Excel templates.

When you create a blank workbook, you must enter all of your data and formulas and format it yourself. Although you're in total control, you may spend more time creating your workbook this way. If there is a template that matches your workbook goals, you might want to try using it instead. Templates are preformatted and are ready for you to start entering data right away.

Creating Blank Workbooks

To get you started creating a blank workbook, let's create a simple workbook that tracks your grocery store purchases for a month. To do so, follow these steps:

1 Launch Excel by finding the Microsoft Office 2001 folder on your hard drive, opening it, and double-clicking the Microsoft Excel icon. This opens the Project Gallery, shown in Figure 11-9. Since your choice defaults to a blank Excel workbook, you don't need to change anything in the Project Gallery.

2 Click OK to create the workbook.

FIGURE 11-9.

Use the Blank Documents template to create a blank Excel workbook

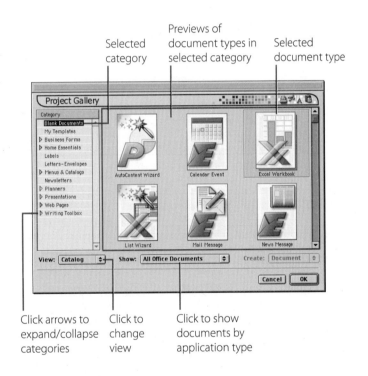

Selected category

Previews of document types in selected category

Selected document type

Click arrows to expand/collapse categories

Click to change view

Click to show documents by application type

3 When finished creating the workbook, Excel will open it and start you out on Sheet1 with cell A1 active (you can tell by the border drawn around the cell). This means that if you start typing right away, your data will be entered in cell A1.

NOTE

Each sheet is separate from the others, so for now, stay on the first sheet.

III

Microsoft Excel

4 With cell A1 still active (if you changed the active cell, just click your mouse cursor on cell A1 to make it active again), enter a date, such as "12/15/00," and press Enter. We'll use this first column to identify when you bought the groceries.

5 Notice how the date is entered and how Excel changes the location of the active cell? Whenever you press Enter or Return, Excel records the date you just entered in the active cell and moves to another. The default direction (which can be changed in Excel's preferences) is down.

6 Make cell B1 active by moving the active cell box to B1 with your arrow keys or clicking on cell B1 with your mouse. Type "Cost" and press Enter or Return. The price for each item bought will go in column B. We'll put the name of the grocery item in column A.

> If you make a mistake entering data, you can use the Undo button to back out of it. If you are entering data, you can also press Esc prior to pressing Enter/Return, and Excel will cancel your data entry for that cell. ·

Now fill out column A, under the date, with several items you have bought. Enter their names but not the price. If the name of an item is long enough, it will run over into the next cell. This doesn't mean the contents become mixed; rather, it is a display oddity. To make your column wide enough to fit your longest item, double-click the border between the column A and column B headers. This adjusts the column width. After you finish, go back and put the price for each item in column B. When you enter the price, don't use a dollar sign. Instead, just enter the number with its decimal point. When you are done entering the prices, select column B by clicking on the column header (where it says "B"), and change the number format to Currency using the Formatting Palette. Do this by clicking the pull-down list beside Format in the number portion of the Formatting Palette and selecting Currency. Figure 11-10 shows you our example.

FIGURE 11-10.

Listing how much groceries cost is easy with Excel

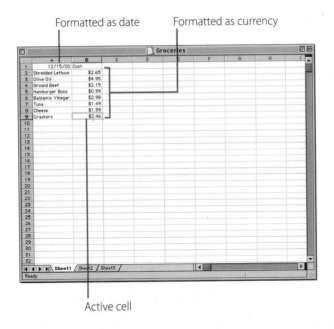

Formatted as date   Formatted as currency

Active cell

Let's finish this example by having Excel total up the cost of the groceries. After the last item in column A, type the word "Total." Make the cell opposite the Total in column B active, and click the AutoSum button on the Standard toolbar. Excel takes a look at your data and guesses which rows or columns you want added up, which is indicated by a flashing border around those cells for you to double-check. It also displays the formula in the active cell that it will use to perform the calculation, as shown in Figure 11-11. Since this is a simple example, Excel should add the correct cells together to arrive at a total. Press Enter or Return. In more complicated worksheets where there may be intervening blank cells or data that shouldn't be added, such as labels or text, Excel may have a harder time identifying the exact cells you want totaled. In such cases, Excel will normally identify one section of a column you want added, but you will need to add additional cells to the selection manually.

III

Microsoft Excel

FIGURE 11-11.

The AutoSum feature, which allows you to add columns of data with the click of a button

Box highlights cells of formula

AutoSum function

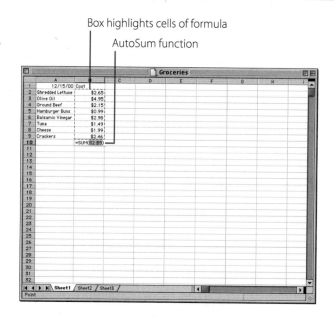

Figure 11-12 shows the final workbook, which is saved as "Groceries."

FIGURE 11-12.

Using the AutoSum feature allows you to see a total for your groceries

Result of AutoSum function

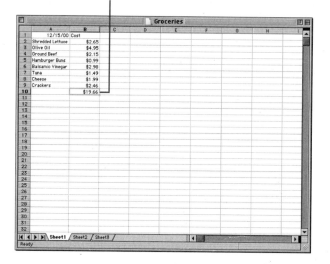

> NOTE
>
> You can change the way your data looks, in a similar fashion as you did it in Word. You can make data bold, italicized, a different font size, and so on through the Formatting Palette.

Using this example as a starting point, you can see how easy it would be to continue adding dates and items and eventually create a grocery list that analyzes how much money you spend per month.

Using Templates in Excel

Excel offers several built-in templates that can make your job of creating a workbook much easier. Even if you don't use them for their intended purpose, you can benefit from opening them up and seeing how they are arranged and formatted.

All the templates are available through the Project Gallery; its Excel-related categories are summarized in Table 11-1.

Table 11-1.   Excel Workbook Templates Available in the Project Gallery.

Category	Effect or Templates
Blank Documents	Allows you to create a blank Excel workbook or use the List wizard. The List wizard launches a three-step process that helps you create a list from new or existing data and put the list in a new or existing workbook.
My Templates	Templates you have created are available here.
Home Essentials	Contains Family Financial and Budget templates.
Planners	Offers Dietary Planner templates.

Follow these steps to use the templates:

1   Launch Excel, and select Excel Documents from the Show drop-down menu. This narrows down your choices to just those available to Excel.

2   Browse through the categories, and choose one that looks interesting. If there is an Excel template available, you'll see it previewed in the main window.

TIP

Categories that can be expanded are shown with an arrow beside them. Click the arrow to reveal what's underneath.

III

Microsoft Excel

3 In Figure 11-13, we've chosen the Moving Cost Calculator template. Click OK when you've selected the type of document you want to create.

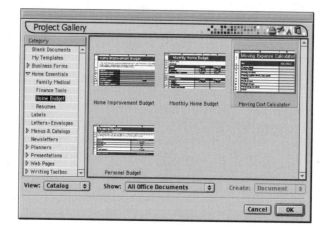

4 When the template is in the main document window, as shown in Figure 11-14, you're ready to start using or customizing it.

Moving Expense Calculator and Log					
Item	Actual Cost	Estimated Cost	Reimbursable?	Tax deductible?	Over/Under
Packers (labor)					at budget
Movers (labor)					at budget
Moving van rental					at budget
Packing supplies (boxes, tape, paper)					at budget
Shipping					at budget
Meals on road					at budget
Mileage and gas					at budget
Pet boarding and airfare					at budget
Airfare					at budget
Hotel					at budget
Rental car					at budget
Telephone charges					at budget
Deposits on services/new accounts					at budget
Long-term storage					at budget
Driver's license					at budget
Vehicle inspection/registration/license					at budget
Vehicle shipping					at budget
Cleaning services (old home)					at budget
Cleaning services (new home)					at budget
Repairs to old home					at budget
Repairs to new home					at budget
Miscellaneous expenses					at budget

5 Select the cells for which you have data, such as the actual cost of items, and begin entering your data. Remember to save your work, and don't forget to use Undo if you make a mistake.

Getting Help

Excel has the same extensive Help system that the other Office applications have, and you use the same methods to get help in Excel as you do in the other applications. You can:

- Ask questions of the Office Assistant by clicking it. (See Figure 11-15.)

FIGURE 11-15.

Search for a term using the Office Assistant

Enter word, phrase, or question, and press Search

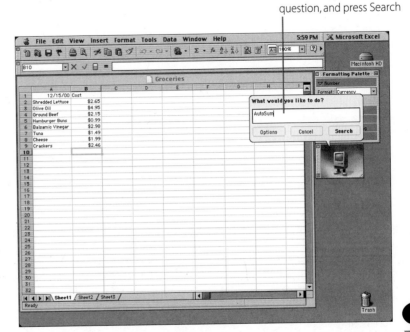

- Rely on pop-up ToolTips (shown in Figure 11-16), which are activated by letting your mouse rest over buttons and other interface elements, to refresh your memory about the names of these elements.

FIGURE 11-16.

Hold your cursor over
a button to see the
ToolTip

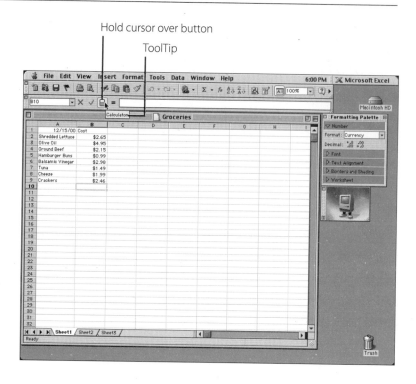

Turn Balloons on and more help appears when your mouse hovers over the different parts of Excel, as shown in Figure 11-17.

FIGURE 11-17.

Enable Balloon Help to
see a description of a
function

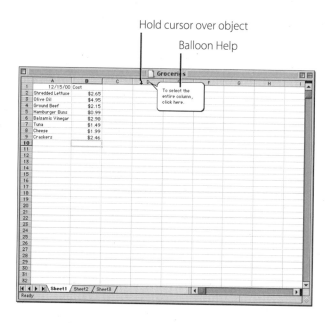

- From the Help menu, select Microsoft Excel Help and ask the Office Assistant a question.

- Select the Help menu, and choose Contents And Index to open the actual help file (as shown in Figure 11-18), where you can browse through the contents or look up a word in the index. Click on a subject in the left pane, and it will expand to give you more choices. Click on an entry that you think will answer your question, and Help will appear in the right-hand side. Click the Index button to see the index.

FIGURE 11-18.

The Help file in Excel

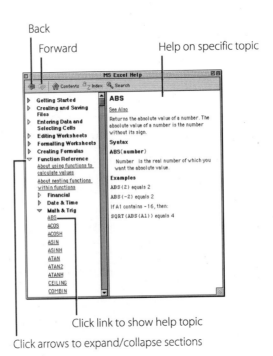

Back

Forward

Help on specific topic

Click link to show help topic

Click arrows to expand/collapse sections

- From the Help menu, select Help On The Web to open your Web browser and display several links to Microsoft's Web site. You can peruse downloads, support, and other information.

III

Microsoft Excel

Entering and Formatting Data

U nlike word processing in an application such as Microsoft Word, you can't just sit down and start typing in Excel. Excel requires a tad more forethought. First, you need to understand how to navigate the worksheet. In other words, since Excel isn't a blank piece of paper like a Word document, there are special skills and knowledge required to properly move around and select cells for data entry. This chapter discusses navigating and moving around the worksheet. It also discusses how to format the information and delete the contents of cells.

Once you understand how worksheets work, entering data in the form of text and formulas (and later, functions) is easy. It should be because the real power of Excel comes after you enter your raw data. You can compare, manipulate, and analyze your information in a multitude of ways, including graphically with charts. Those features will be covered in later chapters.

Navigating the Worksheet

With time and practice, you'll be able to navigate Excel worksheets without a second thought. If you are just learning Excel or are switching from another spreadsheet program, this section will teach you how to refer to cells and make cells active so that you can enter data in them. It will also teach you about other features that will help you create a workspace you'll be comfortable with.

Understanding Cells and Cell References

Unlike Word, which uses lines, paragraphs, and pages to store information, Excel uses cells. As we mentioned in the last chapter, cells are formed at the intersection of each row and column in a worksheet. Each cell can be 255 characters wide by 409 points high and can contain up to 32,747 characters. Cells are where you will enter data—literally everything in Excel is based around the concept of the cells.

> **NOTE**
>
> In this book, we make frequent comparisons to Word because many people use Word and try to bring that knowledge to Excel. Although a large amount of information you have learned using Word will be helpful—such as formatting concepts and interface features that all Office applications share—some concepts don't translate well. We will indicate these throughout.

A cell's address (the row and column labels) is called a *reference*. The primary method for referring to cells in Excel is the A1 reference style, which uses the column letter and row number to identify a cell. For example, the first cell in a worksheet is in column A, row 1. Therefore, it is called cell A1 (referred to as the A1 reference style throughout).

> **NOTE**
>
> Other programs sometimes use the R1C1 reference style. This style refers to the row and column number to identify a cell. For example, cell E14 (using the A1 reference style) would be called cell R14C5. This is an advantage when you need to use row and column positions *as numbers* in macros.

You can also describe a range of cells with cell references. For example, the first five cells in row 1 are A1:E1 and the 10 cells in column A are A1:A10. You can even refer to a range of cells that spans multiple rows and columns. The first number in the reference identifies the top-left cell and the number following the colon identifies the bottom-right cell. Figure 12-1 illustrates a selected cell range that would be referred to as C5:H23.

FIGURE 12-1.

A selected cell range of C5:H23

Selected cells are highlighted and have a border around them

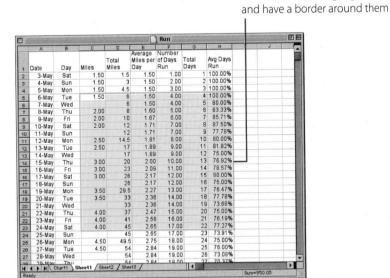

If you need to refer to all of the cells in a row or column, or all of the cells in a range of rows or columns, follow these examples:

- 5:5 refers to all the cells in row 5.

- 5:23 refers to all the cells in row 5 through row 23.

- C:C refers to all the cells in column C.

- C:H refers to all the cells in column C through column H.

Moving Around and Making Cells Active

It's important to note that you can enter data only in a cell that is active. You can distinguish an active cell from an inactive cell by the light border drawn around the active cell, as shown in Figure 12-2.

III

Microsoft Excel

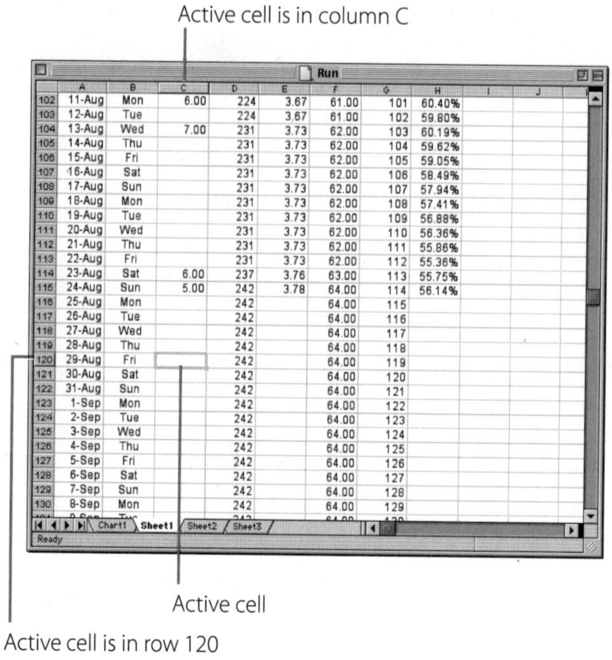

FIGURE 12-2.

An active cell, which has a light border around it

Active cell is in column C

Active cell

Active cell is in row 120

There are a number of ways to move around in the worksheet window and select cells, or make them active. Here is a summary of the techniques:

- Click a cell with your mouse.

- Use your arrow keys to move one cell at a time in the direction of the key you press.

- Use the Page Up or Page Down buttons to move one page in either direction.

- Scroll through your worksheet with the scrollbars.

Navigating worksheets is easy and intuitive if you are using your mouse. Click a cell to make it active, and if the cell you want is not onscreen (for example, if you are working close to the top of the worksheet in cell A15 and need to get to cell A432), use the scrollbars to find it. If you are more comfortable using your keyboard to navigate a worksheet, Table 12-1 summarizes some of the more convenient keyboard shortcuts for moving or scrolling in a worksheet.

Table 12-1. Common Keyboard Shortcuts for Navigating a Worksheet in Excel.

Keyboard Shortcut	Result
Arrow keys	Moves one cell in the direction of the arrow (up, down, left, or right)
Page Up and Page Down	Moves up or down one screen
Option-Page Up or Option-Page Down	Moves one screen to the left or right
Control-Arrow key	Moves to the edge of the currently active data region, which is a range of cells that are bordered by empty cells or the worksheet border
Home	Moves to the beginning of the current row
Control-Home	Moves to the first cell in the worksheet
Control-Delete	Scrolls to and centers (as much as possible, given the cell's location) the currently active cell

Hiding Rows or Columns

Sometimes it's convenient to hide rows and columns in your worksheet. Perhaps you've entered data that you need to use to perform calculations but don't want to display it or have it shown on a printout. The solution is to hide the rows or columns, which can be done by following these steps:

1 Select a cell in the row or column you want to hide.

2 Select the Format menu, and then choose either the Row or Column submenu.

3 Choose Hide from either submenu. The row or column headers on each side of the hidden row or column will change color from black to blue. This lets you know at a glance where you have hidden rows or columns.

 NOTE

If you can't seem to find your hidden rows or columns, look for the change of color in the headers on either side of the hidden row or column. Another giveaway is the fact that the headers will skip numbers or letters. If your column header row goes from A to B to E, then columns C and D are hidden.

When you want to see the hidden rows or columns again, unhide them by following these steps:

1 Select a row or column on one side of the hidden row or column by clicking its header. Hold the mouse button down.

2 Drag your mouse to the right or left so that you select the rows or columns on either side of the hidden row or column.

3 Select the Format menu, and then choose either the Row or Column submenu.

4 Choose Unhide from either submenu.

Switching Between Worksheets

 SEE ALSO

For more information on manipulating worksheets, including renaming, adding, and deleting them, see the "Managing Worksheets" section in Chapter 15, "Working with Worksheets and Workbooks."

You've probably noticed that Excel creates three blank worksheets whenever you create a new workbook. During the course of entering data and creating your own customized workbook, you may even add to or delete from these default worksheets. Because each worksheet is an independent unit, you really should not think of them as pages in a word processing document that allow information to flow freely back and forth. In other words, you can't scroll down or press Page Down until you come to the next worksheet. Rather, you should click on the name tab at the bottom of the main Excel window to change worksheets.

Excel also provides navigation arrows beside the name tabs that allow you to scroll through a lengthy list of worksheets (if you have them). Figure 12-3 illustrates the worksheet name tabs and navigation arrows. Don't be confused by the fact that these worksheet names have been changed from the default and that there are more than three. You can change the name of any worksheet as well as add and delete worksheets.

FIGURE 12-3.

Click on a worksheet name to switch to that worksheet, and use the arrows to navigate if you have a large number of worksheets

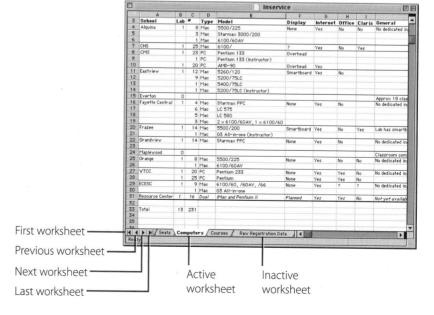

Splitting the Window

Splitting the main workbook window enables you to view (and work on) two to four different areas of the same worksheet at one time. This is especially helpful if the areas are rather far apart. For example, if you are working on a budget or other financial document, you could split the window and refer to the date from a prior quarter in one split while you enter this quarter's data in the second split. You can also split your window to keep row and column headers visible, although freezing panes (covered later in this chapter) also works. Follow these steps to split a worksheet into different windowed areas:

1 Select (by clicking and holding the mouse button down) either the vertical or horizontal Split box (shown in Figure 12-4) at the right side of the horizontal scrollbar or the top of the vertical scrollbar. You'll know when your mouse is over the Split box because the mouse cursor changes shape from an arrow to two parallel lines with arrows pointing up and down or left and right (depending on which Split box you have chosen).

FIGURE 12-4.

Split boxes create divisions in your worksheet

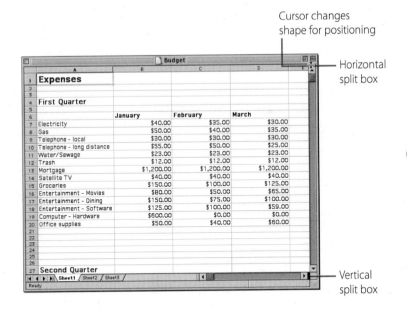

Cursor changes shape for positioning

Horizontal split box

Vertical split box

2 Drag the Split box into the worksheet window.

3 When you are happy with the position of the split, release the mouse button. Figure 12-5 illustrates the split window.

III

Microsoft Excel

FIGURE 12-5.

Splitting the window enables you to refer to and work on areas of the same worksheet that may be far apart

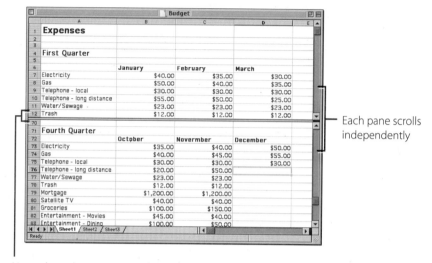

Each pane scrolls independently

Note where the top pane ends and the bottom pane begins

You can split the window into four independently scrollable sections by inserting both a horizontal and vertical split. Each split is also movable. Just click the split and drag it to a new position. If you want to remove the split, double-click it or choose Remove Split from the Window menu.

Freezing Panes

Freezing panes is a bit different from splitting a window. When you split a window, you are creating two to four separate little windows that can each be scrolled. Freezing does as its name implies—it freezes rows or columns in the main window so that they can't be scrolled. The non-frozen rows and columns move as you scroll in the window normally. This is a great benefit when you have a lot of data to enter in your columns or rows but want your labels to be visible. For example, if you use Excel to log your running workouts, after a month or so of entering data, the labels at the top of your columns won't be visible when you enter new data. Assuming you want to see them to remind you what data to enter in which column, freezing those rows keeps them visible, no matter what row you're working in.

Freezing panes can be a bit tricky at first, until you remember the rules that control which rows or columns are frozen. These rules are:

- The rows above the currently active cell (but not including it) will be frozen.

■ The columns to the left of the currently active cell (but not including it) will be frozen.

Therefore, to freeze row 1 and column A (see Figure 12-6), you would first select cell B2, then the choose the Window menu, and finally select Freeze Panes.

FIGURE 12-6.

Freezing panes keeps row or column headers (or other vital information) continually visible

Row 1 is frozen

Column A is frozen

Frozen rows and columns have a dark border

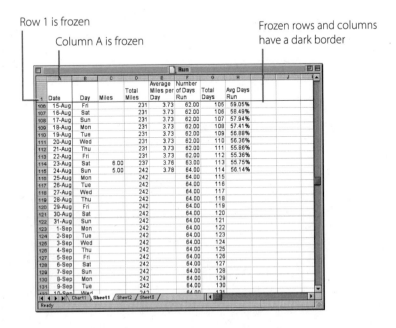

To unfreeze the panes, simply select the Window menu and choose Unfreeze Panes.

 NOTE

It doesn't make any difference which cell is active when you choose to unfreeze panes.

Entering Data

Unlike Word, you don't just sit down with Excel and start typing in information. That's not to say you have to create a blueprint on paper before you can start creating a workbook, but you'll have to make a few decisions about where to put your data right away.

Remember, each cell is a discrete "box" that holds information. As such, your information should be discrete. An exercise log is a good example of this. In an exercise log, you don't put everything in one cell. Instead,

III

Microsoft Excel

you separate the data into categories, which are contained in the worksheet columns, and use the cells under the column headers for each data point. Table 12-2 illustrates a hypothetical running log.

Table 12-2. Hypothetical Running Log.

Date	Day	Miles Run	Total Miles
11 Aug	Friday	3	3
12 Aug	Saturday	2.5	5.5
13 Aug	Sunday	0	5.5
14 Aug	Monday	4	9.5

Table 12-2 illustrates how Excel is superior to Word when doing certain tasks. For example, Excel allows you to create and extend data series, such as the date. If you want to add dates to extend the series to December 31, you don't have to enter each date individually. Rather, you can extend the data series, and Excel automatically enters each new date in a new cell.

Entering Text

Entering text is fairly straightforward, whether the amount is large or small. Simply select a cell to make it active and begin typing. Of course, the more text you enter in one cell, the higher the chances are that you'll have to expand the column width or enable text wrapping so that the text will all be displayed in the cell without "bleeding" over to other columns or being hidden. Enable text wrapping in a cell by following these steps:

1   Select the cell you want the text to wrap in.

2   Choose the Format menu.

3   Select Cells.

4   Select the Alignment tab.

5   In the Text Control area, click Wrap Text.

6   Click OK to finish.

You can quickly change a column's width by clicking the border of the column header (where the column labels are, such as A, B, and C) and dragging it to the desired width. If you double-click the border, the column will expand to fit the largest cell in the column.

As you enter more data, you will run across the AutoComplete feature, shown in Figure 12-7. Excel remembers each data point you enter, and as you type the first few characters of another cell, if the contents match a cell that was previously entered, Excel will prompt you with a small menu with the possible matches. To accept an entry, use your down arrow key to scroll to the match and press Return. Keep typing if the data you're entering is unique and not in the list.

FIGURE 12-7.

Starting an entry with a letter that has started other entries enables the AutoComplete feature

C triggers AutoComplete

Pop-up menu with AutoComplete choices

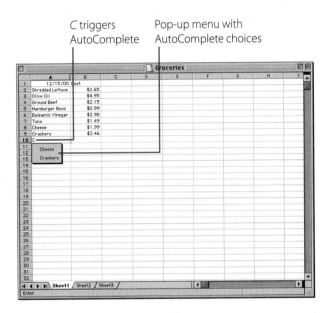

Spell Checking

Although you may not equate spell-checking with a worksheet, you should take advantage of this feature. Select the Tools menu, and choose Spelling (or press F7) to begin checking your worksheet. The Spelling dialog box opens, as shown in Figure 12-8, and enables you to address each potentially misspelled word and correct it or ignore it.

 TIP

If you aren't at the top of the worksheet when you begin your spell check, Excel will check from the active cell downward and then ask you if you want to continue checking at the beginning of the sheet. Click Yes at this prompt to ensure you've checked everything on your worksheet.

III

Microsoft Excel

FIGURE 12-8.

Spell-checking is a valuable tool, even in Excel workbooks

Misspelled word

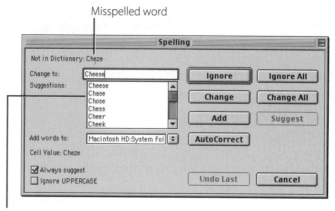

Select a suggestion and then click Change or Change All

AutoCorrect

AutoCorrect is a handy feature that is actually a "real-time" spell checker. As you enter text, if you make a misspelling that is in Excel's list of commonly misspelled words, Excel will automatically correct your entry. Select the Tools menu and choose AutoCorrect to open the AutoCorrect dialog box (see Figure 12-9) to see the words Excel will automatically correct for you, to add or delete words, or to turn the feature off.

FIGURE 12-9.

AutoCorrect corrects misspelled words as you type and can be customized by adding or deleting words or phrases of your own choosing

Click to enable AutoCorrect

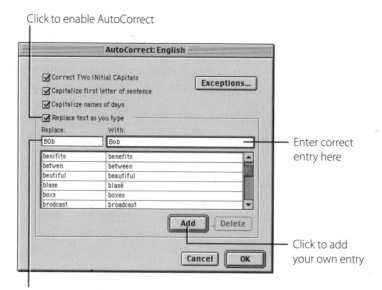

Enter correct entry here

Click to add your own entry

Enter new AutoCorrect entry

Entering Numbers, Dates, and Times

Entering numbers is as easy as entering plain text. Just select a cell to make it active and enter the number. Negative numbers should be preceded by a minus sign (–), and decimals should come after a decimal point (.).

Dates are easy to enter, but you may want to format your dates so that they are displayed the way you want. If you enter a date, such as 6/13, and want it to be displayed as 13-Jun, select the cell (before or after you enter the data), choose the Format menu, and then choose Cells. Under the Number tab, in the Category listing, choose Date and then select a format from the list in the right page of the dialog box, as shown in Figure 12-10.

FIGURE 12-10.

Enter dates and times as you wish and change their formatting through the Format Cells dialog box

Select different tabs for more formatting options

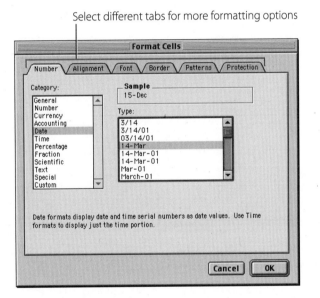

> **NOTE**

You can enter dates and times in just about any manner, and Excel will automatically change them to reflect the formatting you want, such as MM/DD/YY or DD-MMM.

Using Formulas

Formulas are mathematical expressions that perform an action on numbers or the contents of a cell. In Excel, formulas are always preceded by an equal sign (=). For example, a formula to add 1 to 1 would be expressed as =1+1. If you enter that in a cell, Excel will evaluate the

III

Microsoft Excel

expression and display the result. If you select the cell again, you'll see the formula in the Formula bar near the top of the screen. The easy way to enter formulas is simply to select the cell and enter the formula, making sure to include the equal sign. If you leave the equal sign out, Excel thinks you're entering text and will display the numbers you have typed, such as 1+1 from the example above. Figure 12-11 illustrates each of these points.

FIGURE 12-11.

Entering a formula correctly, incorrectly, and seeing the result

Note the formula with the correct entry

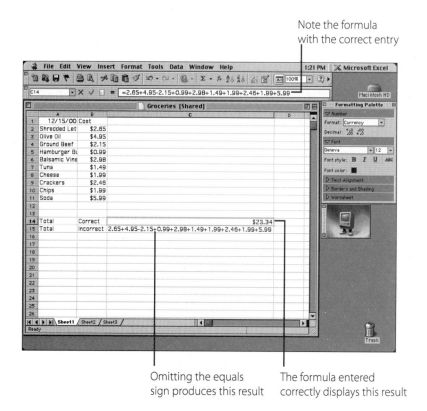

Omitting the equals sign produces this result

The formula entered correctly displays this result

> **NOTE**
>
> You can also use the Formula bar to enter formulas. Select a cell to make it active, click the Edit Formula button (the equal sign) to begin, and then enter your formula. Excel displays the result of your formula and allows you to accept it by clicking an OK button or to abort it by clicking Cancel. This can be a bit cumbersome so you may want to just enter the formula in the active cell.

You're not restricted to simple addition of constants in formulas. You can create just about any formula you can think of, as well as substitute cell references for constants. For example, =A1/F13 divides the contents of cell A1 by the contents of cell F13 and displays the result in the current cell.

Entering Data in a Series

One of the most convenient features Excel offers is the ability to enter data and automatically extend it in a series. For example, if you need a series of dates, just enter the first date and extend it into a series. Follow these steps to perform this action:

1 Select a cell to make it active.

2 Enter the first number, date, or time in your series.

3 Press Return.

4 Select the cell you just entered and click the fill handle at the lower-right corner of the cell, shown in Figure 12-12.

FIGURE 12-12.

Your cursor changes to a small box with arrows at the corners when you are over the fill handle

Fill cursor

5 Drag the fill handle in the direction you want the series to extend.

6 When your series is complete, release your mouse button and Excel will extend the series automatically, as shown in Figure 12-13.

FIGURE 12-13.

Entering data couldn't be much easier than dragging to fill a series

Original cell   These cells were filled automatically

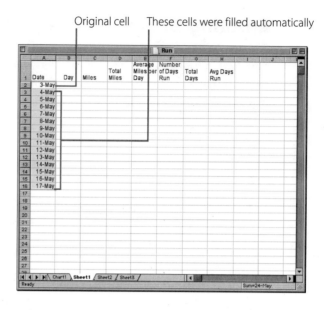

 TIP

Dragging a series of dates and times works well without any other intervention, but if you need to extend numerical values (such as even or odd numbers, or extending the series by more than one at a time) or other types of values (such as extending a date by weeks or months), press Control as you click the fill handle and drag it with your mouse. Excel will open a context-sensitive menu and allow you to choose exactly how the series should be filled.

Editing Existing Data

If you've entered data and want to go back and edit it, simply double-click the cell to make it active and enter edit mode, or select the cell with a single click and then click in the formula bar to edit the cell contents. You can move your cursor within the contents of the cell with your arrow keys or your mouse. When you are finished editing, press Return or click another cell.

Formatting Data

Excel offers two levels of formatting. You should be familiar with the first level because you perform this type of formatting in applications such as Word. Namely, you can change the color, appearance, alignment, and other visual properties of your data. The second, and critically important, formatting level determines how Excel treats the data you have entered. Excel defines the following data categories:

- **General** This is the default format. It doesn't allow you to control how a number is displayed or how many decimal places are shown.

- **Number** This is a general format for numbers, but it allows you some control over how they are displayed. For example, you can set how many decimal places are shown and whether negative numbers are shown in red or with a minus sign in front of them.

- **Currency** This is a general format for currency. It allows you to change the currency symbol and how negative numbers are displayed.

- **Accounting** This is a specialized currency format that lines up the currency symbols and decimal points.

- **Date** This format allows you to format dates in numerous ways. Numbers formatted as dates are treated differently than other, general numbers when used in calculations and series.

- **Time** This format allows you to format times in numerous ways.

- **Percentage** This format formats a number as a percentage and displays the % symbol. For example, .90, when formatted as a percentage, would change to 90%.

- **Fraction** This format allows you to format cells so they are displayed as fractions instead of decimals.

- **Scientific** This format formats cells in scientific notation. 34 would be displayed as 3.40E+01.

- **Text** This format formats the contents of a cell as text, even if it is a number. Once a number is formatted as text, you cannot perform calculations on it.

- **Special** This format contains useful formats for data that don't fit elsewhere, such as Social Security and telephone numbers.

- **Custom** This format allows you to create your own number format so that you can display numbers precisely how you need them. You can select an existing data format and modify it as a custom format.

III

Microsoft Excel

Each category has one or more options that defines how the data will be displayed. For example, you can display time data in the following manners:

- HH:MM, based on a 24-hour clock (16:30)

- H:MM AM/PM (4:30 PM)

- HH:MM:SS, based on a 24-hour clock (16:30:00)

- H:MM:SS AM/PM (4:30:00 PM)

- MM:SS.00, elapsed time in minutes, seconds, and fractions of a second (42:13.5)

- HH:MM:SS, elapsed time in hours, minutes, and seconds (1:42:13)

- DATE H:MM AM/PM, includes the date with the time (6/13/00 7:30 PM)

- DATE HH:MM, includes the date with the time based on a 24-hour clock (6/13/00 19:30)

You can access each of these data types by opening the Format Cells dialog box. To do this, select a cell or range of cells that you want to apply the formatting to, and then select the Format menu and choose Cells. These formatting options are located in the Numbers tab.

 ## Using the Formatting Palette

As you can see from Figure 12-14, the Formatting Palette is broken up into several categories. If a category isn't visible, click the arrow beside its name to expand that section of the palette. The arrow will change and point downwards. Conversely, you can minimize unneeded sections by clicking the arrow so that it points to the right.

Each category serves the following purposes:

- **Number** Allows you to change data categories and decimal places.

- **Font** Controls font properties such as color, size, and font of selected text or cells.

FIGURE 12-14.

The Formatting Palette allows you to format the contents of cells as well as properties of the worksheet

Click arrow to expand/collapse section

■ **Text Alignment** Facilitates placement of text within cells exactly how and where you want it.

■ **Borders And Shading** Controls borders and color to be drawn around and inside cells.

■ **Worksheet** Allows you to change page margins and other printing options.

Using the Formatting Toolbar

The Formatting toolbar is a holdover from previous versions of Excel. Although many of the options are shared with the Formatting Palette, some features, such as the Currency Style and Percentage buttons (which allow you to change the data type for selected cells to currency or percentages with the touch of a button), can't be found on the Formatting Palette.

The Formatting toolbar is not visible by default. To view it, select the View menu, choose Toolbars, and then select Formatting.

III

Microsoft Excel

Other Formatting Menus and Commands

Other formatting menus are available in Excel. These menus, which are found in the Format menu, are:

- **Cells** Opens the Format Cells dialog box, which allows you to choose many different types of formatting options to apply to the selected cell.

- **Row** Allows you to change the size of the selected row or hide and unhide the row.

- **Column** Allows you to change the size of the selected column or hide and unhide it.

- **Sheet** Allows you to rename a worksheet, hide or unhide it, and choose a custom background for the worksheet.

- **AutoFormat** Automatically formats cells in a list.

- **Conditional Formatting** Allows you to set conditions that, when fulfilled, apply certain formats to the cells that meet the conditions.

- **Style** Enables you to select and create different styles to apply to your data.

Deleting Cell Contents

Should you need to delete a cell, select the cell with your mouse to make the cell active (don't double-click it as you will enter editing mode) and press Delete or Clear.

You can also select a range of cells and then select Delete from the Edit menu. When you do this, Excel displays the dialog box shown in Figure 12-15.

FIGURE 12-15.

Excel needs to know what to do with the surrounding cells when it deletes the selection

Choose an option from those shown (Shift Cells Left, Shift Cells Up, Entire Row, or Entire Column), and click OK.

If you want to clear the contents of a cell or range of cells without deleting the actual cells, you should clear the cells rather than delete them. Follow these steps to clear cells:

1 Select the cell or range of cells to clear.

2 From the Edit menu, select Clear.

3 Choose what to clear by picking one of the following submenus:

- **All** Deletes the formatting and contents of a cell, as well as any comment in it.

- **Formats** Clears any formatting in a cell without deleting the information in the cell.

- **Contents** Deletes the contents of a cell but leaves the formatting and any comments intact.

- **Comments** Deletes comments from a cell.

CHAPTER 13

Selecting, Moving, Finding, and Sorting Information

In this chapter you'll learn how to select cells in Microsoft Excel so that you can copy, paste, or move their contents, find and replace information in a workbook, as well as sort and filter information.

Selecting and finding are features used in many applications. In Excel, you must usually select cells in order for a command to function on the cell's contents. Finding (and replacing) is helpful if you have a large worksheet and need to quickly and selectively find and replace information. Meanwhile, sorting and filtering easily rank among the top ten Excel features. Sorting enables you to select a group of cells and sort their contents by a variety of criteria. Perhaps you want a price list to appear in a certain order. Simply sort the list and Excel reorders the list with the prices in ascending or descending order. Filtering enables you to "de-clutter" a list and show only the information you want. For example, say you have a diet log that lists all the food you have eaten each day for the last month. Filtering allows you to show only your lunches, hiding your breakfasts and dinners.

Selecting and Moving Cells

Selecting and moving cells are important tasks to master. You must select cells to perform most actions in Excel, from entering data to deleting a cell's contents. In addition, moving cells is an incredible time-saver. Rather than having to reenter data in a new location, simply copy or cut the same or similar information and paste it in a new location.

Selecting One Cell or Multiple Adjacent Cells

To select one cell, simply click it to make it active. If you want to select multiple cells, follow these steps:

1 Click a corner cell of the cell range you want to select, and hold your mouse button down. This corner cell can be any of the four corners of the rectangle that will comprise your finished selection.

2 Drag your mouse in any direction so that you highlight the cells you want to select, as shown in Figure 13-1. You'll see the highlighting change as you move your mouse, letting you know the exact size of the selection.

FIGURE 13-1.

Drag a box around the cells you want to select

Selected cells are highlighted and have a thick border

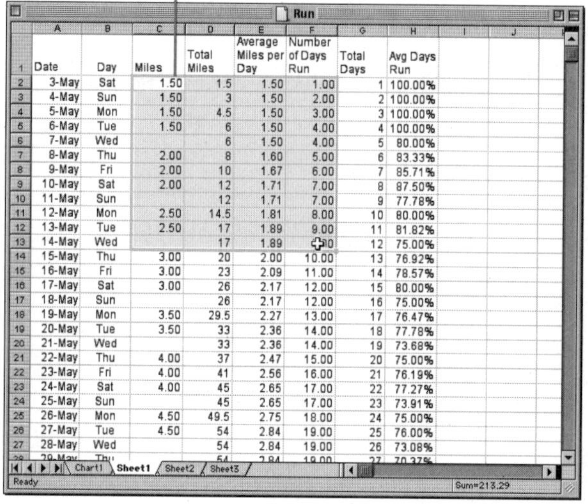

3 Release the mouse button when you've highlighted the cells you want to select.

After you have selected a cell or area, press the ⌘ key as you click on another cell or drag over more cells to add the cell or cells to your original selection.

To select an entire row or column, click its header. To select multiple rows or columns, click a header, hold the mouse button down, drag your mouse so that you highlight the rows or columns you want to select, and then release the mouse button.

Selecting Non-Adjacent Cells

When you need to select non-adjacent cells, you'll find that the normal method of using the mouse to select cells only allows you to select an adjacent range or area of cells. Normally, when you select a range of cells, you click the first cell in the range and drag your mouse to highlight the entire range; there is no way to avoid the fact that the cells must be connected. You must therefore use the keyboard in conjunction with the mouse to select a non-adjacent range of cells. Use the following keyboard and mouse combinations to select non-adjacent cells or ranges of cells:

- **Non-Adjacent Cells** Select a cell with your mouse, hold down the ⌘ key, and then select another cell.

You can release the ⌘ key between selecting additional cells. There is no re-quirement to hold it down when you are not in the process of selecting a cell or range of cells.

- **Non-Adjacent Ranges** Select the first range of cells as you would normally (using your mouse), and then hold down the ⌘ key as you select the second (or more) range. Excel will highlight the selected areas, as shown in Figure 13-2.

FIGURE 13-2.

You can select non-adjacent cells by pressing ⌘ as you click new cells or cell ranges

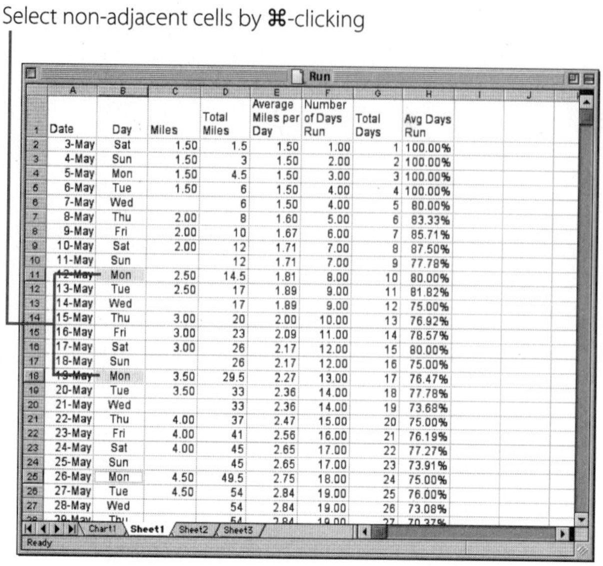

Select non-adjacent cells by ⌘-clicking

Copying, Cutting, and Pasting

Copying information allows you to store the contents of a cell or cell range in the Clipboard so that you can paste it elsewhere. Cutting allows you to move the contents of cells and remove the data from its original location. Pasting transfers previously copied or cut information from the Clipboard to an area in your worksheet. Follow these steps to copy or cut material:

1 Select the cell or cell range you want to copy or cut.

2 Click the Copy (Control-C) or Cut (Control-X) button from the Standard toolbar. If you are copying, you should notice that the cell or cell range now has an animated box surrounding it. This is a reminder so that you don't forget what you've copied. If you are cutting, the same animated box appears, and the contents remain visible until you paste the information elsewhere. If you've made a mistake and want to reselect the cell or cell range again, press Esc to deactivate the selection.

⭐ **TIP**

You can't use the Cut command to delete information from a worksheet (a popular technique people employ while working in Word and other programs) because cutting doesn't actually delete the selected cells until you've pasted them in another location. Use the Clear or Delete keys, or select the Edit menu and choose either Clear or Delete to remove data.

3 Click in the destination cell or select a range of cells that matches the dimensions (in rows and columns) of the copied or cut area.

4 Click the Paste button on the Standard toolbar. (You can also press Control-V.)

Special Pasting

There are times when the default method of copying and pasting information does not do what you need it to. You might be forced to manually enter the new information, format it, perform calculations on it, or transpose it from a row to a column or vice versa. Excel features a Paste Special function that allows you to modify how Excel pastes information. Follow these steps to use Paste Special:

1 Select a cell or cell range to copy.

2 Copy it normally.

3 Choose Paste Special from the Edit menu, which opens the dialog box shown in Figure 13-3.

 **NOTE**

> If you have copied a range of text from another program, the Paste Special dialog box shown in Figure 13-3 may not appear. Instead, you will be given the choice of pasting formatted or unformatted text or graphics or of using other text formatting options such as HTML.

FIGURE 13-3.

You can customize pasting operations with the Paste Special dialog box

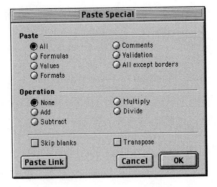

4 Choose an option, summarized in Table 13-1, which will determine how Excel will handle the Paste Special operation.

III

Microsoft Excel

NOTE

The Operation options (in the middle of the Paste Special dialog box) listed in Table 13-1 are only available if you choose to paste All, Formulas, Values, or All Except Borders.

Table 13-1. Paste Special Options.

Paste Options	Pastes...
All	Contents and formatting; the default setting
Formulas	Formulas
Values	The values of formulas but not the formula itself
Formats	Cell formatting only, thereby transferring any applied formatting of the copied cells to the paste area
Comments	Comments attached to the cell only
Validation	Validation rules
All Except Borders	Contents and formatting except border formatting
Operation Options	**Result**
None	Does not perform any additional mathematical operations between the copied and pasted cells
Add	Adds the copied cells to the information in the destination cells
Subtract	Subtracts the value in the destination cell from the value in the copied cell and pastes the result
Multiply	Multiplies the value in the destination cell by the value in the copied cell and pastes the result
Divide	Divides the value in the destination cell by the value in the copied cell and pastes the result
Other Options	**Result**
Skip Blanks	Does not paste blank cells
Transpose	Converts a cell range that is a column to a row or a row to a column when pasted
Paste Link	Links the data you're pasting to the current worksheet

Drag-and-Drop Editing

Although you can use the cut-and-paste commands to move information, Excel also allows you to use your mouse to drag-and-drop cells in new locations. Follow these steps to drag-and-drop cells:

1 Select the cell or cell range you want to move.

2 Move the mouse cursor over the border of the selection until it turns into a hand icon. This indicates that you can now drag-and-drop the selection.

3 Click on the selection, and drag it to a new area.

4 Release your mouse button to drop the selection in its new position. If you drop your selection on existing content, Excel will ask you whether it's ok to overwrite the contents of the destination cell or cells. Click OK to allow it, or click Cancel to abort the operation.

Finding, Sorting, and Listing Information

Finding and sorting are powerful tools that allow you to search for information in your worksheet and sort lists.

Using Find

The Find function is a great time-saver when you are searching for data but don't know exactly where it is in your worksheet. Follow these steps to find the information you're looking for:

1 Select the worksheet you want to search.

2 Choose Find from the Edit menu (or press ⌘-F). This opens the Find dialog box, shown in Figure 13-4.

FIGURE 13-4.

Enter the words or data you want to find to search your worksheet

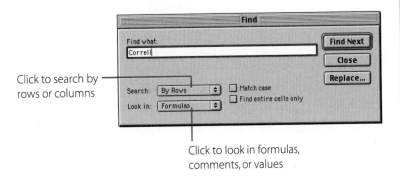

Click to search by rows or columns

Click to look in formulas, comments, or values

Microsoft Excel

3 Enter the words or data you want to find in the Find What field.

4 Choose a search pattern by selecting By Rows (the default) or By Columns from the Search pop-up menu. By Rows searches each row consecutively from left to right, and By Columns searches each column consecutively from top to bottom. If you press and hold down the Shift key when you click Find Next, the direction is reversed to right to left for rows and bottom to top for columns.

5 Choose a container from the Look In pop-up menu. You can search via formulas (the default), values, or comments. The following guidelines will help you choose the appropriate container:

- Choose Comments if you want to search for information in comments.

- Choose Formulas if you want to find information that is present in formulas. (Note that if the cell contains no actual formulas, but instead contains text or numbers, such as "Products" or "2000," Find searches that information.)

- Choose Values to ignore any underlying formulas and search only what is visibly displayed (that is, the value). For example, if the formula =SUM(A1:A20) computes to 42, then 42 is the value. If you search for "A1" in Values (given that this is the only cell with data in it on a worksheet), you will not find it. Conversely, searching for "42" in Formulas will not find it either because it's a value.

- Choose Match Case to make Excel find matches according to case only. For example, if you click Match Case and search for "ACCOUNTS" (uppercase), any occurrences of "accounts" (lowercase) are ignored because the word isn't in the same case.

- Choose Find Entire Cells Only to search for complete cells. For example, if this option is not enabled, and you search for "Smith," then any cell with the word "Smith" in it is found, even if it contains additional data. Clicking Find Entire Cells Only means if you search for "Smith," then only those cells that exactly match what you are looking for are found. In this case, a cell with the words "Smith, Bob" would be ignored, but a cell with the word "Smith" would be found.

- Click Find Next to find the next occurrence of your search information. Excel moves the worksheet (if necessary) to display the match on your screen and makes it the active cell. Click Find Next to keep searching.

 NOTE

You can click Replace to switch to the Replace dialog box.

6 Click Close to finish.

Replacing Information

Replace is a close companion to Find, the only difference being that you are searching for information so that you can replace it. Follow these steps to replace data in your worksheet:

1 Select the worksheet you want to search.

2 Choose Replace from the Edit menu (or press ⌘-H). This opens the Replace dialog box, shown in Figure 13-5.

FIGURE 13-5.

Replace allows you to quickly search for and replace words or data in your worksheet

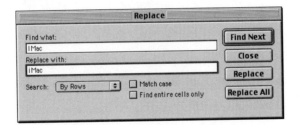

3 Enter the words or data you want to replace in the Find What field.

4 Enter the words or data with which you want to replace the information you are finding in the Replace With field.

5 Choose a search pattern by selecting By Rows (the default) or By Columns from the Search pop-up menu. By Rows searches each row consecutively from left to right and By Columns searches each column consecutively from top to bottom. If you press and hold down the Shift key when you click Find Next, the direction is reversed to right to left for rows and bottom to top for columns.

6 Choose Match Case to make Excel find matches according to case only.

7 Choose Find Entire Cells Only to search for complete cells.

III

Microsoft Excel

8 If you want to preview each case, click Find Next to find the next occurrence of your search information. Excel moves the worksheet (if necessary) to display the match on your screen and makes it the active cell. If you decide to replace it, click Replace. Click Find Next to keep searching.

9 If you don't need to preview each occurrence, click Replace. Excel will find the next match and replace it. Click Replace to cycle through each match.

10 If you're really confident, click Replace All to replace all matches. You don't get a chance to preview replacements, so be careful with this button.

11 Click Close to finish.

Using Wildcards

The trouble with finding information is that sometimes you may not know exactly what you are looking for, or perhaps you want to look for a range of data that may be spelled slightly differently. Wildcards alleviate this problem by allowing you to enter a combination of actual data and placeholders in the form of various wildcards.

Asterisks

Asterisks (*) allow you to match a string of characters. For example, if you want to find all instances of words that begin with R and end with T you can enter R*T in the Find dialog box. This will find any data that has an *R* followed by a *T,* regardless of the number of intervening characters. Thus, it will pick up words such as Robert, rat, recalcitrant, and rotate.

Question Marks

Question marks (?) are a bit more limited in their application. A question mark is a placeholder for a single character. Therefore, entering R?T does not find the same cells as R*T. R?T only finds cells that contain data that have an *R* and *T* separated by a single character, such as the words rat, rotate, and generate. Each additional question mark is a placeholder for another character.

Using Go To

The default method of selecting cells with the mouse or keyboard is indiscriminate. You thus have no control over selecting cells that may be blank or that contain formulas, functions, or special formatting.

This means you have to manually choose cells based on what they contain—a potentially laborious process. In some cases, you may not know whether the cell contains a value or a formula, therefore compounding the problem. Excel has an often-overlooked feature that allows you to selectively choose cells to include in a selection: Go To. To use this feature, follow these steps:

1 Choose Go To from the Edit menu. This opens the Go To dialog box, shown in Figure 13-6.

FIGURE 13-6.

Open Go To, and then click Special to open the Go To Special dialog box

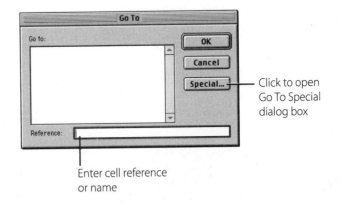

Click to open Go To Special dialog box

Enter cell reference or name

2 Click Special to change the dialog box to Go To Special, shown in Figure 13-7.

FIGURE 13-7.

You can quickly find cells by a wide variety of criteria—not just data–using Go To Special

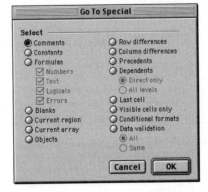

3 Choose a selection criterion. (Table 13-2 summarizes the available options.)

4 Click OK to close the Go To Special dialog box. The cells that match the criterion will be selected in your worksheet.

Table 13-2. **Go To Special Options.**

Option	Meaning
Comments	Selects cells with comments.
Constants	Selects cells with constants, which are cells that do not begin with an equals sign or contain a formula. You can also define the type of constant to go to as Numbers, Text, Logicals, or Errors. (Logicals are constant or formula cells that contain the logical values of TRUE or FALSE and Errors are cells that contain error warnings as a result of an invalid constant or formula.)
Formulas	Selects cells with formulas. You can also define the type of formula you want to select (Numbers, Text, Logicals, and Errors).
Blanks	Selects blank cells up to the last cell that contains formatting or information.
Current Region	Selects a region bounded by blank rows and columns based on the location of the active cell.
Current Array	Selects the current array if the active cell is in an array.
Objects	Selects all graphical objects, charts, and buttons.
Row Differences	Selects cells with different contents than a comparison cell in each row.
Column Differences	Selects cells with different contents than a comparison cell in each column.
Precedents	If the active cell has a formula, this option selects the cells that the formula may reference. You can choose to select only those cells that are directly referenced or search all levels, which selects all the cells referenced by any formulas that the selected cell references.
Dependents	Selects all cells that reference the current cell in a formula. You can choose to select only those cells that are directly referenced or search all levels.
Last Cell	Selects the last cell in the worksheet that has data or formatting applied.
Visible Cells Only	Selects visible cells. (This excludes cells that are hidden.)
Conditional Formats	Selects cells with conditional formatting. You can choose between All, which selects all cells formatted in that way, and Same, which selects only those cells with conditional formatting identical to the active cell.
Data Validation	Selects cells with data validation. You can choose between All, which selects all cells with data validation rules, and Same, which selects only those cells with rules identical to the active cell.

Sorting Data

Sorting allows you to order your data for presentational and analytical purposes. Sorting imposes a predefined order on a list. Follow these steps to sort data:

> **NOTE**
>
> Your data must be in a list for Sort to work. If Excel can't find a list, it will inform you of such and prevent you from sorting. Select a single cell within your list.

1 Choose Sort from the Data menu. This opens the Sort dialog box, shown in Figure 13-8.

FIGURE 13-8.

Enter your sorting criteria (what columns you want to sort and whether you want to reorder them as ascending or descending lists) in the Sort dialog box

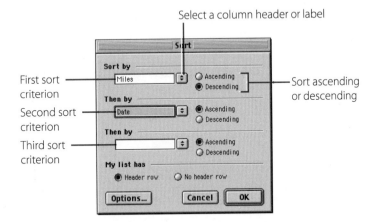

Select a column header or label

First sort criterion

Second sort criterion

Third sort criterion

Sort ascending or descending

2 Choose your sorting criteria by selecting what columns you want to sort. You can choose up to three columns, which are identified by column labels or headers in the Sort By, Then By, and Then By pop-up menus.

3 Choose a sort order, either Ascending or Descending. Ascending sorts numbers and letters from lowest to highest while Descending does the opposite.

4 Choose whether your list has a header row or not. It is somewhat disconcerting when you sort a cell range and then realize that Excel sorted your column header labels along with all the other data. If you catch it, you can undo the sort and try it again. However, to avoid this problem entirely, make sure you sort columns with the header row option enabled.

> **NOTE**
>
> Clicking Options allows you to change the sort order. With Options clicked, you can sort days and months in their correct order (and not alphabetically), make the sort case-sensitive, and change the default sort orientation in columns from top to bottom or in rows from left to right.

5 Click OK to perform your sort.

Using Lists

A list is simply a series of rows that contain related information. For example, the running log shown in Figure 13-9 as an example is a list. Each column contains different information, such as the date, number of miles, and total miles run. Each row contains entries that correspond to the date the runner ran.

FIGURE 13-9.

Create a list by entering your data in organized columns

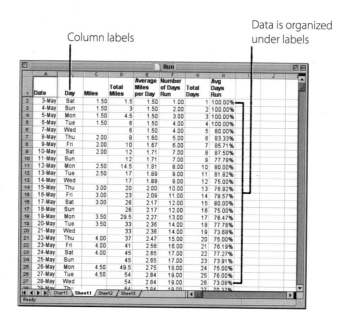

If you want to create a list, you'll find no menu option, button, or other special list interface element. This is because Excel does not require you to use a menu selection or button to create a list. You just do it, and if your list fits the parameters that Excel requires, it will automatically enjoy the benefits of being a list.

The following explains the requirements and conditions your list should fulfill in order to be considered a list in Excel:

- You should have only one list per worksheet for features such as Filtering to work correctly.

- You should include similar information in the same column. For example, a good list column would be "Last Name."

- Your list should not be adjacent to other data on the same worksheet. Use blank rows and columns to keep the list in a distinct region.

- If you have important information you want included with (not in) the list, place it above or below the list rather than beside it.

- When making changes to your list, show any hidden rows or columns. This will prevent you from accidentally deleting information as you edit your list.

- Although this isn't an absolute necessity, create column headers in the first row of your list and format them as text prior to entering the headers. Formatting them as text assures you they will be treated as header text and not list data. The trick here is to format the cells before you enter the headers.

- Create column headers that are formatted differently than the information contained in the list. For example, you could make your column headers a different font, font size, or font style (such as bold). This will not only make them stand out visually, but also help Excel identify them.

- Don't use blank rows or columns within a list because Excel may recognize only part of your list, not the entire list. A technique you should use to separate headers or labels from the list data, or separate sections of your list from each other, is using cell borders to draw a distinction rather than blank rows or columns.

- Avoid using leading or trailing spaces within list data, as this can cause sorting and filtering problems.

Filtering Lists

If your list gets too large, it can become unwieldy. This results in excessive scrolling as you look for data. Fortunately, lists have a feature called a *filter* that allows you to sort and analyze them. These filters help you make sense of and analyze list data by showing and hiding list items based on variable criteria. To use a filter on a list, follow these steps:

1 Select a cell within a list.

2 Choose Filter from the Data menu, and then choose AutoFilter. This causes pop-up menus to appear within the column header rows of your list. These are the filter criteria you can choose to analyze the list with. In addition, a checkmark appears next to the AutoFilter menu to indicate this option is enabled.

3 Select a pop-up menu from one of the column headers.

4 Choose a filter criterion, as shown in Figure 13-10. Excel then hides all list items that do not match the criterion.

III

Microsoft Excel

FIGURE 13-10.

Choose from one of the several AutoFilter criteria to filter your list

Pop-up menu arrows appear after selecting AutoFilter
Click arrows to see AutoFilter menu

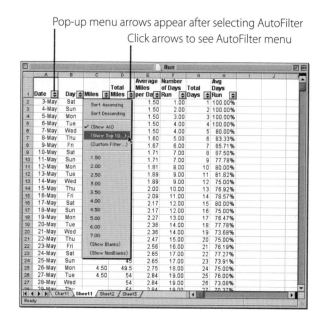

The available criteria are:

- **Show All** This filter shows all list items.

- **Show Top 10** This filter shows the top ten list items or the top ten percent. The column must contain numerical data for this filter to work. Selecting Show Top 10 opens the Top 10 AutoFilter dialog box, shown in Figure 13-11. This dialog box allows you to distinguish between the top ten items or top ten percent and allows you to change the criterion to the bottom ten as well. You can also increase or decrease the number of list items up and down from ten.

FIGURE 13-11.

Accepting the default values will filter your list to show only the top ten items

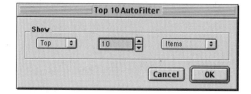

- **Show Bottom 10** This filter is not available from the pop-up menu, but you can choose it by selecting Show Top 10 and changing the settings in the Top 10 AutoFilter dialog box.

- **Custom Filter** This filter opens the Custom AutoFilter dialog box, shown in Figure 13-12. Choosing Custom enables you to use logical comparisons to match list records. The fields on the left-hand side of the Custom AutoFilter dialog box are the "logical operators." Select one to make comparisons between values you enter in the right-hand fields. Available options are Equals, Does Not Equal, Is Greater Than, Is Greater Than Or Equal To, Is Less Than, Is Less Than Or Equal To, Begins With, Does Not Begin With, Ends With, Does Not End With, Contains, and Does Not Contain. When entering the value in the right-hand side of the dialog box, you can use the ? and * wildcards to represent one or more than one character respectively. Use them as you would when searching for information (discussed earlier in the chapter). Finally, you can set more than one condition to use in the filter. Using And results in a filter that has two conditions that must both be true. Use Or if you want to check the cells in the list against two criteria but only one needs to be true to show the cell after it is filtered.

FIGURE 13-12.

Custom filtering allows you to enter your own filter criteria

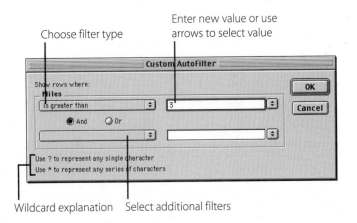

Enter new value or use arrows to select value

Choose filter type

Wildcard explanation   Select additional filters

■ **List Item** This filter shows only the list items that contain the value as shown in the filter. If you've opened up a subsequent AutoFilter dialog box (such as Show Top 10 or Custom Auto-Filter), click OK to close the dialog box and sort the list.

To turn the AutoFilter off, select the Data menu, choose Filter, and then choose AutoFilter (which should have a checkmark). This removes the pop-up menus that were attached to your header row and the checkmark from the AutoFilter menu item.

One final note about filtering When you filter a list that has been used to create a chart, the chart itself (whether embedded in a worksheet or included as a separate chart sheet) is updated to show only those data points that aren't filtered out. For more information on charting, continue on to the next chapter.

III

Microsoft Excel

Creating Charts and Using Functions

Charts and functions are two of the most powerful tools you can employ in Excel. Charts take data from your worksheets and display it in various forms (such as pie charts and line charts) in existing worksheets or in newly created "chart-only" sheets. Charting data is easy and can help you understand both complex and simple data patterns.

Functions are distinctly different from formulas. Formulas, such as =((A1+42)/3.14), are mathematical expressions (or equations) that perform an action on numbers or the contents of a cell. With formulas, you have to create the expression yourself. Functions, such as the oft-used SUM function, are predefined formulas. They are built into Excel and are available whenever you need them. Although functions aren't difficult to use, you do need to know which function will actually achieve the results you desire.

This chapter will help you get started creating charts and will teach you how to select and use functions.

Creating Charts

You create charts with the touch of a button; the hard part is understanding chart terminology and choosing the appropriate chart type for your data. This section will lead you through the most important aspects of creating charts.

Charting Fundamentals

To create a chart, you need data. That data can be organized into one or more *data series*. A data series is a group of related *data points* that have been organized into rows or columns on your worksheet. A data point is simply the value of the data at that point in the series.

In the example running log shown in Figure 14-1, each column is a data series, while each entry in the Average Miles Per Day column (1.00, 1.25, 1.33, etc.) is a data point.

FIGURE 14-1.

A chart with data series and data points

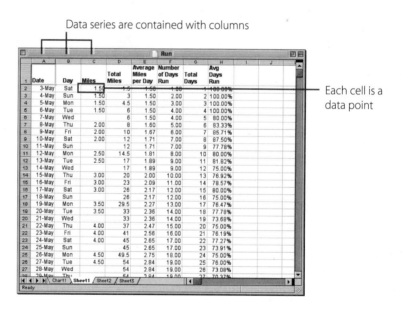

Data series are contained with columns

Each cell is a data point

When plotted on a chart, each data series will be drawn with a different color or pattern. Most charts allow you to plot more than one data series, the exception being the pie chart. Others, such as the stock chart, require that you plot three data series.

When you have data points arranged into data series, you can create any chart in Excel. In order to better use the chart feature, let's review the parts that make up a chart.

Figure 14-2 illustrates a simple bar chart. Notice that this chart is embedded directly into the worksheet, as opposed to being placed on a separate chart worksheet. Embedding charts into worksheets works well when you're charting only a small amount of data, as shown here. Large, complicated charts should use their own worksheet.

FIGURE 14-2.

A simple bar chart embedded in a worksheet

Selected cells have been charted

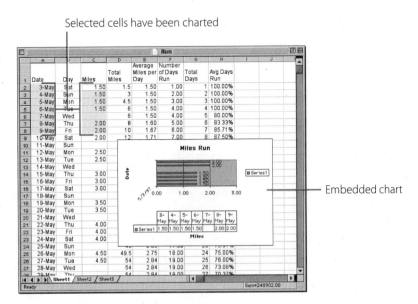

Embedded chart

Types of Charts

There are numerous predefined charts in Excel, each emphasizing different methods of displaying data, and many having special requirements (such as the number of data series needed). The standard predefined charts are summarized in Table 14-1, while the custom predefined charts are listed immediately following the table. You can also create your own chart types based on those already built into Excel.

III

Microsoft Excel

Table 14-1. Predefined Chart Types in Excel.

Standard Chart Type	Best At...
Column	Showing changes over time or comparing items. Categories are placed on the horizontal axis while values are expressed in vertical columns.
Bar	Comparing individual items. Categories are placed on the vertical axis while values are expressed in horizontal bars.
Line	Showing trends over equivalent intervals, normally time. The intervals are normally placed on the horizontal axis while values are shown on the vertical axis. Each data point in a series is connected to form a line.
Pie	Showing the proportion of a series of items in one data series in relation to the sum total. Each data point in the series is reflected as a piece of the pie chart.
XY (Scatter)	Showing uneven clusters of data. You can either chart several data series or show two groups of numbers as a series of X, Y coordinates. Points are plotted at the intersection of each X and Y coordinate.
Area	Showing the magnitude of change over time. The sum total of data values is placed on the vertical axis while time intervals are shown along the horizontal axis. The result is similar to a line chart except the area underneath each line is filled in to emphasize the growth or decay of the data.
Doughnut	Showing the proportion of a series of items in more than one data series in relation to the sum total. Each data point in the series is reflected as a portion of the "doughnut ring" and each ring is a unique data series.
Radar	Comparing the total value of a number of items in different data series. Each category is plotted on a different axis originating from a center point, and the data points from each series are connected to form lines that ring the center point.
Surface	Showing optimum combinations of two sets of data. The surface chart is three-dimensional, although you can view it from above so that it looks two-dimensional. Values are plotted on the two "2D" axes, and the third "3D" axis is used to show the data set that is the outcome of the combination of the other two data series. For example, you could plot temperature and humidity on the 2D axes and plot how far you could run on the 3D axis. You could then visualize the best combination of temperature and humidity that allows you to run the farthest.
Bubble	Showing uneven clusters of two data series while illustrating a third. You can either chart several data series or show two groups of numbers as a series of X, Y coordinates. Points are plotted at the intersection of each X and Y coordinate, the size of which reveals the third data series.
Stock	Showing changes in data points over time, just as a stock price fluctuates over the course of a day.
Cylinder	Anything you would use a bar or column chart for, but instead of bars or columns, cylinders are used.
Cone	Anything you would use a bar or column chart for, but instead of bars or columns, cones are used.
Pyramid	Anything you would use a bar or column chart for, but instead of bars or columns, pyramids are used.

In addition to the standard chart types, there are quite a few predefined types of custom charts. They are:

- **Area Blocks** This is a three-dimensional area chart.

- **B&W Area** This is a grayscale area chart.

- **B&W Column** This is a grayscale column chart.

- **B&W Line—Timescale** This is a grayscale line chart with the area below the line filled in. In addition, the X axis is plotted as a timeline.

- **B&W Pie** This is a grayscale pie chart.

- **Blue Pie** This is an exploded pie chart in shades of blue. The pie pieces in an exploded pie chart don't touch each other as normal pie chart pieces do—they are separated and appear as if they were an "exploded" diagram.

- **Colored Lines** This is a colored line chart on a black background.

- **Column—Area** This is a combination of a column chart and an area chart.

- **Columns With Depth** This is a column chart in which the columns have depth, making the chart look somewhat three-dimensional.

- **Cones** This is a three-dimensional chart with cones.

- **Floating Bars** This chart allows you to plot bar charts with a beginning and end point to each bar.

- **Line—Column** This chart combines line and column charts into one chart.

- **Line—Column on Two Axes** This chart combines line and column charts into one chart, but uses two vertical axes.

- **Lines on 2 Axes** This is a line chart that uses both vertical axes.

- **Logarithmic** This is a line chart that uses a logarithmic axis.

- **Outdoor Bars** This is a bar chart with a "woodsy," outdoor look. The outdoor look is achieved by a green background color and wood textures that are used in the bars in place of solid colors.

- **Pie Explosion** This is an exploded pie chart.

- **Smooth Lines** This is a line chart in which the lines of each data series are smooth rather than being drawn straight from one data point to another.

- **Stack Of Colors** This chart shows several data series in colorful bars.

- **Tubes** This is a stacked bar chart with tubes instead of bars.

Using the Chart Wizard

Having entered your data in a worksheet, follow these steps to create a chart:

1 Select a cell in your list to make it active, or select a range of cells to chart. If you select a cell in your list, the entire list will be charted.

2 Click the Chart Wizard button on the Standard toolbar or select the Insert menu and choose Chart. Either action launches the Chart wizard, shown in Figure 14-3, and starts you at Step 1 of 4: Chart Type. The Chart wizard takes you through four steps to create a chart.

> You can click Finish at any time, and your chart will be drawn with the default values for each option. At that point, you can go back and modify the chart using the Chart portion of the Formatting Palette.

FIGURE 14-3.

Selecting a chart type

Selected chart type

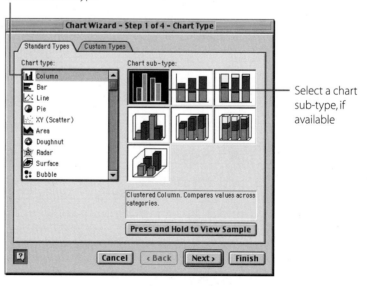

Select a chart sub-type, if available

3 Choose a chart type from the list on the left. If the chart you want isn't a standard type, click the Custom Types tab to see more pre-defined chart types you can choose from.

You can make you own type of chart by creating a built-in chart, customizing it to meet your needs, and then adding it as a user-defined chart in the Custom Types tab of the Chart Type dialog box.

4 Choose a chart subtype from the illustrated list on the right. Chart subtypes modify different aspects of the chart they originate from.

5 Click the Press And Hold To View Sample button to see a preview of your chart as the currently selected type, as shown in Figure 14-4.

FIGURE 14-4.

Previewing your chart

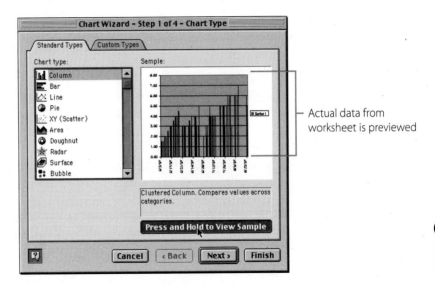

Actual data from worksheet is previewed

6 Click Next to go to Step 2 of 4: Chart Source Data.

You can click Back at any time to go to previous steps and change any of the options you've selected or entered.

7 Enter or modify the data range if it is not correct. (See Figure 14-5.) You can click the small worksheet icon to jump to your worksheet and select a new range of cells if you want.

FIGURE 14-5.

Confirming the data range of the chart

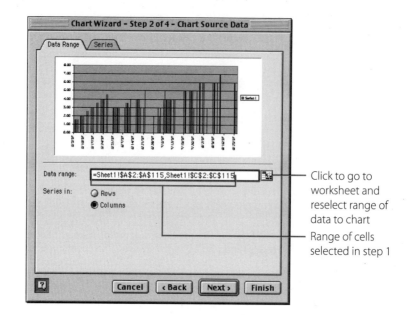

Click to go to worksheet and reselect range of data to chart

Range of cells selected in step 1

8 Choose whether to change how the data series are plotted by clicking the Rows or Columns radio buttons. Excel's default behavior is to plot whichever you have fewer of—rows or columns—in the current data range as a series. For example, if you have four columns which represent four quarters of the year and two rows which contain financial data for this year and last year, each row would form a separate data series. Conversely, if you have two columns which represent weight and height, and 25 rows that contain the measurements, each column would form a separate data series. In the first example you are plotting each year's data—not each quarter—in a data series, and in the second example you are plotting weight and height as the data series—not each set of measurements.

9 Click Next to go to Step 3 of 4: Chart Options.

10 Excel does quite a good job of identifying the correct options to employ to make your chart presentable. In this step, however, you may want to enter additional information or change the default values. Figures 14-6 through 14-11 illustrate each tab present in this step, while the following bulleted items explain the various options. Notice that you can select a tab and enter new information or change the existing options.

NOTE

Not all of the option tabs are available for each chart type, and individual options on tabs that are present may not be usable. For example, if you have selected Pie Chart, you will not see the Axes, Gridlines, or Data Table tabs, while the only available option on the Titles tab is Chart Title.

- **Titles** This tab creates a title for your chart and labels the axes. (See Figure 14-6.) Notice that the wizard updates the preview window to reflect the information you enter.

FIGURE 14-6.

Chart Title options

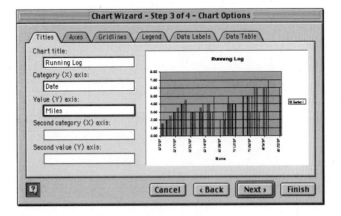

- **Axes** This tab shows or hides the axes and determines whether the X-axis uses a time-scale. (See Figure 14-7.) Notice that the categories (dates) are on the X-axis, and values (miles run) are plotted on the Y-axis.

FIGURE 14-7.

Chart Axes options

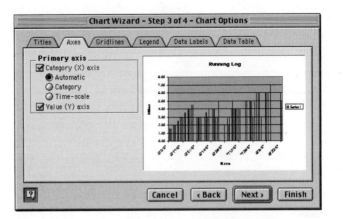

III

Microsoft Excel

- **Gridlines** This tab shows or hides major and minor gridlines for each axis. (See Figure 14-8.)

FIGURE 14-8.

Chart Gridline options

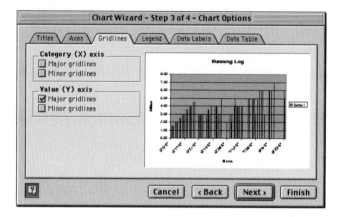

- **Legend** This tab shows or hides a chart legend and allows you to position it relative to the chart. (See Figure 14-9.)

FIGURE 14-9.

Chart Legend options

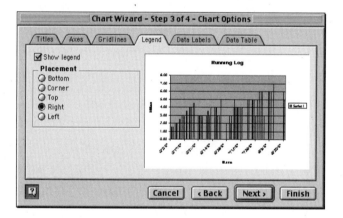

- **Data Labels** This tab shows or hides labels beside your data points and allows you to choose from several different methods of presentation. (See Figure 14-10.) Select the None check box under Data Labels if you are plotting a large number of data points, so that you don't clutter your chart and make it unreadable.

FIGURE 14-10.

Chart Data Label options

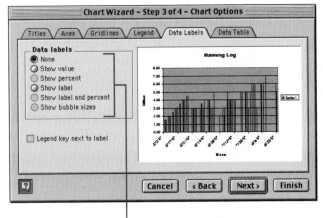

Each type of label appears next to each data point

- **Data Table** This tab shows or hides a data table beneath your chart, which contains the source data in tabular format. (See Figure 14-11.) Leave Show Data Table unchecked if you're plotting a large number of data points.

FIGURE 14-11.

Chart Data Table options

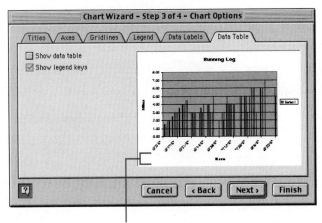

Data table appears below chart

11 Click Next to continue to Step 4 of 4: Chart Location.

12 Choose a location to place your chart, as shown in Figure 14-12. You can elect to place it in a new sheet (which you can name now) or place it as an object in an existing worksheet (which you can select from the pop-up menu).

FIGURE 14-12.

Choosing where your new chart will be located

Enter new name if necessary

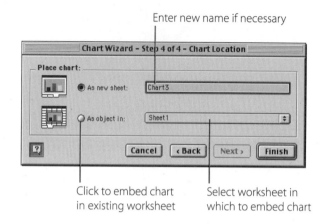

Click to embed chart in existing worksheet

Select worksheet in which to embed chart

13 Click Finish to end the Chart Wizard and create your chart.

Excel creates your chart with the options you've chosen (see Figure 14-13) and places it in the location you specified in the last step of the Chart wizard.

FIGURE 14-13.

Your finished chart

Y-axis label   Gridlines   Data points   Title

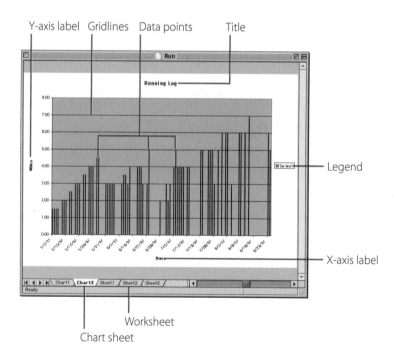

Legend

X-axis label

Chart sheet

Worksheet

Customizing Charts

Once you've created a chart, it isn't set in stone. You can return at any time to modify any aspect of its design or data. Follow these steps to customize charts:

1 If your chart is on a special chart sheet, you can immediately use the Formatting Palette's Chart options. If your chart is embedded in another worksheet, select the chart with your mouse to activate the Chart section of the Formatting Palette, shown in Figure 14-14. If there is more than one chart on a worksheet, make sure you have selected the correct chart.

FIGURE 14-14.

The Formatting Palette with Chart options visible

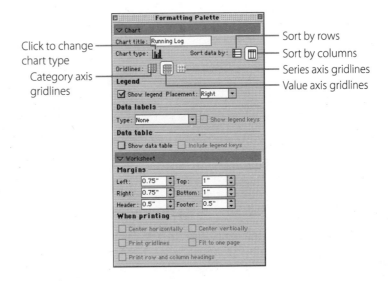

Click to change chart type

Category axis gridlines

Sort by rows

Sort by columns

Series axis gridlines

Value axis gridlines

2 The Chart section of the Formatting Palette is organized into the following functional areas:

- General

- Legend

- Data Labels

- Data Table

You can also use the Chart menu to modify your existing chart. The chart menu contains the following submenus:

- **Chart Type** This submenu corresponds to step 1 of the Chart wizard.

III

Microsoft Excel

- **Source Data** This submenu corresponds to step 2 of the Chart wizard.

- **Chart Options** This submenu corresponds to step 3 of the Chart wizard.

- **Location** This submenu corresponds to step 4 of the Chart wizard.

- **Add Data** This submenu opens the Add Data dialog box (see Figure 14-15) so that you can add new data to the chart. You can enter data manually or click the Range box and then go to a worksheet and select a range of cells to add.

FIGURE 14-15.

Adding new data to your chart

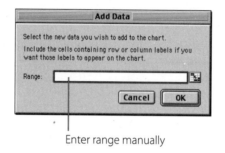

Enter range manually

- **Add Trendline** This submenu opens the Add Trendline dialog box, shown in Figure 14-16, and allows you to add a line on your chart that represents a trend in your data.

FIGURE 14-16.

Adding and configuring a trendline

Click to see advanced trendline options

Selected trend type

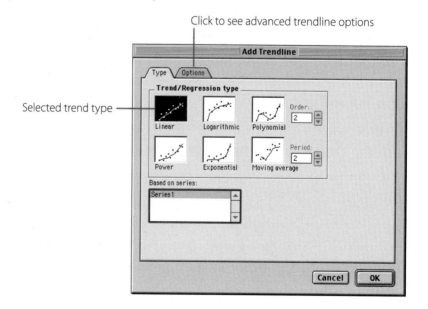

■ **3-D View** This submenu, available only if your chart is three-dimensional, opens the 3-D View Dialog box, which enables you to change the viewing perspective of any three-dimensional chart.

Remember that charts are supposed to represent visually the data you have entered, making interpretation easier. You can highlight or showcase different aspects of the data you've gathered, trends in the growth or decline of certain data series, and much more. Experiment with the different chart types to see which one best emphasizes the point or points you want to make. If you want to start over, select the chart and press Delete, or if the chart is on its own sheet, delete the sheet.

Entering Functions

Functions are predefined formulas that are built into Excel, ready for you to use. For example, rather than manually adding up the values in a given column, or entering a formula (such as =A1+A2+A3), you can use the SUM function to achieve the same result.

Functions are composed of several parts, each of which is necessary for the function to work correctly. For example, the function =SUM(A1:A15, B1:B15) contains all five elements you'll find in functions. They are:

■ The equals sign(=)

■ The function name (SUM)

■ Parentheses to enclose arguments (which are used to evaluate the function)

■ A comma to separate arguments

■ The arguments themselves (A1:A15 and B1:B15)

This function adds the contents of cells A1 through A15 and B1 through B15.

Each function contains unique requirements (also known as the *syntax* of a function), which can be found through the Calculator or Help. For example, the SUM function has the syntax:

SUM(number1,number2,...)

SUM is the function name and each argument (up to 30 in the case of SUM) is separated by a comma. The final result is obtained by resolving each argument and adding them together.

III

Microsoft Excel

An example of a different type of function, known as a logical function, is IF. The syntax for IF is:

IF(logical_test,value_if_true,value_if_false)

IF contains three arguments. The first is a logical test, such as A1>A2. This tests to see whether the value of A1 is greater than the value of A2. The next argument is the value or result to be shown if the test is true, and the final argument is the value or result to be shown if the test is false. For example, in the following function

=IF(A1>A2, "Greater Than", "Less Than Or Equal")

if cell A1 (which contains the number 5) is less than or equal to cell A2 (which contains the number 10), then the text "Less Than Or Equal" will display in the cell where you enter the function (for example, cell C3).

Notice that the text we've entered in the latter two arguments is enclosed in quotes. This is necessary only if you want text to be displayed as a result of the function.

 NOTE

> You can also use numbers, formulas, and other functions within functions.

Deciding Which Function to Use

Deciding which function to use is vital in ensuring that the function gives you an appropriate result. If you need to find the sum total of a column of numbers, for example, the SUM function works well, whereas the AVERAGE function will return the average value of the sum total.

Functions are divided into several broad categories:

- Financial
- Date & Time
- Math & Trig
- Statistical
- Lookup & Reference
- Database
- Text
- Logical
- Information

There are far too many functions to list and describe here, but should you want to explore them, you can use the Calculator, as described below.

Entering Functions

You can enter functions in one of three ways: manually, through the Calculator, or from the menus. Manually entering functions is only advisable when you are familiar with the function you are going to enter and are well-versed in its syntax. To enter functions manually, follow these steps:

1 Select the cell that will contain the function.

2 Press the Equals key (=).

3 Enter the function, complete with any cell references or other values. As you enter the function, you can use your mouse to click on a cell or range of cells that you want to include. Be sure to include all the required arguments and follow the function syntax exactly.

4 Press Return to finish your entry. The *result* of the function will be displayed in the cell (not the function itself). If you want to go back and edit the function, select the cell, and the function will appear in the Formula bar. Click in the Formula bar to edit the function.

> ⭐ **TIP**
>
> You can double-click functions and formulas to edit their contents in the cell rather than in the Formula bar.

An easier way to enter functions is by using the Calculator. To do so, follow these steps:

1 Click the Calculator button on the Formula bar.

2 Click the buttons on the calculator just as you would a real one to perform mathematical operations and enter values.

3 To enter the IF or SUM functions, use the If or Sum shortcut buttons. If you click If, the Calculator changes form, as shown in Figure 14-17.

III

Microsoft Excel

FIGURE 14-17.

Using IF through the calculator shortcut button

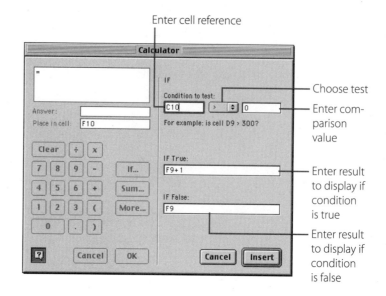

Enter cell reference

— Choose test

— Enter comparison value

— Enter result to display if condition is true

— Enter result to display if condition is false

4 Enter the condition to test and the value to return if the test is True or False, and then click Insert. If you click Sum, the Calculator changes form, as shown in Figure 14-18.

FIGURE 14-18.

Using SUM through the calculator shortcut button

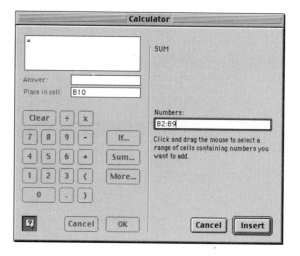

5 Enter numbers, cells, or cell ranges manually or use your mouse to drag a range of cells to the Calculator. Click Insert to finish the function.

6 To find the other functions, click More, which opens the Paste Function dialog box, as shown in Figure 14-19.

FIGURE 14-19.

Choosing a function to find information about it and its syntax

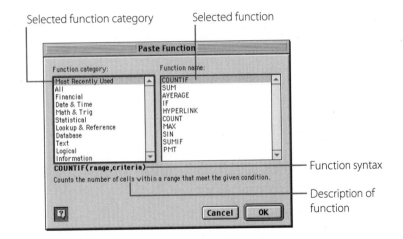

Selected function category

Selected function

Function syntax

Description of function

7 Scroll through the list of function categories on the left, select one, and then select a function from the list on the right. After you select the function, its syntax and a description appear in the dialog box. Read this information carefully if you're not familiar with the function. Click OK to continue.

8 The next screen you see, shown in Figure 14-20, will be unique to each function, although they all work the same.

FIGURE 14-20.

Enter the information required for the function you are using

Elements of function syntax   Enter values manually

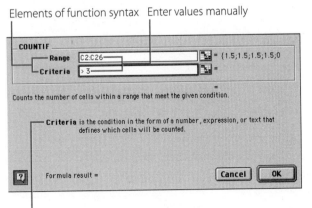

Expanded definition of selected function element

9 In this example we're using the COUNTIF function to count a number of occurrences of a particular value. In this instance, we want to count the number of times a runner has run over 3 miles. Therefore, we have filled out the form to reflect a cell range and criteria, as prompted by the form.

10 Now click OK to finish entering your formula, and return to the Calculator.

11 The Calculator shows your formula, the answer, and where the answer is located. After reviewing this information to ensure its accuracy, click OK.

CHAPTER 15

Working with Worksheets and Workbooks

Worksheets and workbooks are the fabric binding together your creations in Excel. Thus, you need to know how to work with and manage worksheets and workbooks in order to maximize your effectiveness with Excel.

This chapter will cover some of the most important worksheet features, such as naming, moving, adding, and deleting. In addition, we'll discuss some powerful workbook features, such as tracking changes, protecting, sharing, and data validation.

Managing Worksheets

Knowing how to manage worksheets is an important step in customizing Excel so that it better suits your needs. When you open a new, blank workbook, you are presented with three blank worksheets by default, named Sheet1, Sheet2, and Sheet3. As you work on your project, you can add, delete, rename, and move worksheets as you see fit.

> You can access the context-sensitive worksheet name menu, which consolidates many of the worksheet management options, by Control-clicking on any worksheet name.

Let's say you need to manage a district-wide teacher and staff training session for a school. You will most likely need far more than three worksheets to accomplish this task. Figure 15-1 displays seven sample worksheets you may want to create to accomplish such a task. The worksheets in this example are Schedule, Seats, Computers, Courses, Raw Registration Data, Choices, Assignments, and Aliases.

FIGURE 15-1.

Creating a workbook that meets your needs often involves extensive changes to the default numbers of worksheets and their names

	A	B	C	D	E	F	G	H	I	
3	School	Lab	#	Type	Model	Display	Internet	Office	Claris	General
4	Alquina	1	8	Mac	5500/225	None	Yes	No	No	No dedicated ins
5			3	Mac	Starmax 3000/200					
6			1	Mac	6100/60AV					
7	CHS	1	25	Mac	6100/	?	Yes	No	Yes	
8	CMS	1	23	PC	Pentium 133	Overhead				
9			1	PC	Pentium 133 (Instructor)					
10		1	20	PC	AMD-90	Overhead	Yes			
11	Eastview	1	12	Mac	5260/120	Smartboard	Yes	No		
12			9	Mac	5200/75LC					
13			1	Mac	5400/75LC					
14			1	Mac	5200/75LC (Instructor)					
15	Everton	0								
16	Fayette Central	1	4	Mac	Starmax PPC	None	Yes	No		Approx 18 clas
17			6	Mac	LC 575					No dedicated ins
18			5	Mac	LC 580					
19			3	Mac	2 x 6100/60AV, 1 x 6100/60					
20	Frazee	1	14	Mac	5500/200	Smartboard	Yes	No	Yes	Lab has smartb
21			1	Mac	G3 All-in-one (Instructor)					
22	Grandview	1	14	Mac	Starmax PPC	None	Yes	No		No dedicated ins
23										
24	Maplewood	0								
25	Orange	1	8	Mac	5500/225	None	Yes	No	No	Classroom com
26			1	Mac	6100/60AV					No dedicated ins
27	VTCC	1	20	PC	Pentium 233	None	Yes	Yes	No	No dedicated ins
28		1	25	PC	Pentium	None	Yes	Yes	No	
29	ECESC	1	9	Mac	6100/60, /60AV, /66	None	Yes	?	?	No dedicated ins
30			1	Mac	G3 All-in-one					
31	Resource Center	1	16	Dual	iMac and Pentium II	Planned	Yes	Yes	No	Not yet availab
32										
33	Total		13	231						
34										
35										

Schedule / Seats \ **Computers** / Courses / Raw Registration Data / Choices / Assignm

Ready

Renaming Worksheets

You can rename worksheets so that the worksheet name tab at the bottom of the main Excel window better reflects the worksheet's content. It's far easier to remember their contents with a name you choose, rather than Sheet1, Sheet2, and so on. Follow these steps to rename worksheets:

1 Double-click the tab of the worksheet that you want to rename. The current name will become highlighted. You can also Control-click over the worksheet name to open the worksheet shortcut menu.

2 Enter a new name.

3 Click in the worksheet or press Return to accept the new worksheet name.

Moving Worksheets

You can increase the ease of use among different worksheets in a workbook by reordering them so that the ones you work with most are next to each other. Follow these steps to move a worksheet:

1 Click the worksheet tab that you want to move. Hold the mouse button down.

2 Drag the worksheet tab to the left or right with respect to the other worksheet tabs, as shown in Figure 15-2.

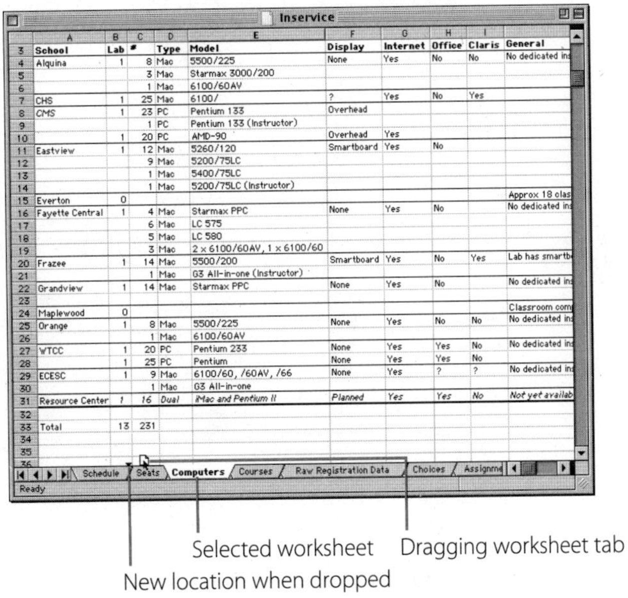

FIGURE 15-2.

Moving worksheets is especially helpful in a file with a large number of worksheets

Selected worksheet   Dragging worksheet tab
New location when dropped

3 Release the mouse button to drop the worksheet in its new location.

Selecting More than One Worksheet

Most of the time you only need to select one worksheet at a time in your workbook. If you need to select more than one worksheet, however, the normal method of selecting a worksheet tab with your mouse doesn't work. To select more than one worksheet, use the following methods:

- **Selecting non-adjacent sheets** ⌘-click each worksheet name to select two or more worksheets that are not adjacent on the worksheet tab display.

- **Selecting several adjacent sheets** Select the first (or last) worksheet of the selection and Shift-click the last (or first) worksheet to select a range of adjacent worksheets. These worksheets will remain selected until you select another single worksheet.

Adding and Deleting Worksheets

When three worksheets aren't enough, you can simply add more. Likewise, if you add too many, or three is too many, you can delete the extras. Follow these steps to add a worksheet:

1   Select a worksheet tab. The worksheet you insert will be placed to the left of the worksheet you select.

2   Select the Insert menu, and choose Worksheet. The new worksheet will appear and be named Sheet*X*, where *X* follows Sheet1, Sheet2, and so on.

> **NOTE**
>
> You can insert a chart as a separate worksheet in the same manner as you insert normal worksheets. Select the Insert menu, and choose Chart. This starts the Chart wizard, which creates your chart. Creating charts is covered in Chapter 14, "Creating Charts and Using Functions."

Follow these steps to delete a worksheet:

1   Select the tab of the worksheet that you want to delete.

2   Select the Edit menu, and choose Delete Sheet. Excel asks you to confirm the deletion; if you click OK, the sheet you have selected will be deleted.

Copying Worksheets

It's sometimes useful to duplicate a worksheet in its entirety rather than copying its contents and pasting them into a new, blank worksheet. You can then rename the copied worksheet and modify it as you wish without affecting the original. To copy a worksheet, follow these steps:

1 Select the worksheet you wish to copy.

2 Select the Edit menu.

3 Choose Move Or Copy Sheet. This opens the Move Or Copy dialog box, shown in Figure 15-3.

FIGURE 15-3.

The moved or copied sheet will appear before the sheet you select

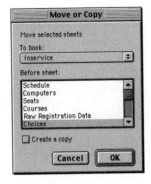

4 If you are copying the worksheet to a new workbook, select that option from the pop-up To Book menu.

5 Determine where the copied worksheet will be located by selecting a worksheet from the Before Sheet list. The copied worksheet will appear before the selected worksheet.

6 Make sure to click Create A Copy; otherwise, the currently selected worksheet will simply be moved to the new location.

7 Click OK to close the dialog box.

Hiding and Unhiding Worksheets

If you have a lot of worksheets and you don't need to use them all right away, you have the option to hide them. All links and references to a hidden worksheet remain in place; you just can't see the worksheet. You can also hide worksheets and protect the workbook if you want to share some, but not all, of the information in the workbook.

III

Microsoft Excel

Follow these steps to hide a worksheet:

1 Select the worksheet you want to hide.

2 Select the Format menu, choose Sheet, and then choose Hide. The worksheet is now hidden.

Of course, you may need to unhide worksheets at a later time. Follow these steps to do so:

1 Select the Format menu, choose Sheet, and then choose Unhide. This opens the Unhide dialog box, shown in Figure 15-4.

FIGURE 15-4.

You can choose a worksheet to unhide in this dialog box

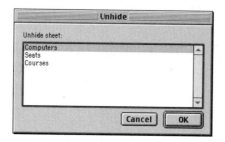

2 Click a worksheet name to select it. (It will become highlighted.)

3 Click OK to close the dialog box and unhide the worksheet.

 NOTE

> You can't unhide more than one worksheet at a time in the Unhide dialog box. Therefore, if you need to unhide several worksheets, you'll have to perform the entire unhide operation repeatedly.

Sharing Your Workbook

Sharing allows two or more people to work on a workbook simultaneously. Obviously, you need a computer network with shared access to a file storage area for this to work. If those conditions are present, enable sharing by following these steps:

1 Select the Tools menu, and choose Share Workbook. This opens the Share Workbook dialog box, shown in Figure 15-5.

2 Click the Allow Changes By More Than One User At The Same Time option.

FIGURE 15-5.

Sharing allows other users to work on the file at the same time

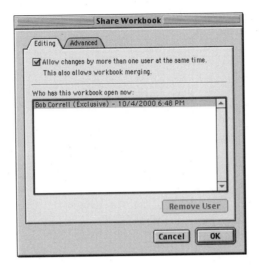

 NOTE

The Advanced tab on the Share Workbook dialog box allows you to track and update changes, as well as determine how conflicts between file versions are resolved.

3 Click OK to finish. You'll be asked to save the worksheet if you haven't yet saved it.

Tracking and Reviewing Changes

As you work with your data, you will most likely make changes to it. Problems can arise in keeping track of all the changes you make to a workbook should you want to verify or have a record of your changes. The Tracking function in Excel allows you to keep track of your changes. It is especially important when more than one person makes changes.

Excel doesn't enable change tracking by default. Thus, if you need to track changes to your data in order to ensure its integrity, enable the Track Changes option. To begin tracking changes to a workbook, follow these steps:

1 Select the Tools menu, and choose Track Changes.

2 Select Highlight Changes. This opens the Highlight Changes dialog box, shown in Figure 15-6.

III

Microsoft Excel

FIGURE 15-6.

The Highlight Changes dialog box, which allows you to specify when, by whom, and where changes are tracked

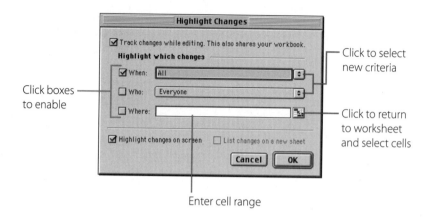

Click boxes to enable

Click to select new criteria

Click to return to worksheet and select cells

Enter cell range

3 Check the Track Changes While Editing box.

A side effect of this action is that your workbook will become shared. "[Shared]" appears in the title bar of the workbook. If you haven't saved your workbook, you'll be asked to when it is shared.

4 You can now identify which changes will be highlighted. Click the When, Who, or Where box to activate the respective options, and then choose how that option will be implemented from the pop-up menu. Table 15-1 summarizes each option category.

Table 15-1. Highlight Changes Options.

Option	Choice or Effect
When	All (Default) tracks all changes from the point when you enable change tracking to the time you disable it. Since I Last Saved tracks changes until you save the file.
	Not Yet Reviewed tracks changes until you review and either accept or reject them.
	Since Date tracks changes from the date that you enter.
Who	Everyone (Default)
	Everyone But Me
Where	Allows you to select a cell or cell range to monitor.
	Enter a cell or cell range reference, or click the small worksheet icon to the right of the pop-up menu and select the appropriate cell or cell range from a worksheet.

(continued)

Table 15-1.   *continued*

Option	Choice or Effect
Highlight Changes On Screen	Cells that have changed are visibly annotated onscreen. When you rest your mouse over the cell, a comment will pop up offering more details.
List Changes On A New Sheet	Displays changes on a separate history worksheet.

5   After you select the options you want, click OK to close the dialog box.

Figure 15-7 shows a workbook with tracking on. Notice how the cells that have changes have a border around them and a comment symbol. This allows you to see immediately how a workbook has been changed. You can hover your cursor over the change to see the details of the change.

FIGURE 15-7.

Highlighting changes literally highlights them onscreen

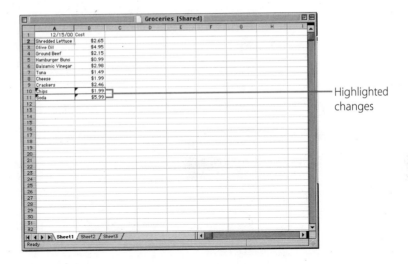

Highlighted changes

Another important aspect of tracking changes is reviewing them and either accepting or rejecting each change. Follow these steps to review changes in a workbook:

1   Open a workbook that has changes highlighted.

2   Select the Tools menu, choose Track Changes, and then choose Accept Or Reject Changes. You may be prompted to save your file, after which the Select Changes To Accept Or Reject dialog box opens, shown in Figure 15-8.

III

Microsoft Excel

FIGURE 15-8.
Decide which changes
to review

Select to change criteria

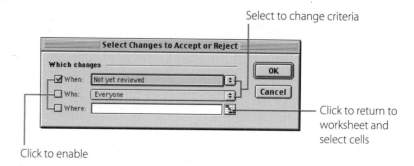

Click to return to
worksheet and
select cells

Click to enable

3 Click OK to continue. This opens the Accept Or Reject Changes
dialog box, shown in Figure 15-9.

FIGURE 15-9.
You can review each
change or accept or
reject them in one fell
swoop

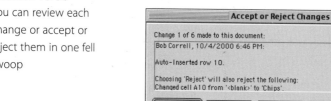

4 You can now choose to accept or reject each change. Clicking
Accept All or Reject All bypasses your review of each change and
either accepts or rejects all changes immediately.

 CAUTION

Accepting or rejecting
all changes without
reviewing isn't recom-
mended. You're track-
ing changes so that
you can review them,
and accepting or
rejecting all of the
changes at one time
prevents you from
doing so.

5 Click Close to complete the process.

If you no longer wish to track changes in a workbook, follow these
steps to turn change tracking off:

1 Open the workbook with change tracking enabled.

2 Select Tools, choose Track Changes, and choose Highlight
Changes to open the Highlight Changes dialog box.

3 Click to uncheck the Track Changes While Editing box.

4 Click OK to close the dialog box. Excel will ask you if you want
to continue to share the workbook (which was required to track
the changes) or make it exclusive to you. Press Yes to unshare
the workbook or No to cancel. If you press No, your workbook
will not be unshared and change tracking will not be disabled.

Protecting Information

It's always frustrating when another person changes your worksheet when you don't want them to. If you don't have change tracking enabled or a backup of your file, it is almost impossible to resurrect your original data. To prevent others from changing your worksheet, protect your information. To do so, follow these steps:

1 Select the Tools menu, and choose Protection.

 NOTE

> If your document is already shared, Protect Shared Workbook is the only option available.

2 Select Protect Sheet. This opens the Protect Sheet dialog box, shown in Figure 15-10.

FIGURE 15-10.

Protect individual sheet contents, objects, or scenarios

3 Check the options you want to protect:

- **Contents** Protects cells and chart items from being changed.

- **Objects** Protects graphic objects on worksheets or charts.

- **Scenarios** Protects the definitions of scenarios used in the worksheet.

4 Enter a password if you like; otherwise, click OK to finish.

5 If you entered a password, confirm it by re-entering it, and click OK.

If you've created a "master" workbook that needs to be shared among a group of co-workers, you'll soon find that they may accidentally change the workbook and destroy your work. If you want people to be able to access a workbook but not make changes, protect the workbook as shown in the steps on the following page.

1 Select the Tools menu, and choose Protection.

2 Select Protect Workbook. This opens the Protect Workbook dialog box, shown in Figure 15-11.

FIGURE 15-11.

The Protect Workbook dialog box

3 Check the options you want to protect.

- **Structure (Default)** Protects the structure of the workbook so that its worksheets can't be moved, deleted, or renamed and so that new worksheets can't be added.

- **Windows** Protects the workbook window so that it can't be resized, moved, hidden, or closed.

4 Enter a password if you like; otherwise, click OK to finish.

5 If you entered a password, confirm it by re-entering it, and click OK.

To protect a *shared* workbook (a workbook that can be opened by several people simultaneously), follow these steps:

1 Select the Tools menu, and choose Protection.

2 Select Protect And Share Workbook. This opens the Protect Shared Workbook dialog box.

3 Click the Sharing With Track Changes option. This option protects your workbook in addition to protecting change tracking.

4 Enter a password if you like; otherwise, click OK to finish.

5 If you entered a password, confirm it by re-entering it, and click OK.

To unprotect a worksheet, workbook, or shared workbook, follow these steps:

1 Select the Tools menu, and choose Protection.

2 Select Unprotect Sheet, Unprotect Workbook, or Unprotect Shared Workbook as appropriate.

3   Enter your password, if necessary. Click OK to continue.

 NOTE

> Passwords are effective tools to protect your workbook, but using them can sometimes backfire. If you forget the password, you won't be able to reverse any protection you enable and may have to re-create your workbook from scratch.

4   In the case of worksheets and workbooks, this is all that is required. For shared workbooks, click Yes when prompted to remove the protection.

Hiding and Unhiding Workbooks

If you need to have several workbooks open at one time, but one or more is getting in the way, simply hide them. To do so, follow these steps:

1   Select the workbook you want to hide.

2   Select the Window menu, and choose Hide.

3   Click OK to finish.

To unhide workbooks, follow these steps:

1   Select the Window menu, and choose Unhide.

2   Select a workbook to unhide from the Unhide dialog box.

3   Click OK to finish.

Using Data Validation

Data is the bedrock of Excel. Entering incorrect data means that you will likely draw incorrect conclusions from it. Despite your best efforts, you (or others) may enter the wrong type of data in a cell. For example, if your worksheet tracks personnel and their number of sick days, vacation days, and the like, entering text in a cell that requires a numerical value will throw your worksheet off. Likewise, unrealistic values can be entered. For example, a telephone number should have ten digits (counting the area code). If someone enters nine or twelve digits, your data is wrong.

If you need to protect the integrity of the data you enter and ensure it is either the correct type or range, you can validate the data. To use data validation, follow the steps on the next page.

1 Select a cell or cells on which to use data validation.

2 Select the Data menu, and choose Validation. The Data Validation dialog box opens.

3 Select a data type to allow by choosing from the Allow pop-up menu, shown in Figure 15-12. Your choices are:

- **Any Value** Accepts any value entered.

- **Whole Number** Accepts only whole numbers.

- **Decimal** Allows decimals.

- **List** Displays a list for the user to choose a value from.

- **Date** The data must be a date.

- **Time** The data must be a time.

- **Text Length** The data is text with a limited length.

- **Custom** Allows you to enter a formula, an expression, or a calculation from another cell to determine valid entries.

FIGURE 15-12.

Choose a type of data to allow

Select to change data type

Select to change condition

Enter values

Select Range box to select cells on a worksheet

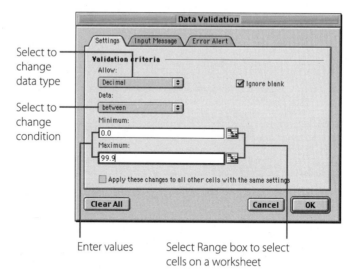

4 Based on your choice, you will be presented with different data criteria. Those listed under the Data menu are:

- Between

- Not Between

- Equal To

- Not Equal To

- Greater Than

- Less Than

- Greater Than Or Equal To

- Less Than Or Equal To

5 Choose one.

6 Next enter minimum and maximum values (if allowed) for your data.

7 If you want to display a message when the cell is selected, switch to the Input Message tab. Enter a title for your message in the Title field, and the message in the Message field.

8 If you want to display an error message if the data entered isn't valid, switch to the Error Alert tab. Enter a title and error message to display.

9 Click OK to close the dialog box.

Now, when someone attempts to enter data in a cell for which data validation rules are enabled, and enters data outside of the limits you've chosen, he or she is presented with the error message you entered, as shown in Figure 15-13.

FIGURE 15-13.

You can program the error message users will receive

Cell with data validation showing incorrect data entered

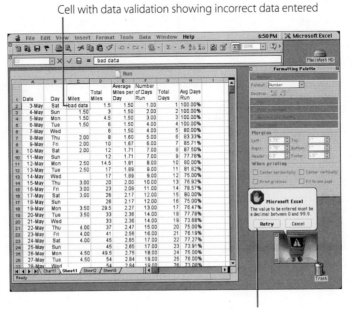

Error message

CHAPTER 16

Customizing
Microsoft Excel

Like all other Office applications, Microsoft Excel is specially designed to allow you to customize it to fit your needs. You can change how the program looks and calculates, choose your editing and color preferences, create custom lists, change the default toolbars, use your own custom creations, and more. Most of these options are available by choosing the Edit menu and selecting Preferences, although some are accessible by means of the Customize command, which is in the Tools menu. This chapter will discuss the various customization options available in Excel.

Modifying Preferences

Much like those in Microsoft Word, the preferences in Excel are organized into functional areas and can be accessed by selecting the Edit menu and then selecting Preferences to open the Preferences dialog box, shown in Figure 16-1.

FIGURE 16-1.

The Preferences dialog box, where many of Excel's preferences are located

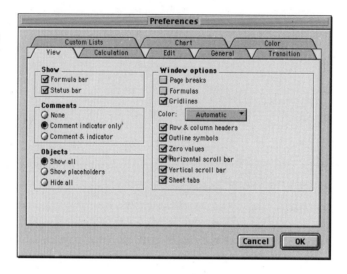

> **NOTE**
>
> The Preferences dialog box opens to the tab you last viewed or the View tab upon first use.

The tabs running across the top of the dialog box are the functional areas that represent most of what you can change in Excel. Click a tab to make it active and to view the preferences associated with it. Most of the time, you can simply check a check box to change a preference. If a check box is checked, the option is enabled; if it is unchecked, the preference is currently disabled. In other cases, you select a choice from a pop-up or a pull-down menu.

> **NOTE**
>
> If you make a mistake while changing preferences, click Cancel instead of OK. Excel won't update the preferences with ones you don't want or are unsure of.

For the remainder of this section, we'll show you each preference tab and briefly explain (if necessary) what each preference category does.

The View Tab

The View tab (shown in Figure 16-1) allows you to modify how Excel's interface is displayed and to toggle other options on or off. The View tab is organized into four areas:

- **Show** Toggles the Formula and Status bars on or off.

- **Comments** Changes how comments are displayed. You can choose to display no comment indicator, display the indicator only, or display the entire comment and indicator.

- **Objects** Either shows objects (such as pictures), shows a place-holder (a blank rectangle so you know something is there), or hides all objects.

- **Window Options** Toggles interface elements on or off, such as gridlines or sheet tabs, and allows you to choose a default color.

⭐ **TIP**

If you have many large objects in a workbook, it may take a lot of memory to display them. Try enabling the Show Placeholders option (or Hide All) to reduce the strain on your computer as you edit your file.

The Calculation Tab

The Calculation tab, shown in Figure 16-2, allows you to customize how and when Excel performs calculations. Calculation options control when Excel recalculates your worksheet. The default value, Automatic, updates calculations every time you change a value, formula, or name. Should you want to, you can change this behavior so that Excel recalculates everything except data tables when you make changes, or you can turn automatic calculation off by selecting Manual.

The Iteration option limits the number of iterations for goal seeking or for resolving circular references. The default values are displayed in Figure 16-2. Workbook options affect the entire workbook and range from updating remote references to accepting labels in formulas.

III

Microsoft Excel

FIGURE 16-2.

You can modify how Excel performs calculations through the Calculation tab

Recalculate entire workbook

Recalculate worksheet

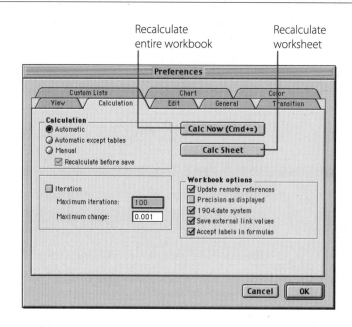

> **NOTE**
>
> The default date system for Excel workbooks created on Macintosh computers starts on January 2, 1904, while the default date system for workbooks using Microsoft Windows is 1 January, 1900. If you are swapping files back and forth between these two platforms and the dates appear wrong, uncheck the 1904 Date System option (or have the person using Windows enable his or her 1904 Date System option).

The Edit Tab

The Edit tab, shown in Figure 16-3, controls your editing preferences. These preferences affect drag-and-drop operations, the direction the active cell moves when you press Return, changes in what century you are referring to with two-digit years, and other editing preferences. (The default value for years specified by two digits is 30, so any year from 00 to 29 will be considered in the 21st century.)

FIGURE 16-3.
You can configure editing preferences through the Edit tab

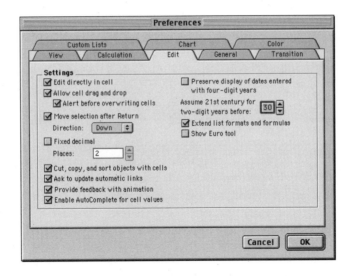

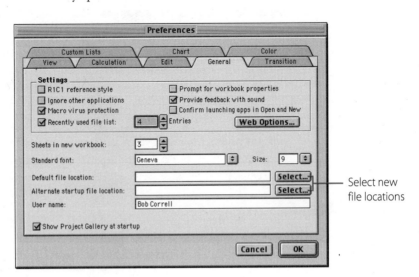

TIP

If you find yourself annoyed by the AutoComplete feature, you can turn it off by unchecking the Enable AutoComplete For Cell Values option. For more information on this feature, see the "Entering Text" section in Chapter 12, "Entering and Formatting Data."

The General Tab

The General tab, shown in Figure 16-4, is a grab-bag of settings that are actually quite useful.

FIGURE 16-4.
You can enable Macro Virus Protection and other general settings in the General tab

Select new file locations

III

Microsoft Excel

SEE ALSO

For more information, see the "Protecting Yourself from Macro Viruses" section in Chapter 9, "Special Tasks in Microsoft Word."

 NOTE

For security purposes, make sure Macro Virus Protection is enabled. Excel will scan each workbook you open for the presence of macros and ask you if you want to enable them. If Macro Virus Protection is enabled, you will have the option of disabling macros in workbooks that you open before the macros execute. Without the protection, macros are automatically enabled and may run without your knowledge.

> You may want to disable the Provide Feedback With Sound option if you work in a crowded office environment and people are looking at you quizzically whenever Excel beeps and boops at you. Although it's a nice feature, it can be distracting to others.

Other particularly useful settings are:

- **Sheets In New Workbook** If you find that three sheets in a new workbook are either overkill or not enough, change the default behavior to a number that suits you.

- **Standard Font** Although the standard font (Geneva, 9 pt) is very easy to read, if you decide to change this setting for corporate or personal reasons, you can easily select a new font type or size.

- **Show Project Gallery At Startup** Disable this option if you don't need the Project Gallery every time you launch Excel.

The Transition Tab

The Transition tab, shown in Figure 16-5, is somewhat misleading. From the name, you might be inclined to think that this tab applies to those transitioning to Excel from another spreadsheet program. In fact, the Transition tab is geared toward the default file type you want Excel to use when you save a file. In other words, the default save-as file type is initially set to Microsoft Excel Workbook. Selecting the Default Save As Type pop-up menu reveals a large number of alternate choices, which range from tab-delimited text to earlier versions of Excel, dBASE, and Lotus 1-2-3 files.

 NOTE

> Be careful when changing the default save-as file type because not all file types will preserve the formatting or other special Excel 2001 features. The differences among the file types are spelled out in the Excel Help system.

FIGURE 16-5.

On the Transition tab, you can choose which format to save your Workbook in

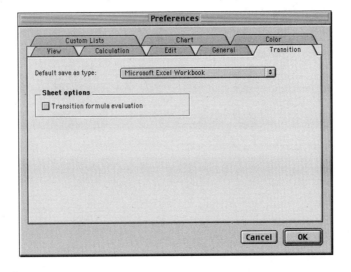

The Transition Formula Evaluation option allows you to open Lotus 1-2-3 files without losing or changing information.

The Custom Lists Tab

The Custom Lists tab, shown in Figure 16-6, allows you to create custom lists that can be sorted and automatically filled as a series. Selecting an existing custom list shows you its individual entries.

FIGURE 16-6.

You can create new types of sortable lists in the Custom Lists tab

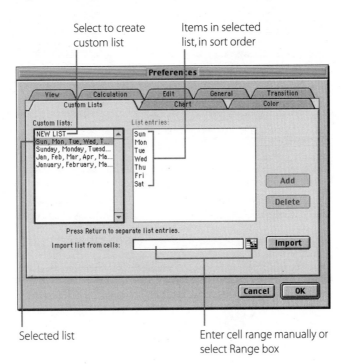

To create a new list, follow these steps:

1 Select New List from the Custom Lists field.

2 Click in the List Entries portion of the dialog box, and enter each new list item. Press Return to start a new line.

3 When finished adding new list entries, select Add.

4 Click OK to close the dialog box.

 NOTE

> Having a hard time thinking of new lists? There are unlimited possibilities, from the seasons of the year, to holidays, to names of people. Although you don't need to create a custom list for everything, if you need to sort a list other than alphabetically (which causes havoc with days and months), a custom list will allow you to sort according to the order in which you enter your custom list.

The Chart Tab

The Chart tab, shown in Figure 16-7, contains options that change the way Excel handles and displays charts.

FIGURE 16-7.

You can modify Charting preferences in Excel in the Chart tab

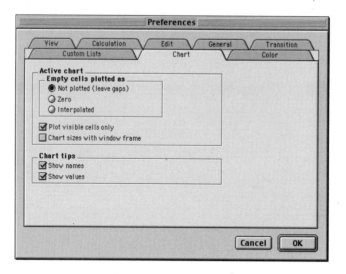

The two major categories of options are:

■ **Active Chart** This option controls how empty cells are plotted, allows you to not plot hidden cells, and determines whether a chart is resized with the main Excel window frame.

■ **Chart Tips** This option toggles names and values on or off for charts.

The Color Tab

The Color tab, shown in Figure 16-8, allows you to modify Excel's default color palette (seen when you select a color picker from a toolbar or menu option) and copy customized color schemes from other workbooks to the one you are working on.

FIGURE 16-8.

The Color tab, which allows you to create new color schemes and use them in other workbooks

Selected color   Click to open Color Picker

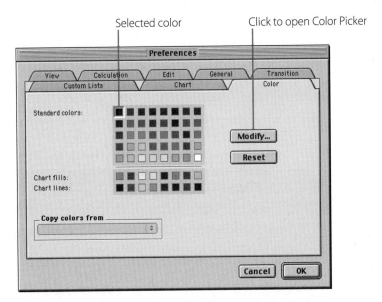

To change the 40 colors that are displayed by default, choose a color you want to change from the Standard colors and click Modify. This opens the Color Picker dialog box, shown in Figure 16-9.

Drag to choose new color

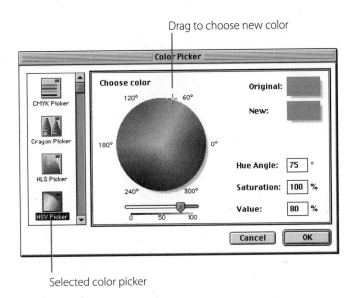

Selected color picker

III

Microsoft Excel

> **NOTE**
>
> You can use the same procedure for changing the colors for chart fills and lines, but in these cases, select a color to change from those displayed as Chart Fills or Chart Lines in the Preferences dialog box.

If you don't like the default HSV Picker, choose a new picker (such as the RGB Picker), choose a new color (or enter new numerical values for the color), and click OK.

> **NOTE**
>
> HSV stands for *Hue Angle*, *Saturation*, and *Value* and is simply another method of identifying the colors that appear on your monitor. The HSV Color Picker uses a color wheel with the primary (red, green, and blue) colors arranged around it, blending into each other as they meet. The Hue Angle determines the color based on its angle on the color wheel. Saturation is determined by moving from the edge of the wheel (100%) to the center (0%, or neutral gray). Value (from 0 to 100) corresponds to the brightness of the color, from black to perfectly bright.

If you make a mistake or want the color palette to revert back to its default state, click the Reset button in the Color tab of the Preferences dialog box.

Should you need to copy the color scheme from another workbook, follow these steps:

1 Open the workbook that has the color scheme you want to copy.

2 Open (or switch to) the workbook that you want to receive the copied color scheme.

3 Select the Edit menu, select Preferences, and choose the Color tab.

4 Select the workbook you opened in Step 1 from the Copy Colors From pull-down list.

> **NOTE**
>
> The Copy Colors From pull-down list is not active unless you have two workbooks open.

5 Click OK to finish.

Customizing Toolbars, Commands, and Appearance

As with the other Office 2001 applications, you can modify Excel's toolbars, commands, and appearance. This triumvirate of options is accessed through using View, Toolbars, and Customize, or using Tools and Customize.

> **NOTE**
>
> For more complete coverage on how to modify toolbars, commands, and appearances, please refer to Chapter 3, "Understanding the Microsoft Office Interface."

III

Microsoft Excel

PART IV

Microsoft Entourage

Setting Up Microsoft Entourage

B efore you can use Microsoft Entourage, you'll want to configure it to work with your existing e-mail accounts, newsgroup accounts, and directory services, as explained in this chapter. Of course, this assumes that you have an Internet account. To complete the Entourage set-up described in this chapter, you will also need the following information: the user name and password that you use to sign on to your Internet account, the names of the incoming and outgoing mail servers, and the name of your news server.

If you don't have this information, contact your Internet service provider (ISP) or your network administrator. Note that Entourage can also be configured to send and receive e-mail from Hotmail accounts and some other Web-based e-mail services. For instructions, see "Setting Up Existing ISP and Hotmail E-Mail Accounts," later in this chapter. If you are switching to Entourage from another e-mail program, you can import your Address Book into Entourage. For help doing this, as well as using and maintaining the Address Book, see Chapter 4, "Using the Address Book."

CHAPTER 17

About E-Mail, Newsgroups, and Directory Services

Like its predecessor (Microsoft Outlook Express 5), you can use Entourage to send and receive e-mail (electronic messages sent over the Internet), as well as read and post messages to *newsgroups* (Internet message lists organized by topic).

E-mail messages can be exchanged between any two people who have Internet access and e-mail accounts. It doesn't matter whether they use the same ISP, an online service such as America Online (AOL), a Web-based e-mail service such as Hotmail, or even different types of computers. Your e-mail address uniquely identifies you on the Internet, in much the same way that your street address uniquely specifies where you live. In addition to your main ISP e-mail account, you may have secondary accounts—with the same ISP, with other ISPs, with your business, or with Web-based e-mail services. Entourage can manage them all.

Newsgroups are message lists that you can read and to which you can contribute, if you like. Each newsgroup has a specific topic, such as video games (for example, *alt.games.video.sega-saturn*), disease support groups (for example, *alt.support.cancer*), or programs (for example, *microsoft.public.excel.macintosh*). You can *subscribe to* (follow) as many newsgroups as you like.

Directory services are Internet search sites—such as Bigfoot (*search.bigfoot.com*) and WhoWhere (*www.whowhere.lycos.com*)—that you can use to search for people, street addresses, and e-mail addresses. Rather than going to the directory services Web sites, you can execute many people searches without leaving Entourage.

Setting Up E-Mail Accounts

This section explains how to configure Entourage to work with your existing ISP and Hotmail e-mail accounts, as well as how to create new Hotmail accounts.

Setting Up Existing ISP and Hotmail E-Mail Accounts

Entourage can send and receive e-mail from two types of accounts: normal ISP accounts and Web-based accounts. And each person who uses Entourage on your computer can use it to handle his or her e-mail from *multiple* accounts. (Note that if you have recently installed Office 2001, the Setup Assistant will run automatically—enabling you to set up your primary e-mail account.)

NOTE

> If you have an America Online account or an account with a Web-based provider who does not provide POP3 server support, you cannot use Entourage to send or receive your e-mail from such accounts. Check your service provider's Help information if you're unsure whether POP3 support is provided.

To configure Entourage to use an existing ISP e-mail account, follow these steps:

1 From the Tools menu, choose Accounts. The Accounts dialog box appears, as shown in Figure 17-1.

FIGURE 17-1.

The Accounts dialog box enables you to manage all your e-mail and newsgroup accounts, as well as directory services

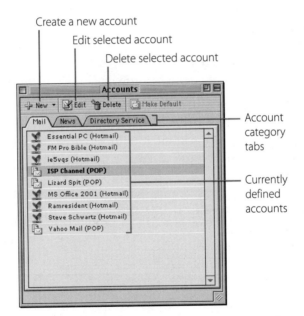

Create a new account

Edit selected account

Delete selected account

Account category tabs

Currently defined accounts

2 Click the down arrow on the right side of the New button and choose Mail. (Or you can switch to the Mail tab and click the New button; open the File menu, choose New, and then choose Account; or press ⌘-N.) The Account Setup Assistant appears, open to the Your Name screen, as shown in Figure 17-2.

FIGURE 17-2.

Enter the name that
you want to appear in
the From line of your
outgoing messages

Enter account information without the
help of the Account Setup Assistant

3 Enter the name you want to use to identify yourself to others.
   (It appears in the From line of all messages received from you.)
   Click the right arrow button to continue.

4 In the Internet E-Mail Address screen, shown in Figure 17-3, click
   the first radio button and enter your complete existing e-mail
   address in the form *username@domain*. Click the right arrow
   button to continue.

FIGURE 17-3.

Enter your existing
e-mail address

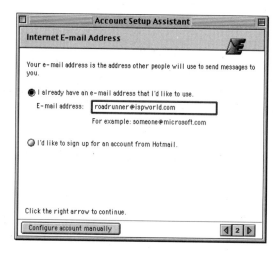

5 In the E-Mail Server Names screen, shown in Figure 17-4, choose the type of mail server used by your ISP: POP (Post Office Protocol, the most common) or IMAP (Internet Message Access Protocol). In the form *server type.domain*, enter the names of the ISP's incoming and outgoing mail servers, such as *pop3.ispworld.com* and *smtp.ispworld.com*. Click the right arrow button to continue.

FIGURE 17-4.

Specify the type of mail server (POP or IMAP) used by your ISP, and the names of the incoming and outgoing mail servers

Specify server type

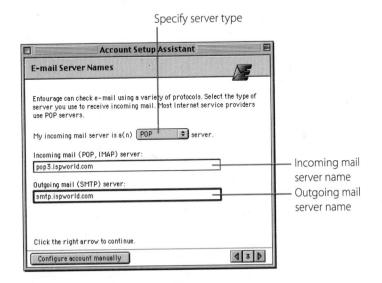

Incoming mail server name
Outgoing mail server name

> **NOTE**

If you aren't sure of the server type and server names, refer to the ISP's sign-up information, check its Web site, or contact its Technical Support group.

6 In the Internet Mail Logon screen, shown in Figure 17-5, enter your user name (everything before the @ symbol in your e-mail address). If you want to be able to log on each time without having to type your password, click the Save Password check box and enter your password in the Password box. Otherwise, you'll be prompted for the password each time you log on. Click the right arrow button to continue.

FIGURE 17-5.

Enter the required logon information for this account

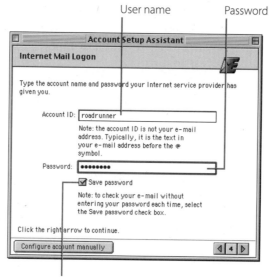

User name   Password

Automatically log on with this password

7 On the Congratulations screen, shown in Figure 17-6, enter a name for the account. (This name is for Entourage identification purposes only. You can call it anything you like.)

FIGURE 17-6.

Name this account and indicate whether it should be included whenever you perform a Send & Receive All

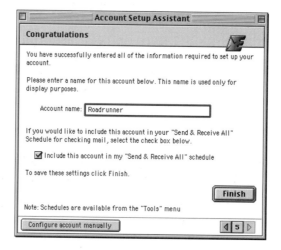

8 If you want mail from this account automatically sent and received whenever you perform a manual or scheduled Send & Receive All, make sure that the check box is checked. Click Finish. The e-mail account is now added to the Accounts dialog box.

To configure Entourage for an existing Hotmail account, follow these steps:

1 Perform steps 1 through 3 of the previous procedure. In step 4, click the first radio button and enter the name of your existing Hotmail account in the form *username @hotmail.com*. Click the right arrow button to continue (shown in Figure 17-3).

2 In the Hotmail Logon screen (see Figure 17-7), enter your user name (everything before the @ symbol in your Hotmail address). If you want to be able to log on each time without having to type your password, click the Save Password check box and enter your password in the Password bar. Click the right arrow button to continue.

FIGURE 17-7.

Enter your Hotmail user name and password

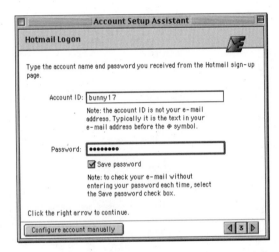

3 On the Congratulations screen (shown in Figure 17-6), enter a name for the account. (This name is for Entourage identification purposes only. You can call it anything you like.)

4 If you want mail from this account automatically sent and received whenever you perform a manual or scheduled Send & Receive All, make sure that the check box is checked. Click Finish. The Hotmail account is now added to the Accounts window.

If you're comfortable with account setup, you can manually configure ISP and Hotmail accounts by clicking the Configure Account Manually button in the Account Setup Assistant. In the New Account dialog box, shown in Figure 17-8, specify the account type and click OK.

FIGURE 17-8.

Specify the account type and click OK

Then fill in the necessary information in the Edit Account dialog box, as shown in Figure 17-9.

FIGURE 17-9.

You can manually configure a new e-mail account (or edit an existing one) in the Edit Account dialog box

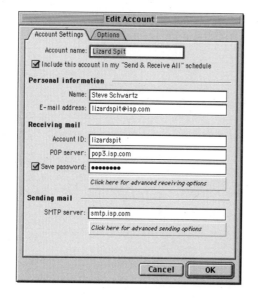

Other Web-Based E-Mail Accounts

Entourage can also be configured to handle other Web-based accounts—as long as the provider offers POP3 servers from which you can send and receive e-mail. (Some do; some don't.) To set up such an account in Entourage, all you need to know is your e-mail address and the names of the mail servers. For Yahoo! Mail, for instance, the incoming (POP) mail server is pop.mail.yahoo.com and the outgoing (SMTP or Simple Mail Transfer Protocol) mail server is smpt.mail.yahoo.com.

When setting up such an account, you may want to enable the Allow On-line Access (Shows Account In Folder List) option by clicking the Options tab in the Edit Account dialog box, shown in Figure 17-10. This will allow you to access the account by clicking its icon in the Folder List, just as you can do with your other e-mail accounts.

FIGURE 17-10.

The Options tab of the Edit Account window allows you to access the account

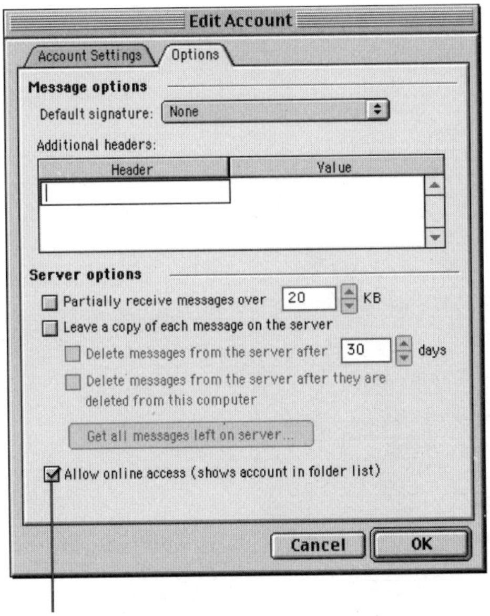

Click to allow online access

Creating a New Hotmail Account

As mentioned previously, Hotmail accounts are free. And unlike your ISP e-mail accounts, you can create as many Hotmail accounts as you like. For example, many Web sites require that you sign up for their services by providing a valid e-mail address. Why put your primary e-mail address at risk when you can subscribe as *someone@hotmail.com*?

You can create new accounts at the Hotmail Web site (*www.hotmail.com*). You can also create them from within Entourage by following these steps:

1 Open the Accounts dialog box, and create a new mail account as described in steps 1 through 3 of configuring Entourage to use an existing ISP e-mail account on page 311.

2 In the Internet E-Mail Address screen (shown in Figure 17-3), click the second radio button, indicating that you want to create a new Hotmail account. Click the right arrow button to continue.

3 In the next screen, click the Hotmail Sign-Up button, click the right arrow button, and then, in the screen that appears, click the Hotmail Sign-Up button. Your Web browser launches and opens to the Hotmail home page, as shown in Figure 17-11.

FIGURE 17-11.

You can sign up for a Hotmail account from this screen, as well as send and receive e-mail from any of your current Hotmail accounts

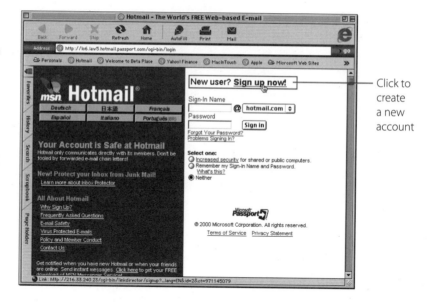

Click to create a new account

4 Click the link to sign up for a new account, and supply the requested information. When Hotmail confirms that the new account has been created, return to the Account Setup Assistant in Entourage.

> **NOTE**
>
> There are already millions of Hotmail accounts. It may take several tries before you come up with a user name that isn't already being used.

5 In the Hotmail Logon screen (shown in Figure 17-7), enter your user name (everything before the @ symbol in your Hotmail address). If you want to be able to log on each time without having to type your password, click the Save Password check box and enter your password in the Password box. Click the right arrow button to continue.

6 On the Congratulations screen (shown in Figure 17-6), enter a name for the account. (This name is for Entourage identification purposes only. You can call it anything you like.)

7 If you want mail from this account automatically sent and received whenever you perform a manual or scheduled Send & Receive All, make sure that the check box is checked. Click Finish. The new Hotmail account is now added to the Accounts dialog box.

Modifying E-Mail Account Options

As with most parts of Microsoft Office, the default account settings of Entourage will satisfy most users. However, if you want to examine or modify the settings, follow these steps:

1 From the Tools menu, choose Accounts. The Accounts dialog box appears. (See Figure 17-1.)

2 Click the Mail tab to view the list of e-mail accounts.

3 Double-click the name of the account you want to examine (or select the account name and click the Edit button). The Edit Account dialog box appears (as shown in Figure 17-9), showing the information that you previously entered in the Account Setup Assistant.

4 Edit the text or change options, as desired.

5 If this is a Hotmail account, as shown in Figure 17-12, you'll note that the Account Settings tab contains a Sending Mail option that's not available for ISP accounts. If you want to store all outgoing messages from this account at Hotmail, rather than on your computer, leave this option checked.

FIGURE 17-12.

You can save copies of outgoing Hotmail messages on your Mac's hard disk or on the Hotmail server

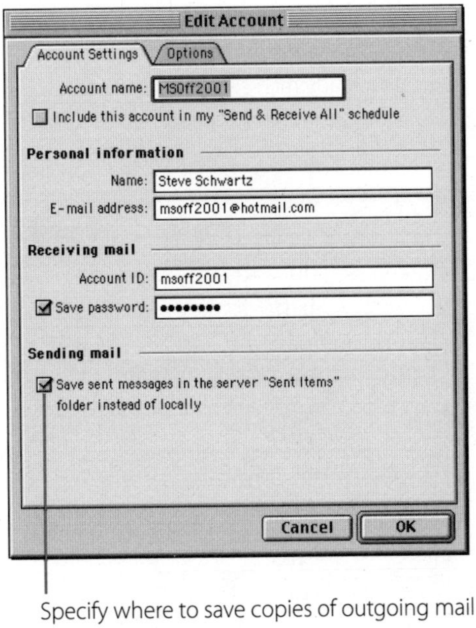

Specify where to save copies of outgoing mail

6 Click the Options tab at the top of the Edit Account dialog box. (See Figures 17-13a and 17-13b.)

FIGURE 17-13A.

The Options tab for an ISP account

Choose a default signature

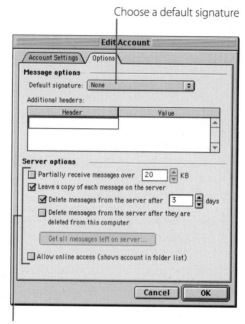

Server message-handling options

FIGURE 17-13B.

The Options tab for a Hotmail account

Default signature

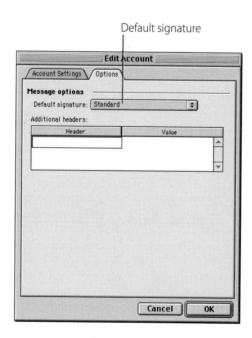

7 Set the following options as desired:

- **Default Signature (ISP or Hotmail)** Choose None or the name of a defined signature (such as Standard) to automatically append the chosen signature to all outgoing messages from the account.

- **Partially Receive Messages Over _x_ KB (ISP only)** If you sometimes receive large messages that you may not want, checking this option causes messages over the specified size to be only partially downloaded to your computer.

> **NOTE**
>
> To tell your mail server how to handle a specific received partial message, select the message in the message list, click the On-Line Status indicator (the envelope icon), and choose an option from the pop-up menu that appears. Alternately, you can open the message in its own window and click an underlined text option, as shown in Figure 17-14.

FIGURE 17-14.
To indicate what you'd like to do with this partial message, you can click Get Entire Message or Delete From Server

Message-handling options

- **Leave A Copy Of Each Message On The Server (ISP only)** Check this option if, for example, you also want to be able to retrieve the same messages from another computer, such as your main system at home or work. You can optionally specify when to delete these messages from the server by clicking either or both of the following two check boxes: Delete Messages From The Server After _x_ Days and Delete Messages From The Server After They Are Deleted From This Computer.

8 Click OK to save all changes, or click Cancel to discard them.

You can delete accounts or choose different default accounts in the Accounts dialog box. To open the Accounts dialog box (shown in Figure 17-1), open the Tools menu and choose Accounts. To delete an existing account, select its name and click Delete.

The *default* e-mail or newsgroup account—the one from which all messages are automatically sent unless you specify otherwise—is shown in boldface in the Accounts dialog box. To make a different account the default, select it and click Make Default.

Setting Up News Server Accounts

Although your primary news server will probably be the one that is provided by your ISP, Entourage can use as many other news servers as you want. Companies such as Microsoft and Symantec, for example, sometimes maintain their own news servers to provide information to customers and to get product feedback. To emphasize this fact, Entourage is pre-configured to use Microsoft's news server.

If you use America Online as your news provider, you must use its software to access newsgroups. Entourage cannot access AOL newsgroups.

Adding a News Server

To add a news server, follow these steps:

1 Open the Tools menu and choose Accounts. The Accounts dialog box appears. (See Figure 17-1.)

2 Click the down arrow on the right side of the New button, and choose News. (Or you can switch to the News tab and click the New button; open the File menu, choose New, and then choose Account; or press ⌘-N.) The Account Setup Assistant appears, open to the Internet News Account screen, as shown in Figure 17-15.

If you manually set up the most recently added account, you will still be in manual mode. To revert to using the Account Setup Assistant, click the Assist Me button in the dialog box that appears.

FIGURE 17-15.

Choose an e-mail address to which replies to your posts should be sent

3 Choose a reply-to e-mail account from the pop-up menu. All replies to your posts will be sent to the chosen address.

4 If you want, you can enter the name of the organization or company with which you're associated. Click the right arrow button to continue.

⭐ **TIP**

When choosing a reply-to e-mail address in step 3, you may want to use a Hotmail or similar account, rather than your personal or company e-mail account. Posting to newsgroups frequently results in *spam* (unwanted advertising e-mail). It's better if spam goes to a secondary e-mail account than to your main one.

5 In the Internet News Server Name screen (shown in Figure 17-16), enter the name of the news server you want to add. (News server names are generally in the form *news.domain*, such as *news.alaskanet.com*.) If the news server does not require you to log on with a user name and password, click the right arrow button to continue. Go to step 7.

FIGURE 17-16.

Enter the name of the news server

6 If this news server *does* require you to log on, click the check box and then click the right arrow button to continue. The Internet News Logon screen appears, as shown in Figure 17-17. Enter your user name. If you want Entourage to provide your password automatically each time you log on to the news server, check the Save Password check box and enter your password. Click the right arrow button to continue.

FIGURE 17-17.

Enter your user name (account ID) and password

7 On the Congratulations screen, shown in Figure 17-18, enter a name for this news server. (This name is for Entourage identification purposes only. You can call it anything you like.)

FIGURE 17-18.

Enter a name to identify this news account

8 Click the Finish button. The news server's name is added to the Accounts dialog box and the Folder List in Entourage's main window.

Subscribing to Newsgroups

The first time you return to the Entourage main screen and click the news server's name in the Folder List, the dialog box shown in Figure 17-19 appears. Click OK to receive the list of newsgroups that are available on the server.

FIGURE 17-19.

Click OK to receive the list of available newsgroups

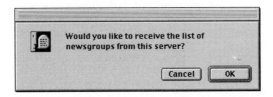

Periodically, you may want to update the newsgroup list by selecting each news server in the Folder list and then clicking the Update List button in the toolbar.

As mentioned previously, you can subscribe to as many newsgroups as you like. (*Subscribing* merely means that you intend to use Entourage to follow the newsgroup regularly.) Subscribing to a newsgroup adds its name to the Folder List, as well as makes the newsgroup readily accessible by opening the View menu and choosing Subscribed Only.

To subscribe to a newsgroup, follow these steps:

1 Click to select a news server in the Folder List of the Entourage window. The names of all newsgroups that are tracked by the news server appear in Entourage's main window, as shown in Figure 17-20.

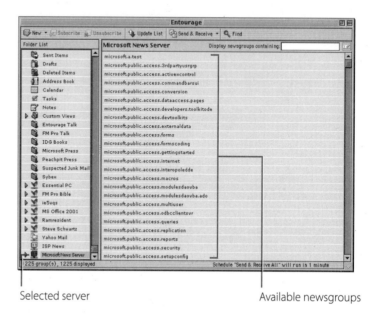

Selected server   Available newsgroups

2 Scroll through the newsgroup list, and click to select the one to which you want to subscribe.

3 Click the Subscribe button, open the Edit menu, and choose Subscribe, or Control-click the newsgroup name and choose Subscribe from the pop-up menu that appears. The newsgroup's name is now displayed in boldface to indicate that it is a subscribed-to newsgroup, and its name is also added beneath the server name in the Folder List.

 **TIP**

Some news servers handle thousands of newsgroups. To find a particular newsgroup or one that contains a given keyword ("Mac," for example), enter the keyword in the Display Newsgroups Containing text box, as shown in Figure 17-21. As you type, the newsgroup list is automatically filtered to show only the newsgroup names that contain the search text. To view the entire list of newsgroups again, click the Clear button to the right of the text box.

FIGURE 17-21.

To filter the newsgroup list, enter a text string in this text box

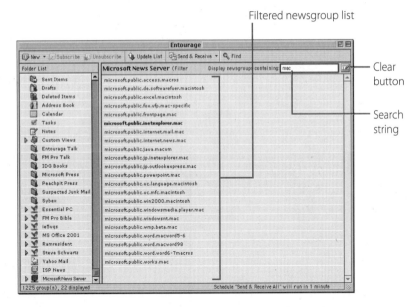

Filtered newsgroup list

Clear button

Search string

If you later decide that you no longer want to subscribe to a newsgroup, select its name and click the Unsubscribe button, open the Edit menu and choose Unsubscribe, or Control-click the newsgroup name and choose Unsubscribe from the pop-up menu that appears.

Adding Directory Services

Entourage comes preconfigured to use four directory services: Bigfoot, Infospace, WhoWhere, and Yahoo! People Search. When you create an e-mail message and issue the Check Names command (by clicking the Check Names button, opening the Tools menu and choosing Check Names, or pressing Shift-⌘-C), the directory services are consulted for possible matches.

While the four directory services will suffice for most users, you can add others, too. Open the Tools menu, choose Accounts, click the Directory Service tab in the Accounts dialog box, click the New button, and then fill in the requested information in the Account Setup Assistant.

You shouldn't count on directory services to be able to find e-mail addresses for you. If a person has a common name, you're liable to find dozens of potential matches—with no way of distinguishing the correct one from the others or determining whether *any* of the matches are actually the correct person. Note, too, that an individual will be listed by a particular directory service only if he or she has completed a Web form *requesting* the listing.

CHAPTER 18

The Calendar and Information Management Features

The presence of a calendar in Microsoft Entourage is a breakthrough for the Macintosh version of Microsoft Office. Now—for the first time—Office enables you to record appointments and, optionally, to set reminders for them. And because the Calendar is integrated with the other Office applications, you can now flag any Microsoft Word, Excel, or PowerPoint document with a reminder to follow it up at a later date and time.

Entourage also enables you to track tasks, write notes to yourself, and create links between Entourage items. Since these options—like the Calendar—are only tangentially related to Entourage's main purposes (sending and receiving e-mail and newsgroup messages), they are all covered in this chapter.

Using the Calendar

To view the Calendar (shown in Figure 18-1), click the Calendar icon in the Folder List, choose Calendar from the Window menu, or press ⌘-4. You can specify the time range you want to display by choosing a command from the View menu: Day, Week, Work Week, or Month. (To display the same view for different dates, click a new starting date in one of the miniature calendars at the top of the window.)

TIP

> To make it easier to view and work with the Calendar, open the View menu and choose Folder List, removing its check mark. When you resume working with e-mail, you can restore the Folder List by choosing its View menu command again.

FIGURE 18-1.

In the Week view of the Calendar, work periods are shown in white; non-work periods are patterned

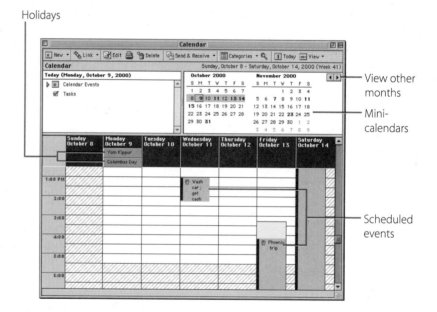

Holidays

View other months

Mini-calendars

Scheduled events

SEE ALSO

You can also view your Calendar by saving it as a Web page to view online using any Web browser, such as Microsoft Internet Explorer. See Chapter 30, "Microsoft Office 2001 and the Web," for instructions.

If you want to see a list of only the scheduled events, holidays, and tasks that fall within the chosen time period (as shown in Figure 18-2), choose List from the View menu.

You can also view a range of dates in the Calendar (from one day to six weeks). Click the start date in a mini-calendar, and then drag to select the end date.

FIGURE 18-2.

In List view, the Calendar shows all events and tasks for the period

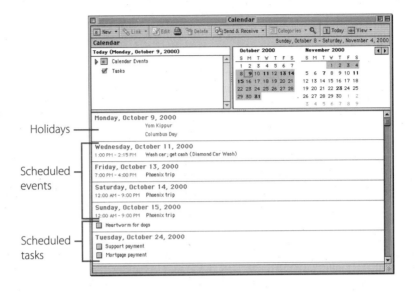

Holidays —

Scheduled events

Scheduled tasks

Creating an Event

To create a new Calendar event, follow these steps:

1 Click the Calendar icon in the Folder List, choose Calendar from the Window menu, or press ⌘-4.

2 Double-click a calendar date (in the mini-calendars or in any view) to create an event for that day. Or if you are viewing the Calendar in Day, Week, or Work Week view, you can double-click a specific time on the chosen date. An untitled event window appears, as shown in Figure 18-3.

FIGURE 18-3.

You schedule an event by filling in the details in this event window

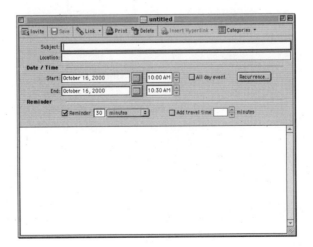

IV

Microsoft Entourage

> **NOTE**
>
> You can also create an event by clicking the New button in the toolbar. By default, the date and time that are currently selected in the Calendar will be treated as the event's starting date and time. Of course, you can change these settings when you define the event.

3 Enter a description of the event in the Subject box.

4 *Optional:* If the event will occur in a particular place, you can enter it in the Location box.

5 If the event will take an entire day, check the All Day Event check box. Otherwise, leave the check box blank and specify a start date/time and an end date/time in the boxes that appear, as shown in Figure 18-3.

6 *Optional:* If you want to be reminded prior to the event's starting time, click the Reminder check box and designate a time interval (in minutes, hours, or days). At the designated time, a pop-up reminder window will appear when any Office 2001 application is running.

7 *Optional:* If you must drive to the event (such as an appointment at your doctor's office), click the Add Travel Time check box and specify the approximate number of minutes travel will require. The start and end times will be adjusted to compensate for travel time.

8 *Optional:* You can enter notes, such as driving directions, in the large text box at the bottom of the event window.

9 Click the Save button, and close the event window.

Creating a Recurring Event

Some events occur more than once. For example, there may be a club meeting on every first and third Tuesday of each month, or you may pay your rent on the first day of every month. Rather than create a separate event and reminder for every occurrence, you can create a single event and reminder but designate it as *recurring*.

To set an event as recurring, click the Recurrence button in an event window. (See Figure 18-3.) The Recurring Event window appears, as shown in Figure 18-4. Specify a recurrence pattern and an optional end date. Click OK to return to the event window. The event will now appear on the Calendar on every affected date and time.

FIGURE 18-4.

You can specify a frequency based on a specific date (every 12th of the month) or a day of the week (every other Thursday), as well as when the recurrences will end

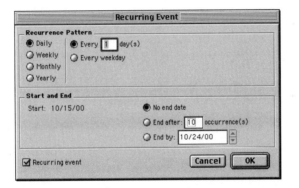

To make changes to a recurring event, locate and double-click one occurrence of the event on the Calendar. (If you want to edit the entire series, you can choose any occurrence. To edit a particular occurrence, double-click that one.) A dialog box appears, asking whether you want to change just this occurrence or the entire series. Select the appropriate option, and click OK. Make whatever changes are necessary.

 NOTE

If you are editing the entire series for a recurring event, you can remove all occurrences by clicking the Delete button in the event window toolbar.

Managing Events

Once you've set an event, there's often more that you must do than occasionally glancing at the Calendar window. Entourage enables you to change an event's time and other details, delete events, respond to and modify event reminders, and issue and respond to event invitations.

TIP

Can't remember when a particular event is scheduled or when it took place? The Find and Advanced Find commands in the Edit menu work in the Calendar, too.

 SEE ALSO

You can instruct the Calendar to automatically delete non-recurring events after they've passed by setting an option in Preferences. See "Customizing the Calendar" later in this chapter.

Modifying and Deleting Events

After scheduling events, you'll frequently need to modify them by changing the date and/or time and adding more details. You can make any modifications you want by double-clicking the event on the Calendar. Make your changes, click Save when you're through, and then close the event window.

> If you just need to change the date or time for an event, you can drag it to a new location on the Calendar. In order to do this, however, you must be in a view that displays both the original date/time and the desired date/time.

To delete an event, click to select it, and then click the Delete button, press Delete, or drag it to the Trash.

Responding To and Modifying Reminders

When you create events and tasks, you can optionally assign a reminder to each one. The reminder will appear at the scheduled date and time—as long as an Office program is running. If an Office program is *not* running, the reminder will appear the next time an Office program is launched.

By selecting a reminder in the Reminders window (as shown in Figure 18-5) and clicking toolbar buttons, you can do any of the following:

- Open the original event or task (enabling you to view and/or edit it).

- Open a document that you've flagged for follow-up in Word, Excel, or PowerPoint. (To do so, open the Tools menu in Word, choose Flag For Follow Up, and set a date/time for when you want to be reminded.)

- Click to set the reminder to *snooze* for five minutes or a different length of time (click the down arrow on the right side of the Snooze button) after which it will reappear.

- Dismiss the reminder.

FIGURE 18-5.

The Reminders window appears when a reminder has been set for an event or task.

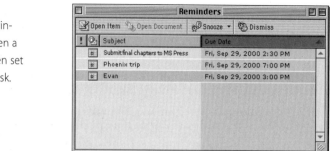

To modify a reminder, open the original event or task and make any desired changes. If you decide that you don't need a reminder at all, remove the check mark from the Reminder check box and click Save.

Inviting Others to an Event

You can also use the Calendar to coordinate group activities, such as meetings and family reunions. Using Entourage's e-mail capabilities, you can notify or invite people to events that you've scheduled on your Calendar, as well as accept or reject invitations from others. Everyone, however, must have an e-mail program that supports Internet Calendaring (iCalendar). Otherwise, the received message will merely display the event title as the subject and the start/end times as the message text.

To issue an invitation, open the event for editing and click the Invite button in the toolbar. Choose or hand-enter the e-mail addresses of the people you want to invite. Add any necessary comments or attachments, and click Send Now.

Incoming invitations arrive in the recipient's Inbox. When an invitation is received by an Entourage user and is opened, as shown in Figure 18-6, the recipient can click one of three buttons: Tentative, Accept, or Decline.

FIGURE 18-6.

If you're sure of your decision, click Accept or Decline; otherwise, click Tentative to suggest that you *may* attend

Response buttons

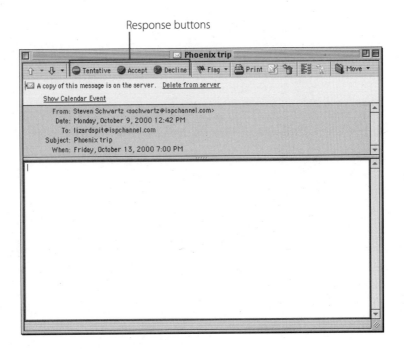

If you—or another host—later want to cancel an event, double-click the event to open it and click the Cancel Invitations button. A dialog box will appear asking: "Do you want to send an update to the attendees?" Click Send to e-mail a cancellation notice to all persons who previously received your invitation.

Customizing the Calendar

You can customize the Calendar by opening the Edit menu, pointing to Preferences, and choosing General. The General Preferences dialog box appears. Click the Calendar tab, as shown in Figure 18-7.

FIGURE 18-7.

You can set Calendar preferences in the Calendar tab of the General Preferences dialog box

Click for help with these settings

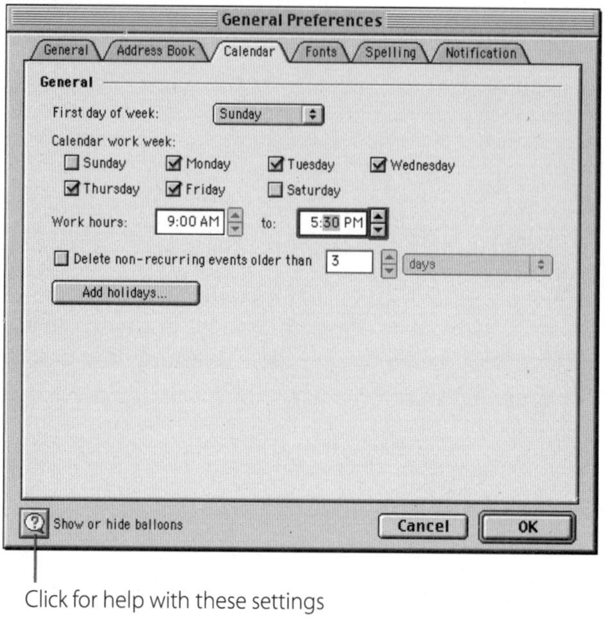

You can set the following Calendar preferences:

- Your choice in the First Day Of Week pop-up menu determines the way the Calendar is displayed when in Week view.

- Check the days in the Calendar Work Week section to match the days of the week you normally work.

- In the Work Hours section, indicate your daily work hours by selecting start and end times.

- To instruct the Calendar to automatically delete normal (non-recurring) events that have passed, click the Delete Non-Recurring Events Older Than check box and specify a time period.

- To include holidays in your Calendar, click the Add Holidays button, select the Holidays file from the list that appears, and click Open. The Add Holidays To Calendar dialog box appears. Click the countries and religions whose holidays you want to add, and then click OK.

> **NOTE**
>
> You can selectively remove holidays that you don't observe or celebrate. Conduct an Advanced Find, and set criteria as shown in Figure 18-8. In the Search Results window, select the holidays you want to remove and click the Delete button (or press the Delete key).

FIGURE 18-8.

This search will list all holidays that are found in the Calendar, enabling you to delete the extraneous ones

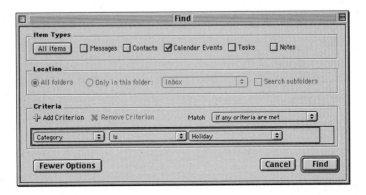

Tracking Tasks

Traditionally, personal information management (PIM) programs relied on a calendar to track appointments as well as items on your to-do lists. While this approach worked reasonably well, it meant that your to-do items had to be assigned to dates—even if they really weren't date-sensitive. For example, although it might be important for you to fix the screen door, you might not want to *schedule* it for a specific date and time.

Although you can use the Entourage Calendar to schedule such tasks as events, you can also create and track them in the Tasks list or window, shown in Figure 18-9. Doing so has the following advantages:

- Tasks can either be undated or have a specific due date. You can schedule a reminder for any task—even ones for which you haven't set a due date.

- Tasks can be marked as completed by checking a box. You can view tasks by completion status, and you can limit displayed tasks to those for today or this week.

- You can set a priority level for each task, as well as assign one or more categories to it.

- Like Calendar events, tasks can be single or recurring events.

FIGURE 18-9.

The Tasks list shows all scheduled tasks, their completion status, their priority, whether they are recurring events, and whether a reminder has been associated with them

Check boxes show completion status

Click a column head to sort the list

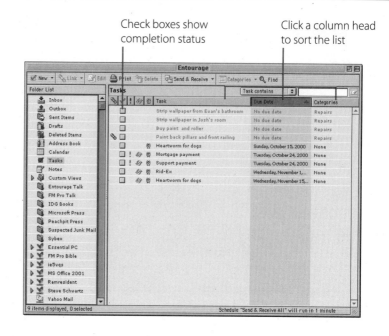

Creating Tasks

All defined tasks are displayed in the Tasks window and list. To create a new task and add it to the Tasks window and list, follow these steps:

1 If the Tasks window or list is active, click the New button; press ⌘-N; or open the File menu, point to New, and choose Task. If any other window or list is active, click the down arrow on the right side of the New button and choose Task, or open the File menu, point to New, and choose Task. An untitled task window appears, as shown in Figure 18-10.

FIGURE 18-10.

All tasks are created and edited in this window

Enter title

Set priority

Choose due date (optional)

Set reminder (optional)

Enter task details

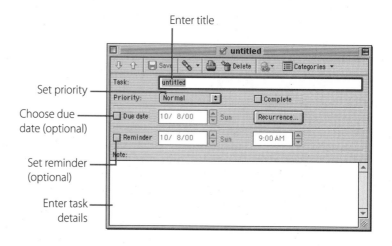

2 At a minimum (for an undated task or to-do item), you must enter a title in the Task text box, save the task (by clicking the Save button), and close the window. All remaining steps are optional.

3 *Optional:* Set a priority for completing the task by selecting an option from the Priority pop-up menu.

4 *Optional:* If you've already completed the task, click the Complete check box. (It's more common to do this when editing a task, but you may be tracking a multi-step project and want to record the steps you've already completed, for example.)

5 *Optional:* If the task has a particular date on which or by which it must be completed, click the Due Date check box and enter a date.

6 *Optional:* If you want to be reminded in advance or at the moment the task must be handled, click the Reminder check box and set a date/time for the reminder. As long as Entourage or another Office application is running when the reminder is triggered, a Reminders window (shown in Figure 18-5) will automatically appear. If an Office application is not running at that time, the Reminders window will be presented the next time you launch an Office application.

7 *Optional:* If you want to elaborate on the task, you can type, paste, or drag the necessary information into the Note area.

8 *Optional:* From the Categories pop-up menu, choose one or more categories to classify the task.

9 Click the Save button, and then close the task window.

Recurring Tasks

Not all tasks are one-time events. Some—such as paying the mortgage, playing bridge, or giving your dog her heartworm pill—recur on a regular basis. By clicking the Recurrence button in the new task window, you can specify the frequency with which the task occurs. (See Figure 18-4.)

Viewing and Editing Tasks

To view the list of tasks (as shown in Figure 18-9), you can click the Tasks icon in the Folder List, choose Tasks from the Window menu, or press ⌘-5. You can specify a particular view of the Tasks list by choosing a command from the View menu, as shown in Figure 18-11.

FIGURE 18-11.

Choose whether all tasks, incomplete tasks, or completed tasks are displayed in the list

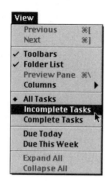

To open a task for viewing or editing, double-click its header. Make whatever changes are necessary, and click the Save button.

You can delete any task—whether it is completed or not. Select its header in the Tasks list or window and then click the Delete button, press the Delete key or ⌘-Delete, choose Delete Task from the Edit menu, Control-click the task and choose Delete Task, or drag the task to the Trash.

If all you want to do is mark a task as completed, you don't need to open the task. Just click the completion check box in the Tasks list or window. You can also change a task's category, priority, or completion status by Control-clicking the task header.

As is the case with other Entourage windows, you can sort the Tasks window by clicking a column header in the Tasks list or window. You can also filter the tasks, or issue Find/Advanced Find commands to identify the tasks that satisfy your search criteria. For instructions, see Chapter 4, "Using the Address Book."

Working with Notes

In addition to tracking tasks and appointments, you can also create notes in Entourage. A *note* is a free-form text document that can contain any type of information you want. Because notes are created in the same way that you create formatted HTML e-mail messages, they can contain headings, bullets, numbered lists, different paragraph alignments, rules, and different fonts and text sizes.

Creating and Editing Notes

SEE ALSO
Although you can use Entourage notes as you would any notepad or memo pad program (that is, to jot down unrelated items), notes can be *very* useful when linked to other items, such as Calendar appointments or e-mail messages. You can learn how to link items in the "Linking Items to Other Items" section later in this chapter.

As with other documents in Office, you can create new notes, as well as go back and edit or delete existing ones. To create a new note, follow these steps:

1 If the Notes folder or window is active, click the New button in the toolbar, open the File menu and choose New and then Note, or press ⌘-N.

   or

   If another folder or window is active, click the down arrow on the right side of the New button and choose Note, or open the File menu and choose New and then Note. A new, untitled note window appears.

2 Identify the note by typing a title in the Title box. (Choose the title carefully. It is the only identifying information that you will see when you switch to the Notes window.)

3 Write the note. Work as though you're using a word processing program. You only have to press Return when you want to start a new paragraph. Otherwise, text automatically wraps as necessary to fit within the dimensions of the note window. You can apply formatting before you begin typing, or you can add it later. (Formatting commands can be chosen from the note's toolbar or from the Formatting menu.)

4 In addition to formatting commands common to many word processing applications, you can also do the following in your notes:

   • Choose a background color by clicking the down arrow on the right side of the Background button.

   • Add a timestamp to the note by clicking the Insert Date & Time button. (If you're recording notes from a series of phone conversations, this is an excellent way to help you keep track of them.)

   • Add a horizontal line (or rule) by clicking the Horizontal Line button.

   • For the page currently being viewed in Microsoft Internet Explorer, insert a Web page address from your stored Favorites or from Internet Explorer's History, by clicking the Insert Hyperlink button.

- Classify the note by choosing one or more categories from the Categories pop-up menu.

5 Save the note by clicking the Save button, choosing Save from the File menu, or pressing ⌘-S. Figure 18-12 shows a completed note.

6 Close the note window by clicking its close box. The new note's title is added to the list in the Notes window.

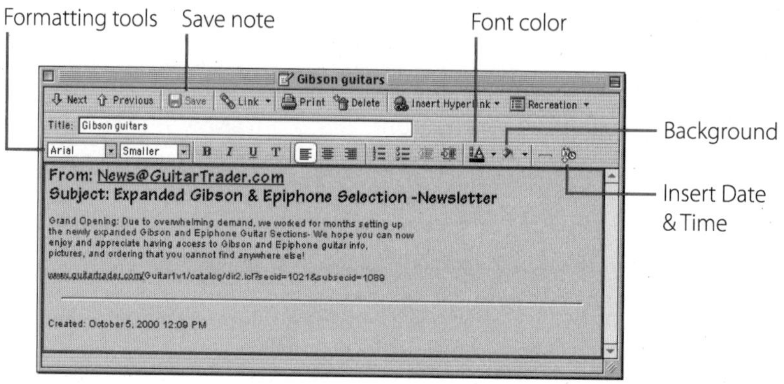

FIGURE 18-12.

A completed note can contain paragraph and text formatting, rules, timestamps, and a background color

Formatting tools   Save note   Font color

— Background

— Insert Date & Time

The composition area of the note window supports drag-and-drop. You can, for example, add the text of an entire e-mail message to the note by dragging the message header from your Inbox into the composition area of the note. You can also do the same thing with selected text from an e-mail message or a Word document. And, of course, copy-and-paste also works.

To view or edit an existing note, follow these steps:

1 Click the Notes icon in the Folder List to open the Notes window, as shown in Figure 18-13. If you prefer, you can open the Notes window by pressing ⌘-6 or choosing Notes from the Window menu.

2 Double-click the note's header in the list. The note opens in its own window.

3 Read and edit the note, as desired. (Note that you can also change the note's title.)

4 If you've made any changes to the note, click the Save button and then close the note window. Otherwise, you can just close the note window.

FIGURE 18-13.

The Notes list is similar in appearance and function to the message header list when using Entourage for e-mail

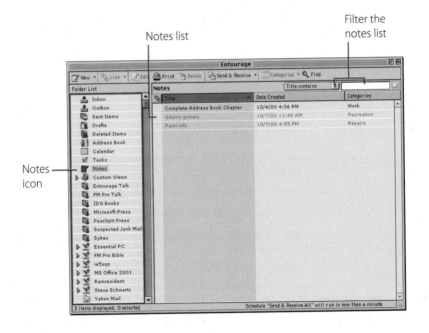

Notes list

Filter the notes list

Notes icon

If you want to delete a note that you no longer need, select it in the notes list and do one of the following:

- Click the Delete button.

- Press the Delete key.

- Press ⌘-Delete.

- Choose Delete Note from the Edit menu.

- Control-click it, and choose Delete Note.

- Drag it to the Trash.

Sorting and Searching the Notes List

As in other Entourage windows, you can sort the Notes list and search for particular notes as follows:

- You can sort the notes in the Notes window or list by title, date created, or category. (Click any of these three column headers to sort by that column.) To change the order of the sort (from ascending to descending or vice versa), click the same column header again.

- To find particular notes or ones that match your criteria, you can filter the Notes list by title or category or—for more sophisticated searches—you can issue the Edit menu's Find or Advanced Find command. Filtering and searches work the same in the Notes window as they do in all other Entourage windows. For instructions, see Chapter 4.

Linking Items to Other Items

As you've seen, Entourage contains many, many components—e-mail, newsgroups, the Address Book, the Calendar, tasks, and notes. While they all are dedicated to managing information, the relationships between them aren't always obvious. The components can easily stand alone and are often used that way.

However, Entourage has a feature called *links* with which you can create connections among all types of Entourage items, as well as create links to files on your hard disk. By creating links, you can avoid duplicating information and manage your projects better. When viewing the relevant Entourage list, the presence of one or more links is indicated by a chain symbol in the Links column.

Here's an example: Suppose you're asked to write a review for *Macworld*. Using Entourage, you can create a task for the article with its due date and a reminder. To make it simple to manage the writing process, you can create links between the task and:

- The Word document in which you're composing the article

- The Photoshop graphics you'll be using for screen shots

- Relevant e-mail messages you've received from the editor and product manager

- The editor's and product manager's contact cards in the Address Book

When the reminder pops up onscreen, you can open any of the linked items by clicking the Links button—enabling you to edit the article or screen shots, review related e-mail messages, or send e-mail to the editor or product manager.

Creating Links

You can link items to existing items, to existing files, and to new items you intend to create, as described in the following lists.

To link an item to an existing item, follow these steps:

1 In the Folder List, click the icon of the list (e-mail, newsgroups, the Address Book, the Calendar, tasks or notes) that contains the item that you want to link to other items.

2 Select the item.

3 Click the down arrow on the right side of the Link button in the toolbar, choose Link To Existing, and then choose the item type to which you want to link: a message, Calendar event, task, note, Address Book contact, address group, or file.

4 The appropriate window opens and comes to the front. (If it does not come to the front, select its name from the Window menu.) A Link Maker window appears, as shown in Figure 18-14.

FIGURE 18-14.

Drag the items you want to link to into the Link Maker window

Drag items here

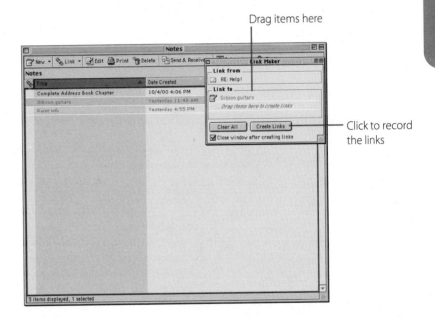

Click to record the links

5 Drag the desired item (or items) into the Link Maker window.

6 Click the Create Links button to record the links.

To link an item to an existing file:

1 Perform steps 1 and 2 from the first list (selecting the Entourage item you want to link to a file).

2 Click the down arrow on the right side of the Link button in the toolbar, choose Link To Existing, and then choose File. A standard file dialog box appears.

3 Select the file and click Link.

To link an item to a new item, follow these steps:

1 Perform steps 1 and 2 from the first list (selecting the Entourage item you want to link to a new item).

2 Click the down arrow on the right side of the Link button in the toolbar, choose Link To New, and then choose the item type to which you want to link. An appropriate window appears, enabling you to create a new e-mail message, Calendar event, task, note, and so on.

3 Create the item as you usually do. (Some items, such as notes and tasks, must be completed by clicking the Save button in the toolbar.)

4 Drag the new item to the Link Maker window, and click the Create Links button.

 **TIP**

Another way to link items is to click in the Links column of any message, task, contact, and so on. You'll see the same Links pop-up menu that appears when you click the Links toolbar button.

Entourage provides an optional automatic link that you may want to take advantage of. You can automatically link all outgoing messages to the recipient's contact card in the Address Book. Open the Edit menu, choose Preferences, and then choose General. You can set this option by clicking the Address Book tab.

Opening Linked Items

To open a linked item, click the down arrow on the right side of the Link toolbar button or click the link icon beside the item. A pop-up menu appears, as shown in Figure 18-15, which lists all items that are linked to the current item. (Notice that each type of item has its own hierarchical menu.) Choose the linked item that you want to open.

FIGURE 18-15.

You can open any link to the selected item by choosing from this pop-up menu

Another way to open linked items—as well as to simultaneously view *all* linked items for the selected item—is to click the Link toolbar button or choose Open Links from the pop-up menu. A Links To window appears, as shown in Figure 18-16. To open any of the displayed links, double-click the link, or select the link and click the Open button.

FIGURE 18-16.

You can manage the links attached to the selected item (viewing, deleting, or adding additional links) in the Links To window

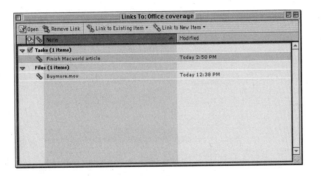

Deleting Links

When particular links are no longer needed, you can eliminate them. To delete links, start by opening the Links To window as explained in the previous section. Select the link you want to eliminate, and click the Remove Link button. (See Figure 18-16.)

CHAPTER 19

Writing and Sending E-Mail

In this chapter, you'll learn to compose and send e-mail messages, as well as reply to and forward messages you've received from others.

Types of E-Mail Messages

Microsoft Entourage enables you to create the following types of messages:

- **New Message** This is a message you are creating from scratch.

- **Reply** A reply is a response to a received message. When you reply to a message, its Subject is automatically set to Re: *original subject*. In order for the recipient to know what you're responding to, his/her original text is generally quoted—denoted by a greater-than character (>) at the start of each quoted line, as shown in Figure 19-1. Entourage automatically quotes the entire original message, but you are free to edit it or delete the irrelevant portions.

- **Forward** You'll sometimes receive messages that you want to forward to other people. The Subject of a forwarded message is normally entitled Fwd: *original subject*.

- **Redirect** A redirected message serves the same purpose as a forwarded message. However, there are two differences. First, while a forwarded message is clearly marked as such (*Fwd:*), a redirected message is identical to the original message. Second, while a forwarded message displays your e-mail address in the From line, a redirected message shows the message's original author in the From line. Use Redirect when a message was sent to you by mistake or if you sent a message to the wrong person.

FIGURE 19-1.

Quoted text from the original message is denoted by a greater-than character (>) in the reply message

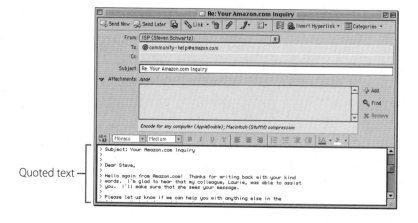

Quoted text —

The process of creating a message is the same, regardless of the type of message. While this chapter focuses on creating *new* messages, you can also use these instructions to help you create replies, forwards, or redirects. All you have to do is select the message header in the message list (or open the message in its own window) and:

- From the Message menu, choose the appropriate command: Reply (⌘-R), Forward (⌘-J), or Redirect (Option-⌘-J).

- Click the appropriate button in the toolbar (Reply or Forward).

- Control-click the message header, and choose a command from the menu that appears. (See Figure 19-2.)

FIGURE 19-2.

When you Control-click a message header, you can choose the type of message action you want to take

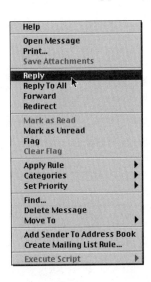

Reply, Reply to Sender, and Reply All

Because Entourage has three Reply commands, you may be confused about each one's purpose. Use Reply to reply only to the person from whom you received the message. Use Reply All to reply to the message author as well as to all other persons in the To and Cc (carbon copy) lines. If the message was from a mailing list, use Reply To Sender to reply to the message's author, rather than to the mailing list.

Message Quoting and Attribution

When replying to or forwarding a message, message quoting and message attribution text are dependent on the settings in the Reply & Forward tab of the Mail & News Preferences dialog box shown in Figure 19-3. (Open the Edit menu, choose Preferences, and then choose Mail & News.)

FIGURE 19-3.

Reply & Forward preferences

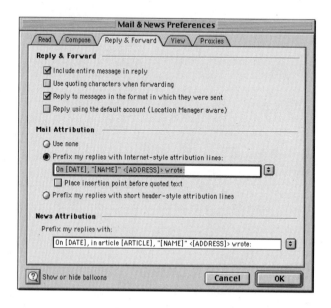

The following are the Reply & Forward preferences:

- **Include Entire Message In Reply** The original message text is automatically included in the reply. (This is a common practice, enabling the recipient to see what you're responding to.) Like other message text, you are free to edit the text or delete unnecessary portions.

- **Use Quoting Characters When Forwarding** Enable this option to precede each line of a forwarded message with a greater-than character (>). Note that since the forwarded text is preceded with the header "Forwarded Message," this isn't necessary.

- **Reply To Messages In The Format In Which They Were Sent** Message formatting (plain text vs. HTML) is set based on the format of the original message.

- **Reply Using The Default Account** When checked, all replies are automatically sent from your default e-mail account, regardless of the account to which the message was sent. Normally, you will not check this option.

IV

Microsoft Entourage

■ **Mail attribution** This is a text header that precedes the text to which you're replying. You can elect to use none; a text string of your design that can include the author's date, name, and e-mail address (as shown in Figure 19-4); or a normal Internet header.

FIGURE 19-4.

This form of attribution text quickly summarizes the original message's delivery information

Attribution text —

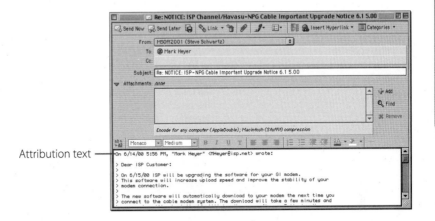

Addressing the Message

Addressing an outgoing message consists of filling in three sections of the message header as follows:

■ Specifying at least one message recipient in the To, Cc, or Bcc boxes

 NOTE

Recipient addresses in the Bcc (*blind carbon copy*) box are hidden from all other recipients of the e-mail.

■ Entering a Subject (or title) for the message

■ Choosing a From e-mail address (if you have multiple e-mail accounts)

Although Entourage provides many shortcuts for completing the message header, you'll create a new message by doing one of the following:

■ With the Inbox or another e-mail account selected in the Folder List, click the New button in the toolbar.

■ Click the down arrow on the right side of the New button in the toolbar, and choose Mail Message.

- From the File menu, choose New and then choose Mail Message.

- Press ⌘-N. (This works only when the Inbox or another e-mail account is selected in the Folder List.)

- Press Option-⌘-N. (This works no matter what is currently selected in the Folder List.)

A new, untitled message window appears, as shown in Figure 19-5. Unless a secondary e-mail account was selected in the Folder List when you issued the New Message command, the From line contains your default e-mail account. The cursor is positioned in the To line.

FIGURE 19-5.

A blank new message window

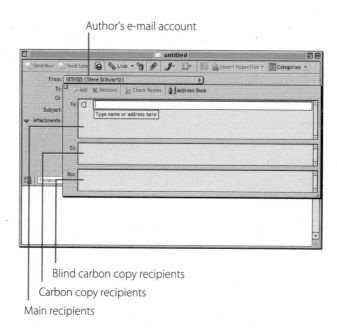

Author's e-mail account

Blind carbon copy recipients

Carbon copy recipients

Main recipients

To complete the message header, follow these steps:

1 If the recipient has a contact record in your Address Book, begin typing any part of his or her name or e-mail address. All possible matches from the Address Book are presented in a drop-down list, as shown in Figure 19-6. If the recipient's name is in the list, click to select it. The cursor drops to the next line, enabling you to specify an additional To recipient, if you like.

FIGURE 19-6.

As you type, Entourage presents all matching names and addresses from your Address Book

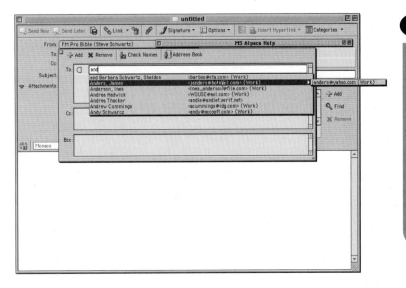

IV

Microsoft Entourage

If the recipient is *not* in your Address Book, type or paste his or her complete e-mail address into the To line and press Tab. The cursor drops to the next line, enabling you to specify an additional To recipient, if you want.

If you prefer to select recipients directly from the Address Book, click the Address Book button. The Address Book appears in the right side of the window, as shown in Figure 19-7. To add a recipient, drag his or her name into the To, Cc, or Bcc box.

FIGURE 19-7.

If you want, you can display the Address Book and then select recipients from it

Address Book pane

2 To add Cc or Bcc recipients, press Tab or click in the Cc or Bcc areas of the message header.

3 Click the address section's close box. The cursor drops into the Subject box.

4 Enter a Subject for the message.

> If you later need to change the recipient list, click in the address section. To delete a recipient, select his or her name and click the Remove button. To add a recipient, click in the To, Cc, or Bcc box (as appropriate) and then click the Add button or tab to the next blank line. To move a recipient between the To, Cc, and Bcc areas, drag his or her name to the correct area.

More Ways to Address a Message

You can also address a message by doing any of the following:

- Open the Address Book by selecting or double-clicking it in the Folder List, by choosing Address Book from the Window menu, or by pressing ⌘-2. Control-click a name and choose New Message To.

- Open the Address Book, select a name, and choose New Message To from the Contact menu.

- Drag a person's name from the Address Book into the appropriate section of the message header (To, Cc, or Bcc).

- Click a *mailto* link (shown in Figure 19-8) found on a Web page or in the text of a received e-mail message. (A mailto link specifies an e-mail address. When clicked, a mailto link launches your e-mail program and addresses a new message to the recipient specified by the link.)

FIGURE 19-8.

Mailto links are frequently embedded in messages—in the header text, body, or signature

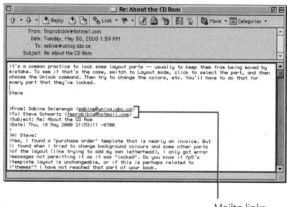

Mailto links

To, Cc, and Bcc Recipients

As you can see, there are three classes of recipients you can specify when creating a message. Persons in the To box are the primary recipients; persons in the Cc (carbon copy) box are secondary recipients; and persons in the Bcc (blind carbon copy) box are recipients who are invisible to all other recipients—as well as to other Bcc recipients.

Note that while you must have at least one recipient for each message, he or she can be listed in the To, Cc, or Bcc box. For example, if you don't want any of the recipients to know who received this message, you can enter all of their e-mail addresses in the Bcc line.

The Message Body

Type or paste the message text into the bottom half of the message window. Entourage works just like a standard word processing program. As you type and edit, words automatically wrap to the next line as needed. You only have to press Return when you want to begin a new paragraph.

Like other modern e-mail applications, Entourage can send and receive two types of messages: *plain text* (messages without paragraph formatting using a single font, size, and style for text) and *HTML* (messages with paragraph formatting and multiple fonts, sizes, and styles for text). All e-mail programs can interpret plain text messages. HTML messages can only be read by more advanced e-mail programs or with a Web browser.

Whether an outgoing message is plain text or formatted HTML depends on your Mail & News Preferences settings (in the Compose and Reply & Forward tabs) and on whether you've manually chosen a different format for the current message, as follows:

- When creating a new message, the default mail format is used, as specified in the Compose tab of the Mail & News Preferences dialog box (shown in Figure 19-9). If you prefer to use the alternate mail format for this message, choose HTML from the Format menu or click the Use HTML button above the message area, if it is visible.

- When replying to or forwarding a message, the format is determined by the setting for Reply To Messages In The Format In Which They Were Sent, found in the Reply & Forward tab of the Mail & News Preferences dialog box. (See Figure 19-3.) If you prefer to use the alternate mail format for this message, choose HTML from the Format menu or click the Use HTML button above the message area, if it is visible.

Whether the HTML formatting toolbar is visible above the message area depends on the relevant setting in the Compose tab of the Mail & News Preferences dialog box. (See Figure 19-9.)

FIGURE 19-9.

New e-mail messages are automatically formatted to match the setting in the Mail & News Preferences dialog box

Default e-mail message format

When typing or editing an HTML message, you can choose fonts, styles, colors, and sizes; adjust paragraph formatting settings; add horizontal rules; and add a message background color from the HTML formatting toolbar or from the Format menu. As with a word processing program, you can freely mix fonts, paragraph formats, and other formatting options.

If you have a document that was created in a drag-and-drop–enabled program (such as Word), you can select text in that document and drag it into your e-mail message. If you set the message format to HTML prior to dragging the text, the fonts, sizes, and styles will be retained. Note that you can also copy and paste formatted text into an HTML message.

TIP

When writing a message, you can also drag-and-drop selected text *within* the message, making it easy to rearrange sentences and paragraphs without having to cut and paste.

Adding Attachments

E-mail messages can optionally contain one or more *attachments* (document files and/or programs sent via e-mail). If you want to e-mail a copy of a business proposal or some recent pictures, you can attach them to an e-mail message.

 NOTE

Many ISP mail servers have a maximum size limit for incoming e-mail messages. It's a good practice to check with your recipients before e-mailing large files to them (bigger than 1MB, for example).

To add an attachment to a message, follow these steps:

1 In the message window, expand the Attachments box by clicking the tiny triangle, shown in Figure 19-10.

FIGURE 19-10.

To view the list of attached files, you can expand the Attachments box

Click to show/hide Attachments box

Add Attachments button

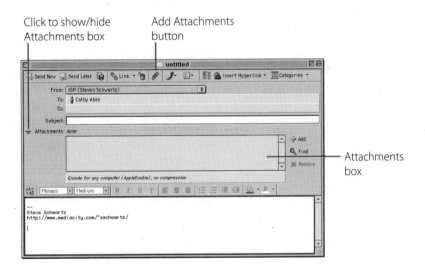

Attachments box

2 Add an attachment by doing any of the following:

- Click the Add button.
- Click the Add Attachments button.

- From the Message menu, choose Add Attachments (or press ⌘-E).

- Drag a file icon into the Attachments box.

3 If you use one of the first three methods, the Choose Attachment dialog box appears, as shown in Figure 19-11. Select a file and click Choose.

FIGURE 19-11.

Navigate to the drive and folder in which the file is located, select it, and then click Choose

	Choose Attachment	
⊆ PB3400	▼	🗁 📖 🕓
Name		Date Modified ⬜
📘 Tranquility		10/10/99
▷ 📓 FAXstf Pro 5.0		6/12/99
🐾 *FileMaker Pro*		10/16/99
▷ 🗋 FileMaker Pro 5 Folder		10/16/99
▷ 🗋 FMsync		5/18/00
▷ 🗋 Fonts		7/20/99 ▼
Select files to attach		
⓪	Open	Cancel	Choose

4 To add other attachments, repeat steps 2 and 3.

▷ NOTE

If you change your mind about sending one or more of the attachments, select them in the Attachments box and click Remove.

5 Change the encoding, compression, and compatibility settings, if desired.

- The default encoding, compression, and compatibility settings are displayed beneath the Attachments box. To change the default settings, open the Edit menu, choose Preferences, choose Mail & News, click the Compose tab, and click the Click Here for Attachment Options button in the Attachments section of the dialog box, as shown in Figure 19-12. To ensure that your attachments can be opened on either a Mac or on Windows, choose Any Computer (AppleDouble) as the encoding method and None for the compression method.

② SEE ALSO

For information about opening and viewing attachments in received messages, see Chapter 20, "Reading and Managing E-Mail."

- To change these settings for only the current message, click the long button beneath the Attachments box, as shown in Figure 19-13.

FIGURE 19-12.

You can specify the default encoding, compression, and compatibility settings for attachments

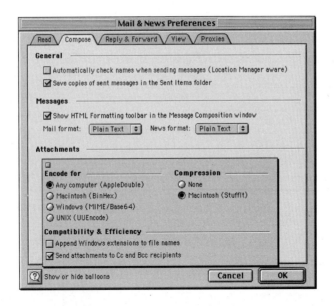

FIGURE 19-13.

You can change the encoding, compression, and compatibility settings for the current message

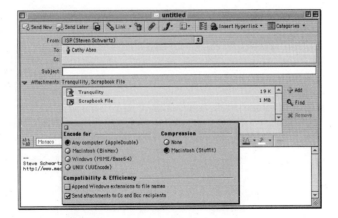

Attachment Encoding and Compression Settings

All messages delivered over the Internet must be encoded. You can send attachments to a Mac using AppleDouble or BinHex encoding, and to a PC using AppleDouble or Multipurpose Internet Mail Extensions (MIME) encoding. If you don't know the recipient's computing platform, use AppleDouble encoding.

You can only use StuffIt to compress attachments into an archive if you have Aladdin System's StuffIt Deluxe installed on your Mac. (To open a StuffIt archive, the recipient must have StuffIt Expander, StuffIt Deluxe, or a similar program. Windows users will not be able to open StuffIt archives unless they have Aladdin Expander for Windows—free from *www.aladdinsys.com/expander/expander_win_login.html*).

Signatures and Priorities

The following sections discuss two additional options you may want to use in your messages: adding personal signature text to the end of messages, and specifying a priority (to alert the recipient to the message's importance).

Adding a Signature

A *signature* is one or more lines of text that you use to conclude an e-mail message or newsgroup post. A signature can contain your name, a Web site address, your contact information, a witty saying, or anything else you want. You can create as many different signatures as you want, assign a default signature to automatically be appended to messages from a given account, manually attach a signature to a message, or instruct Entourage to assign signatures to messages on a random basis.

Creating Signatures

You can create a signature by editing the default signature (named *Standard*) or by designing and naming new ones. To create a signature, follow these steps:

1 From the Tools menu, choose Signatures. The Signatures window appears, as shown in Figure 19-14.

FIGURE 19-14.

The Signatures window lists all defined signatures

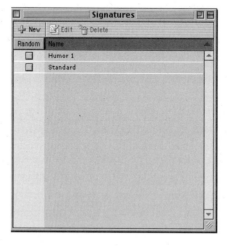

2 To edit the Standard signature, select its name and click Edit. To create a signature from scratch (using a name of your choosing), click the New button. A window appears in which you can create the signature. (See Figure 19-15.)

FIGURE 19-15.

You can create as many new signatures as you like, as well as edit existing ones

Enable/disable HTML formatting

Signature identifier

Include in random signature list

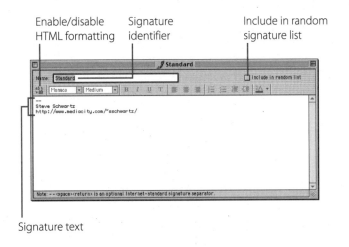

Signature text

3 Specify a name for the signature in the Name text box.

4 Signatures can be plain text or formatted (HTML). To create a formatted signature, click the Use HTML button above the text window. (When HTML is enabled, items in the window's formatting toolbar are enabled.) Type your signature in the text box.

5 *Optional:* If you want to use Entourage's random signature feature and want this signature to be available randomly, click the Include In Random List check box.

6 Click the window's close box. You will have an opportunity to save the new or edited signature.

7 Click the Signatures window's close box.

TIP

If you create an HTML signature and attach it to a plain text message, it is automatically converted to plain text in order to match the message format. Since this is the case, you might as well create *all* signatures in HTML format.

Designating Random Signatures

If you like, you can designate several signatures as members of your "random" list. You can then instruct Entourage to automatically append one of the signatures—at random—to all outgoing messages for a given account or manually append one to the message you're currently writing.

To designate a signature a part of the random list, open the Tools menu and choose Signatures. Check the box before the signature name to include the signature in the random list, as shown in Figure 19-16. You can also add or remove a signature from the random list when you are creating or editing the signature. (See Figure 19-15.)

FIGURE 19-16.

Click the check box for any signature to make it a member of the random list

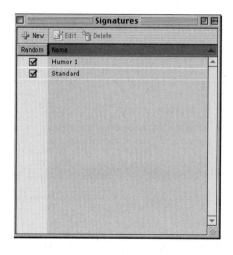

Specifying a Default Signature

Every e-mail and newsgroup account can have a default signature that is automatically appended to every outgoing message. To specify a default signature for an account, follow these steps:

1 From the Tools menu, choose Accounts. The Accounts window appears, as shown in Figure 19-17.

FIGURE 19-17.

Select an account to edit from the Accounts window

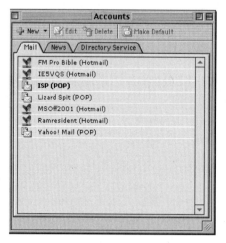

2 Select an account and click Edit (or double-click the account name). The Edit Account window appears.

3 Click the Options tab at the top of the window, as shown in Figure 19-18.

FIGURE 19-18.

Choose a default signature from this pop-up menu

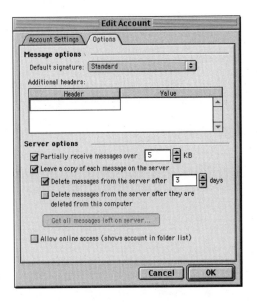

4 To specify a default signature for this account, choose one from the Default Signature pop-up menu. Choose None if you don't want a default signature. Otherwise, choose a named signature or Random (if you've added at least one signature to the Random list).

5 Click the OK button to save your changes.

6 Repeat steps 2 through 5 for your other e-mail accounts, if you want.

> **NOTE**

You can also specify a default signature for each newsgroup account by following the same procedure.

Manually Assigning a Signature to a Message

To manually append a saved signature to the current message, choose Signature from the Message menu and then choose the signature you want to use. You can also select a signature by clicking the Signature toolbar button. The chosen signature is appended to the bottom of the message. If a default or another selected signature is already at the bottom of the message, the newly chosen signature replaces it.

Setting a Priority

If you want, you can specify an importance (*priority*) for any outgoing message. How—or even whether—the priority will be noted by the recipient depends on his or her e-mail program. To set a priority for an open message, choose it from the Priority submenu of the Message menu or the Options toolbar button. (See Figure 19-19.) A priority indicator appears immediately beneath the message's toolbar, as shown in Figure 19-20.

FIGURE 19-19.

You can choose a message priority in the Priority submenu

FIGURE 19-20.

The message priority is indicated above the message header

Priority indicator

> **NOTE**
>
> By default, every message is assigned a Normal priority. Setting a different priority does *not* affect the message's delivery. It merely serves as an indicator of the message's importance.

If you examine the message header list, you'll note that priority is also shown there. (See Figure 19-21.) See Table 19-1 for an explanation of what the different priority symbols represent.

FIGURE 19-21.

The third column in the message list shows the priority symbol which has been assigned to each message

Priority symbols

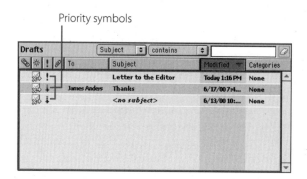

Table 19-1. Priority Symbols.

Priority Setting	Priority Symbol
Highest priority	Red exclamation point
High priority	Orange exclamation point
Normal priority	Blank
Low priority	Light blue down arrow
Lowest priority	Dark blue down arrow

 TIP

Another way to assign a priority to a message is to Control-click in the priority column of any message header in the message list and choose a priority setting from the Set Priority submenu. You can alter the priority for a message regardless of whether it has already been sent or is a message that you've received. To sort the messages in a folder by priority, click the Priority heading (the exclamation point) above the message list.

Sending the Message

When you've finished writing your message, you can send it in any of the following ways:

- **Send Now/Post Now** To send the message immediately, click the Send Now toolbar button, open the Message menu and choose Send Message Now, or press ⌘-K. (If the message is addressed to a newsgroup rather than to an individual, the button and command read Post Now and Post Message Now.)

 NOTE

If you aren't connected to the Internet when you perform a Send Now/Post Now, Entourage acts as if you've chosen Send Later/Post Later. The message is automatically stored in your Outbox until the next time you connect and perform a Send All or Send & Receive All.

- **Send Later/Post Later** To store the message in the Outbox until the next time a Send All or a Send & Receive All is performed (either manually or via a schedule), click the Send Later toolbar button, open the Message menu and choose Send Message Later, or press Option-⌘-K. (If the message is addressed to a newsgroup rather than to an individual, the button and command read Post Later and Post Message Later.)

NOTE

To send the messages in the Outbox manually, open the Send & Receive submenu of the Tools menu and choose Send All (Shift-⌘-K) or Send & Receive All (⌘-M).

■ **Save a Message as a Draft** If you aren't ready to send the message, you can store it in the Drafts folder—completing and sending it at another time. To store a message as a draft, open the File menu and choose Save (⌘-S), Save As, or Close (⌘-W). Or you can just click the message's close box. As long as you elect to save the message when prompted, it will be moved to the Drafts folder. (See Figures 19-22a and 19-22b.) When you're ready to complete and send the message, open the Drafts folder, edit the message, and then send it using any of the previously described methods.

FIGURES 19-22A.
When you save a message as a draft, this explanatory dialog box appears

FIGURE 19-22B.
When you close a message window, click Save to store the message in the Drafts folder, Don't Save to discard it, or Cancel to continue editing the message

Checking Your Spelling

Prior to sending a message, you can use the Office spell checker to correct any spelling errors or typos you have made. The manner in which spell-checking works depends on settings in the General Preferences dialog box, shown in Figure 19-23. To display the dialog box, open the Edit menu, choose Preferences, and then choose General. Click the Spelling tab in the General Preferences dialog box that appears.

Here are some of the most important spelling preference settings:

■ **Check Spelling As You Type** When checked, potentially misspelled words in the message are marked with squiggly red underlines. (See Figure 19-24.)

- **Always Check Spelling Before Queuing Outgoing Messages** If this option is checked and you issue a Send Now, Post Now, Send Later, or Post Later command, a spell check is automatically performed.

- **Suggest From Main Dictionary Only** When unchecked, suggested corrections can also be drawn from a designated custom (user-created) dictionary. Otherwise, suggestions are restricted to words found in the Office main dictionary.

- **Custom Dictionary** Click the Dictionaries button to locate the desired custom dictionary to use in combination with the main dictionary.

FIGURE 19-23.

You can set or view your spelling preferences in the General Preferences dialog box

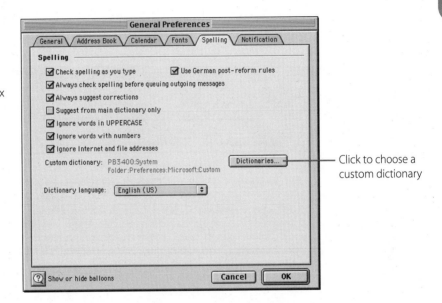

Click to choose a custom dictionary

FIGURE 19-24.

When you've enabled the Check Spelling As You Type option, each word is automatically spell-checked when you complete the word

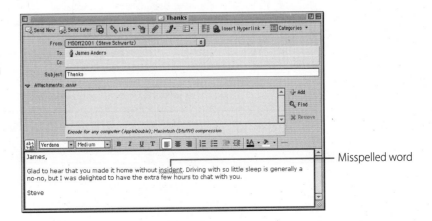

Misspelled word

To manually request a spell check for the current message, choose Spelling from the Tools menu or press Option-⌘-L. If no text is selected, the spell check starts at the beginning of the message. On the other hand, if text is selected, the spell check is restricted to that text. When the selected text has been checked, you are given the option to check the rest of the message.

Whether the spell check is automatic or manual, the process is the same. When Entourage identifies a suspect word, the Spelling dialog box appears. (See Figure 19-25.)

FIGURE 19-25.

The Spelling dialog box appears when Entourage identifies a suspect word

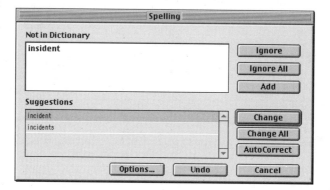

For each potentially misspelled word, you can do the following:

- Click Ignore to accept the word as correct in this instance only.

- Click Ignore All to accept the word as correct in all instances found in the message.

- Click Add to accept the word as correct and add it to the current custom dictionary (so it won't be flagged in future messages).

- Click Change to substitute the highlighted word in the Suggestions list for this instance of the misspelled word.

- Click Change All to substitute the highlighted word in the Suggestions list for all instances of the misspelled word found in this message.

- Click AutoCorrect to add this misspelling to Office's AutoCorrect list. (If you later misspell the same word in the same way—*thier* rather than *their*, for example—it will automatically be corrected.)

NOTE

> If you ignore a misspelled word and later recheck the message, the word will be assumed to be correct.

Checking Addresses Using Directory Services

If you don't have a current e-mail address for a recipient, you can use one of several directory services to search for the person's e-mail address. Any person's name (such as William Jones) entered into the To, Cc, or Bcc line is considered an unknown if it isn't found in your Address Book. Unknown names are preceded by a question mark (?) in the message header.

By setting an option in the General tab of the Mail & News Preferences dialog box, you can instruct Entourage to consult a directory service automatically when an unknown name is encountered. If you are composing a message, you can also manually check all unknown names by clicking the Check Names button, choosing Check Names from the Tools menu, or pressing Shift-⌘-C. For more information on using directory services, see Chapter 18, "The Calendar and Information Management Features."

Filing Outgoing Messages

When creating and sending a message, there are several storage options available to you:

- **Save Message To Sent Items Folder** By default, as soon as each outgoing message is sent from the Outbox, the message is stored in the Sent Items folder. If you'd rather not save your outgoing messages, open the Edit menu, choose Preferences, choose Mail & News, click the Compose tab in the Mail & News Preferences dialog box that appears (shown in Figure 19-9), and remove the check mark from the Save Copies Of Sent Messages In The Sent Items Folder option.

- **Save Message To A Different Folder** Regardless of whether Entourage normally saves outgoing messages in the Sent Items folder, you can direct individual outgoing messages to a different folder. Before sending the message, open the Message menu, choose After Sending, Move To, and then Choose Folder. The Choose Folder window appears, as shown in Figure 19-26. Select a destination folder and click Choose.

FIGURE 19-26.

Use the Choose Folder dialog box to route the message to a folder other than one of the standard Entourage folders

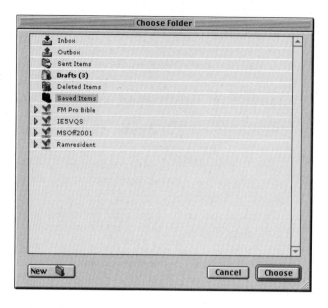

 **NOTE**

Even after a message has been sent, you can move it to a different folder by dragging it into a folder in the Folder List. You can also move a message by selecting it in the Sent Items Folder and then choosing the Move To command from the Message menu, or by clicking the Move button in the toolbar.

After Your Messages Have Been Sent

After you've sent a message, you can view it by checking in the Sent Items folder. If a message was not delivered properly, you can also elect to resend it—to the same or a different address.

Viewing Sent Messages

By default, copies of all your sent messages are stored in the Sent Items folder. (This is determined by a setting in the Compose tab of the Mail & News Preferences dialog box.) To examine any of your sent messages, click the Sent Items folder in the Folder List and select the message header. Unless you manually delete sent messages, they will remain indefinitely in the Sent Items folder.

> **NOTE**
>
> Some types of Web-based e-mail accounts, such as Hotmail, also have a Sent Items folder. Refer to the e-mail service's instructions to determine whether sent items are automatically saved or whether you must issue a command each time to save them.

Resending a Message

You can resend any message—as long as you were the original author and it was sent from a point of presence (POP) account. Being able to resend a message is useful if the original was addressed to the wrong person, you forgot to attach important files, or it simply failed to arrive at its destination (because of a server error, for example).

To resend a message, follow these steps:

1 Highlight the message header in the message list, or open the message in its own window.

2 From the Message menu, choose Resend. (If the message is open in its own window, you can also click the Resend button in the toolbar, as shown in Figure 19-27.) A copy of the message opens in its own window.

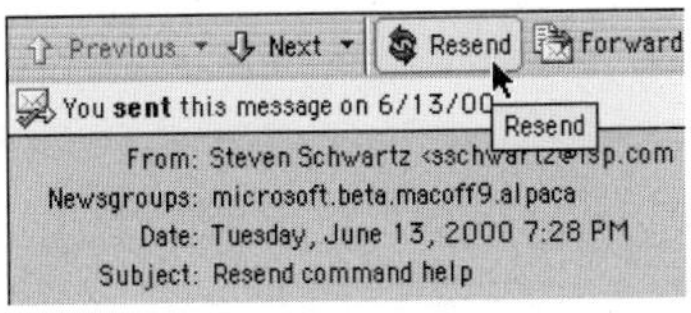

FIGURE 19-27.

The Resend button allows you to resend an e-mail message

3 Make any necessary changes to the message, and send it with the Send Now or Send Later command. (Note that if the message was a newsgroup post, the equivalent commands are Post Now and Post Later.)

Reading and Managing E-Mail

I f you're like most users, you'll find that the majority of your time in Microsoft Entourage will be spent reading and handling incoming e-mail. In this chapter, you'll learn about the different ways that you can retrieve waiting e-mail, read your messages, work with attachments, and manage your e-mail.

Retrieving E-Mail

As long as you are connected to the Internet and Entourage is running, you can retrieve incoming e-mail in two ways:

- Automatically by executing a schedule.

- Manually by issuing a send/receive command or manually executing a schedule.

Entourage includes a Send & Receive All schedule for sending and retrieving all waiting e-mail. At fixed time intervals, the Send & Receive All schedule checks for, and then downloads, new mail. To view this schedule, open the Tools menu, choose Schedules, and then double-click the Send & Receive All schedule. (See Figure 20-1.) For help modifying this schedule, see Chapter 23, "Customizing Microsoft Entourage for E-Mail and Newsgroups."

FIGURE 20-1.

A Send & Receive All schedule

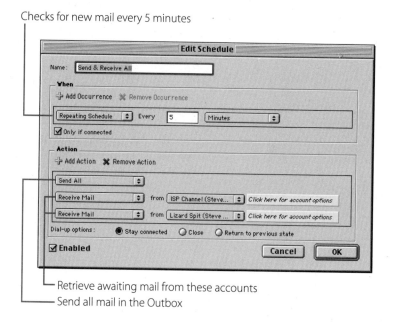

Checks for new mail every 5 minutes

Retrieve awaiting mail from these accounts
Send all mail in the Outbox

To manually check for and retrieve new e-mail, you can do any of the following:

- Perform a Send & Receive All by opening the Tools menu, pointing to Send & Receive, and then choosing Send & Receive All; clicking the Send & Receive button; clicking the down arrow on the right side of the Send & Receive button and choosing Send & Receive All; pressing ⌘-M; or by opening the Tools menu, pointing to Run Schedule, and then choosing Send & Receive All. New e-mail from all accounts associated with the Send & Receive All schedule will be downloaded.

■ Perform a send/receive for any e-mail account by opening the Tools menu, pointing to Send & Receive, and then choosing the account name. (See Figure 20-2.) Alternately, you can click the down arrow on the right side of the Send & Receive button and choose the account from the pop-up menu that appears.

FIGURE 20-2.

Retrieving messages from a single account

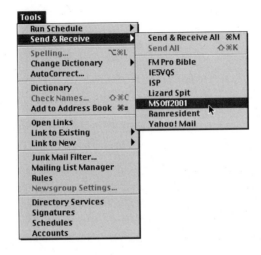

TIP

Another way to manually retrieve e-mail from a Hotmail or IMAP-based account is to click the account name in the Folder List, expand the folder, and then click the desired account folder (such as the Inbox).

■ Manually run any other receive schedule you've defined by opening the Tools menu, pointing to Run Schedule, and then choosing the name of the schedule.

TIP

If you didn't tell Entourage to store an account's logon passwords, you will be prompted for a password each time Entourage does a send/receive for the account. To allow Entourage to send and retrieve e-mail without requesting your password, open the Tools menu, choose Accounts, double-click the account name in the Accounts dialog box, enter the account's password as shown in Figure 20-3, and then click OK.

FIGURE 20-3.

You can instruct Entourage to save and use your log-on password

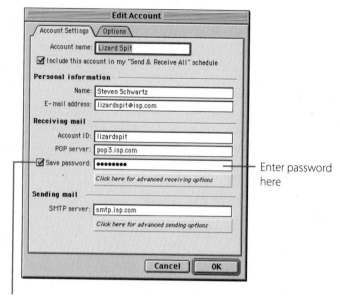

Enter password here

Save password to use automatically

When new e-mail arrives, it is automatically stored in a folder, shown in Figure 20-4. Messages addressed to your POP accounts appear in the main Inbox folder. Messages addressed to other accounts (Hotmail, IMAP, and others) are routed to their respective account folders.

FIGURE 20-4.

When a folder or an account contains un-read messages, its name is displayed in boldface

Unread e-mail indicator

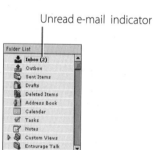

 TIP

You can edit the text of any incoming message by selecting the message header (or opening the message in its own window), opening the Message menu, and choosing Edit Message. You can use this technique to add notes to messages, for example.

⭐ **TIP**

To store particular types of incoming messages in different folders, you can create *message rules*, as explained in Chapter 23. For example, you could automatically route all messages from family members to a special Family folder.

Reading and Managing Incoming Messages

Of course, the point of retrieving your e-mail is to read it and—if necessary—respond to it. (Responding to messages is discussed in Chapter 19, "Writing and Sending E-Mail.") Reading messages is a simple process and is explained below.

Parts of the Entourage Window

The Entourage main window is divided into three parts, as shown in Figure 20-5.

FIGURE 20-5.

Parts of the Entourage window

Folder List   Currently selected header   Message list

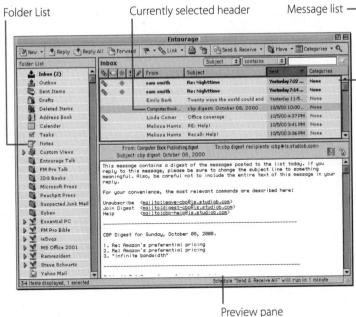

Preview pane

The Folder List contains all the Entourage default folders (such as the Inbox, Outbox, and Sent Items), all user-created folders and accounts, and icons for important Entourage components (such as the Address Book and Calendar). If a folder name is shown in boldface, it means that it holds unread or unsent messages. If a number is also shown, it means that the folder contains that many unread or unsent messages. To view the contents of a folder, click the folder in the Folder List.

The Message List displays the headers of all messages in the currently selected folder. The headers let you easily identify the message's author and subject, and when it was sent. Unless you have changed the standard viewing preferences, headers for unread messages are shown in boldface and read messages are normal text. To sort the message headers, click any of the headings above the message list. If you click a heading a second time, the sort order is reversed.

> You can sort by the From heading to quickly find all messages from a particular person. To do so, click the From column heading.

You can use the Preview Pane to read the message for the currently selected header in the message list. Certain attachments, such as some types of pictures and movies, are automatically displayed in the preview pane. For more information about attachments, see "Working with Attachments" later in this chapter.

Reading Messages

The process of reading a message—whether it's a new message that has just arrived in your Inbox, one that you've stored for safekeeping in another folder, one that you've previously sent, or one that's sitting in the Delete Items folder—is always the same:

1 In the Folder List, select the folder that contains the message you want to read. The message headers for that folder are displayed in the message list.

2 Scroll through the message list until you see the message you want to read. (You can scroll through the list by using the scroll arrows, scroll box, PageUp and PageDown keys, and so on.)

3 Click the header of the message that you want to read. (See Figure 20-5.) You can also select a message header by pressing the up and down arrow keys. The message for the selected header appears in the preview pane. (If the preview pane isn't visible, open the View menu and choose Preview Pane.)

4 To scroll through the message, you can use the scrollbar or press spacebar (to scroll down) and Shift-spacebar (to scroll up).

5 To read additional messages in this folder, return to step 2. To read messages in another folder, return to step 1.

In addition to reading new messages that are delivered to your Inbox, you can read messages in any folder—even those that are in the Deleted Items folder. Select the folder in which the message you want to read is stored, and then click its header in the message list.

Reading in the Preview Pane vs. in a Separate Window

While you'll find it convenient to read most messages in the preview pane, you can also open any message in its own window. The advantage of doing this is that you can devote the entire screen to the message, making it easier to read. To open a message in its own window, double-click the message header in the message list; select the header and choose Open Message from the File menu; press ⌘-O; or select the header and press Enter.

To read additional messages in the same window, click the Previous or Next buttons in the toolbar; choose Previous from the View menu (⌘-[) or choose Next from the View menu (⌘-]); or click the down arrow on the right side of the Previous or Next button and choose a command, as shown in Figure 20-6. When you're done reading messages, click the message window's close box.

FIGURE 20-6.

Reading messages

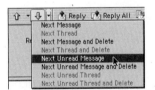

Marking Messages as Read or Unread

Entourage provides several ways for you to determine visually which messages you've read and which ones are still waiting to be read. As mentioned previously, new or unread messages are distinguished in the message list by the presence of boldface. Depending on the settings in the Read tab of the Mail & News Preferences dialog box, shown in Figure 20-7, messages are automatically marked as read after they've been displayed in the preview pane or after they've been displayed in the preview pane for a set number of seconds. (Note that Entourage treats the act of opening a message in its own window as if you'd previewed it.)

FIGURE 20-7.

You can automatically mark messages as read by setting options in the Read preferences

Automatically mark messages as read

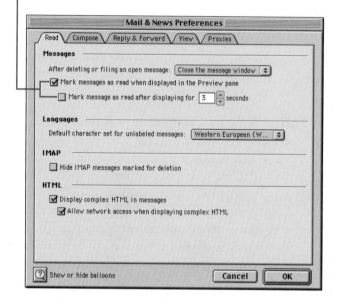

> **NOTE**
>
> If neither of these two Messages preferences are set, the only way a message's status ever changes to read is if you open the message or manually mark it as read, as described below.

You can change the status of any message by Control-clicking the message header and then choosing Mark As Read or Mark As Unread. You can also accomplish this by selecting the message header and choosing the command from the Message menu: Mark As Read (⌘-T) or Mark As Unread (Shift-⌘-T). But why would you want to change a message's read status? You might want to mark a message as unread to remind yourself that you need to respond to it. And there are messages that you regularly receive (such as ones from mailing lists or subscription services) that you seldom read. Marking them as read will tell you that you've already "handled" them.

> **NOTE**
>
> As with most other message-handling commands, you can simultaneously mark multiple messages as read or unread by Shift-clicking or ⌘-clicking them before issuing the Mark As Read or Mark As Unread command.

Changing Your Viewing Options

While the Entourage standard viewing settings will suffice for the majority of users, you can use several techniques to make message reading more enjoyable and productive.

- Depending on your needs, the default column headings above the message list may not give you all the information you require. If you don't use categories, you could eliminate the Categories column, for example. To add or remove columns, select them from the View menu by choosing Columns, as shown in Figure 20-8.

FIGURE 20-8.

To add or remove column headings, select column names by opening the View menu and choosing Columns

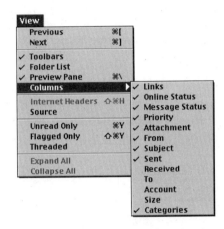

 TIP

You can rearrange the column headings by clicking and dragging them to the desired position. You can change the width of a heading by clicking its right edge and then dragging.

- You can restrict the messages that are shown in the message list by choosing a command from the View menu: Unread Only (⌘-Y) restricts the list to new and unread messages; Flagged Only (Shift-⌘-Y) shows only messages that you have manually flagged or that have been flagged by applying a message rule; and Threaded sorts messages by Subject and lists them alphabetically, enabling you to see all the messages in one place, regardless of when they were sent or received. (Click a triangle in the message list to expand or collapse a thread.) See "Organizing Your Messages" later in this chapter for assistance with flagging messages.

NOTE

To reverse the effects of the Unread Only, Flagged Only, or Threaded commands, choose the same command again. It may be necessary for you to re-sort the message list by clicking the appropriate column heading.

- To make it easier to read a particular message, you can increase or decrease the size of the font used to display the message. Select the message header and then, from the Edit menu, choose Decrease Font Size (Shift-⌘-minus) or Increase Font Size (Shift-⌘-equals sign). To change the display font and size for all messages, open the Edit menu, point to Preferences, choose General, click the Fonts tab (shown in Figure 20-9), and change the HTML Messages and Plain Text Messages settings.

- You'll sometimes notice that the text of a message has ugly line breaks, is littered with quote characters (>), or is difficult to read because it's all in uppercase. You can correct many such problems by opening the Edit menu and choosing a command from the Auto Text Cleanup submenu.

FIGURE 20-9.
The body text of all messages will be displayed in these two fonts and sizes, depending on whether they are HTML (formatted messages) or Plain Text (unformatted messages)

Formatted message font

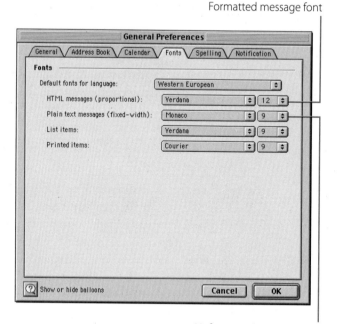

Unformatted message font

Finding Messages

Although you can readily scroll through the items in your message folders to find recently received or sent messages, finding older ones can be a challenge. Luckily, Entourage has several tools that enable you to search by subject, category, and e-mail address. You can even search for text inside messages.

Filtering the Message List

Most of the searches you'll want to perform can be conducted by choosing options from the pop-up menus above the message list. (This is referred to as *filtering*.) To filter the current message folder to display only matching subjects, categories, or e-mail addresses, follow these steps:

1   Click the first filter criteria pop-up menu above the message list, shown in Figure 20-10. You can search the Subject line of each message, the From or To addresses, or the Category.

2   Click the second filter criteria pop-up menu. If you are searching within the Subject, From, or To fields, you can choose Contains or Starts With. Category-based filtering can identify all messages assigned to a specific category. They are executed immediately after you choose a category.

3   When searching within the Subject, From, or To fields, enter a search string in the filter criteria text box. The search is conducted as you type, and the matching headers are displayed in the message list.

FIGURE 20-10.

Choose options to filter the message list

Reminder that a filter is in effect

Filter criterion

Click to restore message list

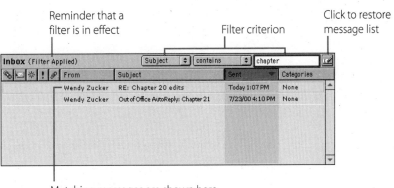

Matching messages are shown here

To restore the message header list after performing a Category search, choose All from the second filter criteria pop-up menu. To restore a search of the Subject, From, or To fields, click the Clear button beside the filter criteria text box.

Performing a Simple Search

Using the Edit menu's Find command (or by pressing ⌘-F), you can perform most basic searches, including:

- Searching the currently selected or open message for a text string.

- Searching the currently selected folder (or all folders for the chosen account) for messages that contain a particular text string in the Subject, as part of the e-mail address, or—optionally—in the message body.

To search the current message for a text string, follow these steps:

1 From the Edit menu, choose Find or press ⌘-F. The Find dialog box appears, as shown in Figure 20-11.

2 Enter a search string in the Find text box.

3 Click the Current Item radio button to restrict your search to text contained in the currently selected message.

4 Click the Find button. The first instance of the search string is highlighted in the message—if it is found. Otherwise, Entourage beeps to indicate that the string wasn't found.

5 To search for additional occurrences of the text string, press ⌘-G.

FIGURE 20-11.

Searching for a text string within the current message

Search current message   Search string

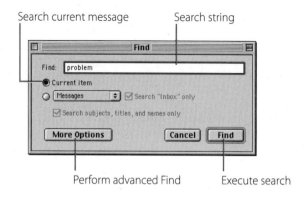

Perform advanced Find   Execute search

To search a folder or all folders in an account for a message that contains a particular text string, follow these steps:

1 If you want to search a single folder, select the folder in the Folder List.

2 Open the Edit menu and choose Find, or press ⌘-F. The Find dialog box appears. (See Figure 20-11.)

3 Enter a search string in the Find text box.

4 Click the second radio button, and choose Messages from the pop-up menu.

5 To restrict your search to messages in the current folder, be sure that the Search *current folder name* Only check box is checked. To search all message folders for this account, remove the check mark.

6 To restrict the search to the contents of the Subject, To, and From fields, check the Search Subjects, Titles, And Names Only option. To include the message body text in the search, remove the check mark.

7 Click Find. Entourage executes the search and displays the matching message headers in the Search Results window, as shown in Figure 20-12.

FIGURE 20-12.

Search results are displayed in a separate window

Matching messages

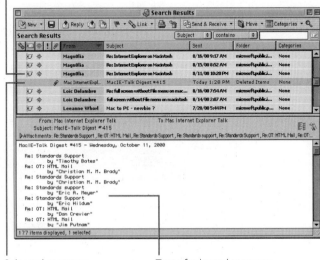

Selected message   Text of selected message

8 Click any message header to view the message in the preview pane. To find the original search text within the message, execute another Find in which you use the same search string but restrict the search to the current message.

9 When you're finished, click the Search Results window's close box.

Think of the Search Results window as a special case of the normal Entourage main window. Essentially, it's just a filtered list of message headers. You can work with these messages in much the same way that you work with them in the Entourage main window.

Performing an Advanced Search

To perform a more advanced search in which you can specify multiple search criteria and examine other message components (such as attachments, the Cc or Bcc lines, and so on), follow these steps:

1 If you want to search a single folder, select the folder in the Folder List.

2 From the Edit menu, select Advanced Find or press Option-⌘-F. A different version of the Find dialog box appears, as shown in Figure 20-13.

FIGURE 20-13.
Performing more precise searches with the advanced version of the Find dialog box

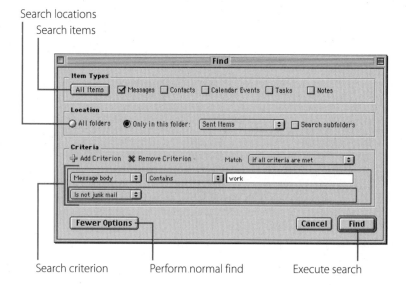

IV

Microsoft Entourage

3 In the Item Types section, check the Messages option (if you want to restrict your searches to messages only).

4 In the Location section, click All Folders to search all folders in the current account simultaneously.

or

To restrict your search to one folder, choose the folder name from the pop-up menu. To also search subfolders of the selected folder, click the Search Subfolders check box.

5 In the Criteria section, enter one or more search criteria by choosing pop-up menu options and typing in text boxes. (To add another criterion, click the Add Criterion button. To delete a criterion, select it and click the Remove Criterion button.)

6 Choose an option from the Match pop-up menu to specify how the search criteria will work together.

7 Click Find. Entourage executes the search and displays the matching messages in the Search Results window. (See Figure 20-12.)

8 Click any message header to view the message contents in the preview pane. To find the original search text within the message, execute another Find in which you use the same search string but restrict the search to the current message.

9 When you're finished, click the Search Results window's close box.

 TIP

You can switch between a Find and an Advanced Find by clicking the More Options or Fewer Options button in the Find dialog box.

Working with Attachments

Some incoming messages may contain *attachments*—files such as pictures, movies, word processing documents, and programs that are transmitted along with the text message. Messages that contain attachments are marked in the message list with a paper clip icon, as shown in Figure 20-14.

FIGURE 20-14.

Messages that contain attachments are marked with a paper clip

Attachment symbol

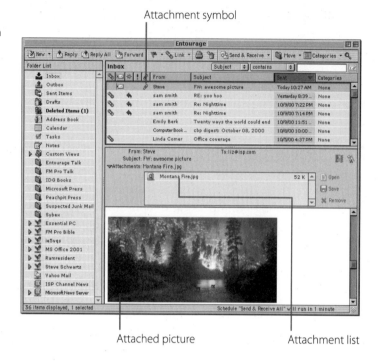

Attached picture

Attachment list

Attached pictures and movies can automatically be displayed in the preview pane, as long as they are in a QuickTime-compatible format, such as JPEG, GIF, MOV, MPEG, or AVI. To display pictures and movies, you must set an option in the View tab of the Mail & News Preferences dialog box, as shown in Figure 20-15.

In many cases, picture attachments can be handled entirely within the preview pane. You only have to open or save a picture or movie attachment if you'd like to view or edit it in another program, such as Photoshop or QuickTime Player. Other types of attachments, such as word processing documents and programs, can be opened or saved by following the instructions in the next several sections.

FIGURE 20-15.

Enable this preference
to display attached
pictures and movies in
the preview pane

Show pictures and movies

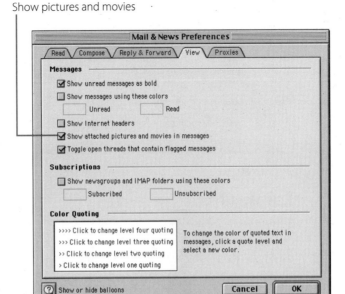

<CAUTION>

You should note that
executable attach-
ments (programs and
installers) are the most
frequent carriers of
viruses. You should
always use an anti-
virus program to scan
such programs before
opening them. You
have little to worry
about when opening
pictures, however.

Opening Attachments

You can open a document attachment to view or edit it in the program
that created it. You can also open programs and encoded or com-
pressed files using the same procedure. To open an attachment, follow these steps:

1 Select the message header in the message list, or open the message in its own window.

2 Click the Attachments triangle to expand the Attachments box.
The list of all attached files and their sizes appears.

3 To open an attachment, select it and click the Open button. A
warning dialog box appears, as shown in Figure 20-16.

4 Click Open to continue. The file opens in an appropriate program, if one exists on your Mac. If the attachment is a program,
it launches.

FIGURE 20-16.

When opening any attachment, this warning appears

Opening: LEESAMOD.jpg

Some files can contain viruses or otherwise be harmful to your computer. It's important to be certain that this file is from a trustworthy source.

Are you sure you want to open this file?

☐ Don't show this message again

[Cancel] [Open]

Saving Attachments

Although you can open attachments from within Entourage, important ones are best saved to your hard disk. (As long as you don't delete the message, its attachment will always be available to you.) To save an attachment, select it in the Attachments list and click the Save button. A warning dialog box appears, similar to the one displayed when opening an attachment. Click Save to continue, choose a location in which to save the file, and then click Save.

Entourage provides other ways to save attachments, too. You can drag them onto your desktop, or you can open the Message menu and choose Save All Attachments.

Deleting Attachments

While you may want to keep a message, you may not want to waste disk space storing its attachments. To delete a single attachment, select it in the Attachments box and click Remove. To delete all attachments, open the Message menu and choose Remove All Attachments.

If you don't need to save the message, you can simultaneously delete it *and* its attachments by deleting the message.

Printing Messages

Entourage provides two ways for you to print a selected message. To print a message using the most recent print settings (bypassing the normal and Entourage-specific Print dialog boxes), open the File menu and choose Print One Copy, or press Option-⌘-P.

SEE ALSO

For more information about printing, see Chapter 2, "Microsoft Office Basics."

To set or change options prior to printing, follow these steps:

1 Click the Print button, choose Print from the File menu, or press ⌘-P. A special Entourage Print dialog box appears, as shown in Figure 20-17.

2 Click check boxes to set print options, as desired. The effects of the options are shown in the Preview box.

3 Click OK. The normal Print dialog box for your printer appears.

4 Specify any additional options you want, and click Print.

FIGURE 20-17.

The Print dialog box in Entourage

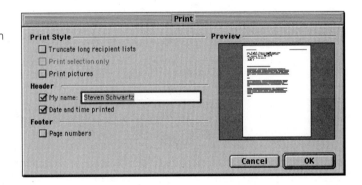

Organizing Your Messages

While no one will ever *insist* that you organize your messages, you'll quickly discover that there are excellent reasons for getting organized if you're a regular e-mail user. Imagine your Inbox or Sent Items folder with 1427 messages in it. What's the likelihood that you can quickly find the message you're looking for by simply scrolling through the headers?

In addition to the organizing procedures discussed in this section, Entourage provides several advanced ways to organize messages automatically. For information about creating message rules, employing the Junk Mail Filter, and managing messages from mailing lists, see Chapter 23.

Creating New Folders

The simplest way to impart organization to your e-mail is to create additional folders for storing different types of messages. You can create folders that are based on projects (Budget or Office 2001 Book) or groups of people (Family, Coworkers), for example. To create a new folder, open the File menu, choose New, and then choose Folder; click the down arrow on the right side of the New button and choose Folder; or press Shift-⌘-N. An "untitled folder" appears in the Folder List. Rename it whatever you'd like.

You can also create *subfolders*—folders nested inside of other folders. For example, a Work folder might contain subfolders named Assignments, Budget, and Coworker Mail. To create a subfolder, select the main (or *parent*) folder in the Folder List, open the File menu, and choose Subfolder from the New submenu; or click the down arrow on the right side of the New button and choose Subfolder.

If you make a mistake and create a new main folder when you meant to make a subfolder, just drag the new folder to its intended parent folder.

Moving Messages

After you receive or send a message, you can sometimes make it easier to locate again by moving it to a more appropriate folder. For example, rather than just leaving Web site registration confirmations lying loose in your Inbox, you could create a Registrations folder in which to store them.

To move a message to a different folder, you can drag the message header onto the destination folder in the Folder List; you can choose a destination folder by opening the Message menu and choosing an option from the Move To submenu; or you can Control-click the message header and choose a destination folder by choosing the Move To submenu.

 # Categorizing Your Messages

One simple way to organize your messages is to assign categories to the important ones. A *category* is a classification, such as Family, Friends, Work, Personal, or Recreation. In addition to the categories provided by Entourage, you are free to create your own.

Headers of categorized messages are color-coded in the message list, making them easy to spot. You can assign more than one category to some messages, if you like. You can also sort the message list by category, or filter it to show only messages from a particular category, as shown in Figure 20-18.

FIGURE 20-18.

Filtering the message list to show only messages that have been assigned a particular category

Filter by category

Inbox (Filter Applied)	Category	Personal			
🏷 ⬜ ❄ ! 📎	From	Subject	Sent ▼	Categories
	sam smith	RE: Outage	Yesterday 9:57...	Person...
	sam smith	RE: Fried eggs	Yesterday 9:55...	Person...
	sam smith	RE: Call	Yesterday 5:14...	Person...
	sam smith	RE: flood	Yesterday 5:05...	Person...
	sam smith	Re: flood	Yesterday 2:20...	Person...
📎 ↩	sam smith	Re: flood	Yesterday 2:15...	Person...
	sam smith	Re: flood	Yesterday 2:11...	Person...
	sam smith	RE: Hi there!	6/14/00 12:38	Person

To assign a category to one or more messages, select the message header or headers in the message list. Then click the down arrow on the right side of the Categories button, shown in Figure 20-19, or open the Edit menu and choose a category from the Categories submenu.

FIGURE 20-19.

Assigning a category to the current message by choosing it from the Category button's pop-up menu

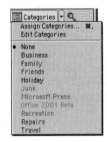

To create your own categories or edit the current ones, follow these steps:

1 Open the Edit menu, point to Categories, and then choose Edit Categories. The Categories window appears, as shown in Figure 20-20.

2 To add a new category, click the New button and then enter a name for the category. A new color is automatically assigned to the category. To change the color, click the down arrow on the right side of the category's color box.

3 To delete a category, select it and click the Delete button. Click Delete in the confirmation dialog box that appears.

4 To change a category name, select the category and click its name a second time.

FIGURE 20-20.

You create, edit, and delete categories in the Category window

Category names

Associated message header colors

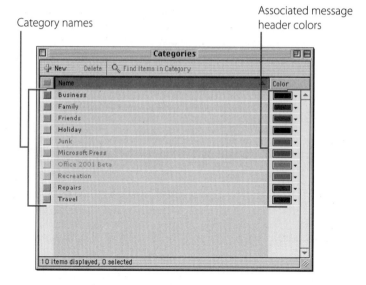

When you delete a category, any messages or other items to which you've previously assigned the category will have that category removed. If the items have not been assigned additional categories, their category will be shown as "None."

To sort the message list by category, click the Categories heading above the list. To reverse the sort order, click the heading a second time. (If the Categories heading isn't visible, open the View menu, point to Columns, and then choose Categories.)

To filter the message list so it shows only a single category, click the first pop-up menu above the message list and choose Category. Choose a category from the second pop-up menu.

Searching by Category

Entourage also enables you to search for categories and, optionally, create custom views based on the search results. To search for all messages, contacts, calendar events, tasks, and notes for a given category, open the Categories window by opening the Edit menu, pointing to Categories, and then choosing Edit Categories; select a category; and click the Find Items In Category button. A Search Results window appears, as shown in Figure 20-21, presenting the results in alphabetical order by title.

FIGURE 20-21.

The Search Results window following a category search

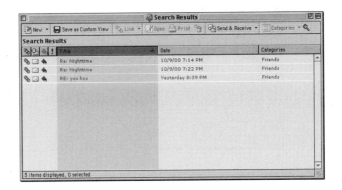

If you want to be able to repeat the same category search easily, click the Save As Custom View button. The Edit Custom View dialog box appears. (See Figure 20-22.) Name the view, remove any unnecessary item types, and then click OK. The new view is added to the Custom Views folder in the Folder List. To repeat this search in later sessions, expand the Custom Views folder and click the search's name.

FIGURE 20-22.

You can create a custom view based on this search

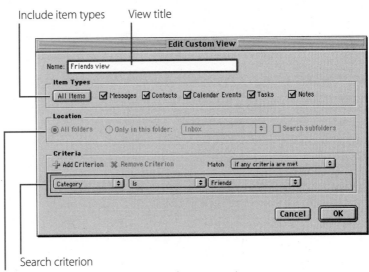

Include item types   View title

Search criterion

Specify folders (when searching only for messages)

Another way to make messages stand out is to assign a priority to them manually by choosing one from the Priority submenu of the Messages menu. You can also *flag* messages, which marks them with a tiny flag icon. (See Figure 20-23.)

FIGURE 20-23.

Messages can be flagged manually or as a result of having a message rule applied to them

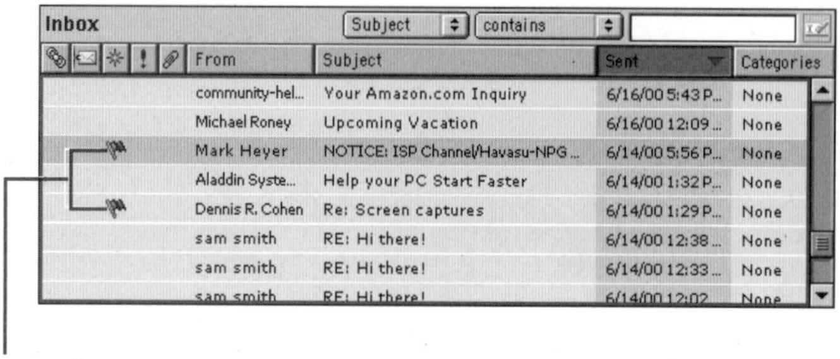

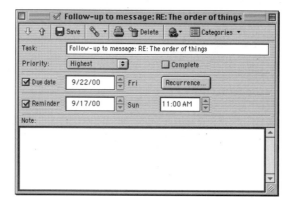

Flagged messages

To add or remove a flag, select the message header and click the Flag button in the toolbar (or the Flag button's down arrow). To set follow-up options for a message (due date, reminder, and/or priority), as shown in Figure 20-24, select the message header, click the down arrow on the right side of the Flag button, and choose Flag For Follow-up.

FIGURE 20-24.

A flagged message can have specific follow-up settings, such as a due date

Deleting Messages

To avoid unnecessarily wasting disk space, and to protect your privacy, it's a good idea to delete any messages you don't need to keep. To delete a message, select the message header or open the message in its own window and then do any of the following:

■ Click the Trash button in the toolbar.

■ Press Delete or ⌘-Delete.

- From the Edit menu, choose Delete Message.

- Drag the message header into the Deleted Items folder or the Trash.

- Control-click the message header and choose Delete Message.

 TIP

> You can delete multiple messages by ⌘-clicking or Shift-clicking them and then following one of the deletion procedures. When reading messages in their own windows (rather than in the preview pane), you can also delete the current message by clicking the down arrow on the right side of the Previous or Next toolbar button and choosing one of the Delete commands, such as Next Message and Delete.

Deleted messages aren't immediately deleted. They are simply moved into the Deleted Items folder. To delete them permanently, you must empty the Deleted Items folder. You can do this by:

- Control-clicking the Deleted Items folder in the Folder List and choosing Empty 'Deleted Items.'

- Clicking the Deleted Items folder in the Folder List, selecting the items you want to delete, and then following one of the previously mentioned message deletion procedures.

    or

- Running the Empty Deleted Items Folder schedule by opening the Tools menu, pointing to Run Schedule, and then choosing Empty Deleted Items Folder.

 TIP

> You can also delete any *folder* you've created. Deleting a folder simultaneously deletes all messages that it contains.

Automatically Emptying the Deleted Items Folder

By default, the Empty Deleted Items Folder schedule can only be run manually. To make it more useful—and secure—you can change it to a schedule that automatically empties the folder each time you quit Entourage. From the Tools menu, choose Schedules, double-click the Empty Deleted Items Folder schedule (to edit it), and in the When pop-up menu, change Manually to On Quit.

Reading and Managing Newsgroup Articles

A rticles posted to newsgroups are the equivalent of public e-mail messages. Everyone who opens or subscribes to the newsgroup to which an article is posted can read it. This chapter will help you understand the process of reading newsgroup articles, as well as organizing and saving them. When referring to newsgroups, the terms *post*, *message*, and *article* all mean the same thing. They are used interchangeably in this book, as well as in magazines and other books.

Reading Posts

Reading newsgroup posts is similar to reading e-mail, as explained in the following steps. The procedure differs slightly depending on whether you subscribe to the newsgroup or not.

To read articles in a newsgroup to which you subscribe, follow these steps:

1 Click the news server name from the Folder List to expand it. All the newsgroups you've subscribed to are listed beneath the news server's name, as shown in Figure 21-1.

FIGURE 21-1.

Select a newsgroup to view by clicking its name in the Folder List

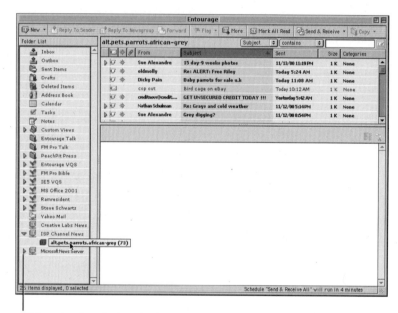

Click to view list of subscribed-to newsgroups

2 In the Folder List, click the name of the newsgroup you want to view. New message headers for the newsgroup are automatically downloaded and added to the message list.

3 To read a post, click its header in the message list. Microsoft Entourage sends instructions to the news server to download the message to your computer, as shown in Figure 21-2.

FIGURE 21-2.

Entourage downloads
your selected
messages to your
computer

As soon as the message has finished downloading, its text appears in
the preview pane, as shown in Figure 21-3.

FIGURE 21-3.

You can read the text
of the selected mes-
sage in the preview
pane

Preview pane

⭐ **TIP**

You don't have to wait for the current message to download before clicking
other message headers. Click as many as you like; they will *all* download. Although you can also use the up and down arrow keys in the message list to
move from post to post, doing so tells Entourage that you want to read *every*
post that you touch. Using the mouse to click just the ones you want to read
will save time (and disk space) by not requiring Entourage to download unnecessary posts.

You can also read posts in newsgroups to which you *don't* subscribe
by following these steps:

1 In the Folder List, click the name of the news server that
    handles the newsgroup you want to read. The list of available
    newsgroups appears, as shown in Figure 21-4. If you want to see
    whether any new newsgroups have been added or older ones
    eliminated, click the Update List button in the toolbar.

IV

Microsoft Entourage

FIGURE 21-4.

The first step in locating a newsgroup is to display the list of all available newsgroups for the news server

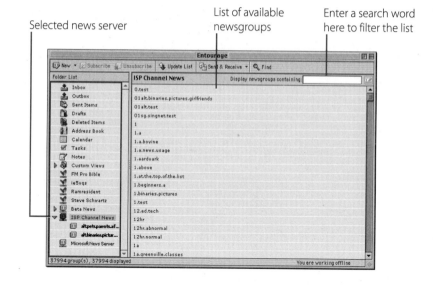

Selected news server

List of available newsgroups

Enter a search word here to filter the list

2 To locate the newsgroup you want to view, scroll through the list until its name is in sight or type part of its name in the Display Newsgroups Containing box, shown in Figure 21-4.

3 Select the newsgroup of interest by clicking its name in the list.

NOTE

If you're positive that this is the newsgroup you're searching for, you can subscribe to it by clicking the Subscribe button.

4 To open the newsgroup and download its message headers, double-click the newsgroup name, from the File menu choose Open *newsgroup name* or press ⌘-O. The newsgroup opens in its own window.

5 To read a post, click its header in the message list. Entourage sends instructions to the news server to download the message to your computer. As soon as the message has finished downloading, its text appears in the preview pane.

TIP

As with e-mail messages, you can read any article in its own window by double-clicking its header in the message list. You can then move from message to message by clicking the Next or Previous buttons, shown in Figure 21-5.

FIGURE 21-5.

If you prefer, you can read newsgroup messages in a separate window rather than in the preview pane

View previous message

View next message

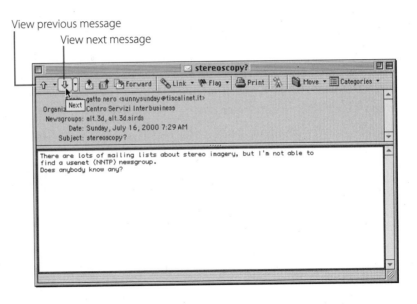

Working Offline: A Thing of the Past

Previous versions of Outlook Express had features that made it easy to work offline with newsgroups. (Working *offline* refers to those times when you are not connected to the Internet.) Because Internet accounts were often expensive, and based on how long they were connected, users would log on to their Internet accounts, download new newsgroup message headers, disconnect from the Internet, mark the messages they wanted to retrieve, reconnect to download the marked messages, disconnect, and then read the messages at their leisure. True, it was complex—but it was a money-saver.

Because most Internet accounts are no longer time-based and newsgroup reading is on the wane, offline newsgroup-related features and support have been eliminated in Entourage. To mark messages for downloading, you must be online. If you attempt to read a new message while offline (by clicking its message header), a dialog box appears, as shown in Figure 21-6. Click Work Online to reconnect and stay connected to the news server, click Override to temporarily reconnect, or click Cancel to remain offline.

FIGURE 21-6.

If you try to read a new message while offline, you'll be asked if you want to connect to the Internet

Handling Attachments

Some messages—particularly those in any of the newsgroups that have the word *binaries* in their names—contain file attachments. Although the most popular attachments are pictures (such as JPEG and GIF files), an attachment can be any kind of file.

Any picture attachment in a format that Entourage understands (such as JPEG, GIF, or PNG) will automatically be displayed in the preview pane after it is downloaded. Those attachments, as well as files of other types, are listed in the Attachments area of the message window, as shown in Figure 21-7. To open or save a newsgroup message attachment, select its file icon and click Open or Save (as explained in the instructions in Chapter 20, "Reading and Managing E-Mail").

FIGURE 21-7.

All file attachments are listed by name in the Attachments list

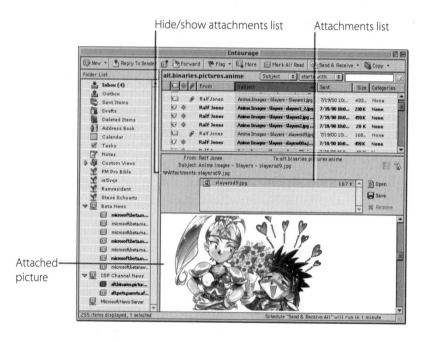

Hide/show attachments list

Attachments list

Attached picture

⭐ **TIP**

Multi-part attachments (attachments that, because of their size, are uploaded to the newsgroup as a series of smaller pieces) are relatively common in picture, movie, and audio newsgroups. Entourage is not designed to download and combine multi-part attachments. In fact, Entourage incorrectly shows the first attachment as a complete file that, when you try to open it, displays an error message. The simplest way to combine multi-part attachments is to identify the messages in Entourage which—when combined—contain all the attachment pieces, and then run MT NewsWatcher (available from *www.best.com/~smfr/mtnw*) to download and combine the pieces.

Changing Your View of the Message List

Because newsgroup messages are public, you've probably noticed that there is no way to delete them. However, by setting different views in Entourage and marking messages as having been read, you can restrict the list to just the articles you're interested in. The following are a few techniques to help you view newsgroup messages:

- **Sort by Sent Date rather than by Subject** This technique will quickly show you the newest messages posted to the newsgroup. (Click any heading above the message list to sort by it. Click it a second time to reverse the sort order.)

- **From the View menu, choose Unread Only (or press ⌘-Y)** This view only displays messages you haven't already read. A message can be marked as read by viewing it or by selecting its header and choosing Mark As Read from the Message menu (or by pressing ⌘-T).

- **From the View menu, choose Threaded** Use this command to group an initial message with all the responses it has received. To expand a thread in the message list, click the triangle that precedes the initial message, as shown in Figure 21-8.

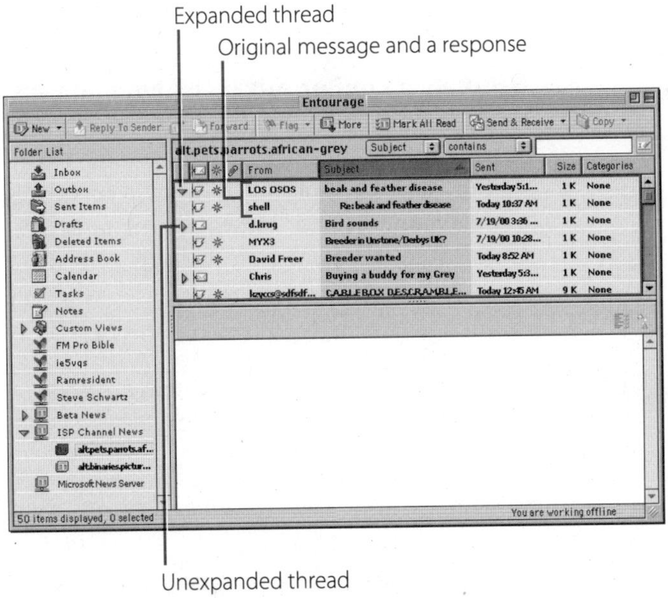

FIGURE 21-8.

Messages in a thread are marked with a triangle icon, which you can click to see all the responses for a message

Expanded thread
Original message and a response

Unexpanded thread

- **From the View menu, choose Flagged Only (or press Shift-⌘-Y)** If you've manually flagged some messages by choosing Flag from the Message menu, or have designed rules to flag messages automatically, use this command to restrict the message list to flagged items only.

■ **Filter the message list** You can filter the message list to show only the messages that are from a particular individual, or whose subject contains a particular word, as shown in Figure 21-9. To view the entire message list later, click the Clear button. See Chapter 20 for more information on filtering the message list.

FIGURE 21-9.

By typing a word in this box, you can filter the message list to show only the messages that interest you

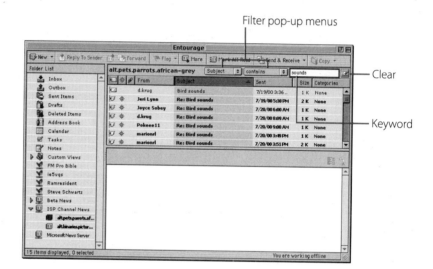

■ **Create a Find or Advanced Find and save it as a custom view** If the standard options for filtering, sorting, and otherwise restricting the message list aren't sufficient, you can create a custom view to display only what you want, such as all messages originating from a particular person or domain (*microsoft.com*, for instance). By saving the search results as a custom view, you can reuse the view whenever you want without having to go through the steps to recreate the desired list of messages.

You can simultaneously mark several messages as read by Shift-clicking or ⌘-clicking them and then choosing Mark As Read from the Message menu. If you want to mark *all* visible messages in a newsgroup as read, choose Mark All As Read from the Message menu (or press Option-⌘-T). Following either of these commands by choosing Unread Only from the View menu is an excellent way to eliminate unwanted messages from the message list.

Copying and Saving Important Messages

Old newsgroup messages are eventually removed from news servers. If a message is important to you—because it provides some helpful information, strikes you as funny, or whatever the reason—you can make a permanent copy of it by either saving it as a file or by copying it into an Entourage folder. Doing either has the added advantage of allowing you to read the message even when you aren't connected to the Internet.

To save a newsgroup message as a file (in most cases so it can be read by someone else, or on a computer that doesn't have Entourage installed), follow these steps:

1 Select the message's header in the message list.

2 From the File menu, choose Save As. The Save Message dialog box appears, as shown in Figure 21-10.

FIGURE 21-10.

Use the Save Message dialog box to specify a name, location, and format for a message you're about to save

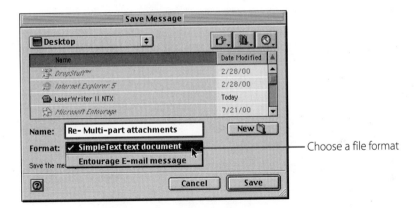

Choose a file format

3 Select a location in which to save the file.

4 By default, the message subject is proposed as the file name. You can change it by editing the text in the Name box, if you wish.

5 Choose a format for the message file from the Format pop-up menu. You can either create a file that can be read with SimpleText—a free text-editing program that is included with every version of the Apple system software—or one that must be opened with Entourage.

6 Click the Save button.

Saving a newsgroup message in an Entourage folder, on the other hand, is faster and involves fewer steps than saving a newsgroup message as a file. Note, however, that the saved message can be read only on the current computer. To save a newsgroup message in an Entourage folder, follow these steps:

1 Select the message header in the message list.

2 Do one of the following:

- Drag the message header onto the destination folder in the Folder List.

   or

   From the Message menu, point to Copy To and then choose Copy To Folder (or press Shift-⌘-M). The Copy To Folder dialog box appears, as shown in Figure 21-11. Select a folder and click Copy.

FIGURE 21-11.

Select a destination folder for the message and click Copy

Selected folder ——

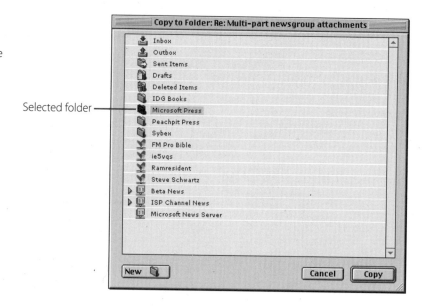

A copy of the message is stored in the destination folder. To read the copied message later, simply open the folder in which it was stored and click its header in the message list.

Posting to Newsgroups

Unlike exchanging e-mail messages with friends, you're under no obligation whatsoever to contribute to newsgroups. No one knows the ones to which you subscribe, so the people who follow the newsgroup aren't sitting there wondering why you're reading messages but not posting any of your own. However, while there may be many newsgroups that you just read—checking *comp.sys.mac.forsale* for hot deals on Macintosh hardware, for example—there may also be newsgroups in which you'll want to take an active part. You can submit new posts and respond to others' posts as you see fit.

Posting a New Message

If you've ever written an e-mail message, you already know how to write a message to a newsgroup. The only difference is that the message is addressed to one or more newsgroups (where it will be posted for everyone to read), rather than to an individual.

To create a new message for a newsgroup, follow these steps:

1   Open the newsgroup to which you want to send the message. (Note that you don't have to subscribe to a newsgroup before you can send a message to it.)

2   Click the New button in the toolbar, choose News Message from the New submenu of the File menu, or press ⌘-N. A new, untitled message window appears, as shown in Figure 22-1. The To line already contains the name of the selected newsgroup. If you don't want to send it to other newsgroups or individuals, skip to step 6.

FIGURE 22-1.

A newsgroup message window contains a News Account line in the header, and the To line contains the name of the destination newsgroup

News account pop-up menu

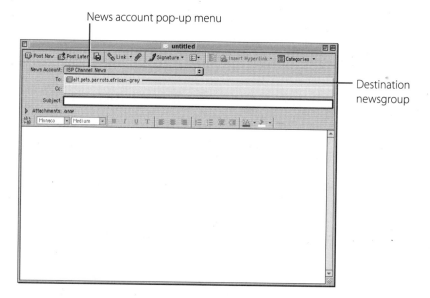

Destination newsgroup

> **NOTE**

The message will automatically be addressed to the correct newsgroup *only* if you are viewing that newsgroup when you create the message (as indicated in step 1).

3   By default, the currently active news account/server is listed in the News Account line. If you wish to send the message through a different news account, choose its name from the News Account pop-up menu.

IV

Microsoft Entourage

4 To send the message to additional newsgroups simultaneously, click the To box, click to select the next blank line (shown in Figure 22-2), and type or paste the newsgroup's name into the box.

FIGURE 22-2.

Addressing the post to one or more newsgroups

Destination newsgroups go here

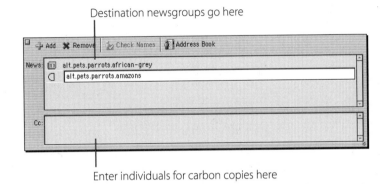

Enter individuals for carbon copies here

5 If you want to send a copy of the message directly to one or more people, click the Cc (carbon copy) box and enter the recipients' e-mail addresses.

6 Click the To window's close box when you are done adding newsgroups and/or Cc recipients.

7 Fill in the Subject line, and compose the message.

8 If desired, you can enclose an attachment by following the instructions presented in Chapter 19, "Writing and Sending E-Mail."

9 To post the message to the newsgroup immediately, click the Post Now button (shown in Figure 22-3), choose Post Message Now from the Message menu, or press ⌘-K.

or

To post the message at a later time (that is, the next time you perform a Send & Receive All—manually or via a schedule), click the Post Later button (shown in Figure 22-3), choose Post Message Later from the Message menu, or press Option-⌘-K.

FIGURE 22-3.

Posting a message

NOTE

> As with regular e-mail messages, you can format a newsgroup post as plain text or HTML, insert links to Web pages and e-mail addresses, and add a sig-nature. Although you will usually be viewing messages from the destination newsgroup when composing your posts, you aren't *required* to do so. You can also address a post by typing the newsgroup's name in the To line or by se-lecting the name from your Address Book. If so, be sure to select the correct news account from the pop-up menu.

Replying to a Message

An easy way to begin participating in an interesting newsgroup is by adding your two-cents' worth to an ongoing discussion. For instance, if someone posts a message asking a question to which you know the answer or have an opinion, jump right in.

When replying to a newsgroup message, you have three options:

- You can post your reply to the newsgroup (where it can be read by everyone).

- You can respond (via e-mail) to the author of the message directly.

- You can post your reply to the newsgroup while simultaneously e-mailing a carbon copy to the author of the message.

Which option you choose depends on the situation. Here are a few simple rules to help you decide what to do:

- If you want your reply to be private, respond directly to the author.

- If the reply would also be of interest to the readers of the news-group, direct the response to them, too.

- If the response is merely part of a general discussion and it isn't essential that the original author sees your comments, direct it only to the newsgroup.

To respond to a post, begin by selecting the message header in the message list and then do one of the following:

- To post your reply to the newsgroup (where it will become part of the message thread), click the Reply To Newsgroup button in the toolbar (shown in Figure 22-4), choose Reply from the Message menu, or press ⌘-R.

FIGURE 22-4.

Click a button to choose a recipient

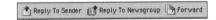

- To reply only to the author, click the Reply To Sender toolbar button, choose Reply To Sender from the Message menu, or press Option-⌘-R

- To reply to the newsgroup *and* send a copy of the reply to the author (as shown in Figure 22-5), choose Reply To All from the Message menu or press Shift-⌘-R.

FIGURE 22-5.

When you choose the Reply To All command, your message is automatically addressed to the original newsgroup and a copy is e-mailed to the message's author

Destination newsgroup

Author of original message

Because posting to newsgroups puts your e-mail address at risk for receiving a flood of *spam* (unwanted advertising-relating messages), many newsgroup authors use bogus e-mail addresses. Don't be surprised if some of your replies bounce back to you as undeliverable. If this happens, be *sure* that you resend the message to the newsgroup so the author will have a chance to see your response. (On a similar note, if you don't want to receive direct replies to your posts, do what the others do. Use a fake e-mail address or create a Hotmail one that you use exclusively for newsgroups.)

> **NOTE**
>
> Whether you're posting a reply or starting a new message *thread* (discussion), it's important for you to know that newsgroup message delivery isn't as fast as normal e-mail. It takes time for your message to appear in the message list. If it doesn't appear when you click the More button, wait a bit and then check again.

Posting Etiquette

After observing a particular newsgroup for a few days, you should have a good sense of what the implicit "rules" are for posting to it. Following are some general principles that you should find helpful.

Top Ten Posting Do's and Don't's

1 Even if you normally use HTML formatting for your e-mail messages, you should generally stick to plain text messages for newsgroup posts. All newsgroup readers can handle plain text, while only the more advanced ones (such as Entourage) can interpret HTML.

2 When replying to a message, do *not* change the Subject line. If you do, your reply will be treated as the start of a new thread rather than a continuation of the one to which you're replying.

3 When writing a reply, be sure to quote the relevant parts of the original message. Otherwise, if readers view your message out of sequence, they may not have any idea what you're talking about. However, don't quote unnecessary material from the original author's message. Deleting the parts that aren't relevant to your comments will keep the post to a reasonable size, ensuring that others won't have to waste time downloading extraneous material.

4 Keep your posts on topic. Repeating a great joke that you found on the Internet is appropriate only when sent to a joke-related newsgroup.

5 Don't send advertisements to *any* newsgroups unless you are certain that they are directly related to the newsgroup topic and that they are welcome.

6 Don't waste bandwidth. Although you can simultaneously address a post to multiple newsgroups, try to pick the one (or two) to which the message is most relevant. A regular follower of dog-related newsgroups, for example, is liable to subscribe to several such newsgroups. He or she won't be pleased when your message is spotted in every one of those newsgroups.

7 Don't send test posts to regular newsgroups. If you just want to see how one of your newsreader functions works (such as encoded attachments), send your test posts to a newsgroup that is specifically designed for testing, such as *microsoft.test*.

8 Should you include attachments with your posts? Only if it is a newsgroup devoted to attachments, such as the many *alt.binaries* (picture) newsgroups, or if other users specifically request that you post a particular file.

9 Copyright laws apply to the Internet, too. Never post pictures, music, or other materials that you did not create.

10 Making public attacks on a message author may subject you to similar attacks. If you disagree, be polite. Better still, keep the disagreement private by e-mailing the author directly.

Customizing Microsoft Entourage for E-Mail and Newsgroups

A lthough you'll probably learn to use Microsoft Entourage as is, at some point you will probably want to customize it to better suit the way you work. Following the instructions in this chapter, you will be able to set preferences, modify the message list display, filter incoming junk mail, create automatic schedules, apply message rules to manage incoming mail, manage e-mail from mailing lists, and enhance Entourage with AppleScripts.

Setting Preferences

As is the case with many other Macintosh programs, you set *preferences* in Entourage to specify the manner in which you want the program to behave. Entourage has two types of preferences: General and Mail & News. *General preferences* govern how Entourage behaves in all settings —whether you're using the calendar to set reminders, displaying e-mail messages, or doing anything else. *Mail & News preferences* govern e-mail and newsgroup-specific behavior. While the standard (or *default*) preference settings will probably be fine for you, there are still a few that you may want to explore or change, as explained in the following sections. Because there are so many preferences, we'll discuss only the ones that are likely to be important to you.

Are you unsure about the function of a preference option? Click the Show Or Hide Balloons button at the bottom of any Preferences dialog box. Then when you pass the cursor over any preference item, a cartoon balloon with an explanation appears, as shown in Figure 23-1.

FIGURE 23-1.

Click Show Or Hide Balloons for help with setting preferences, or click it a second time to turn off Balloon Help

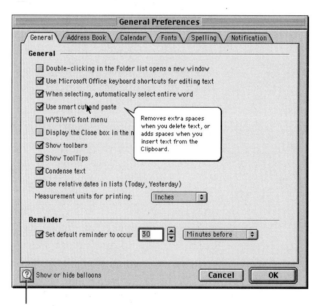

Turn Balloon Help on or off

General Preferences

To set or view General preferences setting, open the Edit menu, point to Preferences, and choose General (or press ⌘-semicolon). The General Preferences dialog box appears, open to the most recently modified tab, as shown in Figure 23-1. To set or view preferences for a different section of the General Preferences dialog box, click the tabs at the top of the dialog box. When you are through making changes, click OK to accept them or Cancel to ignore them.

The following are some General preference settings that you may want to change from the Entourage defaults:

- **General tab: Set Default Reminder To Occur** When you create a new reminder, Entourage proposes the time period specified by this setting. For example, if you set the preference to 30 Minutes Before, every new reminder you create will appear 30 minutes before the event. If you need more or less time, you can change this setting to a different number of minutes, hours, or days (as shown in Figure 23-1). Note that you can still specify a different reminder period for every new reminder you create.

- **Address Book tab: Default Area Code** To save typing time, you can specify a default area code that will automatically be added to every new contact address card for which you don't specify an area code. You can also ensure that all phone numbers are uniform. See Chapter 4, "Using the Address Book," for instructions.

- **Calendar tab** If you work a non-standard workweek (something other than Monday through Friday) or want to view the calendar with something other than Sunday as the first day of the week, you can make changes in this section of the dialog box, as shown in Figure 23-2.

- **Fonts tab** If you don't like the default fonts or font sizes used to create formatted (HTML) and unformatted (plain text) messages, to display onscreen lists in Entourage (such as the message list), or to print plain text messages and similar items, you can choose different fonts and sizes here, as shown in Figure 23-3.

FIGURE 23-2.

Use the Calendar tab to indicate your work-week and to customize the calendar

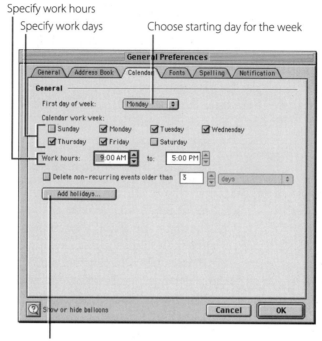

Specify work hours

Specify work days

Choose starting day for the week

Click to import religious and country-specific holidays

FIGURE 23-3.

Choose default fonts for displaying messages and lists

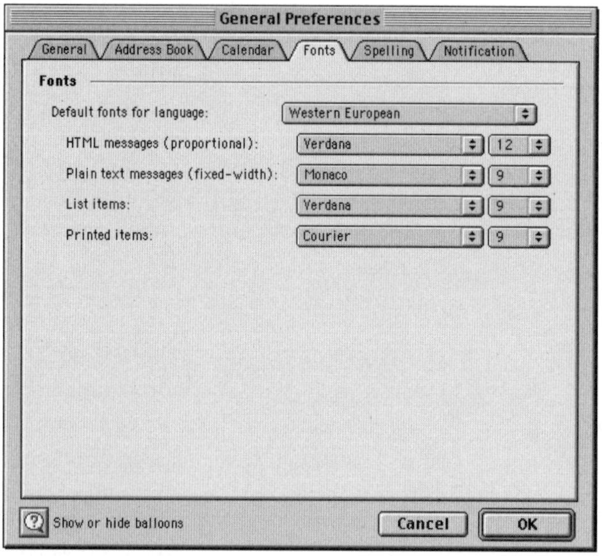

- **Spelling tab** Click this tab, shown in Figure 23-4, if you want Entourage to perform a spell check automatically on every outgoing message or if you want to specify a different user dictionary.

FIGURE 23-4.

Use the Spelling tab of the General Preferences dialog box to specify automatic spelling options and words to be ignored

Choose a user dictionary

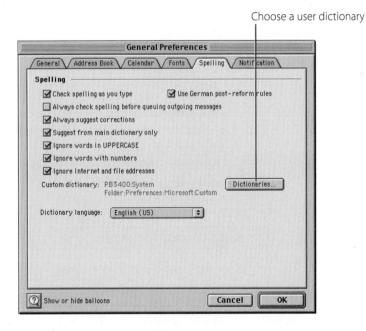

■ **Notification tab: Require Confirmation When Deleting**
If you're tired of being asked if you're sure that you want to delete something (messages, contacts, and so on), remove the check mark from this preference, shown in Figure 23-5.

FIGURE 23-5.

Set your e-mail sound and confirmation preferences on the Notification tab

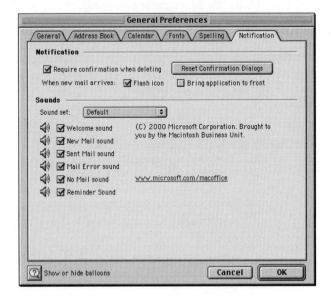

IV

Microsoft Entourage

- **Notification tab: Reset Confirmation Dialogs** If you've permanently dismissed some Entourage dialog boxes by clicking their Don't Show This Message Again check box, you can restore the missing dialog boxes by clicking this button.

- **Notification tab: Sounds** You can examine or change the sounds that play when new mail arrives or when a reminder is triggered. To hear any of the designated sounds, click the speaker icon to the left of the event check box. To play no sound for an event, remove its check mark. To specify a different sound set, choose one from the pop-up menu. (Random assigns a different random sound for each event.)

Adding Custom Sound Sets

You can add custom sound sets by dragging them into the Entourage Sound Sets folder (found by opening the Documents folder and then opening the Microsoft User Data folder). Until Entourage-specific sound sets begin to appear, you can use Outlook Express 5 sound set files. However, you'll need to open the sound set files in a utility program (such as FileTyper) and change the Creator to OPIM.

Mail & News Preferences

To set or view Mail & News preferences, open the Edit menu, point to Preferences, and choose Mail & News (or press Shift-⌘-semicolon). The Mail & News Preferences dialog box appears, open to the most recently modified tab, as shown in Figure 23-6. To set or view preferences for a different section of the Mail & News Preferences dialog box, click the tabs at the top of the dialog box. When you are through making changes, click OK to accept them or Cancel to ignore them.

The following are some Mail & News preference settings that you may want to change from the defaults:

- **Compose tab: Messages** If you generally create plain text messages rather than formatted HTML messages, you may want to remove the check mark from the Show HTML Formatting Toolbar In The Message Composition Window check box, shown in Figure 23-7. You can also choose separate default formats for new e-mail and newsgroup messages (either plain text or HTML). Choose the format you use the most.

IV

Microsoft Entourage

FIGURE 23-6.

Set e-mail and newsgroup-related preferences in the Mail & News Preferences dialog box

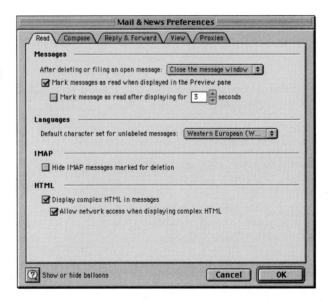

FIGURE 23-7.

The Compose tab of the Mail & News Preferences dialog box

Pick default formats for e-mail and newsgroup messages

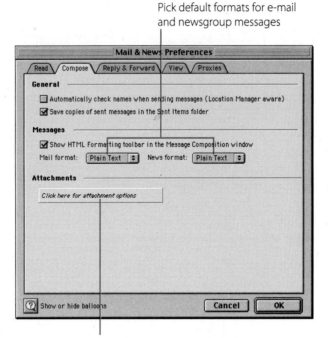

Specify default settings for attachments

- **Compose tab: Attachments** Click the Click Here For Attachment Options button to view the default options for attachments. You can still set attachment options differently for every new message, but you should select the options here that you will use for *most* messages. For instance, if most of your messages are sent to Windows users, you may want to check the option to add Windows extensions to all attached files. (Doing so won't affect file readability when received by a Mac user.)

- **Reply & Forward tab: Mail Attribution/News Attribution** When replying to an e-mail message or newsgroup post, you can preface the original author's text with a text string that includes the date of the message, the author's name, and/or his or her e-mail address, as shown in Figure 23-8. You can edit the attribution text if you want and insert the Date, Name, and Address placeholders by choosing them from the pop-up menus. If you prefer, you can use normal message header information to mark the original message (the most common approach) or display no message attribution text.

FIGURE 23-8.

Use the Reply & Forward preferences to specify options for replying to or forwarding received messages

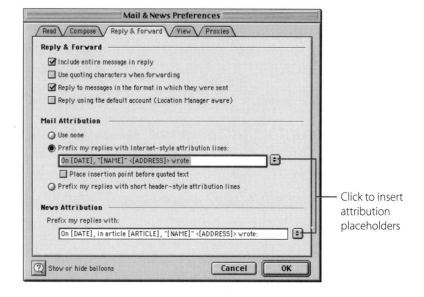

Click to insert attribution placeholders

■ **View tab: Message and Subscription Colors** Figure 23-9 shows that Entourage normally distinguishes unread from read messages by displaying message headers in boldface and normal type, respectively. You can optionally choose colors for read and unread message headers, as well as distinguish newsgroups to which you've subscribed from those to which you haven't subscribed. Click the appropriate check box to enable mail or newsgroup colors, and then click a box (Unread, for example) to pick a color.

FIGURE 23-9.

When color differentiation is enabled, you can pick colors from pop-up lists

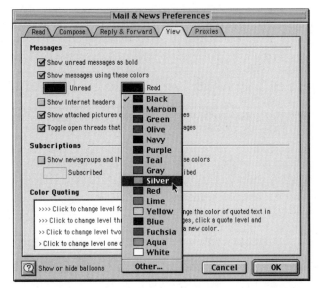

■ **Proxies tab** If you must access the Internet through a firewall or your Internet service provider (ISP) requires that you use a proxy server, click the Proxies tab, shown in Figure 23-10. Your network administrator or ISP will give you the addresses of their Web, e-mail, and/or secure proxy servers. If there are some sites that you must go to directly—bypassing the proxy servers— enter their addresses in the Exceptions text box. Separate each such address from the next by using a comma or space.

FIGURE 23-10.

Proxy preferences are
for users who must
access the Internet
indirectly by passing
through proxy servers

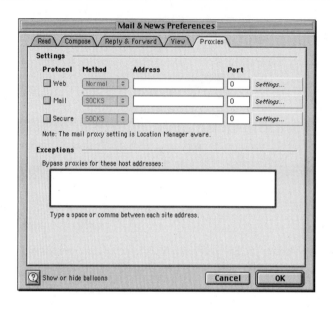

Customizing the Message List

Although you can't customize the Entourage toolbars, you can make
some changes to the message list display:

- **Adding or removing column headings** To add or remove
  column headings, click the View menu, point to Columns, and
  choose the heading to add or remove. (Checked columns are
  displayed; unchecked columns are hidden.)

- **Resizing and moving column headings** To alter the size of a
  column heading, move the cursor to the heading's right edge.
  The cursor changes to a double-headed arrow. Click and drag to
  the left (reduce) or right (enlarge), as shown in Figure 23-11. To
  move a heading to a new position, click and drag it to the left
  or right and then release the mouse button. A vertical dotted line
  shows where the heading will appear.

- **Changing the amount of screen space devoted to the message list, preview pane, and folder list** The size of the panes
  in the Entourage window can be changed as you see fit. Move
  the cursor over the double lines that separate any two sections
  of the window. The cursor changes to a double-headed arrow.
  Click and drag to the left, right, up, or down as appropriate.

FIGURE 23-11.

To resize a column in the message list, click to the right of the column and then drag

Drag cursor to change column size

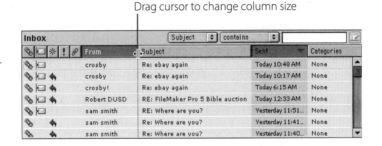

Another way to customize the display is by removing unnecessary elements. You can show or remove elements (toolbars, Folder List, or Preview Pane) by choosing them from the View menu.

Using the Junk Mail Filter

If you aren't careful to whom you reveal your primary e-mail address, you may find that you're receiving large quantities of unwanted e-mail. At best, such e-mail can be annoying and make it difficult to identify the messages that you *do* want to read. At worst, it can be extremely embarrassing. Do you really want to try to explain why you're receiving unsolicited e-mail from porn sites?

If you find yourself receiving e-mail that you didn't request, you can use the Junk Mail Filter to mark certain incoming messages as junk mail automatically. You can also instruct the Junk Mail Filter to handle such messages by marking them as read and/or performing an AppleScript (such as moving them to the Deleted Items folder or a Junk Mail folder).

To activate and set up the Junk Mail Filter, follow these steps:

1 From the Tools menu, choose Junk Mail Filter. The Junk Mail Filter dialog box appears, as shown in Figure 23-12.

2 To activate the filter, click the Enable Junk Mail Filter check box.

3 Move the sensitivity slider to the desired position. As you drag it further to the right, more mail will potentially be classified as suspected junk.

FIGURE 23-12.

You can enable or disable the Junk Mail Filter and set its sensitivity in this dialog box

Drag to change the filter's sensitivity

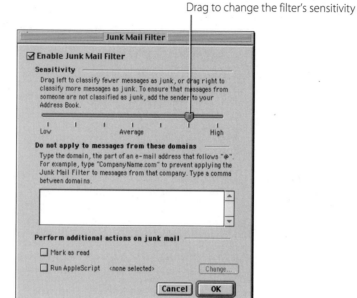

4 To keep mail from particular companies, institutions, or Internet providers from being classified as junk, enter their domains in the center text box. Separate each domain from the next with a comma, such as *internetworld.net, adobe.com, hnrc.tufts.edu.*

5 To specify automatic actions that the filter will perform on suspected junk messages, click one or both of the bottom check boxes.

6 Click OK.

7 If you changed the previous settings in the Junk Mail Filter dialog box, a new dialog box appears, as shown in Figure 23-13. Click Apply, to filter or refilter the messages in your Inbox, or click Don't Apply, to enable the filter but not check your old messages.

FIGURE 23-13.

Set or change the filter's sensitivity to apply the new settings to current messages in your Inbox

> NOTE

Messages from people and companies who are listed in your Address Book will never be classified as junk.

Whenever the Junk Mail Filter examines your messages, it indicates suspected junk messages in two ways. First, a special icon is displayed in the message header's Priority column, as shown in Figure 23-14. Second, when you view the message (in the preview pane or a separate message window), a line is added at the top of the message.

FIGURE 23-14.

Messages suspected of being junk mail are marked with a special icon, and a yellow line is displayed when the message is viewed

Junk mail icon   Line added to suspected junk mail

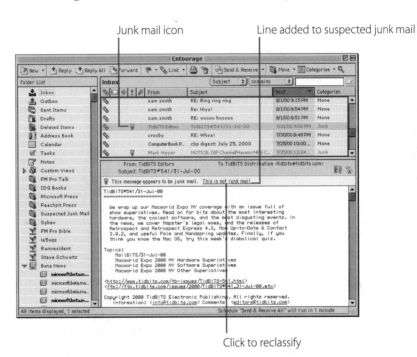

Click to reclassify

If the message isn't junk mail, click the This Is Not Junk Mail text and choose an option in the This Is Not Junk Mail dialog box, shown in Figure 23-15. The options are as follows:

- **Add Sender To Address Book** Messages from Address Book contacts are never mistaken for junk mail.

- **Create A Mailing List Rule** Choose this option if the message is from a mailing list.

- **Classify All Messages Sent From The Sender's Domain As "Not Junk"** Use this option to add trusted domains to the junk mail exception list. Normally, you'll want to reserve this for ISPs and corporate domains, such as *microsoft.com.*

- **Just Classify This Message As "Not Junk"** Choosing this option merely reclassifies the selected message as not junk. Additional messages from the same person may still be classified as junk.

FIGURE 23-15.

Specify how you want to handle this particular message and avoid classifying additional messages from the same person or company as junk

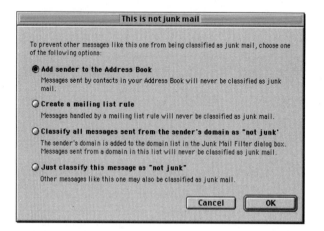

It may take you a couple of tries to get the Junk Mail Filter sensitivity just right. One way to determine quickly whether a new setting is optimal is to let it screen the existing messages in your Inbox. If it marks more than a couple of messages as junk that really aren't junk, the sensitivity is too high. If it misses more than a few of the real junk messages, the sensitivity is probably too low.

The best way to avoid unwanted e-mail is to create a free account in Hotmail, Yahoo!, or another Web-based service, and use that account for all online registrations, newsgroups, and chat services. Use your primary e-mail account only to send and receive messages from family, friends, and trusted business contacts.

Creating and Using Schedules

You've already learned that you can retrieve waiting messages from an e-mail account by opening the Tools menu and choosing the account name from the Send & Receive submenu. This manual approach is useful, but it isn't nearly as nice as having Entourage *automatically* check for new mail—without your intervention. To instruct Entourage to perform various e-mail and newsgroup actions automatically, you create *schedules*. Every schedule consist of two parts:

- **When** The times, periods, or events that will trigger the schedule's execution.

- **Actions** The actions that will be performed when the schedule is executed.

Any schedule can be triggered in multiple ways and can perform multiple actions. You can create as many schedules as you like. Each schedule can be executed automatically (based on timing or an Entourage event, such as startup or quitting) or manually, by opening the Tools menu and choosing the schedule name from the Run Schedule submenu, as shown in Figure 23-16.

FIGURE 23-16.

Schedules—automatic or manual—can also be executed by choosing them from the Run Schedule submenu

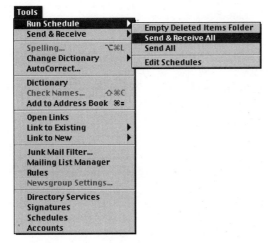

The easiest way to learn how to create schedules is to examine the ones that are installed with Entourage. Using the Send & Receive All schedule as an example, we will modify it to send and receive mail automatically at program startup and every two minutes while Entourage is running. To do so, follow these steps:

1 From the Tools menu, choose Schedules. The Schedules dialog box appears, as shown in Figure 23-17.

FIGURE 23-17.

Choose an existing schedule to edit from the Schedules dialog box

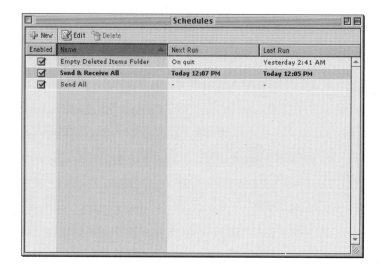

2 To view or modify an existing schedule, select it and click Edit (or double-click the schedule name). In this example, open the Send & Receive All schedule. The Edit Schedule dialog box appears, as shown in Figure 23-18.

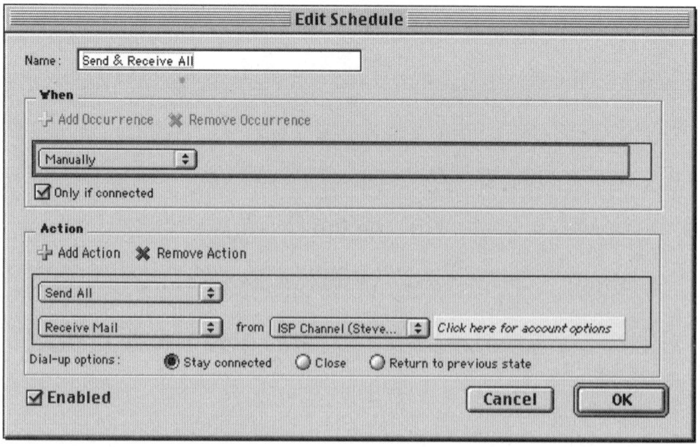

FIGURE 23-18.

The Send & Receive All schedule sends all mail that is in the Outbox

3 Any defined schedule can be executed manually by opening the Tools menu and choosing the schedule name from the Send & Receive submenu. As such, you can change the Manually option to something more useful, such as At Startup, by choosing that option from the pop-up menu in the When section.

> All new schedules default to Manually as the execution method. Until you change this occurrence method to something else, you *cannot* add more occurrences.

4 To make this schedule even more useful, let's add another occurrence to the When section. Click Add Occurrence, and set it for Repeating Schedule Every 2 Minutes. (Feel free to choose a longer interval.)

5 Be sure that Only If Connected is checked. Otherwise, Entourage will attempt to make a dial-up connection to your ISP whenever this schedule is executed.

6 If this is your only e-mail account, there is no need to change the settings in the Action section. If you have more accounts that you'd like to check automatically, click Add Action and duplicate the Receive Mail action for each account.

7 Click OK to save the schedule changes. The modified schedule is shown in Figure 23-19.

FIGURE 23-19.

The revised Send & Receive All schedule automatically checks two accounts every two minutes for new e-mail

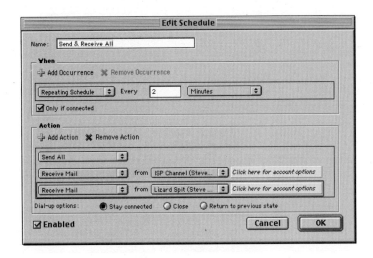

Of course, you'll undoubtedly want to create schedules of your own. For example, if you have several Hotmail or Yahoo! e-mail accounts, you can check them for new mail each time you launch Entourage. The following are the general steps to create a new schedule:

1 From the Tools menu, choose Schedules. The Schedules dialog box appears, as shown earlier in Figure 23-17.

2 To create a new schedule, click the New button. The Edit Schedule dialog box appears, as shown in Figure 23-20.

FIGURE 23-20.

You can create new schedules in the Edit Schedule dialog box

Specify times or events that will trigger the schedule

Name the schedule

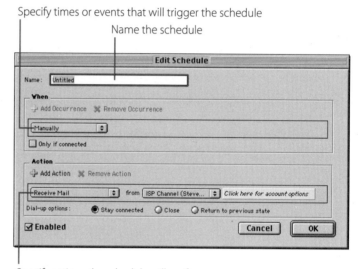

Specify actions the schedule will perform

3 Enter a name for the schedule in the Name text box.

4 Specify the events or times at which the schedule will execute by clicking the Add Occurrence button in the When section or by choosing different options for currently defined occurrences.

The When options are as follows:

- **Manually** Executed only when you choose the schedule name from the Run Schedule submenu of the Tools menu.

- **At Startup and On Quit** Runs at Entourage's startup or when you quit the program.

- **Timed Schedule** Executes only at the specified days of the week and time combinations (for example, Mondays, Wednesdays, and Fridays at 9 AM, 2 PM, and 5 PM).

- **Repeating Schedule** Runs every so many minutes, hours, or days.

- **Recurring** A daily, weekly, or monthly schedule that repeats until a condition is satisfied (until a particular date or number of occurrences have passed).

5 Click the Only If Connected check box to restrict the schedule's execution to those times when you are already connected to the Internet. Otherwise, Entourage will be forced to try to make a connection for you whenever the schedule executes.

 TIP

> If you occasionally read messages or use Entourage for other things while offline (such as scheduling tasks, for example), be sure to check the Only If Connected check box. Doing so will prevent Entourage from automatically attempting to dial.

6 Specify the actions to be performed by clicking the Add Action button in the Action section or by choosing different actions for those that are already defined. Actions include:

- **Receive Mail** Receives all awaiting e-mail messages.

- **Receive News** Downloads new headers from a particular news server for selected newsgroups.

- **Send All** Sends all messages from your Outbox.

- **Run AppleScript** Runs a specified script.

- **Delete Mail** Deletes messages from the Deleted Items folder (or any other folder) that are older than a specified number of days.

- **Launch Alias** Runs a selected program or opens a particular document.

7 Click a Dial-Up Options radio button to indicate what should happen after the schedule has executed.

8 To enable the schedule, click the Enabled check box. To disable the schedule, remove the check mark. (You can always enable the schedule later.)

 **TIP**

> If you think you'll never need a given schedule again, select its name in the Schedules dialog box and click the Delete button. If there's a chance that you'll use it again at some point, disable it instead.

Creating and Applying Message Rules

Normally, when you receive a new e-mail message, you must review it manually and decide what you want to do with it. You might read it or simply mark it as read, print it, create a reply, move or copy it to a different folder, or delete it, for example. If you think for a few moments, however, you'll recognize that there are certain types of mail on which you always perform the same action. Using Entourage rules, you can automate the handling of many messages.

A *rule* consists of one or more criteria that, when satisfied, triggers one or more automatic actions. Figure 23-21 shows a rule that automatically scans incoming e-mail, checks to see if "Office 2001" is part of the Subject text, creates a new Address Book record for the person, adds him or her to an e-mail group named Office 2001 Readers, and moves the message into the Microsoft Press folder. If we later want to contact everyone who e-mailed comments to us concerning the book, we can send them all a message by addressing it to the Office 2001 Readers group.

FIGURE 23-21.

You can easily create your own mail rules by looking for keywords in message subject lines, for example

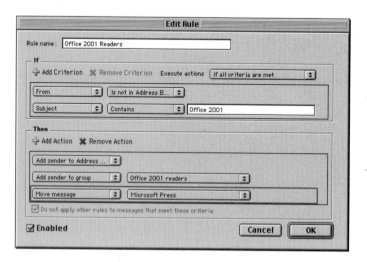

In Entourage, you can create rules that are applied to incoming mail from POP accounts (normal ISP accounts), incoming mail from IMAP

accounts, incoming mail from Hotmail accounts, new newsgroup messages, or outgoing messages. To create a rule, follow these steps:

1 From the Tools menu, choose Rules. The Rules dialog box appears, as shown in Figure 23-22.

FIGURE 23-22.

You can create new rules, as well as edit, disable, or delete existing rules in the Rules dialog box

Enabled rule   Rule types

Currently
defined rules

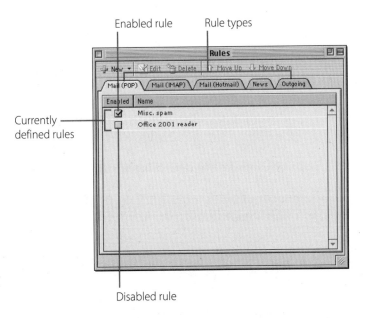

Disabled rule

2 Click the tab that corresponds to the type of rule you want to create.

3 Click the New button at the top of the dialog box. The Edit Rule dialog box appears, as shown in Figure 23-23.

FIGURE 23-23.

You can create or modify rules in the Edit Rule dialog box

Specify criteria   Name the rule   Execute rule under this condition

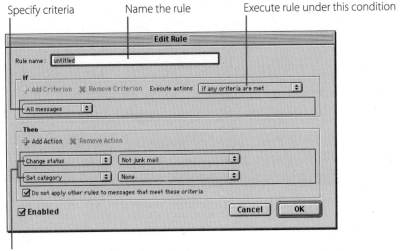

Specify actions to perform when criteria are met

4 Enter a name for the rule in the Rule Name text box.

5 Specify criteria in the If section by changing the default criterion (All Messages) and then adding others by clicking Add Criterion, as necessary.

6 Specify actions to be carried out by changing or removing the default action in the Then section and then adding others by clicking Add Action, as necessary.

7 At the right side of the If section, choose a criteria handler from the pop-up menu.

8 Click OK to save the rule.

To delete an existing message rule, select it in the Rules dialog box and click Delete. To change the settings for a rule, select it in the Rules dialog box and click Edit. To temporarily disable a rule, select it in the Rules dialog box and click the Enabled check box to remove the check mark.

Managing Mailing Lists

Think of a mailing list as a newsgroup that is conducted via e-mail. Like newsgroups, mailing lists are organized around a central topic, such as computer book writing, jokes, or a given program, such as Photoshop or FileMaker Pro. Each day (or at intervals designated by the mailing list owner), subscribers receive copies of all the messages that everyone has sent to the mailing list. Depending on the manner in which you subscribed, you may receive a separate copy of each message or a daily *digest* (in which the entire day's messages are grouped together in a single e-mail message).

If you are using a POP mail account, you can use the Mailing List Manager to set handling options for mailing lists to which you subscribe. To do so, follow these steps:

1 In the message list, highlight a message from the mailing list.

2 From the Tools menu, choose Mailing List Manager. The Mailing List Manager dialog box appears, as shown in Figure 23-24.

FIGURE 23-24.

The Mailing List Manager dialog box lists all mailing lists it's controlling

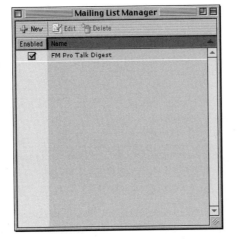

3 Click the New button (or press ⌘-N). The Edit Mailing List Rule dialog box appears, open to the Mailing List tab, as shown in Figure 23-25. Much of the basic information for the mailing list is automatically filled in for you.

FIGURE 23-25.

The mailing list address and handling options for the messages are specified in the Edit Mailing List Rule dialog box

Handling options   Address from which messages will arrive

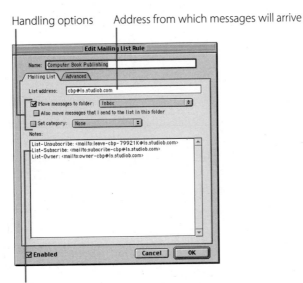

Notes about mailing list

4 Fill in any incomplete information, such as the list's name. You can optionally designate a special folder in which to store list messages, as well as store your own messages to the list in the same folder (rather than in the Sent Items folder).

⭐ **TIP**

> To avoid cluttering your Inbox, you may want to direct all messages from a mailing list to a special folder that you've created for that purpose. (You can also direct mailing list messages to a particular folder by creating a message rule, as explained previously in the "Creating and Applying Message Rules" section.)

5 *Optional*: If you want to specify additional list handling and reply options, click the Advanced tab at the top of the dialog box. Some advanced options that you may want to change include the following:

- If you want to automatically mark as read messages from the list, click the Mark As Read check box.

- If you receive individual messages from the list rather than a digest, you can add a prefix to the subject to make the messages easier to sort and locate in the message list.

- To avoid receiving your messages to the list twice (in the Sent Items folder and again from the list), click the Delete Copies Of Incoming Messages That I Sent To The List check box.

- To specify a different default reply behavior (when responding to a message in the list), check boxes in the When Replying section of the dialog box. (In general, however, the default behavior specified by the list itself is the one you'll want to use.)

6 Be sure that the Enabled check box is checked.

7 Click OK to save the handling instructions for the message list.

⭐ **TIP**

> Unless it's imperative that you see incoming messages from a mailing list the moment they're posted, see the list's instructions for subscribing in digest mode. Otherwise, if it's a popular list, you may find yourself inundated with individual messages each day.

Using AppleScripts

You can use a programming language called AppleScript to modify or customize Entourage's behavior. AppleScript is included with every version of the MacOS software. AppleScripts enable you to perform complex action sequences within scriptable programs such as Entourage.

If you examine the Scripts menu (denoted by the script icon between the Window and Help menu), you'll see several useful scripts. (See Figure 23-26.) All scripts that have been placed in the Entourage Script Menu Items folder are automatically added to the Scripts menu. (You can find this folder by opening the Documents folder and then the Microsoft User Data folder.) Double-click any of these scripts to open and view them in Script Editor (as shown in Figure 23-27), an editing program that is installed along with AppleScript.

FIGURE 23-26.

You can execute Entourage AppleScripts by choosing them from this menu

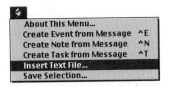

FIGURE 23-27.

Double-click any AppleScript to view it in the Script Editor

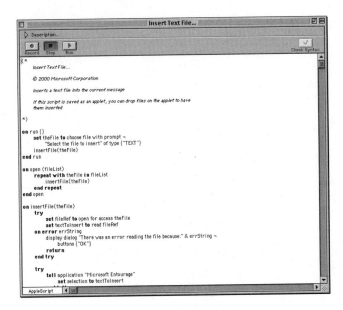

If you're an enterprising programmer, you can design your own AppleScripts. Otherwise, there are many sources of usable scripts on the Internet. To learn more about AppleScript programming in general, visit *www.apple.com/applescript/*.

Introducing Microsoft PowerPoint

Microsoft PowerPoint is an application that creates presentations (high-tech slide shows) that you can display onscreen, print out, turn into 35mm slides, or make into movies. With a little effort, you'll find that PowerPoint is one of the most valuable components of the Office 2001 package. While overhead projectors and 35mm slides have a certain old-school charm, it is far easier to create a more compelling presentation in PowerPoint. And, once you create it, you can easily modify it to meet your particular needs.

This chapter will introduce you to the many features of PowerPoint. We will discuss the various views used in the application and will get you started in creating your own slide show.

Working in PowerPoint

PowerPoint offers various views that enable you to create a presentation. You can access these views by selecting the View menu and choosing one of the following four submenus:

- Normal

- Slide Sorter

- Notes Page

- Slide Show

There are also view buttons at the bottom of the main PowerPoint window. Click the appropriate button to take you to the following views:

- Normal view

- Outline view

- Slide view

- Slide Sorter view

- Slide Show view

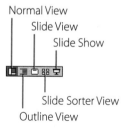

Using the Normal View

The Normal view is where you will spend much of your time creating the slides that make up your presentation. The Normal view has three panes in its main window, as shown in Figure 24-1.

- **Slide pane** This pane shows your slide and allows you to enter and edit information on it.

- **Outline pane** This pane shows the organization of your presentation and displays an outline of the content.

Drag-and-drop slides in the Outline pane to change their order in your presentation, or click on a slide to have it appear in the Slide pane.

■ **Notes pane** This pane allows you to enter notes to accompany your presentation. You can use these notes as speaker notes or in a handout.

FIGURE 24-1.

The Normal view

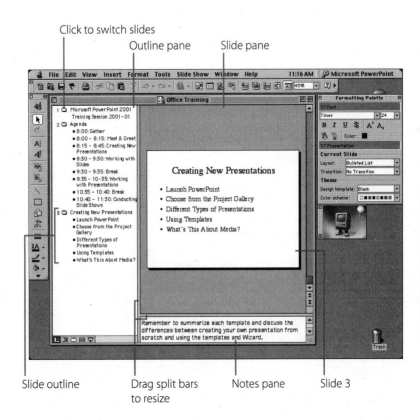

Using the Outline View

The Outline view, shown in Figure 24-2, offers a distinctly different view than the Normal view. The same three panes (Slide, Outline, and Notes) are present, but they have been resized to emphasize the Outline pane. This helps you organize and develop the content of your presentation, while keeping the distraction of the Slide pane to a minimum.

FIGURE 24-2.

The Outline view emphasizes the outline of your presentation

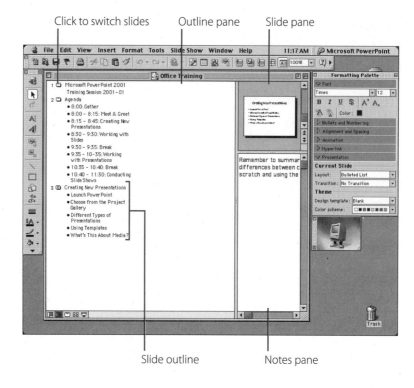

Click to switch slides   Outline pane   Slide pane

Slide outline   Notes pane

Using the Slide View

The Slide view, shown in Figure 24-3, emphasizes the slide itself, giving it more screen space than any of the other views. In this view, the Outline pane is present but you can only see the slide and slide number by default, while the Notes view is hidden. Use the Slide view when you need a large amount of area to work on your slides.

NOTE

You can click and drag the borders of the panes to resize them yourself. You can even access the Notes pane from the Slide view by dragging the bottom border (just above the view buttons) upward.

FIGURE 24-3.

The Slide view emphasizes the slides in your presentation, giving you a large work area

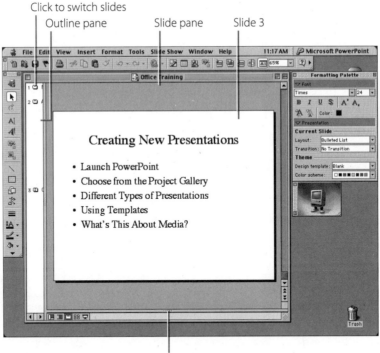

Click to switch slides

Outline pane   Slide pane   Slide 3

Drag split bar to see notes

SEE ALSO

Slide transitions are discussed in greater detail in Chapter 28, "Customizing Microsoft PowerPoint."

Using the Slide Sorter View

The Slide Sorter view, shown in Figure 24-4, helps you organize your presentation. You can see each slide in your presentation as a small thumbnail and even drag-and-drop slides to create a new order. *Slide transitions* (special effects that introduce a slide during a slide show) are also evident by the small transition icon just below slides that have this effect. Click the icon to see it in action.

FIGURE 24-4.

The Slide Sorter view allows you to organize your presentation

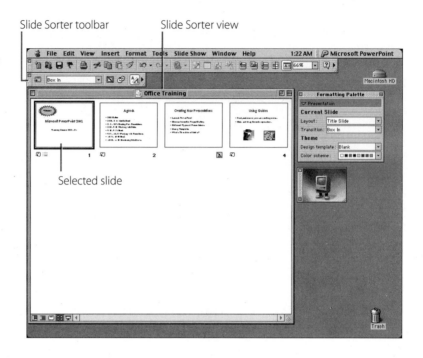

There are a few other useful tricks available in the Slide Sorter view.

- You can start a slide show from any slide in your presentation by clicking the slide in the Slide Sorter view, and then initiating a slide show by pressing the Slide Show button at the bottom of the document window.

- You can hide slides that you don't want included in the slide show so that they still appear in the Slide Sorter view (so you don't forget them). These hidden slides will have a crossed-out icon underneath them.

❓ SEE ALSO

Refer to Chapter 27, "Managing and Conducting Presentations" to learn how to hide slides during a slide show.

Using the Slide Show View

The Slide Show view is the final view in PowerPoint. You can't create or edit slides in this view; its purpose is to show each slide in the order you have chosen, with the transitions and special effects you have created. Notice that the slide takes up your entire screen in the Slide Show view.

Creating Presentations

PowerPoint presentations hold the slides that you will display, print out, or turn into movies. Your first step, then, is to create the presentation that will contain the slides you will use. Once you create your presentation file, you can add slides and enter and format the content of each slide. You can build presentations on your own, much like creating a new, blank document in Word, or you can base your presentation on a template you choose from the Project Gallery.

Building a Presentation on Your Own

The easiest—and paradoxically the most difficult—method of creating a presentation is to build your own. It's easy because the steps you need to take to get the presentation up and running are short and simple. It's difficult because you do the lion's share of the work as you add your own slides, content, and thematic formatting.

Using Templates

A large number of templates have been prepared for you to use in creating your presentations. These templates, found in the Project Gallery and summarized in Table 24-1, are available in both content and design variations. Design templates take care of all the factors that influence the visual appearance of a presentation (color scheme, background, location of presentation elements, and so forth), while Content templates primarily manufacture generic slides that help you choose the overall organization of your presentation.

Table 24-1. PowerPoint Templates Available in the Project Gallery.

Category	Description
Blank Documents	Templates that allow you to create a blank PowerPoint presentation or use the AutoContent wizard.
My Templates	Templates that you have created are available here.
Presentations	Contains a multitude of templates arranged into Content and Designs categories. The Content templates are the same as those used by the AutoContent wizard.

To create a presentation based on a PowerPoint template, follow these steps:

1 If you already have PowerPoint running, select the File menu and choose Project Gallery (or press Shift-⌘-P). Otherwise, launch PowerPoint and the Project Gallery will appear.

2 Select the Presentations category from the list of categories in the Project Gallery. The Presentations category will expand to show its two subcategories (Content and Designs) when you select it.

3 Select either Content or Designs, and the appropriate templates appear.

4 Select a template, as shown in Figure 24-5.

FIGURE 24-5.

Most PowerPoint templates are found in the Presentations category

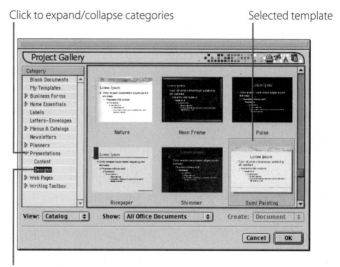

5 Click OK to create a presentation based on the template you've chosen. If you've chosen a template of the Content type, the presentation will be created and appear ready for you to edit. If you've selected a template from the Designs listing, the presentation opens and prompts you to create a new slide. (See Figure 24-6.)

FIGURE 24-6.

Choose a slide layout from the New Slide dialog box

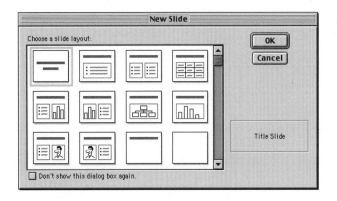

6 Choose a slide layout by clicking on a slide preview. A Title Slide is chosen for you by default.

7 Click OK to finish.

Now you're ready to add content and additional slides until you've finished your presentation.

Using the AutoContent Wizard

The AutoContent wizard is perhaps the speediest way to put a presentation together. It guides you through three steps that help you choose a general content type for the presentation you are creating. It also offers you expert design options along the way. To use the AutoContent wizard, follow these steps:

1 If you already have PowerPoint running, select the File menu and choose Project Gallery (or press Shift-⌘-P). Otherwise, launch PowerPoint and the Project Gallery will appear.

2 Select the Blank Documents category from the list on the left side of the Project Gallery.

3 Click AutoContent Wizard from the list on the right. You will probably have to scroll up to see the AutoContent wizard because the default blank PowerPoint Presentation is near the bottom of the list and the AutoContent wizard is at the top.

V

Microsoft PowerPoint

4 Click OK to launch the AutoContent wizard. The Presentation Type screen asks you to choose which type of presentation you want to create, as shown in Figure 24-7.

FIGURE 24-7.

First choose a presentation category, and then find a type that matches your needs

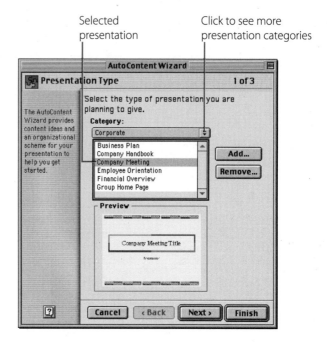

Selected presentation

Click to see more presentation categories

5 Choose a presentation category from the Category pop-up menu. When you choose a category, such as Corporate, a list of the available presentation types (which are also templates) is shown below the pop-up menu.

> **NOTE**

The All category lists all individual presentation types.

6 Choose a template from the list. (Notice that the template is previewed in the Preview window.)

7 Click Next to continue to the Presentation Media screen.

8 Choose the medium that will carry your presentation from the options presented, as shown in Figure 24-8. Your four options are:

- **On-Screen Presentation** Optimized for display on your monitor, or through a projector system to a television or screen. Color, graphics, and special effects can be used to their greatest effect in this option.

- **Black And White Overheads** Optimized for printing your presentation in black and white on overhead slides. Since you will be printing this presentation, special care is taken to minimize the use of effects that will be lost on the printed product, and objects and text are drawn so that they do not require inordinate amounts of ink to print. This medium places a premium on legibility.

- **Color Overheads** As with the black and white overheads, only color is used. Take care not to choose this medium if you don't have a color printer.

- **35mm Slides** Optimizes your presentation for 35mm slides, which are ideal for large audiences in formal settings, and where a 35mm projector is available but computer connectivity to a projection system is absent. You'll have to send your presentation file out to a service bureau to be processed into 35mm slides if you don't have this capability at your business.

FIGURE 24-8.
The presentation media will affect how your slides are optimized

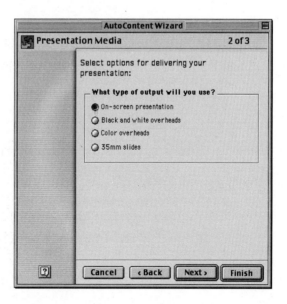

9 Click Next to go to the Presentation Title And Footers screen.

10 Enter the title for your presentation in the Presentation Title box, as shown in Figure 24-9.

FIGURE 24-9.

Enter the information
you want to appear
on the Title slide

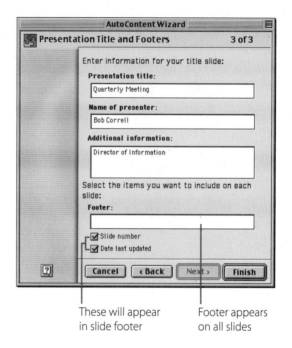

These will appear   Footer appears
in slide footer   on all slides

11 Enter the name of the presenter, if desired, and any additional information you want included underneath that person's name (job title, company, etc.) in the appropriate boxes. (See Figure 24-9.) The presenter's name will appear on the Title slide, with the additional information placed just below the presenter's name.

12 To include in the footer of each slide any additional information, such as the file name or the location where you are presenting your slide show, enter the information in the Footer box.

13 The last two options (the Slide Number and the Date Last Updated) are checked by default. This information is placed at the bottom of every slide. Uncheck them if you want to leave them off.

14 Click Finish to end the AutoContent wizard. PowerPoint will now create your presentation. When PowerPoint is finished creating your presentation, it will open it in Normal view for you to edit, as shown in Figure 24-10.

FIGURE 24-10.

The AutoContent wizard creates presentations with content and art included

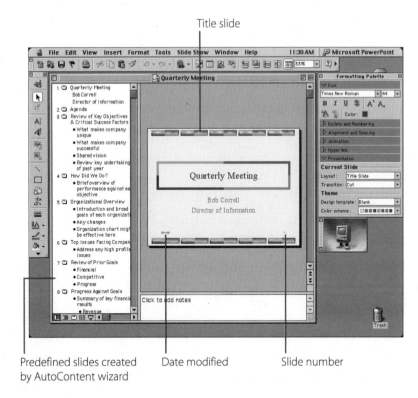

Title slide

Predefined slides created by AutoContent wizard

Date modified

Slide number

The AutoContent wizard is a great way to get started in PowerPoint, but don't think you have no work left to do. Since all of the content (except for the title, presenter's name, additional information, and footer) is generated by the wizard, you'll have to modify the presentation to include your own content, add or delete slides if necessary, and configure the presentation (if you're going to use it onscreen) to meet your individual needs.

Creating Slides

Microsoft PowerPoint is all about creating slides. Slides are the meat and potatoes of any presentation, whether you turn the presentation into a movie or print it out in the form of a handout. This chapter teaches you how to create and delete slides, add your own content in a variety of forms and formats, and use master slides to make global changes to the formatting of your slides. We'll walk you through adding the following types of content to your slides: text; tables; charts, including organizational charts; Clip Art; and other media, such as pictures and movies.

Working with Slides

Any presentation goes through a variety of stages—from conception to drafts to the final product. As you work through these stages, you should become familiar with all aspects of working with slides.

Adding and Deleting Slides

Adding slides is an easy process—one that will become second nature after only a few attempts. To add a slide, follow these steps:

1 Select the slide in your presentation that will come immediately before the slide you want to add.

2 Click the New Slide button on the Standard toolbar. The New Slide dialog box appears, as shown in Figure 25-1.

FIGURE 25-1.

Slide layouts contain preformatted areas for your content

Selected slide

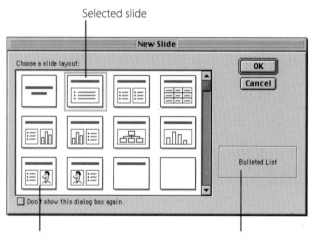

Click a slide layout to see its description   Slide description

3 Scroll through the list of slide layouts until you find the type you want and select it with your mouse, or use your arrow keys to move between the different slide layouts.

With the exception of the Title Slide, Blank, and Large Picture, each slide has a title at the top, with the content arranged underneath it.

4 Click OK to insert the slide in your presentation.

Decoding the Slide Layouts

You can get a good idea of the way the slide is laid out by looking at the slide layout list. Titles appear as gray boxes, while other content has a border around it and an illustration of what it looks like. Text and lists appear as small bullets next to squiggly lines, charts have three columns, Clip Art is represented by a picture of a man's head, and media clips are represented by scene markers (like those they use in the film industry). When you select a slide type, a description will appear on the right-hand side of the dialog box.

Deleting slides is easier than adding them. To delete a slide, follow these steps:

1 Select the slide you want to delete by clicking on it in the Outline pane or scrolling to it in the Slide pane. If you need to delete multiple, consecutive slides, hold down the Shift key as you click the first and last slides in the Outline pane.

You cannot select more than one slide if they aren't consecutive.

2 Select the Edit menu, and choose Delete Slide. Your slide will now be deleted.

Should your presentation contain more than one master slide, deleting all slides that reference a particular master will delete that master slide from your presentation. See "Using Master Slides" later in this chapter.

Inserting Slides from Another Presentation

If another presentation has a slide you need in the presentation you are working on now, there is no need to copy the original slide's contents and paste them into the new presentation or re-create them from scratch. Instead, insert the slide into your new presentation by following these steps:

1 Select the Insert menu, and then choose Slides From File. This opens the Choose A File dialog box, shown in Figure 25-2.

V

Microsoft PowerPoint

FIGURE 25-2.

Choose a presentation that contains slides you want to insert, and insert all or selected slides

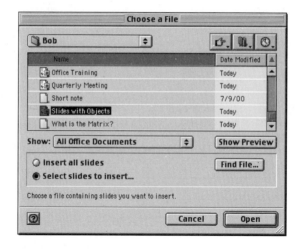

2 Navigate to the presentation from which you want to insert slides, and select the presentation.

3 Click the Insert All Slides option button if you want to insert the entire presentation in your open file; otherwise, click Select Slides To Insert.

4 Click Open to continue. If you choose to insert all the slides, PowerPoint will insert them immediately following the selected slide in the active presentation. If you choose to insert selected slides, the Slide Finder opens, as shown in Figure 25-3.

FIGURE 25-3.

Select one or more slides to insert into your open presentation

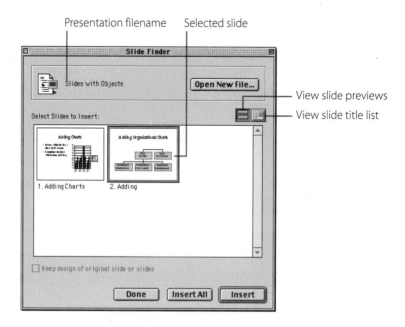

5 Choose a slide from the Select Slides To Insert preview. A box will appear around any slides you choose. To choose more than one slide, hold down the Shift key as you click more slides.

You can change the way the slides are previewed by clicking the small buttons above the slide preview. The Slide Sorter button on the left, active by default, shows the slides in order, with their titles beneath them. To select more than one non-adjacent slide in the Slide Sorter view, Shift-click the slides. The Outline button on the right switches to an outline view. In this view, the presentation outline is on the left and a preview of the currently selected slide is on the right. To select more than one non-adjacent slide in the Outline view, ⌘-click the slides.

6 Click Insert to insert the selected slides into your presentation.

7 Click Done to close the dialog box.

Using Guides

Guides are convenient lines that you can use to align objects on your slides. When guides are visible and you drag objects such as text boxes or pictures near them, the objects snap to the guides and are neatly aligned. Guides appear when you are working on your slide, but they do not appear in your presentation. Select the View menu and choose Guides to view the guides. To move the guides, follow these steps:

1 Position your cursor over a guide.

There is no visual feedback that indicates when your mouse is directly over a guide. You must click to find out whether it is positioned correctly or not. If the cursor changes from the default arrow to a measurement and small directional arrow when you click and hold, you've positioned your mouse correctly. If not, reposition your mouse and try again.

2 Click and hold your mouse on the guide. The cursor will change form, as shown in Figure 25-4, and will appear as a directional arrow indicating where you are dragging the guide; numbers will tell you how far you are dragging it from the center of the page.

The guide numbers use the same units the ruler is set to use, which by default is inches. You can change the units from inches to centimeters, points, or picas by selecting the Edit menu, choosing Preferences, and selecting a different ruler unit from the pop-up menu on the View tab.

V

Microsoft PowerPoint

FIGURE 25-4.

Movable guides allow you to align objects precisely onscreen

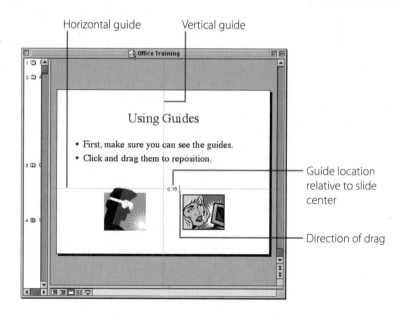

Horizontal guide Vertical guide

Guide location relative to slide center

Direction of drag

3 When you've positioned the guide in the location you want, release your mouse button to "drop" the guide.

To insert more guides on a slide, follow these steps:

1 Position your cursor over a guide.

2 Hold down the Option key, and click the guide to select it. Continue to hold the Option key down as you drag the new guide to its location.

3 Release your mouse button first to drop the guide, and then release the Option key.

To delete guides, follow these steps:

1 Select the guide you want to delete.

2 Drag it off the slide, and release your mouse button.

Reapplying or Changing Slide Templates

You can reapply or change the slide template (the slide layout that you choose when you create a slide) for any slide in your presentation. Simply select the slide to make it active, and then click the Slide Layout button. The Slide Layout dialog box will appear and prompt you to choose a new layout for the slide. After the new slide layout is applied, the slide's contents will be rearranged as best they can to fit the new slide layout.

Adding Content

No slide would be complete without your own content. As you add new slides to your presentation, consider what sort of content you want to add, and make your slide layout selection based on that decision.

Entering and Formatting Text

Text is easy to enter, and if you're familiar with Microsoft Word or any other word processing program, you won't need much guidance. Simply click in the fields—also called text boxes or title boxes—that prompt you to add text, and begin typing. The placeholder text will disappear automatically—there is no need to delete it yourself. Notice that in Figure 25-5 we haven't entered a title yet, but we are working on the body of the slide.

FIGURE 25-5.

Click in a placeholder to make it active, and begin entering your text

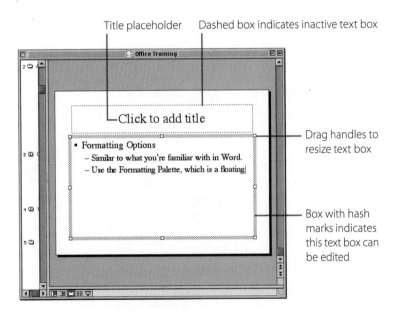

Title placeholder   Dashed box indicates inactive text box

Click to add title

• Formatting Options
  – Similar to what you're familiar with in Word.
  – Use the Formatting Palette, which is a floating

Drag handles to resize text box

Box with hash marks indicates this text box can be edited

When you first click in the text box, its appearance changes to alert you that you are in editing mode for that particular object. A hashed line and drag handles appear around the box so that you are aware of which object you are editing. A blinking insertion cursor displays where text will appear when you begin typing. To change the size of a text box, simply drag the box handles.

To format your text, use the Formatting Palette, shown in Figure 25-6. Use the Formatting Palette in PowerPoint just as you would in other Office applications. You can change text and other presentation properties, such as the following:

- Font style, size, and color

- Bullets and numbering

- Alignment and wrapping

> If you want to change the appearance of all of the titles or body text, don't use the Formatting Palette. Rather, change their formatting on the Slide Master instead. This saves you a lot of work. Use the Formatting Palette to add specific emphasis or alignment to small amounts of text.

You can also insert hyperlinks that respond to mouse events such as On Mouse Click and On Mouse Over. In addition, you can apply a design template or theme to a slide.

FIGURE 25-6.

The Formatting Palette in PowerPoint

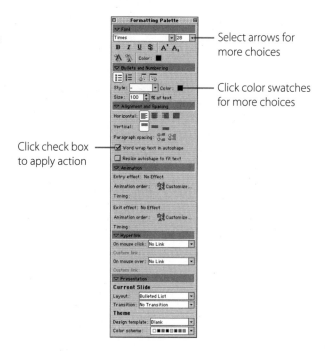

Select arrows for more choices

Click color swatches for more choices

Click check box to apply action

NOTE

To increase the level of interaction in slide shows, PowerPoint allows you to control when an animation or slide transition occurs, and what happens when you click or move the cursor over an object or area within the slide or when you click on hyperlinked text. (For example, when you click the mouse button, you can begin animation or continue to the next slide in the slide show.) Furthermore, each object in a slide can have an action that is triggered when clicked or when the cursor moves over it.

Adding Tables

Tables help organize information on your slides. Tables work best when they are not overused. Thus, don't create tables with too many rows or columns, or too much information, because they will be difficult to read. To add a table, follow these steps:

1 Create a new slide using the Table layout.

2 Double-click the table placeholder in the slide. This opens the Insert Table dialog box, shown in Figure 25-7.

FIGURE 25-7.

Choose the number of rows and columns you want your table to have

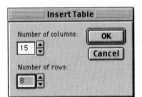

3 Choose the number of rows and columns you want to include in your table.

4 Click OK to finish. PowerPoint updates your slide to contain the table with the dimensions you specified, and displays the Tables And Borders toolbar, shown in Figure 25-8.

Microsoft PowerPoint

V

FIGURE 25-8.

Enter your content in the table cells

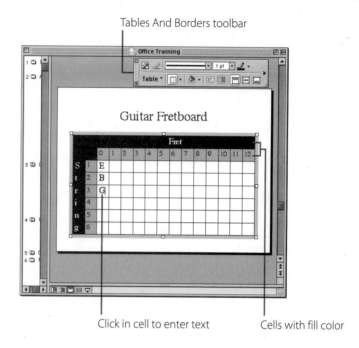

Tables And Borders toolbar

Click in cell to enter text

Cells with fill color

? **SEE ALSO**

For more information on creating tables, see Chapter 8, "Adding Tables, Columns, and Graphics."

5 Use the Tables And Borders toolbar to modify the table's properties. If the Tables And Borders toolbar doesn't automatically appear, choose View, Toolbars, and then Tables And Borders.

6 Click in a cell to add your content.

Adding Charts

Charts usually display numerical data in graphical form. Rather than forcing you to create this graphic in PowerPoint, PowerPoint does the work for you. For example, you can chart your company's quarterly sales and include the chart in your PowerPoint presentation by entering the data in Microsoft Graph and allowing it to create the chart for you. To add a chart, follow these steps:

1 Create a new slide using one of the layouts that contains a chart placeholder.

2 Double-click the chart placeholder in the slide. This opens Microsoft Graph, as shown in Figure 25-9, with "dummy" data already entered. The default chart is a 3-D column chart.

NOTE

> PowerPoint remains running and visible on your screen as Microsoft Graph launches. PowerPoint was hidden for Figure 25-9, however, to keep the figure from becoming too busy. If you want to hide everything except Graph as you work on your chart, select the Application menu and choose Hide Others. When you quit and return to PowerPoint from Graph, PowerPoint will automatically become visible again.

FIGURE 25-9.

Microsoft Graph, which functions in similar ways to charting in Microsoft Excel, allows you to insert detailed charts in your presentation

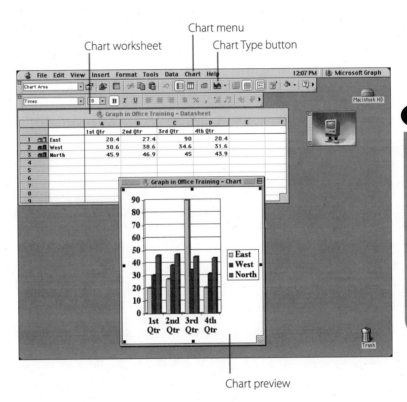

Chart menu

Chart worksheet

Chart Type button

Chart preview

SEE ALSO

Microsoft Graph works just like Excel. For more detailed information on making charts in Excel, refer to Chapter 14, "Creating Charts and Using Functions."

3 Enter new data in the Chart worksheet window, which looks like an Excel worksheet.

4 Modify the chart type, if desired, using the Chart Type button.

5 Modify other chart preferences by choosing Chart Options from the Chart menu.

6 To update the chart in your slide, select the File menu and choose Update. You can then switch tasks to your PowerPoint presentation to see the results.

7 When you are done with the chart, select the File menu and choose Quit & Return To *Presentation* (where *Presentation* is the file name of the presentation to which you have added the chart).

Adding Organizational Charts

Rather than draw all the boxes and connecting lines to form an organizational chart yourself, insert a slide that contains an organizational chart into your presentation, and then edit the chart to match your organization. Follow these steps to add an organizational chart:

1 Create a new Organization Chart slide.

2 Double-click the "org chart" placeholder in the slide. This opens MS Organization Chart 2.1 with "dummy" data already entered. (See Figure 25-10.)

FIGURE 25-10.

The Organization Chart enables you to create detailed organizational charts without having to draw them yourself

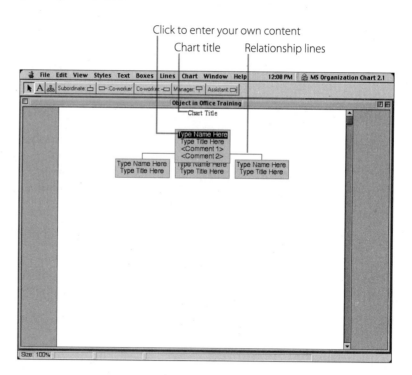

3 Select the Chart Title, and enter one of your own.

4 Click in each box, and enter the appropriate organizational data.

5 To add more boxes, click a box type from among the buttons at the top of the window, and then click the box on the chart that you want to attach the new level of organization to, as shown in Figure 25-11. For example, if you want to attach a subordinate to a particular box, first click the Subordinate button and then click the box on the chart that will appear *above* (or beside) the new box in the organization.

FIGURE 25-11.

You can add different levels of organization to your chart

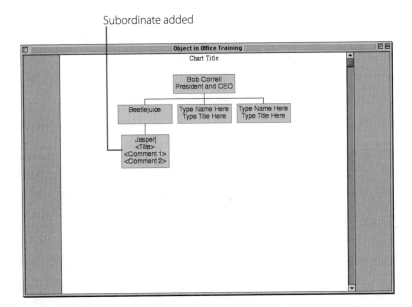

6 Continue adding and editing boxes to mirror your organization.

⭐ **TIP**

If you want to change the style of the organizational chart, select the Styles menu and choose a different method of presenting the data. You can choose from several Group styles in addition to Assistant and Co-Manager.

7 If you want to preview your work in your presentation, select the File menu and choose Update *Presentation* (where *Presentation* is the file name of the presentation to which you have added the chart). This will update your slide in PowerPoint so you can preview your work in the actual side without having to quit MS Organization Chart 2.1.

8 When finished, select the File menu and choose Close & Return To *Presentation*.

Adding Clip Art

Clip Art is a favorite among PowerPoint users. It's fast, easy to use, and offers a wealth of visually compelling graphics that will make your presentation stand out. Adding Clip Art is much easier than creating it yourself. Follow these steps to add Clip Art:

1 Create a new slide using one of the layouts that contains a Clip Art placeholder.

2 Double-click the Clip Art placeholder in the slide. This opens the Clip Gallery, shown in Figure 25-12.

FIGURE 25-12.

The Clip Gallery contains hundreds of clips for you to use

Preview of clips in selected category

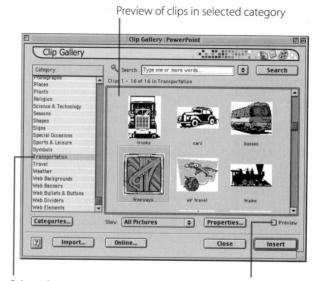

Selected category

Click to show large preview of clip

3 Select a category of art from the list on the left, and then click a clip in the right-hand side of the window.

4 Click Insert to insert the Clip Art in your presentation.

You can resize the Clip Art by selecting it and using the drag handles to change its dimensions. To alter other aspects of the Clip Art, use the Picture toolbar. If the Picture toolbar does not appear, select the View menu, choose Toolbars, and then select Picture to make it visible.

Adding Pictures and Media

Pictures and movies can really make your presentation stand out. Aside from the "pizzazz factor," you may be able to convey your message more meaningfully and effectively through the use of images, both still (pictures) and moving (media clips). Follow these steps to add pictures and other media to your slide:

1 Create a new slide of a type that contains a picture or media clip in its layout.

2 Double-click the placeholder in the slide. This opens the Choose A Picture dialog box, shown in Figure 25-13 (or the File Finder dialog box, in the case of media clips).

FIGURE 25-13.

Choose a picture from your computer to insert into your presentation

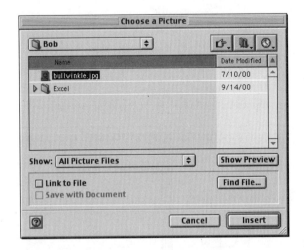

3 Find the picture or media clip you want to insert in the slide on your computer, select it, and click Open.

PowerPoint inserts the picture or media clip in your slide, where you can change its shape or alter other properties by using the toolbars provided. If you are inserting a movie, PowerPoint asks you if you want the movie to play automatically. If not, you'll have to click it during your presentation to play it.

Using Master Slides

As we alluded to earlier, PowerPoint presentations are built around master slides. These slides contain text formatting information such as font style, color, or size as well as the onscreen position of placeholders. This information is applied to all slides in your presentation. If you want to change the font of all your titles, make the change to the Slide Master instead of churning through all your slides and making the changes one by one.

Select the View menu, choose Master, and then choose Slide Master to open the master slide for editing, as shown in Figure 25-14.

FIGURE 25-14.

Use the master slide to apply formatting to each slide in your presentation

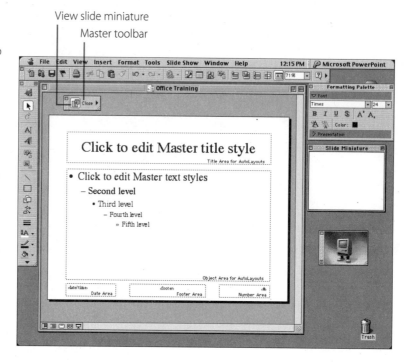

Notice the placeholders that appear instead of the content you may have been working on? Each placeholder has a specific purpose:

- Use the *slide title* placeholder to format the titles that appear on your slides.

- Use the *slide text* placeholder to apply text formatting that appears in the text boxes on your slides.

- Use the *background* placeholder to insert a graphic on the master slide and have it appear on each slide in your presentation.

- Use the *date footer* placeholder to format the default date and time footer.

- Use the *footer* placeholder to format the main footer area.

- Use the *number* placeholder to format the slide number footer.

It is important to note that you don't normally enter any content on the master slide other than to insert a background picture.

NOTE

In some cases, you might want to enter text on the master slide, such as "Draft" or "Preliminary," if you know you're going to change it but don't want it as a header or footer.

Insert a background picture by selecting the Insert menu, choosing Picture, selecting From File, and then using the same procedures that you would use to insert any other picture in your presentation. Follow these steps to modify the formatting of the other placeholders:

1 Switch to the Slide Master view by selecting the View menu, choosing Master, and then selecting Slide Master.

2 Click in a placeholder to make it active and to enter text-editing mode.

3 Select the text in the placeholder.

4 Change the formatting as desired using the Formatting Palette, shown in Figure 25-15.

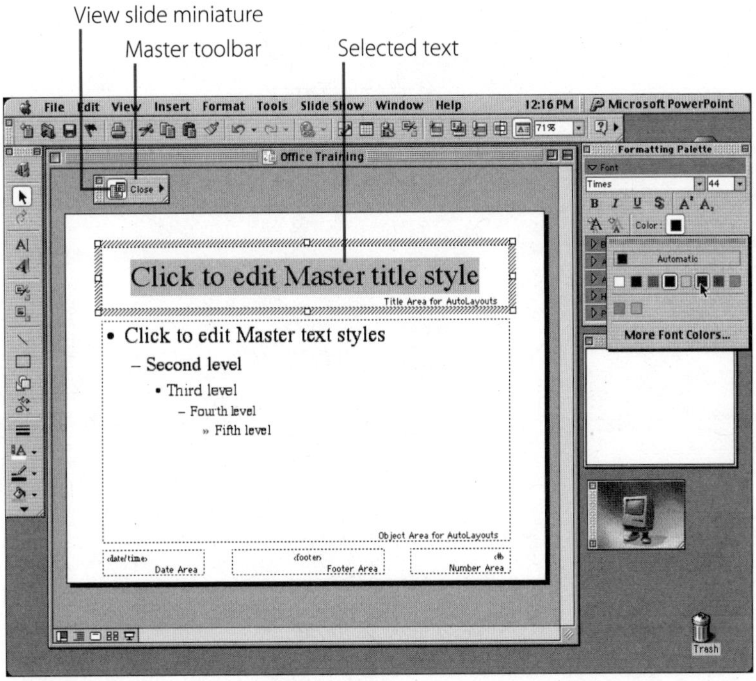

FIGURE 25-15.

Select the text in the placeholder, and format it to reformat all items of like type in your presentation

View slide miniature

Master toolbar   Selected text

5 Click in another placeholder to make other changes until finished.

6 Click the Close button on the Master toolbar to return to your slides. They will be automatically updated with the new formatting.

You can use three other master slides to modify your entire presentation:

■ **Title Master** This master allows you to format your title slides differently than the rest. (See Figure 25-16.) Modify the Slide Master first, then use the Title Master to change your title slides. If you haven't applied a design template to your presentation or master slide (from the Theme section of the Formatting Palette), the Title Master is unavailable.

FIGURE 25-16.

The Title Master creates a unique title slide appearance for your presentation

■ **Handout Master** This master contains placeholders for information that appears on each page of a handout. (See Figure 25-17.)

FIGURE 25-17.

The Handout Master contains placeholders for handouts

Master toolbar

Handout Master toolbar

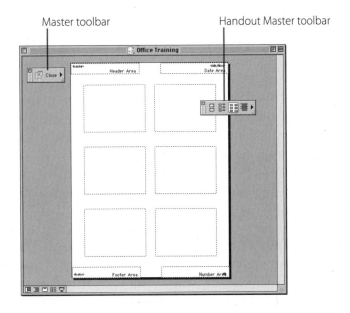

■ **Notes Master** This master contains placeholders for information that appears on each page of your notes. (See Figure 25-18.)

FIGURE 25-18.

The Notes Master contains placeholders for notes pages

Master toolbar

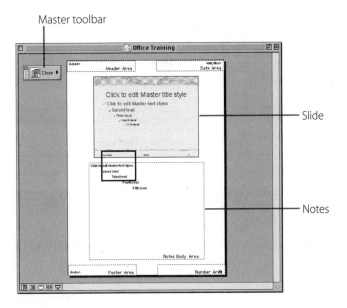

Slide

Notes

Modify each of these master slides as you would the Slide Master.

CHAPTER 26

Using Colors, Drawings, and Animations

We've all heard it said that a picture is worth a thousand words. The same can be said of Microsoft PowerPoint slides. This chapter will teach you how to spruce up your presentation by selecting and applying pleasing color schemes, drawing shapes to help you make your point, and using animations to make your slide shows more interesting.

Adding or Modifying Color Schemes

Color schemes are sets of eight coordinated colors that are applied to different elements of the slides in your presentation. Choosing a color scheme greatly reduces your workload as you create your presentation because when you choose it, everything is colored automatically for you thereafter. For example, if you choose a color scheme that has a yellowish background and blue title text, each slide in your presentation, and that you create from that point on, will use that color scheme.

Applying a Color Scheme

To take advantage of color schemes, you must choose one scheme and apply it to one or more slides in your presentation. Color schemes are dependent on the design template you have chosen. For example, if you've chosen Bold Stripes as your theme, you will have different color schemes available to you than you would with other themes.

Follow these steps to apply a color scheme to a slide:

1 Open your presentation, and select the slide you want to modify from one of the views.

2 Select the Format menu, and choose Slide Color Scheme. This opens the Color Scheme dialog box, shown in Figure 26-1.

FIGURE 26-1.
Choose a color
scheme to apply to
your slides

Selected color   Color scheme preview
scheme   shows colors used

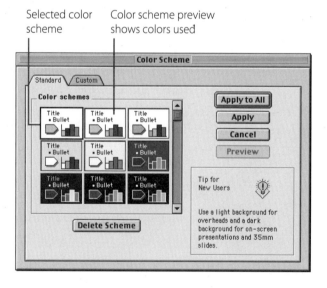

3 There are several predefined color schemes available on the Standard tab. Click on one to choose it.

4 Click Preview to see the color scheme drawn on your slide in the main PowerPoint window.

Drag the Color Scheme dialog box out of the way to see the preview better.

5 Click Apply to apply the color scheme to the currently selected slide. Click Apply To All to apply the color scheme to all slides in your presentation.

You can also apply a color scheme by selecting one from the Color scheme pop-up menu on the Formatting Palette. Should you select the pop-up menu, small color swatches will be displayed for you to choose from. Select one to apply to all slides in your presentation.

Creating a Custom-Made Color Scheme

If the set of predesigned color schemes isn't adequate, you can create one from scratch by following these steps:

1 Open your presentation, and select the slide you want to modify from one of the views.

2 Select the Format menu, and choose Slide Color Scheme. This opens the Color Scheme dialog box.

3 Select the Custom tab, as shown in Figure 26-2.

FIGURE 26-2.

The Custom tab allows you to create your own color schemes or to modify existing ones

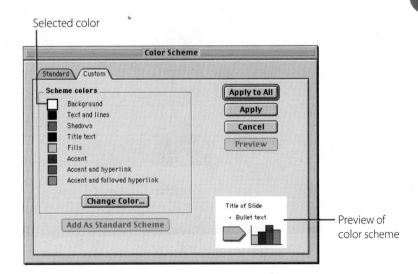

Selected color

Preview of color scheme

4 The items that you can set colors for are listed in the Scheme Colors section. They are:

- Background

- Text And Lines

- Shadows

- Title Text

- Fills

- Accent

- Accent And Hyperlink

- Accent And Followed Hyperlink

5 Click the color swatch beside the name of the item you want to change.

6 Click the Change Color button. This opens the Color Picker dialog box, shown in Figure 26-3.

FIGURE 26-3.

Choose a Color Picker, and then define the color you are adding

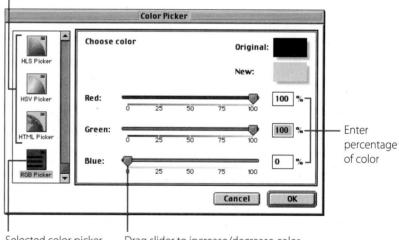

Other color pickers have different methods for defining colors

Enter percentage of color

Selected color picker   Drag slider to increase/decrease color

7 Select a Color Picker from the list on the left. For this example, we've chosen RGB Picker, which is the standard for computer monitors. Use HTML Picker if you plan to use your presentation on the Web, as it will allow you to pick only Web-safe colors. CMYK Picker is used for professional printing, and the Crayon Picker brings out the "lighter side" of choosing colors by allowing you to select crayons with names like "Moss" and "Mildew" for your colors.

8 Use the tools unique to the Color Picker you've chosen to create a new color. In our example in Figure 26-3, we can use sliders or enter the numerical value in the percent field.

9 Click OK when you're satisfied. The new color will take the old color's place in the color swatch beside the item name.

10 Continue modifying the various Scheme Colors items until you're finished.

11 Click Preview to see how the new color scheme looks on your actual slides.

12 Click Add As Standard Scheme if you want your new color scheme to appear on the Standard tab with the others.

13 Click Apply to apply the new color scheme to the currently selected slide. Click Apply To All to apply the new color scheme to all the slides in your presentation.

Using Backgrounds

You can choose a wide variety of colors, shades, patterns, and textures to add to the backgrounds of your slides by following these steps:

1 Open your presentation, and select the slide you want to modify from one of the views.

2 Select the Format menu, and choose Background. This opens the Background dialog box, shown in Figure 26-4.

V

Microsoft PowerPoint

FIGURE 26-4.

Create interesting
background effects by
using the Background
dialog box

Preview shows currently
selected color

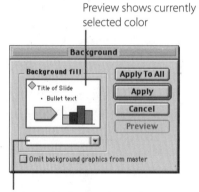

Select color from pop-up menu

3 Select a color from the pop-up menu below the slide preview
portion of the Background dialog box. You have several options
to choose from:

- **Automatic** This option lets PowerPoint select background
colors automatically, depending on the color scheme or
theme you've chosen.

- **Current Theme** Select a color from the eight colors displayed in this menu. These are the colors of the current
theme.

- **More Colors** Select More Colors to open the Color Picker
dialog box if the color you want to use is not present.
Choose a new color, and click OK.

- **Fill Effects** Select Fill Effects if you want to add fill effects
such as shading or textures.

4 *Optional:* If you select Fill Effects, the Fill Effects dialog box
opens. This dialog box has four tabs:

- **Gradient** The Gradient tab allows you to create a color gradient. Clicking One Color, as shown in Figure 26-5, prompts
you to choose a color. Select a color from the pop-up menu
and use the slider to make the color darker or lighter.
Clicking Two Colors prompts you to select two colors to
make up the gradient. Clicking Preset allows you to choose
from a large number of predesigned background gradient
effects, as shown in Figure 26-6. Next choose a shading
style, such as Diagonal Up, from those listed. Finally click
on any of the variants that are previewed in the Variants
portion of the dialog box.

FIGURE 26-5.

Create transitions
between one or more
colors with the
Gradient tab

Choose how many
colors to use

Click to select
different color

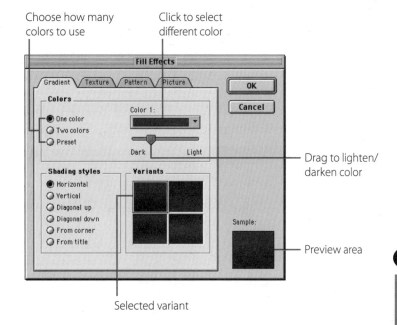

Drag to lighten/
darken color

Preview area

Selected variant

FIGURE 26-6.

The Preset Colors
button reveals a
large number of pre-
designed gradients for
you to choose from

Click to see
different presets

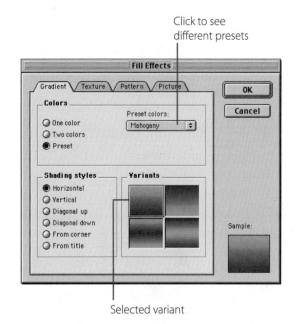

Selected variant

- **Texture** The Texture tab allows you to choose a texture as
  your background. Click a texture from those shown. (See
  Figure 26-7.)

FIGURE 26-7.
The Texture tab allows you to choose a texture for your background

Click to select different texture

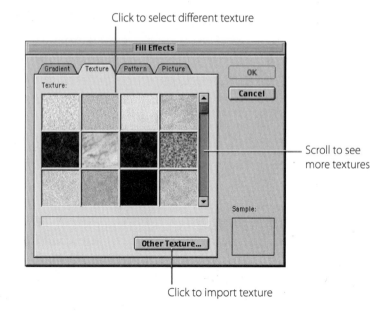

Scroll to see more textures

Click to import texture

- **Pattern** The Pattern tab allows you to choose a pattern created by two colors. Choose a pattern from those displayed, and then choose the two colors (Foreground and Background) that will make up the pattern, as shown in Figure 26-8.

FIGURE 26-8.
The Pattern tab enables you to choose a pattern defined by two colors of your choice

Click to select different pattern

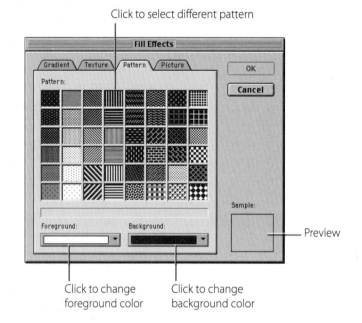

Preview

Click to change foreground color

Click to change background color

- **Picture** The Picture tab allows you to select a picture from your computer as your background. (Click Select Picture to find and choose a picture.)

Click OK when you are finished choosing a Fill Effect.

5 Click Preview to see how the new color scheme looks on your actual slides.

6 Click Apply to apply the new color scheme to the currently selected slide. Click Apply To All to apply the new color scheme to all the slides in your presentation.

Applying Design Templates

Design templates go a step further than color schemes. They are completely coordinated design and color schemes that have been created professionally. Follow these steps to apply a design template to your presentation:

1 Open your PowerPoint presentation.

2 Select a design template (such as Blank or Artsy) from the Design Template pop-up menu on the Formatting Palette.

3 If you choose Select Template from the list, the Choose A File dialog box opens in the folder where your design templates are located, as shown in Figure 26-9.

FIGURE 26-9.

Choose a design template to apply to your presentation

4 Select a design template, and click Apply.

Drawing and Manipulating Graphics

Should you need to add line art or other graphical objects to your slides, there is no need to launch a separate graphics program to draw the object and import it into PowerPoint. PowerPoint comes with a powerful array of drawing tools. The AutoShapes are shapes—such as circles, squares, stars, and arrows—that you can draw quite easily. Follow these steps to draw an AutoShape:

1 Select the slide you want to add a drawing to, and switch to an appropriate view.

 TIP

The Slide view gives you the most room to work with.

2 Click a shape to draw from the Drawing toolbar, as illustrated in Figure 26-10.

FIGURE 26-10.
The Drawing toolbar contains a large number of drawing tools for you to use

Click to show menu

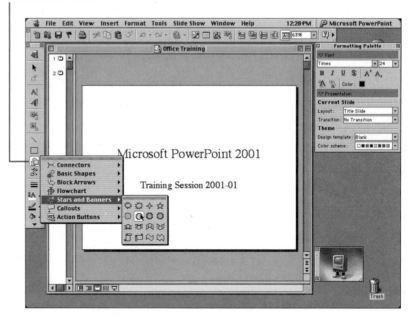

3 There are several types of shapes you can choose to draw:

- Lines

- Rectangles

- AutoShapes (including Connectors, Basic Shapes, Block

Arrows, Flowchart, Stars And Banners, Callouts, or Action Buttons)

4 Draw your object by clicking on the slide and dragging to form lines, rectangles, or other shapes. When you release your mouse button, the object is rendered onscreen.

5 You can change the color and other properties of the object you just drew. Select the object by clicking it. (Alternatively, you can select a color or formatting option first and then draw your object). Depending on what you want to do, you can:

- Resize an object by clicking on one of the drag handles and dragging in the direction to which you want the object to enlarge or shrink.

- Click on the object's adjustment handle (a small yellow diamond) to change the most prominent feature of a shape. Not all shapes have adjustment handles, but in the case of a doughnut, the adjustment handle increases or decreases the size of the opening in the middle.

- Select a new fill color by clicking the down arrow on the right side of the Fill Color button on the Drawing toolbar and selecting a new color or effect.

- Change the lines of the object by selecting new line types from the Drawing toolbar.

- Enter text in your object by selecting the object and typing the text.

> **NOTE**

Some of these properties (such as Fill Color) can be changed from the Drawing toolbar as well as the Formatting Palette. Which device you use depends on your personal preference.

Applying Animations

PowerPoint allows you to animate text, graphics, sounds, movies, charts, and other objects on your slides in order to draw attention to them or control the flow of a slide (by hiding text and displaying it when you click a button). Follow these steps to quickly apply animations to objects on your slides:

1 Open your presentation, and select the slide that you want to animate.

2 Select the object to which you want to apply the animation. This can be any item on your slide, such as the title, buttons, text boxes, or graphics.

3 Select the Slide Show menu, select Animations, and select an animation from the following list:

- Custom
- Fly In
- Fly Out
- Fly In/Out
- Drive In/Out
- Camera
- Flash Once
- Laser Text
- Typewriter
- Reverse Order
- Drop In/Out
- Wipe Right
- Dissolve
- Split Vertical Out
- Appear

If you want more control over the animation, follow these steps:

1 Open your presentation, and select the slide that you want to animate.

2 Select the Slide Show menu, and choose Animations.

3 Select Custom from the list under the Animations submenu. This opens the Custom Animation dialog box. The Custom Animation dialog box has three major areas and three tabs, as shown in Figure 26-11.

FIGURE 26-11.

The Custom Animation dialog box gives you fine control over your animations

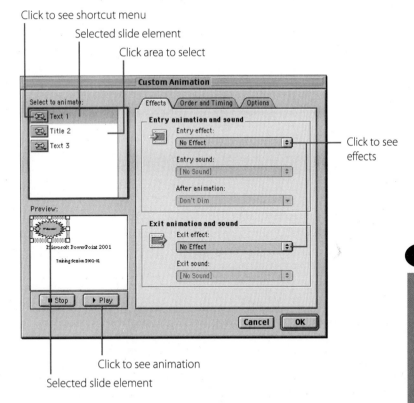

4 Select an object to animate (such as your title) from the Select To Animate list in the upper-left portion of the dialog box.

5 Select entry and exit animation effects for the selected object from the pop-up menus in the Entry Animation And Sound or Exit Animation And Sound areas of the Effects tab. You can be as creative as you like, adding entry and exit effects as well as sound. You can choose from a number of effects, some with several variations.

6 At any time, you can click the Play button in the preview window to see how your animation will look.

7 Select the Order And Timing tab, shown in Figure 26-12, to control which objects begin their animations first and when the animation starts. (This only applies if there are multiple animations on the slide.)

8 Select an object, and use the arrow buttons to move it up or down the Animation Order list.

9 Determine whether you want the Start Animation to begin On Mouse Click or Automatically, *x* Seconds After Previous Event by clicking on the appropriate option.

10 Select the Options tab, shown in Figure 26-13, to choose options specific to the effect and object you are animating. In the case of the title, the options pertain to how the text will enter the screen.

11 Click OK to finish creating the animation.

FIGURE 26-12.

The Order And Timing tab allows you to set the order and timing of your animations

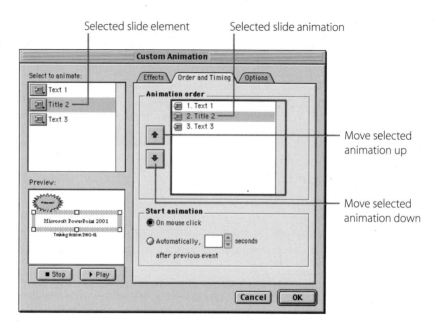

Selected slide element   Selected slide animation

Move selected animation up

Move selected animation down

TIP

If you use a lot of animations that require you to click your mouse to start them, make sure to practice relentlessly. Because one default method of advancing slides is to click the mouse (the other is pressing the Spacebar), you might forget about the animations and think you are advancing slides when in fact you are just starting an animation.

NOTE

In some cases, such as with objects, there are no options available when you select the Options tab.

FIGURE 26-13.

The Options tab has options specific to the object and effect you've chosen

Click to see shortcut menu

Selected slide element

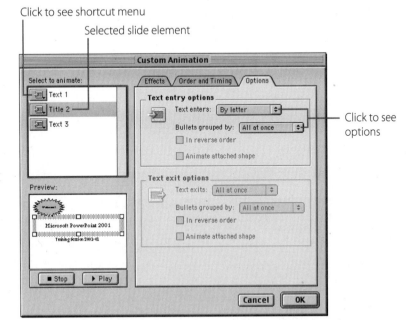

Click to see options

Managing and Conducting Presentations

Slide shows, or presentations, are where "the rubber meets the road" in Microsoft PowerPoint. All the time and effort you spend creating a masterful presentation will come into play when you finally give the presentation. To alleviate the pressure, make sure you set up your slide show well in advance, and practice, practice, practice. This chapter will help you set up and present a slide show, and create other types of presentations for your audience.

Setting Up a Slide Show

Select the Slide Show menu, and then choose Set Up Show to open the Set Up Show dialog box, shown in Figure 27-1. The Set Up Show dialog box allows you to set up each slide show in a variety of ways.

FIGURE 27-1.

You can define your show type, choose which slides to view, and determine how the slides are advanced in the Set Up Show dialog box

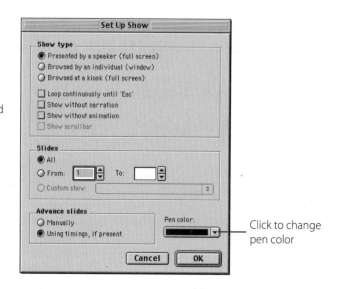

Click to change pen color

The Set Up Show dialog box is divided into four main areas. The options you can choose from in this dialog box are:

- **Show Type** This option allows you to choose a venue (full screen or windowed), and to choose whether to repeat your slide show in a loop, include narration, or include animations.

- **Slides** This option allows you to pick the slide range you will use in the show.

- **Advance Slides** This option allows you to decide whether the slides will advance automatically or manually.

- **Pen Color** This option allows you to select a different annotation pen color. The pen allows you to draw on slides during a slide show.

 NOTE

To use the pen, Control-click a slide during your slide show (or click on the pop-up menu in the lower-left corner of the presentation), select Pointer Options, and select Pen. This enables the annotation pen, which you can draw with on the slide using your mouse.

Using Transitions

Transitions are special effects, such as Wipe Down (which reveals the slide by "uncovering" it from the top down), that appear between slides and reveal the next slide during a slide show. They are more exciting than having the next slide simply pop up.

 NOTE

> Transitions are fun, but they can sometimes overpower the actual presentation. Be careful that the transitions don't dominate the presentation so much that nobody remembers what you are actually saying.

To set transitions for each slide, follow these steps:

1   Switch to the Slide Sorter view by clicking the Slide Sorter View button or by choosing Slide Sorter from the View menu.

2   Click on a slide to select it.

3   Select a slide transition from the Slide Transition Effects pop-up menu on the Slide Sorter toolbar. Because there are so many transitions to choose from, we won't list them here. The names are self-explanatory, so experiment with different ones until you find one you like.

 TIP

> If you have a hard time choosing a transition, select Random Transition from the Slide Transition Effects pop-up menu. PowerPoint will then randomly choose transitions during your slide show.

Using Action Buttons

Action buttons allow you to create interactive presentations that respond to user actions (for example, clicking the button). Action buttons also give you the option to link to separate files, presentations, slides, or the Internet. They are similar to the buttons on your Web browser and hyperlinks on a Web page. You can create buttons that go back a slide, go to the beginning of the show, or open another file. During your presentation, you or a person viewing the slide show can use the mouse to click or hover over an action button. Follow these steps to add action buttons to your presentation:

1   Switch to the Normal or Slide view by clicking the appropriate View menu or button.

V

Microsoft PowerPoint

2 Select the Slide Show menu.

3 Select the Action Buttons submenu.

4 Select an action button to use on your slide. You can choose from the following options:

- Custom

- Home

- Help

- Information

- Previous Slide

- Next Slide

- First Slide

- Last Slide

- Last Slide Viewed

- Document

- Sound

- Movie

5 Use your mouse to click and drag on your slide to create the action button, as shown in Figure 27-2.

FIGURE 27-2.

You can create action buttons for increased interactivity during slide shows

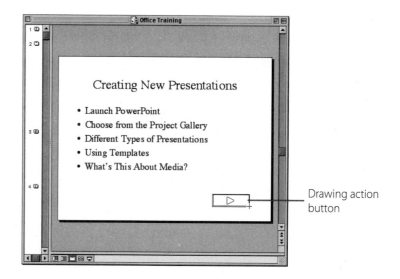

6 When you release your mouse button, the Action Settings dialog box pops up, as shown in Figure 27-3, showing you the Mouse Click tab.

FIGURE 27-3.

Configure your action button to do what you want it to

Click to choose different action

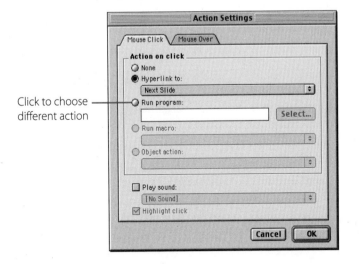

7 Review the action taken when the button is clicked in the Action On Click area of the dialog box. You can change the default action to any one of several possible values. You can hyperlink to another slide, a Web page on the Internet or your intranet, an e-mail link, or another program entirely. You can also play a sound when the button is clicked.

8 Select the Mouse Over tab, and select other actions that you want to occur when you move your mouse over the button during the slide show.

9 Click OK to finish.

Hiding Slides

You may have slides in your presentation that you don't want shown during a slide show. Rather than delete them from your file, you can hide them by following these steps:

1 Click the Slide Sorter View button to enter Slide Sorter view.

2 Click the Hide Slide button on the Slide Sorter toolbar. The Slide Sorter displays an icon over the slide number underneath the slide, as shown in Figure 27-4, to indicate it will be hidden during a slide show.

V

Microsoft PowerPoint

FIGURE 27-4.

Hidden slides are still displayed in the Slide Sorter, but they have a hidden icon to remind you they won't be seen during a slide show

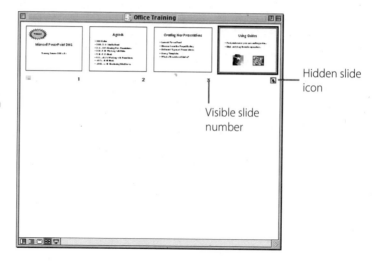

Hidden slide icon

Visible slide number

Conducting the Slide Show

The slide show is where you get a chance to impart to your audience whatever knowledge you have chosen. To conduct a slide show, follow these steps:

1 Open your presentation in PowerPoint.

2 Although it isn't necessary to be in a particular view, most people find that the Slide Sorter view is the best place to start. Switch to the Slide Sorter view by clicking the Slide Sorter View button or choosing Slide Sorter from the View menu.

3 Click the first slide in your presentation.

Take special care to select the first slide to be shown during your slide show. If you accidentally select a different slide, your slide show might begin on that slide.

If you want to end your presentation before the last slide, press Esc. This closes the slide show and returns you to PowerPoint in the view you were in prior to launching the show.

4   Click the Slide Show button on the View toolbar at the bottom of the screen. This begins the slide show.

5   Click your mouse or press the spacebar to advance through each slide, unless your slide show is timed and you have set the slides to advance automatically.

6   During your show, wiggle your mouse if you need to access the pop-up menu or Slide Navigator (if you have the option enabled), as shown in Figure 27-5.

FIGURE 27-5.

The pop-up menu and Slide Navigator can be accessed by wiggling your mouse

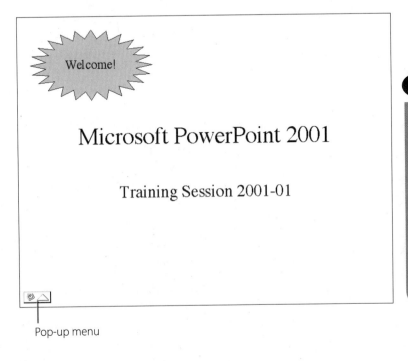

Pop-up menu

7   When you reach the last slide, do not advance the presentation unless you don't mind the audience seeing the PowerPoint interface. This is often why it's good to end on a black slide or a slide that you won't forget is the end.

Recording a Narration

Narrations allow you to create a slide show that can literally present itself. To record a voice narration that will accompany your presentation, follow these steps:

1   Select the Slide Show menu, and choose Record Narration. This opens the Record Narration dialog box, as shown in Figure 27-6.

V

Microsoft PowerPoint

FIGURE 27-6.

Recorded narrations can be linked or embedded in your PowerPoint file

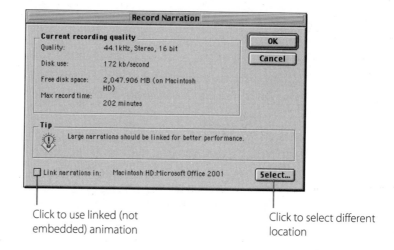

Click to use linked (not embedded) animation

Click to select different location

2 The top portion of the dialog box shows information about the recording as it is currently set up. You see:

- **Quality** This is given in kHz (kilohertz, which is the sampling rate in thousands of samples per second), stereo/mono (which is the number of channels recorded), and the number of bits devoted to each audio sample.

- **Disk Use** This takes the recording parameters given above and translates them into how many KB of disk space will be required for each second of your recording.

- **Free Disk Space** This is reported from your hard disk.

- **Max Record Time** This takes into account the amount of disk use and free hard disk space.

3 As the dialog box indicates, large narrations should be linked (rather than embedded in your PowerPoint presentation file) so that the performance doesn't suffer. If your narration falls into this category, click the Link Narrations In check box.

NOTE

You should experiment with linking vs. embedding recorded narrations to determine where you get the best performance in relation to the convenience of embedding the narration in your file. This is a judgment call that depends on the length, size, and quality of your recording as well as the capabilities of your computer (or the system that will be used during the actual presentation).

4 If you are linking your narration, click the Select button and choose a folder to store the narration file in. Navigate to the folder you want to store your narration in, and select Choose. You will then be returned to the Record Narration dialog box.

5 Click OK to close the Record Narration dialog box. Your presentation will now be shown in a slide show.

6 Speak into your microphone (internal or external), and record a narration for each slide. When your slide show is completed, PowerPoint will prompt you with a final question.

7 Click Yes to the first question asking you to save slide timings with the narration.

8 If you clicked Yes to the first question, you'll be asked another question. Click Yes to see the timings in the Slide Sorter view.

Setting Presentation Timing

A timed presentation presets the amount of time each slide is shown before automatically proceeding to the next slide. This means you don't have to fiddle with a mouse during the presentation or have someone advance the slide for you. A timed presentation also allows you to create a self-running presentation. You can either set the timing of your presentation from the Slide Sorter or you can set the slide show timing by using rehearsal timings. The second method is especially useful if you are recording a narration.

To set the timing of your presentation using the Slide Sorter, follow these steps:

1 Click the Slide Sorter View button to enter the Slide Sorter view.

2 Select a slide in the Slide Sorter to add a timing value.

3 Click the Slide Transition button on the Slide Sorter toolbar to open the Slide Transition dialog box, as shown in Figure 27-7.

4 In the Advance section of the dialog box, click Automatically After and enter the number of seconds you want the slide to be displayed in the Seconds field.

FIGURE 27-7.

Slides can be configured to advance automatically

Click to see more transitions

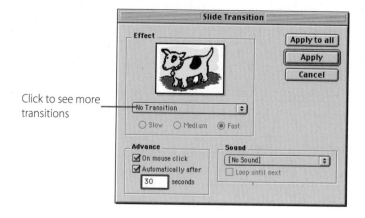

5 Click Apply to finish or Apply To All to set that time for every slide in your presentation.

Rehearsing a Timed Presentation

Rehearsing a timed presentation allows you to practice a slide show in which each slide is viewed for a predetermined amount of time as defined in the Slide Sorter. Rehearsing is useful even in situations where the slides aren't timed because the rehearsal process times your overall presentation. You can even use this information to set slide timings if you change your mind. Rehearsing allows you to see which slides you may be spending too much time on and therefore alter your narration. In addition, since you will be previewing the slide transitions, animations, and action buttons that may be present in your slide show, you can see which ones may be distracting or take too much time. After your rehearsal, return to your slides and "fine-tune" any problems.

> **NOTE**

If you do not need to time your presentation, there is no need to use this procedure. Just start a slide show normally by clicking the Slide Show button, and practice on your own.

Follow these steps to rehearse your timed presentation:

1 Select the Slide Show menu.

2 Choose Rehearse Timings. This launches the slide show and displays a clock in the lower-right corner of the screen that shows the elapsed time for each slide. The clock resets when you advance to the next slide.

 NOTE

> Conducting a timed rehearsal will allow you to use the rehearsed timings to set the timing of your presentation.

3 Conduct your presentation, and advance through each slide normally. If you want to abort the rehearsal, press Esc. Press No when asked to record the timings.

4 When you are finished, the total time you have taken for your presentation will be displayed in a dialog box that asks whether you want to record the slide timings. Click Yes to accept or No to reject.

5 If you clicked Yes, you will be asked whether you want to review the timings in the Slide Sorter view. Click Yes to accept or No to reject.

Creating Other Types of Presentations

Although slide shows are often the primary method of imparting information to your audience, PowerPoint 2001 offers several other methods of transmitting this information.

Creating QuickTime Movies

To turn your presentation into a movie, follow these steps:

1 Select the File menu, and choose Make Movie. This opens the Save dialog box, shown in Figure 27-8.

V

Microsoft PowerPoint

FIGURE 27-8.

Save your presentation as a QuickTime movie

2 Choose a file name for your movie. If you plan to save your movie in the same folder as your PowerPoint presentation, make sure to give it a different name; otherwise, you will overwrite the PowerPoint file with the movie.

3 Select a location on your hard disk to save your movie.

4 Click Use Current Settings if your movie preferences are already set; otherwise, leave the Adjust Settings option (the default) enabled.

5 Click Next. If Adjust Settings was chosen, the Movie Options dialog box appears, as shown in Figure 27-9.

FIGURE 27-9.

You can choose movie options in the Movie Options dialog box

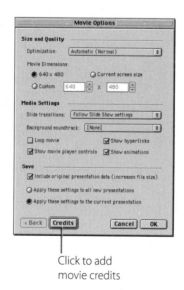

Click to add
movie credits

6 The Movie Options dialog box is divided into three areas. Change the options to meet your needs.

Movie options and credits are discussed more fully in Chapter 28, "Customizing Microsoft PowerPoint."

7 Click the Credits button to add credits to your movie. Click OK to close the Movie Options dialog box entirely, or click Back to return to the main Movie Options dialog box.

8 Click OK to return to the Save dialog box.

9 Confirm that your file name and location is correct, and click Save.

From the Director's Chair: Tips for Making PowerPoint Movies

The following are tips for making a PowerPoint movie:

- Use slide transitions, not slide animations. They do not work together, and QuickTime transitions look better than animations. If you really need to animate something, use different slides, resulting in a frame-based animation effect.

- Slides should have different backgrounds. For example, make your slide with two alternating color backgrounds or different photos. If slides have the same background, you are not using QuickTime transitions to their full effect.

- Do not use large screen sizes. Try 800 x 600 (at most 1024 x 768). This helps transitions play smoothly.

- When using QuickTime transitions, experiment with the repeat and border size settings to achieve interesting results.

- General presentation guidelines also apply here: use no more than three to six bullets per slide, remember that pictures speak louder than words, and also remember that a professional color scheme and font choices significantly add to the power of your presentation.

- Having a good background soundtrack adds punch to a presentation.

- It is also important that slide timings be set appropriately; otherwise, a presentation will run too quickly because the movie does not wait for mouse-clicks before proceeding to the next slide.

Creating Web Presentations

Follow these steps to create a Web page from your PowerPoint presentation:

1 Select the File menu, and choose Save As Web Page. This opens the Save dialog box, shown in Figure 27-10.

V

Microsoft PowerPoint

FIGURE 27-10.
Save your presentation as a Web page

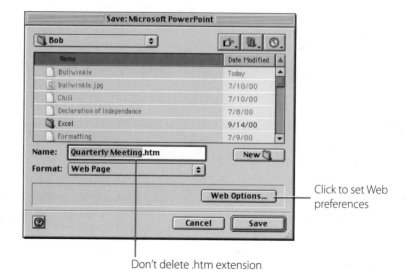

Don't delete .htm extension

Click to set Web preferences

2 Enter a new name for your presentation if you want. It is not always necessary to change the presentation name because Web pages require that the three-letter .htm extension (or the four-letter .html extension) be appended to the file name and automatically enters the extension in the Save dialog box. This allows you to keep the same name as your presentation file, which would have either the .ppt extension (which identifies it as a PowerPoint file for Microsoft Windows users) or no extension at all.

3 Choose a new location to save your Web page on your hard disk, if you want.

4 Click Web Options to open the Web Options dialog box, shown in Figure 27-11.

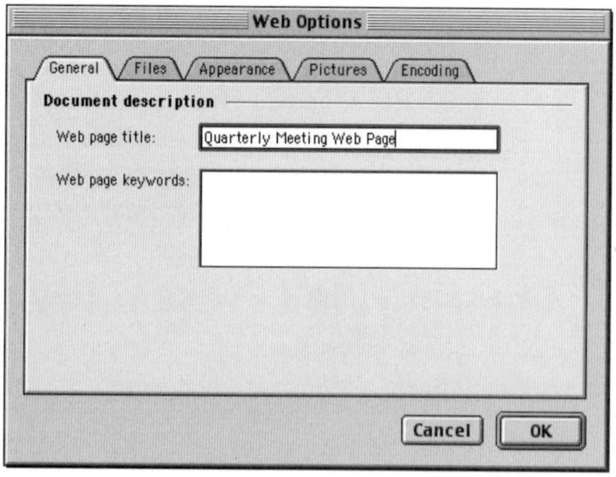

FIGURE 27-11.
Define your Web page options in the Web Options dialog box

SEE ALSO

Web options are discussed more fully in Chapter 28.

5 Select the tabs present in the Web Options dialog box, and make the changes to the preferences that you want.

6 When you are done with the Web Options, click OK to return to the Save dialog box.

7 Click Save to save your presentation as a Web page.

TIP

Select the File menu, and choose Web Page Preview before you save your presentation as a Web page to see how the slides appear in your Web browser.

Creating Handouts

Follow these steps to print handouts for your audience:

1 Create your presentation normally.

2 Select the View menu, and select the Master submenu.

3 Select Handout Master, which changes the view to the Handout Master, as shown in Figure 27-12.

FIGURE 27-12.

You can modify options that you want to appear on every handout page in the Handout Master

Master toolbar   Handout Master toolbar

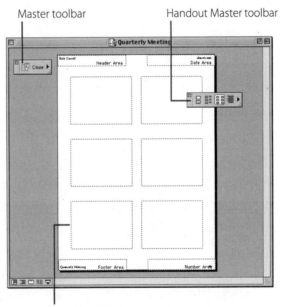

Location of slides

4 Preview the different layouts provided by clicking the positioning buttons of the Handout Master toolbar. You can choose one of four types of layouts:

- 2 slides per page

- 3 slides per page

- 6 slides per page

- Outline

 SEE ALSO

Handouts print the slides only, not any presentation notes you may have added. See the "Creating Slides with Notes" section later in this chapter for information on how to print notes pages.

5 Make any additions or changes to the Handout Master. You can add text, graphics, headers and footers, page numbers, and other information that will only be seen when you print the handouts—nothing added here will modify your slides in any way.

6 When finished, you can click the Close button on the Master toolbar to return to your presentation or leave the Handout Master visible.

7 Select the File menu, and choose Print.

> **NOTE**

Your Print dialog box may look different from the one shown in these figures depending on the model printer you have, but the steps will remain the same.

8 Select Microsoft PowerPoint from the pop-up menu just below the Printer, as shown in Figure 27-13.

FIGURE 27-13.

You can choose to print 2, 3, or 6 slides per page

Select Microsoft PowerPoint

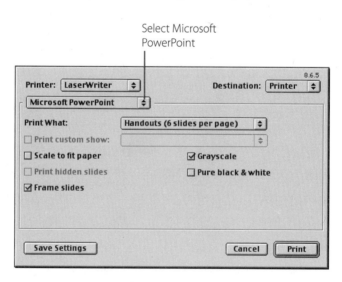

9 Select the type of handout you want to print (2, 3, or 6 slides per page or Outline) from the Print What pop-up menu.

10 Click Print.

Creating Slides with Notes

Follow these steps to create and print notes pages:

1 Create the slides in your presentation, and enter notes to accompany each slide in the notes pane of the Normal, Outline, or Notes Pages views.

2 Select the View menu, and select the Master submenu.

3 Select Notes Master to open the Notes Master page, shown in Figure 27-14.

FIGURE 27-14.

You can modify options you want to appear on every notes page in the Notes Master

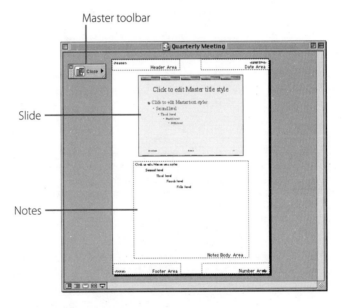

4 Modify the Notes Master page as you see fit. You can add text, graphics, headers and footers, and page numbers, as well as change the global formatting (font style, size, color, etc.) of your notes.

5 Click the Close button of the Master toolbar when finished to return to your presentation.

6 Select the File menu, and choose Print.

7 Select Microsoft PowerPoint from the pop-up menu, as shown in Figure 27-15.

FIGURE 27-15.

Select Notes Pages to print your notes pages

Select Microsoft PowerPoint

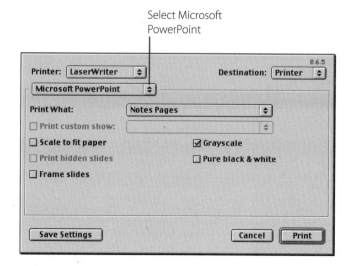

8 Select Notes Pages from the Print What pop-up menu.

9 Click Print.

CHAPTER 28

Customizing Microsoft PowerPoint

Microsoft PowerPoint's major preferences are organized into functional areas, just as they are in other Office 2001 applications. You can access them through the Edit menu under Preferences. Selecting the Preferences menu opens the Preferences dialog box, shown in Figure 28-1.

FIGURE 28-1.
You can modify PowerPoint's options in the Preferences dialog box

Most tabs organize preferences into functional areas

Click pop-up menus to see more choices

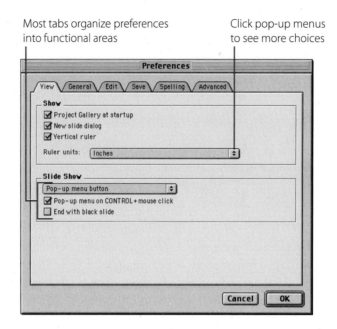

> **NOTE**

The Preferences dialog box opens to the tab you last viewed or to the View tab upon first use.

The tabs running across the top of the dialog box are the functional areas that contain the options you can change. Click a tab to make it active and to view the preferences associated with it. Most of the time you can simply check a check box to change a preference. If a check box is checked, the option is enabled; if it is blank, then the preference is currently disabled. Some options use pop-up menus to define choices or text-entry fields. Select a choice from a pop-up menu or enter text in a text-entry field to identify your preferences.

> **NOTE**

If you make a mistake while changing preferences, click Cancel instead of OK; PowerPoint won't update any of the preferences.

The following sections describe each preference tab and briefly explain what each preference category does.

The View Tab

The View tab contains options that relate to what you see onscreen when you are creating your presentations in PowerPoint and conducting slide shows. The view tab is organized into two areas:

- **Show** This area allows you to disable the Project Gallery when you launch PowerPoint; to disable the New Slide dialog box (which allows you to choose a layout) when you create a new blank presentation or add slides; to show or hide the vertical ruler; and to configure the ruler's measurement units (in inches, centimeters, points, or picas).

> **NOTE** Points and picas are units of measurement used in the print industry. A point is approximately 1/72 of an inch, and a pica is approximately 1/6 of an inch.

- **Slide Show** This area allows you to choose whether a pop-up menu, Slide Navigator, or no slide show controls appear onscreen during your presentation. It also allows you to set a pop-up menu to appear when you Control-click onscreen during a presentation, as well as to end your slide show with a black slide.

The General Tab

The General tab, shown in Figure 28-2, allows you to set general PowerPoint preferences and modify movie and Web options. The general options range from enabling or disabling sound feedback to linking sounds larger than a certain size (rather than embedding them, which could cause your file size to balloon dramatically). You can also allow animated GIFs to play in slide shows. Animated GIFs are graphics used on the Web. They are a single file containing from one to a large number of "still frames," which are animated so that the image looks like a movie.

FIGURE 28-2.

Set general preferences in the General tab

? SEE ALSO

For more information on macro viruses, see Chapter 9, "Special Tasks in Microsoft Word."

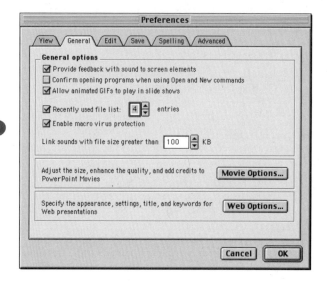

When you click the Movie Options button, the Movie Options dialog box appears, as shown in Figure 28-3.

FIGURE 28-3.

Configure the movie options if you plan to save your presentation as a movie

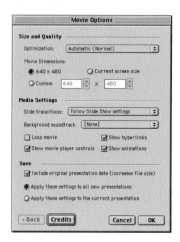

The Movie Options dialog box is divided into three areas:

- **Size And Quality** This area allows you to optimize your movie according to a variety of criteria. You can choose automatic (or normal) optimization, or optimize the movie to reduce file size, ensure smooth playback, or maintain the highest quality. You can also determine the dimensions of your movie in this area of the dialog box.

NOTE

> Not all computers are created equal. If you are working on a very powerful Macintosh and plan on transferring your presentation with one or more movies to another, less powerful computer, you should optimize your movie for smooth playback.

- **Media Settings** This area contains options that determine how your movie will implement slide transitions in the presentation (using the presentation's transitions or QuickTime transitions) and whether you want to add a background sound track, loop the movie, show the movie player controls, show hyperlinks, or show animations.

- **Save** This area configures whether PowerPoint saves the original presentation data with the movie. It also allows you to set whether PowerPoint will apply these preferences to the current presentation or to all new presentations.

Clicking the Credits button on the Movie Options dialog box displays a dialog box for you to enter the credits of your movie, as shown in Figure 28-4. Enter the appropriate information in the fields provided, and click OK to close the Movie Options dialog box entirely or click Back to return to the main Movie Options dialog box.

FIGURE 28-4.

Enter your movie credits in the Movie Options dialog box

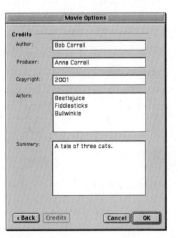

Clicking the Web Options button opens the Web Options dialog box, shown in Figure 28-5.

FIGURE 28-5.

The View tab in the Web Options dialog box

Enter search keywords

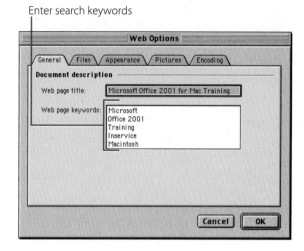

The Web Options dialog box has five tabs, which break down the Web preferences into these areas:

- **General** This tab allows you to give your Web page a title and enter keywords that will be used by search engines to determine the content of your Web pages.

- **Files** This tab contains save and browser support options, which allow you to update hyperlinks when your presentation is saved. This tab also allows you to save your file in PowerPoint format when you save it as a Web page (so that you can go back and edit it in PowerPoint at a later time), and it offers three levels of Web browser support.

> **NOTE**
>
> When it comes to Web browsers, the "big two" are Microsoft Internet Explorer and Netscape Navigator. You can't go wrong supporting either or both of these browsers, but if your organization (if you have one, that is) has standardized to a particular browser, you can choose not to support the others, which reduces the overall file size of your Web page and speeds its load time in Web browsers. Organizations standardize their internal Web browsers to streamline software installation and troubleshooting, in addition to taking advantage of the unique capabilities of particular Web browsers, which aren't always compatible.

- **Appearance** This tab controls the default view (full screen or normal), colors, and full-screen options, such as graphic navigation buttons and button placement locations.

■ **Pictures** This tab allows you to choose to support the PNG graphics file format. This is the latest standardized Web graphic file format, which takes the best of what GIFs and JPEGs have to offer (transparency and animation for GIFs and millions of colors for JPEGs) and combines them into one standard. This area also allows you to choose the size and composition (laptop or desktop) of a target monitor.

■ **Encoding** This tab determines which text encoding you want to save your Web page in. The default is Western European (Macintosh).

Click OK to return to the Preferences dialog box.

The Edit Tab

The Edit tab, shown in Figure 28-6, controls options that affect editing.

FIGURE 28-6.

The Edit tab

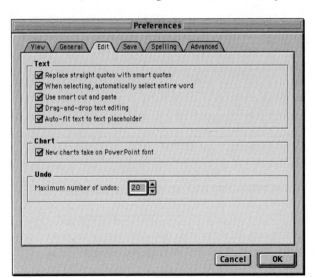

The Edit tab is divided into three areas:

■ **Text** This area contains the standard Office text-editing options, such as replacing straight quotes with smart quotes (smart quotes are angled into the text they enclose), selecting and pasting options, drag-and-drop editing, and auto-fitting text.

■ **Chart** This area has just one option, which causes new charts to take on the PowerPoint font.

■ **Undo** This area lets you change the maximum number of "undos" you can perform (when clicking the Undo button on the Standard toolbar).

NOTE

> The larger the number of undos you use, the more memory PowerPoint will require to keep track of all your changes. If you are working on a computer with little memory, you might reduce the number of undos from the default of 20 to 10 or fewer.

The Save Tab

The Save tab, shown in Figure 28-7, contains some of the more important preferences that can rescue you in an emergency.

FIGURE 28-7.

The Save tab

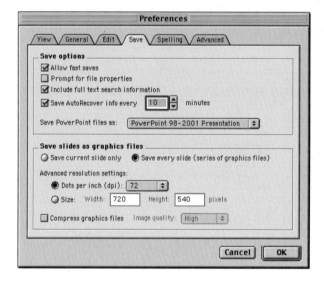

The Save tab is organized into two areas:

■ **Save Options** This area controls how and when PowerPoint saves your files, including how often to save AutoRecover information. A very important option in this tab is the Save PowerPoint Files As option. If you need to send your file to another person or are going to be presenting it on another computer, you should check to see what version of PowerPoint they have. Once you have that information, you can save your file in a compatible format. Those available are:

   • PowerPoint 98-2001 Presentation

   • Microsoft PowerPoint 2001 Movie

   • PowerPoint 4.0 Presentation

NOTE

AutoRecover information is used to recover your file if your computer crashes. Although you should save your work often, AutoRecover helps you if you forget.

■ **Save Slides As Graphics Files** This area contains options that take effect when you save your presentation, or a slide within your presentation, in graphics form (as opposed to the standard PowerPoint format). You can choose to change the default from saving every slide to saving the current slide, alter the resolution of the graphic, and compress your graphics files (with a corresponding quality).

TIP

Don't change the default resolution unless you're going to print your graphics out at high resolution. Most computer monitors will display only 72 to 100 dots per inch (dpi), as opposed to the 1200 dpi that many printers can print. When the dpi gets larger than the monitor will support, it expands the graphic accordingly so as to display each dot.

The Spelling Tab

The Spelling tab, shown in Figure 28-8, controls the spelling preferences found in PowerPoint. These spelling preferences are similar to the preferences found in the other Office 2001 programs.

FIGURE 28-8.

The Spelling tab

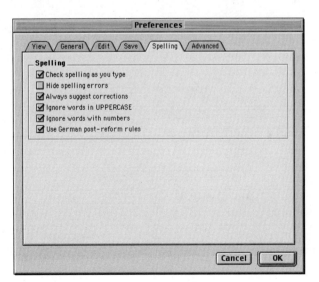

Microsoft PowerPoint

Two of the most troublesome spell-checking preferences are enabled by default: Ignore Words In UPPERCASE and Ignore Words With Numbers. Keep this in mind when conducting a spell check. There's nothing more frustrating than misspelling a word in your title that happens to be in uppercase and is therefore skipped by the spell checker.

The Advanced Tab

The Advanced tab, shown in Figure 28-9, is broken down into three areas:

- ■ **File Locations** This area allows you to set the default file locations for your presentations and recorded narrations.

- ■ **User Information** This area allows you to customize PowerPoint with your name and initials.

- ■ **Multiple Masters** This area allows you to have multiple masters (and therefore designs) for your presentations, and enables the design of a slide to follow the slide itself when you copy it to a new presentation.

FIGURE 28-9.

The Advanced tab

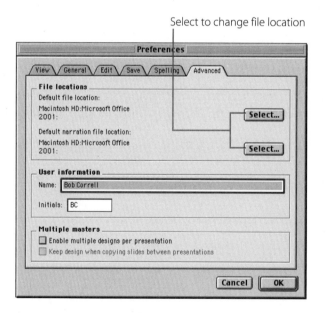

Select to change file location

Customizing Toolbars, Commands, and Appearance

As with other Office 2001 applications, you can modify PowerPoint's toolbars, commands, and overall appearance. Select the View menu, choose Toolbars, and then choose Customize to open the Customize dialog box, shown in Figure 28-10. The three tabs (Toolbars, Commands, and Appearance) allow you to modify or create new toolbars, add buttons to toolbars or menus, and choose between a MacOS Theme Compliant appearance or the default Office 2001 Appearance, respectively.

FIGURE 28-10.

The Customize dialog box allows you to modify toolbars, menus, commands, and appearances

Visible toolbars   Selected toolbar

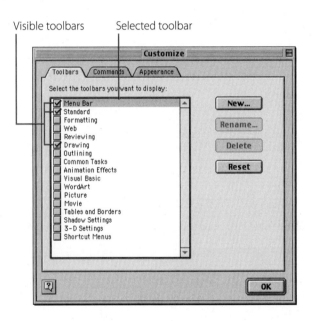

PART VI

Mastering Microsoft Office 2001

CHAPTER 29

Linking Environments via Linking and Embedding

Microsoft Office 2001 has a feature that's similar to the former Macintosh system software feature known as Publish & Subscribe. As explained in this chapter, by using *linking and embedding*, you can add text, charts, and graphic objects from Office programs (and other applications that support linking and embedding) into other Office documents.

Introducing Linking and Embedding

Think of linking and embedding as accomplishing the same task as copying and pasting, but with these bonuses:

- A copied-and-pasted item maintains no link to the original document; it is a static entity in the new document. Embedded objects become a part of the new document, but they remember where they were created. You can double-click any embedded object to edit it in the program in which it was created.

- Linked objects *do* maintain a link to the original document. If you modify the document on which the linked object was based, it can be automatically or manually updated in the new document, or you can choose to leave it unchanged.

- Linked objects aren't saved as part of the new document unless you break the link. Instead, the Office document into which they're linked makes note of the original item's location. Thus, if you need to reduce the size of your Office documents, use linking (rather than copying or embedding the material).

- Linked objects do not merge with the document. They are treated the same as a floating graphic and have handles around their edges. (See Figure 29-1.) You can move and resize an object, and—if you add it to a Word document—you can specify how the surrounding text should wrap around it.

FIGURE 29-1.

An embedded object has handles, like other objects

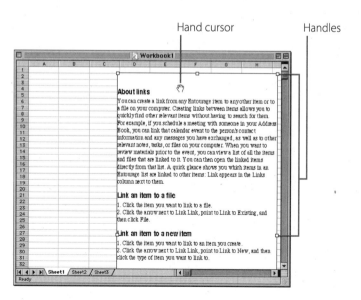

NOTE

You can link or embed objects created in any application that supports linking and embedding—not just ones from Office applications. When choosing an object to insert, Office lists all supported object types from the linking-and embedding-capable programs found on your Mac.

Other Ways to Link Office Environments

In addition to linking and embedding, Office 2001 provides the following features that enable you to commingle elements of the Office environments:

- You can insert *hyperlinks* in documents that—when clicked—fetch a particular Web page in your browser or address a new e-mail message in Microsoft Entourage.

- Any Office document can be flagged for follow-up, which sets a dated/timed reminder for you in the Entourage Calendar.

- Calendar reminders will automatically pop onscreen when launching or running *any* Office application, not just Entourage.

- Entourage enables you to link any item, such as an e-mail message, note, or task, to virtually any other item, including other Office files.

- The Entourage Address Book is also accessible from Microsoft Word.

Embedded Objects

As mentioned, embedded objects aren't linked to their original document. Even if the original document on which an object is based changes, the embedded object remains unchanged. Embedded objects, however, *do* maintain a link to the program in which they were created. If you double-click an embedded object (such as an Excel chart), the object opens for editing in the creating program and *then* reflects the change. Like linked objects, embedded objects can be created from scratch or inserted from an existing file.

VI

To insert a graphic, do not use the Object command (as explained in the following steps). Instead, open the Insert menu, choose Picture, and then choose the type of graphic you wish to insert.

To embed an object into a document, follow these steps:

1 Position the cursor at the spot in the document where you wish to insert or create an object.

2 From the Insert menu, choose Object. The Object dialog box appears, as shown in Figure 29-2.

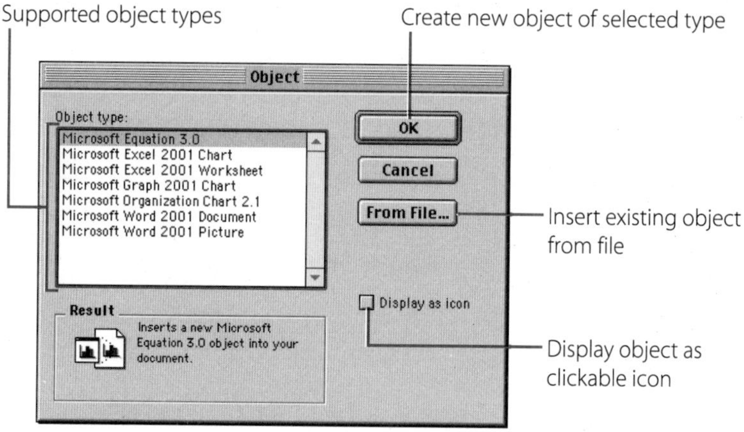

FIGURE 29-2.

Select an object to insert from the list of all installed programs that support linking and embedding

Supported object types

Create new object of selected type

Object

Object type:
Microsoft Equation 3.0
Microsoft Excel 2001 Chart
Microsoft Excel 2001 Worksheet
Microsoft Graph 2001 Chart
Microsoft Organization Chart 2.1
Microsoft Word 2001 Document
Microsoft Word 2001 Picture

OK
Cancel
From File...

Insert existing object from file

Result
Inserts a new Microsoft Equation 3.0 object into your document.

Display as icon

Display object as clickable icon

3 To create a new object from scratch, select the type of object you wish to create and click OK. The chosen object is inserted into the document.

or

To insert an object from a file, click From File. The Insert As Object dialog box appears, as shown in Figure 29-3.

4 Select a file, and click Insert. The chosen file is inserted into the document.

An object can appear as it normally would (as a worksheet, for example), or you can elect to display it as an icon that recipients of the document can double-click to view the actual object. To represent the object as an icon, click the Display As Icon check box in either the Object or Insert As Object dialog box.

FIGURE 29-3.

Select the file name of the object you want to insert

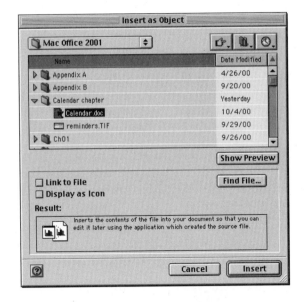

To edit an inserted object and have Word, Excel, or PowerPoint recognize that the object has changed, double-click the object. The appropriate program will automatically open. (Note that if the object is a graphic, it may open within the current Office application.)

Creating an Object from a Part of a Document

While objects are often created from entire documents, you can also create them from a part of a document. To do so, follow these steps:

1 Open the document from which you want to create the object.

2 Copy or Cut the desired part of the document, such as some selected text or an Excel chart.

3 In a Word, Excel, or PowerPoint document, click the spot where you want to insert the object.

4 From the Edit menu, choose Paste Special. The Paste Special dialog box appears, as shown in Figure 29-4.

5 To create an embedded object, click the Paste radio button. To create a linked object, click the Paste Link radio button.

6 In the As list, select the format in which the object should be pasted and then click OK.

FIGURE 29-4.

Choose a format to use for the pasted object

Create embedded object

Select format for object

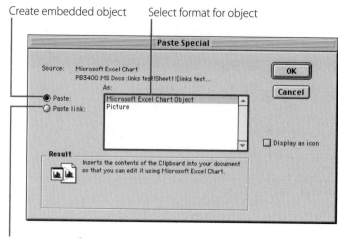

Create linked object

Linked Objects

Unlike embedded objects, linked objects can only be created from existing files. To insert an object into a Word, Excel, or PowerPoint document and link it to its original document, follow these steps:

1 Position the cursor at the spot in the document where you wish to insert the object.

2 From the Insert menu, choose Object. The Object dialog box appears, as shown in Figure 29-2.

- Click the From File button. The Insert As Object dialog box appears, as shown in Figure 29-3.

- Select a file, click the Link To File check box, and click Insert. The chosen file is inserted into the document as a linked object.

 NOTE

You can also create a linked object by opening the Insert menu and choosing File or selecting the Picture submenu and choosing From File. Then click the Link To File check box in the dialog box that appears.

Editing and Updating a Linked Object

The purpose of linking an object rather than just embedding it is that changes made in the object's originating document can be reflected in the object—that is, if you or someone on your network modifies the Excel chart on which an object has been based, the chart object will change to reflect the edits. You can open a linked object for editing by double-clicking it, opening the Links dialog box and clicking Open Source, or opening it directly from within the application in which it was created.

> **NOTE**
>
> If you try to open an object whose file has been deleted or is not available on the computer, an error message appears informing you that the object cannot be edited.

When you initially insert a linked object, it is set to update automatically whenever the originating document changes. It will do so moments after you save the original document. And whenever you open a document that contains automatically updating links, all linked objects are checked for changes at that time.

If you want, you can change any link so it updates only on your command. To do so, follow these steps:

1 From the Edit menu, choose Links. The Links dialog box appears, as shown in Figure 29-5, listing all defined links for the current document.

2 Select the link you want, and click the Manual radio button.

3 Click OK to accept the change.

FIGURE 29-5.

You can change the updating method for any link in the Links dialog box

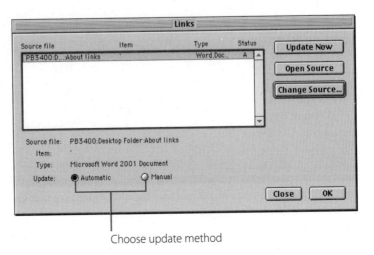

Choose update method

Once you've changed a link from automatic to manual, you must return to the Links dialog box whenever you want to update the link. Click the Update Now button, and then click OK.

You can also *break* some types of links (changing a linked object into a static, embedded object that will no longer update). Open the Edit menu, choose Links, select the link, and click the Break Link button, shown in Figure 29-6.

FIGURE 29-6.

To turn a linked object into an embedded object, click the Break Link button

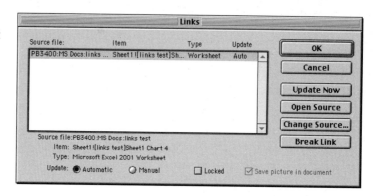

Modifying Objects

Regardless of whether an object is linked or embedded, you can move, resize, or edit it by following these directions:

- To move an object, click once to select it. The cursor changes to a hand. (See Figure 29-1.) Click the object, and drag it to a new position on the document page.

- To resize an object, click once to select it and then drag one of the handles in the desired direction. (See Figure 29-1.) Click a middle handle, and drag it to change the object's height or width. Click a corner handle, and drag it to resize the object proportionately.

- To edit an object, double-click it. The object opens in the program that created it. (If it's a graphic, it may open in the current application.) When you're finished editing, click the object document's Close box. The changes are instantly reflected in the object. (You can open a linked object in other ways, too, as described in "Editing and Updating a Linked Object" earlier in this chapter.)

CHAPTER 30

Microsoft Office 2001 and the Web

I f you have an Internet account, you'll appreciate the Web features in Microsoft Office 2001. For instance, within Microsoft Word, you can open Web pages from the Web, an intranet, or your hard disk. If you enable the Web toolbar in any Office application, you can use its features to launch Microsoft Internet Explorer and fetch a particular Web page. Other capabilities are listed starting on the following page.

Here are some other things you can do with the Web features in Office 2001.

- You can embed hypertext links in Word and Microsoft Excel documents that, when clicked, cause your—or anyone else's—default Web browser to launch and fetch the Web page. You can also embed mailto links that, when clicked, create a new e-mail message addressed to the link's recipient.

- You can insert other standard Web page items (called *HTML objects*) into Word documents, such as pictures, working buttons, and auto-scrolling text.

- You can save any Word document, Excel worksheet, or Microsoft PowerPoint presentation as one or more HTML files, suitable for posting and viewing on the Web. You can get an idea of what an Office document will look like on the Web by choosing Web Page Preview from the File menu. A Web version of the document is generated and opens in your default browser.

- You can publish your Microsoft Entourage calendar as a Web page.

- You can summon Help for Office applications from the Microsoft Web site, as explained in Chapter 2, "Microsoft Office Basics."

Opening a Web Page from the Internet

To open a Web page from the Internet in Word, open the File menu, choose Open Web Page, enter the address (also called a *URL*, or Uniform Resource Locator) of the page in the Open Web Page dialog box, and then click OK. The page is downloaded from the Internet and displayed in Word as an editable document, as shown in Figure 30-1. You can use cut-and-paste, add or delete text, and change the document's formatting, as desired. If you click a text or graphic link in the downloaded document, your default Web browser launches to fetch the page.

 TIP

> Fonts in downloaded Web pages are sometimes ridiculously small when viewed in Word. If you have difficulty reading a page, you can increase the magnification level by choosing a larger percentage from the Zoom pop-up menu in the Standard toolbar. You can also change the magnification by opening the View menu and choosing Zoom.

FIGURE 30-1.

You can view a
downloaded Web
page in Word

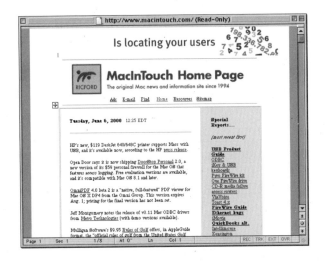

 TIP

If you want to download a Web page that you've previously downloaded with
Word, click the button at the right side of the Open Web Page dialog box and
then choose the page's address from the pop-up list.

Another way to view a Web page or create an e-mail message from
within Word, Excel, or PowerPoint is to enable the Web toolbar, shown
in Figure 30-2. You can launch Internet Explorer to view a particular
page by choosing it from the Favorites or Go pop-up menus. You can
also type the address into the Address text box and then press Enter or
Return, or you can select the address from the pop-up menu of recently
typed addresses.

VI

Mastering Microsoft Office 2001

FIGURE 30-2.

You can launch your
browser by clicking
or typing in the
Web toolbar

Go to home page

Choose from favorites

Enter/choose
Web address

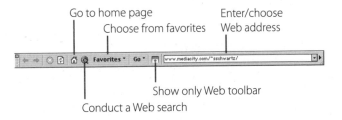

Conduct a Web search

Show only Web toolbar

Embedding Hypertext Links in Documents

Office 2001 enables you to embed hypertext links (referred to as *hyper-links* by Office) to Web pages and e-mail addresses in your documents.
When clicked, the hyperlinks perform appropriately whether the docu-
ment is viewed in Office or with a Web browser. When you pass the

cursor over an embedded hyperlink, as shown in Figure 30-3, the cursor changes to a pointing hand, indicating that the link is *active*—that is, you can click it. If you've attached explanatory text to the hyperlink (called a *ScreenTip*), the text automatically pops up when the cursor is passed over the hyperlink. The process of creating ScreenTips is discussed in the steps below.

FIGURE 30-3.

By default, embedded hyperlinks are displayed as blue, underlined text

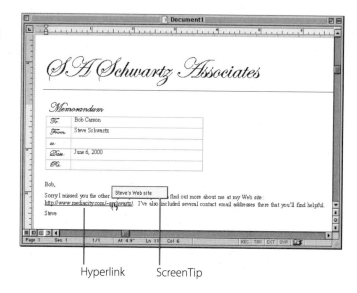

Hyperlink   ScreenTip

To add a hyperlink to a document, follow these steps:

1 Position the cursor at the spot in the document where you want to add the link.

2 From the Insert menu, choose Hyperlink (or press ⌘-K). The Insert Hyperlink dialog box appears, as shown in Figure 30-4.

3 Click the tab for the kind of hyperlink you're creating: a link to a Web Page, to a Document on your hard disk or network, or to an E-mail Address.

4 In the Link To box, enter the complete link to the Web page, Internet item, or e-mail address.

5 Web page addresses begin with *http://*, File Transfer Protocol (FTP) sites begin with *ftp://*, and e-mail addresses must be in the form *username@domain*, such as *marcia496@microsoft.com*. If you want to link to a page you've saved as one of your Internet Explorer Favorites or a recently visited page that is stored in Internet Explorer's History, click the Favorites or History buttons and choose from the list boxes.

FIGURE 30-4.

Create a Web page
hyperlink

Display this link text (rather than address)
Type or paste page address
Enter pop-up description
for the link

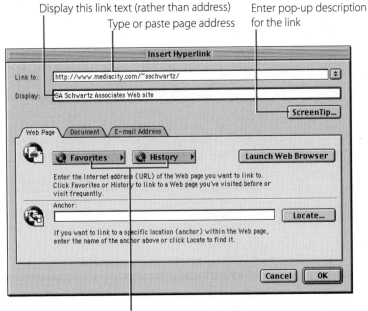

Pick a link from Favorites or History

6 If the link is to an e-mail address, enter the To address and, optionally, the message Subject in the dialog box, as shown in Figure
30-5. The proper information will automatically be transferred to
the Link To box at the top of the dialog box.

FIGURE 30-5.

Create an e-mail (or
mailto) hyperlink

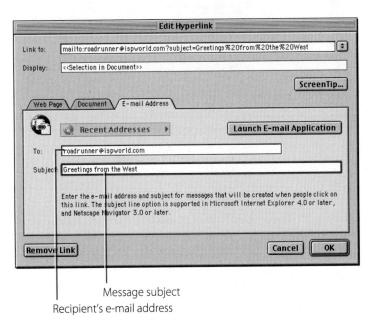

Message subject
Recipient's e-mail address

7 In the Display box, enter the text that will be displayed in the document. (By default, the display text is the Web page address or e-mail address.)

> Often, the purpose of entering a text string in the Display box is to display friendly text, such as "Steve's home page," rather than the actual page address.

8 *Optional:* To add explanatory text that will pop up when the cursor is passed over the hyperlink, click the ScreenTip button.

9 Click OK.

> You can also type hyperlinks directly into any document. As long as the text is recognized by Office as a hyperlink, Office will treat it as such. To modify settings for any embedded hyperlink, select it and choose Hyperlink from the Insert menu. To convert a hyperlink into normal (non-clickable) text, select the hyperlink, open the Insert menu, choose Hyperlink, and then click the Remove Link button in the Edit Hyperlink dialog box. (Another way to open the Edit Hyperlink dialog box is by Control-clicking the Hyperlink. In the pop-up menu that appears, choose Hyperlink, and then choose Edit Hyperlink.)

Embedding HTML Objects in Word Documents

If you intend to save a Word document as a Web page, you can insert HTML objects, such as working buttons, list boxes, and auto-scrolling text into the text. When saved as a Web page and viewed in a browser, these objects will function as they do in any other Web page you might see on the Internet.

To insert an HTML-compatible object into a document, position the cursor where you want to add the object, open the Insert menu, choose HTML Object, and then choose the object of your choice from the submenu. Fill in the information in the dialog box that appears.

Note that inserted HTML objects will not be displayed or may display incorrectly when viewed in Word. They appear and function only when the document is saved as a Web page and viewed in a browser. See the following section for instructions on saving a Word document as a Web page.

NOTE

As an alternative, you can open the File menu and choose Web Page Preview to open the document in your browser without first saving it as a Web page.

Saving a Document as a Web Page

If you have your own Web site or want to put information up on your company's intranet, you can save any Word, Excel, or PowerPoint document as a Web page (commonly called an *HTML file*). To save the current Office document as a Web page, follow these steps:

1 From the File menu, choose Save As Web Page. (An alternate way to save the current document as a Web page is to choose Save As from the File menu and choose Web Page from the Format pop-up menu in the Save dialog box.) A Save dialog box appears, as shown in Figure 30-6 and Figure 30-7.

FIGURE 30-6.

Saving a Word document as a Web page

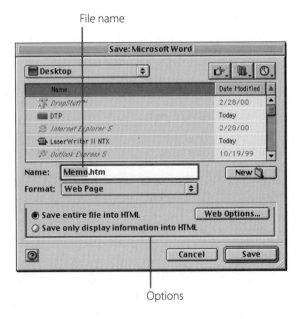

File name

Options

FIGURE 30-7.

Saving an Excel worksheet as a Web page

File name

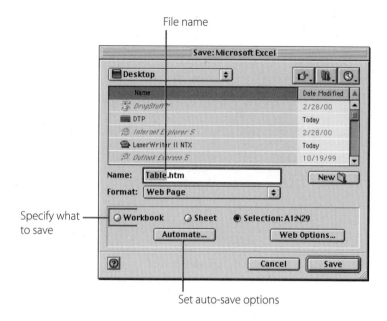

Specify what to save

Set auto-save options

2 Rename the Web page file, if you want, or accept the proposed name (*document file name*.htm).

NOTE

> Every Web page file name must end with an .htm or .html extension. Since Macs don't use extensions to identify file types, either .htm or .html is fine (although Mac Web pages frequently end with .html).

3 Select the options you want by clicking a radio button at the bottom of the dialog box and the Web Options button.

- When saving an Excel worksheet as a Web page, you can save the entire workbook, the current worksheet, or the currently selected range of cells. If you want to make sure that the saved Web page is always up-to-date, click the Automate button. Then choose to automatically save a copy as a Web page each time you do a normal save or to update the Web page on a set schedule.

- When saving a Word document as a Web page (via the Save As Web Page command), you can save in two formats. To save just the information needed to display the page properly on the Web, click the Save Only Display Information Into HTML radio button in the Save dialog box. If you believe you may later want to view or edit the document in Word with all the original Word formatting intact, click the Save Entire File Into HTML radio button.

4   Click Save.

Excel worksheets are saved as tables. PowerPoint presentations are saved as slide shows and include controls for moving from slide to slide, as shown in Figure 30-8.

FIGURE 30-8.

When viewed in a browser, PowerPoint presentations contain familiar controls

Outline controls   Slide controls

To see what Word, Excel, or PowerPoint documents will look like in a browser, open the File menu and choose Web Page Preview.

Publishing Your Calendar on the Web

If you want to share your calendar with others or simply post it on your own Web site so you can refer to it when you're on the road, at the office, or at home, you can use the Save As Web Page command to create an HTML version of it. To do so, follow these steps:

1 Launch Entourage, and choose Calendar from the Window menu.

2 From the File menu, choose Save As Web Page. The Save As Web Page dialog box appears, as shown in Figure 30-9.

FIGURE 30-9.

Set options in the Save As Web page dialog box

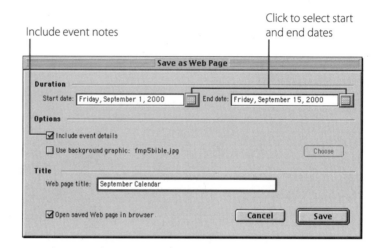

3 In the Duration section of the dialog box, click the two calendar icons to select a Start Date and End Date for your calendar.

4 In the Options section, click the Include Event Details check box if you want your appointment notes to be included in the calendar. If you want to include a background graphic, check the Use Background Graphic check box and select an image from your hard disk.

 **TIP**

Uncomplicated, light-colored graphics work best as background images. Other backgrounds may make it difficult to read your calendar.

5 In the Title section, enter a title for the Web page.

6 If you'd like to immediately view the resulting Web page in your browser (as will normally be the case), check the Open Saved Web Page In Browser check box.

7 Click Save. If you checked the check box in Step 6, your browser launches and displays the calendar, as shown in Figure 30-10.

FIGURE 30-10.

Your Entourage calendar can be saved as a detailed, clickable Web page

View next month   List of events

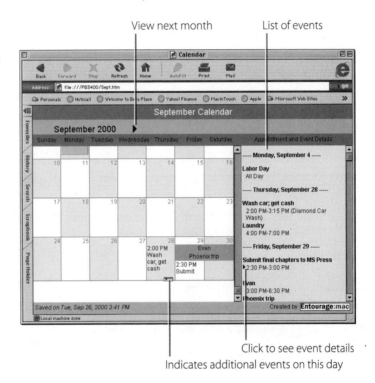

Click to see event details
Indicates additional events on this day

After creating a Web page from your calendar, you have two options:

■ You can view the calendar on this or any other computer. Copy the .htm file and the folder by the same name (SeptCalendar.htm and the SeptCalendar folder, for example) to the computer on which you want to view it. Open the .htm file on that computer using Internet Explorer or another advanced browser.

■ You can post the calendar to a Web site or company intranet. You'll need to upload the .htm file and the folder of supporting files to your Web server. Normally, this is done by using an FTP program, such as FTP Client or Fetch. Depending on where you wish to post the calendar, see your Internet service provider or systems administrator for instructions.

VI

Mastering Microsoft Office 2001

Publishing Your Calendar

If you're familiar with publishing material on the Web and have access to space on a server (such as might be provided by your company or an Internet service provider), you may want to attempt this task on your own. Here's the basic procedure:

1 Launch your FTP program, and log on to your Web server. (If you don't have an FTP program, there are freeware and shareware FTP programs available for download. Search the Macintosh section of *www.download.cnet.com*, for example.)

2 Switch to your main Web directory on the server.

3 Copy the calendar .htm file to that directory, as well as the folder of support files by the same name. (You want the folder and its contents to remain intact on the server; that is, if you have created a calendar called Sept.htm, you want the associated Sept folder to become a new directory on the server.)

4 Launch your Web browser and visit the new calendar page on the Web. Since the page is not linked to any of your other pages, you'll have to type its full address in your browser's Address box.

TIP

If your graphics aren't visible when you open your page in Internet Explorer 5, try this solution: Use an FTP program to change all the graphic .gif file names to uppercase. (An image named monthr.gif would be changed to MONTHR.GIF, for example.)

Configuring Microsoft Office in a Multi-User Setting

Although Microsoft Office 2001—like its predecessors—was not designed as a network or workgroup suite, it does have several useful network- and workgroup-relevant features that will be discussed in this chapter. For instance, multiple users can share the same copy of Office on a single computer—each maintaining a separate identity. Multiple reviewers can edit a document with each reviewer's changes distinguished from the others' changes. Also, users can open shared Office documents over a network.

Configuring Office for Multiple Users

In many settings—such as the home, office, or classroom—a single computer is sometimes shared among several users. To distinguish one user from another, each person can create an *identity*. With identities, each person's preferences, Address Book, Calendar, and e-mail are kept separate. If you share a Mac among several family members or co-workers, for example, each one can have an identity.

When you installed Office, Microsoft Entourage automatically created an identity for you. If you open the Address Book, you'll see that your name has an *i* symbol next to it, as shown in Figure 31-1, denoting that this contact card represents your identity. If you don't see this symbol, edit your contact card (or create one, if necessary), select the contact in the Address Book, and then choose This Contact Is Me from the Contact menu.

FIGURE 31-1.
Your contact record in the Address Book— your identity— is denoted by the *i* symbol

 Steven Schwartz

Microsoft Word, PowerPoint, and Excel also use identities. The active identity determines the author of the current document, as well as the person inserting comments and making revisions. When you attempt to use the Address Book to insert address information into a document, the current identity determines the Address Book that's used. If any user has set reminders for a document, identities ensure that only that person/identity receives the reminders.

 NOTE

> Identities merely provide a convenient way for multiple users of the same computer to distinguish their e-mail messages and Office documents from those of other users. Identities do *not* use passwords nor do they provide any sort of security for your data. *Any* user can access any other user's information via the Switch Identity command. If you need security, consider purchasing a program for that purpose. As an alternative, you may want to upgrade to MacOS 9, since it has built-in multi-user password and security features.

 TIP

> You can also edit your identity in Word's Preferences dialog box. Open the Edit menu, choose Preferences, and then click the User Information tab.

Creating an Identity

Follow these steps to create an identity for another user:

1 Quit all other running Office applications and launch Entourage.

2 In Entourage, open the File menu and choose Switch Identity (or press Shift-⌘-Q). The dialog box shown in Figure 31-2 appears.

FIGURE 31-2.

When switching or working with identities, Entourage closes the current user's connections with the mail and newsgroup servers

3 Click the Switch button. The dialog box shown in Figure 31-3 appears.

Whether a dialog box appears or a balloon beside the Office Assistant appears depends on whether the Office Assistant is currently enabled.

FIGURE 31-3.

All identity maintenance is done using this dialog box

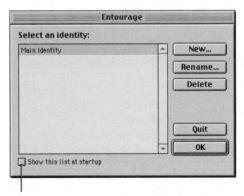

Choose an identity each time you launch

4 Click the New button to create the new identity.

5 In the dialog box that appears, enter a name for the new identity and select the initial settings you'd like to use for the identity from the pop-up menu. You can choose either the Entourage defaults or base the initial settings on another identity. Since the latter option duplicates the identity's accounts, this is useful primarily if you also share the accounts. Click OK.

6 The Entourage Setup Assistant appears. Step through the dialog boxes to enter the person's contact and e-mail information.

CAUTION

Although identities separate each user's data from everyone else's, they do not prevent one user from viewing another user's Calendar or e-mail.

Switching Identities

Think of Entourage as "identity headquarters." Not only do you use Entourage to create identities, you must also use it to switch from one identity to another. When a different user wants to take over the Mac, he or she must follow these steps:

1 Close all Office 2001 programs (except for Entourage—assuming that it is already running).

2 Launch or switch to Entourage.

3 Open the File menu, and choose Switch Identity (or press Shift-⌘-Q). The dialog boxes shown in Figure 31-2 and Figure 31-3 appear.

4 Choose an identity, and click OK. Entourage identifies the current user by displaying his or her identity name in the Entourage window's title bar.

Identity Maintenance

You can also rename identities, delete ones that are no longer needed, and decide whether Entourage should prompt for the appropriate identity each time it runs.

- To rename an identity, open the File menu and choose Switch Identity. Highlight the identity you want to rename, click Rename, enter a new name, and click OK.

- To delete an identity, open the File menu and choose Switch Identity. Highlight the identity you want to delete, click Delete, and click Yes in response to the warning you receive.

- To request that Entourage prompt you for the appropriate identity each time it is launched, open the File menu and choose Switch Identity. Click the Show This List At Startup check box, and then click OK.

NOTE

If you don't elect to choose an identity each time Entourage is launched, it automatically uses the *last* identity used.

Working with Office 2001 in Workgroups

There are no workgroup-specific features in Office 2001—that is, multiple users cannot simultaneously edit the same document. However, the following workgroup-like features are available:

- As with virtually every other type of Macintosh document, you can store Office 2001 documents in shared folders. This enables other users on the network to open, read, and—unless the document is designated as read-only—edit the documents.

- Documents can contain linked objects. For instance, a Word document could contain an Excel worksheet. When the worksheet is changed (by you or another user), the worksheet can be set to update automatically in the Word document.

- Word documents are frequently passed among several people. For example, a group could be co-writing a screenplay. Rather than having each person work on separate documents, you could pass the same document to each person and turn on the Word revision tracking feature. Other Word features that offer related capabilities include adding user comments and highlighting selected text.

Sharing Documents on a Network

The official way to share Office documents over a network is to use a Macintosh system software feature called *file sharing*. To open a file that resides on someone else's computer, several conditions must be true. First, file sharing must be enabled on the target computer. Second, the drive or folder in which the document is stored must be designated as a shared drive or folder. Third, the user who wishes to open the document must log on to the target computer. Follow these steps to use file sharing:

1. If you are currently running an application, switch to the desktop. (Choose Finder from the Application menu in the right-hand corner of the menu bar.)

2. To designate a drive or folder on the target folder as shared, click to select the drive or folder. Then from the File menu, point to Get Info and choose Sharing. An Info window appears, as shown in Figure 31-4.

VI

Mastering Microsoft Office 2001

FIGURE 31-4.

To set up sharing for a drive or folder, display its Info window

 Click here to share this item

3 Click the Share This Item And Its Contents check box.

4 Click the Info window's Close box.

NOTE

Steps 1 through 4 only need to be performed once for any folder or drive.

5 If file sharing isn't on, open the File Sharing control panel by opening the Apple menu, pointing to Control Panels, and choosing File Sharing.

6 Click the Start/Stop tab, shown in Figure 31-5. To turn on File Sharing, click the appropriate Start button.

7 Close the File Sharing control panel.

NOTE

Steps 5 through 7 need to be performed only when file sharing is off. Unless you or another application has turned it off, file sharing will automatically re-start each time you turn on or reboot your Mac.

FIGURE 31-5.

Use the File Sharing control panel to turn sharing on or off

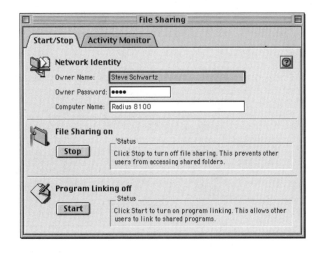

Once file sharing has been turned on, all authorized users can connect to the computer and open any document in a shared folder or drive. If you later want to end file sharing, perform steps 5 and 6 but click the Stop button.

To connect to a shared folder or drive, follow these steps (assuming that your connection isn't already open—indicated by the presence of a shared drive or folder icon on your desktop):

1 From the Apple menu, open the Chooser accessory.

2 Click the AppleShare icon on the left side of the Chooser window, shown in Figure 31-6.

FIGURE 31-6.

To connect to a network drive, start by opening the Chooser

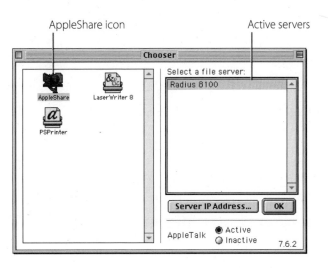

3 Select the target computer's name, and click OK. A log-on dialog box appears, as shown in Figure 31-7.

FIGURE 31-7.
This dialog box enables you to log on to the network

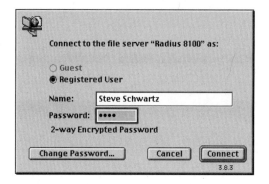

4 Log on to the computer by entering your network user name and password. Click Connect. (If you need assistance, see your network administrator.)

5 Select the drive or drives you wish to open, and then click OK.

6 Close the Chooser window. The selected drives from the target computer should be visible on your desktop. You can now use them and any shared files they contain.

A folder that has been specifically set for sharing is displayed with a special icon, as shown in Figure 31-8. However, if the entire *drive* has been set for sharing, individual folders within the drive will not have special icons—even though they can be shared also.

FIGURE 31-8.
A shared folder displays a special icon

Shared folder

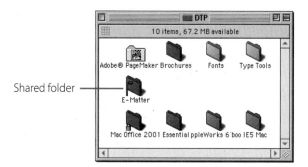

Whenever several users want to work with the same document at the same time, the first user who opens it is in charge. Although both people can freely edit the document, only the first person can save it to the same location from which it was opened.

When a second or later user attempts to open a shared document that is already open, the dialog box in Figure 31-9 appears. He or she can either open a copy of the document by clicking OK, or can click Cancel. If the second user attempts to save the copy while the original is still open, a warning is displayed and he or she must either change the document's name, save it in a different location, or abort the save.

FIGURE 31-9.

The selected document is already being edited by another user

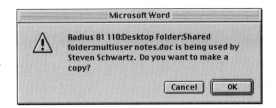

In some instances, the original user will make changes to the document, save, and then close it—while other users may still have it open. If another user attempts to save the document at that point, another dialog box appears, as shown in Figure 31-10.

FIGURE 31-10.

To avoid overwriting the previous user's changes when you save, rename the document or save it in a different folder

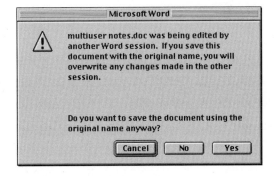

? SEE ALSO

For additional comments on sharing Office documents, see Chapter 15, "Working with Worksheets and Workbooks."

For further instructions on setting up file sharing, designating drives and folders as shared, logging on to a networked computer, and opening shared documents, see your network administrator or search MacOS Help for "networking."

As you can see, allowing multiple users to edit and save a shared document can be confusing. In addition, there is the possibility that if several people are working on the document at the same time, everyone's edits—other than those made by the last person to save it—will be lost. For this reason, it may be more prudent to turn on revision tracking and pass the document from one person to the next. This enables all users to see the changes that have been suggested by other contributors. Then one person can take responsibility for determining which changes will be accepted and which will be rejected.

VI

Mastering Microsoft Office 2001

Documents with Linked Objects

? SEE ALSO

For information on linking and embedding objects in Office documents, see Chapter 29, "Linking Environments via Linking and Embedding."

If multiple people are working on a project, you can use Office's ability to link objects to display the work of several people in a single document. Of course, you don't *need* a group to do object linking. There's nothing that says you can't be the author of all the linked objects yourself—which is probably more common.

Tracking Changes in Word

When a document is being passed between two or more people for comments and additional editing, Word provides the following features that enable all these users to insert comments, highlight important material, and determine what material has been changed—as well as who changed it:

- You can add a comment to any piece of text by highlighting the text, opening the Insert menu, choosing Comment, and then typing your comment text. When another user opens the document and passes the cursor over the commented text, the comment pops up, as shown in Figure 31-11. The reference marks for each reviewer's comments are denoted by a different color. You can see all of the document comments by opening the View menu and choosing Comments.

FIGURE 31-11.

Passing the cursor over commented text displays the comment

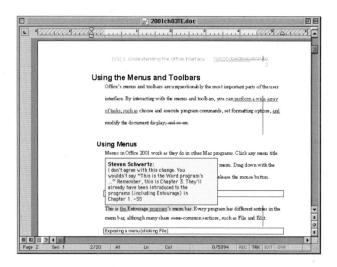

- To make passages stand out, you can highlight the text. Select the text, and then choose a highlight color from the Highlight palette in the Formatting toolbar, shown in Figure 31-12. To apply a different color highlight, click the down arrow on the right side of the Highlight button to pick a color.

FIGURE 31-12.
Select text and click the Highlight button to apply the currently chosen color

Highlight button

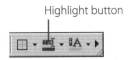

- Another way for multiple users to work on a document is for each of them to work independently on a copy of the document. Then, an editor can review everyone's edits by opening their documents, choosing Merge Documents from the Tools menu, and deciding which changes to accept and which ones to reject.

- When tracking changes is enabled, Word adds revision marks that show all insertions, deletions, and changes in formatting to the document, as shown in Figure 31-13. Each reviewer's changes are shown in a different color.

FIGURE 31-13.
Revisions are denoted by change bars, struck-through text, and underlined text

Deleted text   Inserted text   Change bar

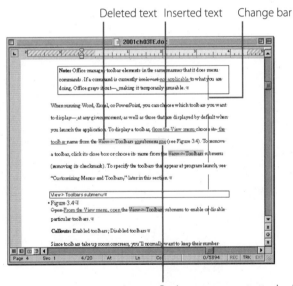

Reviewer comment attached

? SEE ALSO

For a discussion of using Word's change tracking features, see Chapter 10, "Customizing Microsoft Word," and Chapter 15.

- The Compare Documents command (found in the Track Changes submenu of the Tools menu) provides change tracking when you've forgotten to turn the feature on. If two users are working on the same document, you can compare the newer version to the older one by using this command. Revision marks appear, just as if you'd turned on change tracking.

VI

Mastering Microsoft Office 2001

Sharing Data with Other Applications

Most Microsoft Office users start out simple. The Office documents they initially create may never leave their computer. Or, if they do, they're typically in the form of a printout or fax. As users become more adept at working with Office, many recognize that their documents do not need to be created and used in a vacuum, so to speak. Office documents can contain pictures created in other applications or incorporate information from other Office documents. In addition, users discover that there's sometimes a need to share their documents with others. And other people may send them files, too.

This chapter explains how Office 2001 documents can be opened by earlier versions of Office (and vice versa); Office documents can co-exist in non-Office environments (and vice versa); and selected data can be exchanged with other documents, applications, and the Desktop.

Exchanging Files with Office Users

To keep things as simple as possible for Office users, Microsoft has retained the same file formats for Microsoft Word, Excel, and PowerPoint since Office 97. Thus, as an Office 2001 user, you'll find that—without any necessary conversions—you can open any Word, Excel, or PowerPoint document that was created in Office 97, Office 98, or Office 2000. Similarly, if you give your Office 2001 files to users of any older version of Office (from 97 through 2000), they will be able to open your files, also.

If you use any features or formatting options that are unique to Office 2001, however, those elements will be disabled when the document is opened in an earlier version of Office. If the document is later re-opened in Office 2001, those elements will be re-enabled.

 NOTE

> When you intend to give an Office file to a Windows user, you should add the appropriate three-character extension to the end of its name. For example, Word files should end with a *.doc* extension. Windows uses the extension to determine which program will open the file. When saving a file, you can instruct any of your Office 2001 applications to add the correct extension for you by clicking the Append File Extension check box in the Save dialog box, as shown in Figure 32-1. Note that the Save dialog box only appears the first time you save a new document and whenever you choose the Save As command from the File menu.

FIGURE 32-1.

You can add the correct Windows extension to a file name when you save the file

.doc extension

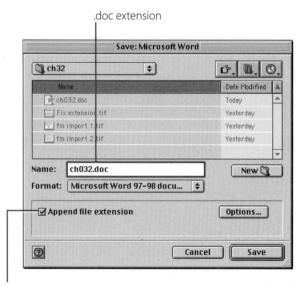

Add a Windows extension to the file name

TIP

If the recipient has a version of Office that is older than Office 97, you will still be able to read his or her files. To ensure that the recipient can also read *your* files, save a copy of each document in the version of Office that the person has, such as Word 6.0/95.

Exchanging Files with Non-Office Users

Of course, not everyone you'll want to share your Office files with will be an Office user. This section discusses several ways that you can share your files with non-Office users. The method you choose will depend on what programs the recipient has, as well as whether he or she merely wants to be able to view and print the files, or wants to edit them, too.

Office-Compatible Applications

Like Office, most competing programs save their files to disk in a proprietary format. Nevertheless, because Office is so pervasive on both the Mac and PC, many of these same programs will be able to open, import, or insert Office files into their existing documents. To see if a program can read Office files, check its documentation. You should also look for and try out the program's Open, Import, and/or Insert commands. If the program can handle Office documents in this manner, you won't have to do a thing to your files before giving or transmitting them to the recipient.

Saving a Document in an Alternative Format

On the other hand, if the recipient's program cannot read Office 2001 files, the next approach is to resave them, while in Office, as a format that the person's program *can* read. (To determine what alternative file formats a program can read—in addition to its own format—check the program's manual, as well as any Open, Import, or Insert commands.)

For example, when you issue the Save As command in Word to open the Save dialog box (as shown in Figure 32-2), you can save your document in an earlier Word format, as Rich Text, or as a Text Only document. Many word processing programs can read Rich Text documents, which will have the advantage of retaining the original formatting. Text Only documents, on the other hand, can be read by *any* word processing program or text editor.

TIP

When resaving an Office document, try to choose the most complex, feature-rich format that the intended recipient's program can interpret. For example, although Text Only documents can be read by virtually any Macintosh or Windows program, such documents will contain no fonts or character styles.

FIGURE 32-2.

In the Save dialog box, you can choose a file format from the For-mat pop-up menu

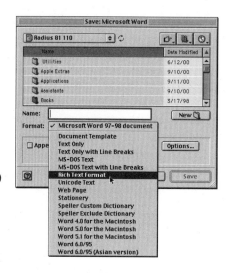

⊗ CAUTION

When When using the Save As command to resave a document in a different format, be sure to give the file a different name or ex-tension, or save it to a different folder on your hard disk! Other-wise, you will over-write your original document.

Some users may also have *file translation software* installed on their computer. On the Mac, for instance, DataViz (*www.dataviz.com*) sells a utility called MacLinkPlus that enables programs to open many types of Mac and Windows documents, as well as to export or save in those same formats. If the recipient uses MacLinkPlus or a similar Mac or PC utility, ask the person which translators it includes and then resave your Office documents in one of those supported formats.

⍰ SEE ALSO

For instructions on saving a Word, Excel, or PowerPoint file as a Web page, see Chapter 30, "Microsoft Office 2001 and the Web."

Saving a Document as a Web Page

Since most computers have a Web browser installed (such as Microsoft Internet Explorer or Netscape Navigator), you can open the File menu in several of the Office 2001 applications and choose the Save As Web Page command to create an HTML file that can be opened, viewed, and printed in any browser. Note that the recipient does *not* need to be connected to the Internet when opening such a Web page.

NOTE

Some browsers—such as recent versions of Microsoft Internet Explorer—will allow you to copy text from a Web page and paste it into another application (such as a word processor). Although this will indeed enable the user to edit the text, this is far from an ideal method of making editable data available to someone. A better approach is to simply save the file in an editable format that the user's software can handle—as described earlier in this chapter in the "Saving a Document in an Alternative Format" section.

? **SEE ALSO**

For details on creating a QuickTime Movie from a PowerPoint presentation, see Chapter 27, "Managing and Conducting Presentations."

Creating a QuickTime Movie

This view-only solution is available only to PowerPoint users. By choosing the Make Movie command from the File menu, you can convert a presentation into a QuickTime movie that is viewable on a Mac or a PC. Of course, the recipient must have an appropriate movie viewer installed, such as QuickTime Player or Movie Player (Mac), or Windows Media Player (PC).

Importing Non-Office Documents into Office

Getting your files to another person in a format in which they can be read is an easier task than doing the reverse—that is, opening or inserting non-Office documents into Office. If a friend or colleague needs you to be able to open his or her non-Office word processing or spreadsheet document in your copy of Office, ask him or her to save the document as a Word or Excel file, if possible. If that isn't an option, check the Word and Excel Open dialog boxes for file formats they can read. If your colleague doesn't have one of the supported programs, perhaps he or she can still resave the file in one of the supported formats. (Word can open some AppleWorks 5 word processing documents and plain text files. Excel can open Lotus 1-2-3 files and some AppleWorks 5 word processing documents.) If you think you'll regularly receive non-Office documents, there are two other solutions. First, have the other person purchase Office. Second, one of you can buy file translation software.

 TIP

Although the Open dialog box doesn't list it as a supported file format, Excel can also open Web pages (HTML files).

Inserting Items into Office Documents

By choosing commands from the Word, Excel, and PowerPoint Insert menus, you can add graphics (art from Office's Clip Gallery or your own images), movies, and text files to a document.

To insert a text file into an existing Word document, follow these steps:

1 Move the cursor to the spot in the document where you want to insert the new text.

2 From the Insert menu, choose File.

3 In the Insert File dialog box, shown in Figure 32-3, select the file and click Insert. You can limit the file list to one type of file by choosing it from the Show pop-up menu.

FIGURE 32-3.

Select a file to insert into the current document

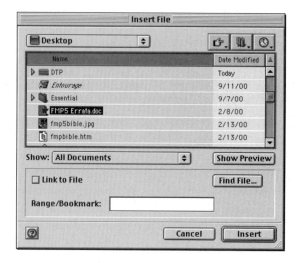

To insert a picture or clip art image into a Word, Excel, or PowerPoint document, position the cursor where you want the image to be inserted, open the Insert menu, select Picture, and then choose either Clip Art or From File.

- If you selected Clip Art, the Clip Gallery appears, as shown in Figure 32-4. Choose an image, and click Insert.

- If you selected From File, the Choose A Picture dialog box appears, as shown in Figure 32-5. Select any supported image file, and click Insert.

FIGURE 32-4.

Office includes an extensive array of clip art that you can use in your documents

FIGURE 32-5.

To help you select the correct image, the Choose A Picture dialog box can also show a preview of the picture

Preview

Show/hide image preview

 NOTE

If you click the Link To File check box in the Choose A Picture dialog box and later modify the inserted picture, Office will automatically update the document to show the revised image.

To insert a QuickTime-compatible movie or audio track into a Word or Excel document, position the cursor where you want the movie to be inserted, open the Insert menu, select Movie, and then choose the movie file that you want to insert.

VI

Mastering Microsoft Office 2001

To insert a movie into a PowerPoint presentation, switch to the appropriate slide, open the Insert menu, open the Movies And Sounds submenu, and choose either Movie From Gallery or Movie From File. (Choose Movie From Gallery if you previously saved the movie into the Clip Gallery. Choose Movie From File if the movie is stored on your hard disk.)

 **NOTE**

Many blank PowerPoint slides contain areas that are reserved for graphics or movies. To insert a graphic or movie into such a slide, double-click the appropriate area, shown in Figure 32-6.

FIGURE 32-6.

You can double-click where indicated to insert a movie into a PowerPoint slide

Double-click to add a media clip

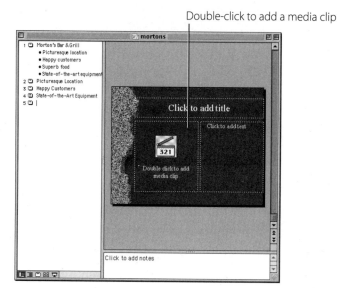

Using Drag-and-Drop

Office 2001 applications do an exceptional job of supporting *drag-and-drop*, a Mac system software feature. When an application is drag-and-drop–enabled, you can do any of the following:

- Drag selected text or objects from one place in a document to a different place. (This performs the equivalent of a cut and paste.)

- Drag selected text or objects from one open Office document into another. (This copies the selected items to the second document).

- Drag selected text or objects from a document onto the Desktop, creating a clippings file. (This copies the selected items to a new file on the Desktop. You can open any clippings file by double-clicking its icon.)

- Drag text or objects from other open applications that are drag-and-drop–enabled into the current Office document. (This copies the selected items into the Office document). You can also use this procedure to copy items in Office documents into the documents of other applications.

- Drag a clippings file from the Desktop into an open Office document.

- Drag the desktop icons of other compatible files (such as JPG graphics, for example) from the Desktop into an open Office document. (This performs the equivalent of opening the Insert menu and choosing the appropriate command, such as File.)

 TIP

If you simply want to open a non-Office document in an Office application (rather than inserting it into an existing document), you can try dragging the document's icon onto the Office application's icon. If Office can understand the file format used by the document, the Office application's icon will turn dark, the program will launch, and the document will open. (Of course, you can also determine if the document is compatible with Office by using the Open command within the Office application and trying to open the file.)

Importing FileMaker Pro Data into Excel

Because of FileMaker Pro's popularity on both Macs and PCs, Microsoft made special efforts to ensure that Excel could translate FileMaker databases into worksheets—enabling users to do additional processing of selected data, such as creating charts and performing advanced calculations. To open a FileMaker Pro 5 database in Excel, follow the steps on the following page. (Note that the import procedure requires that FileMaker Pro be installed on the same machine as Office.)

VI

1 **If you already have a worksheet open in which you want to insert FileMaker Pro data:** From Excel's Data menu, open the Get External Data menu and choose Import From FileMaker Pro. In the Choose A Database dialog box, select the database and click Open.

or

If you want to create a new worksheet from a FileMaker Pro database: From Excel's File menu, choose Open. In the Open dialog box, click the Show pop-up menu and choose FileMaker Pro Files. Navigate to the drive and folder that contains the FileMaker Pro database, select it, and click the Open button.

2 In either case, FileMaker Pro launches and opens the database. The FileMaker Import wizard appears, as shown in Figure 32-7.

FIGURE 32-7.

The opening dialog box for the FileMaker Import wizard

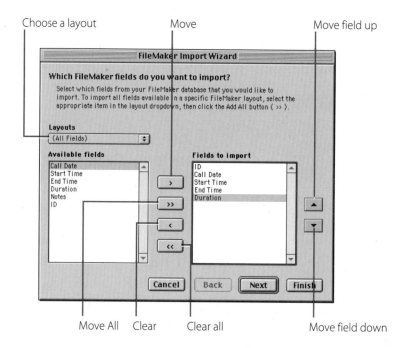

3 To restrict the field list to those fields that are used in a particular layout, choose the layout name from the Layouts pop-up menu. As an alternative, choose (All Fields) to list every field that was defined in the database—regardless of whether it is used in one, several, all, or no layouts.

4 Select fields to import by choosing them in the Available Fields list and clicking the Move (>) button—transferring it to the Fields To Import list. To choose all fields for the selected layout simultaneously, click the Move All (>>) button. To delete a field from the Fields To Import list, select it and click Clear (<). To delete all fields from the Fields To Import list simultaneously, click the Clear All (<<) button.

5 Fields will be imported into Excel in the order in which they appear in the Fields To Import list. To change a field's position in the list, select it and click the Move Up (^) button or the Move Down (v) button.

6 If you'd like to import only a subset of records, click the Next button and continue with step 7. To import all records, click Finish and go to step 8.

7 You can specify up to three criteria for selecting records to import, as shown in Figure 32-8. To indicate that multiple criteria must all be fulfilled, click the And radio buttons. To indicate that *any* of the criteria must be fulfilled, click the Or radio buttons. Click the Finish button.

FIGURE 32-8.

You can specify the records you want to import

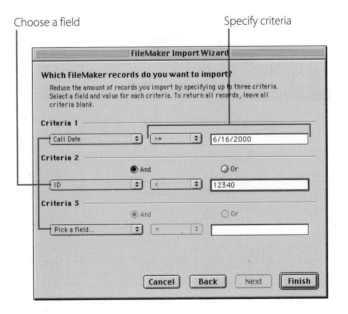

Choose a field   Specify criteria

8 If you began this process by opening the FileMaker Pro database with the Open command, the database is automatically imported into a new worksheet.

or

If you opened the database using the Get External Data command, the dialog box shown in Figure 32-9 appears.

FIGURE 32-9.

This dialog box appears when you initiate the FileMaker conversion process by using the Get External Data command

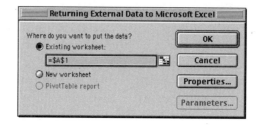

9 You can respond in either of these ways:

- Click the Existing Worksheet radio button, and type the starting cell address in the form shown (or simply click the starting cell).

- Click the New Worksheet radio button to import the database into a new worksheet.

10 To complete the process, click OK.

 NOTE

FileMaker Pro can also open Excel worksheets via its Open command. A similar series of dialog boxes appears. For additional instructions, refer to the FileMaker Pro 5 documentation and Help.

Installing and Updating Microsoft Office 2001

This appendix briefly discusses installing and updating Office 2001. It also explains how to install Microsoft Internet Explorer 5, the Web browser included with Office 2001.

Installing Microsoft Office 2001

Installing Office 2001 consists of three basic steps: copying the Office 2001 applications to your hard disk, installing optional Value Pack add-on software, and running Microsoft Office First Run to install Microsoft system software components. To install Office 2001, follow these steps:

1 Insert the Microsoft Office 2001 CD into your CD-ROM drive. Open the CD's window (if it doesn't open by itself), shown in Figure A-1.

FIGURE A-1.

Contents of the Office 2001 CD

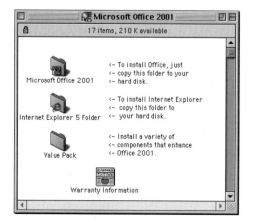

2 Review the installation instructions and compatibility notes in the Read Me folder (found inside the Microsoft Office 2001 folder.) The Read Me files open in SimpleText (a text-editing program from Apple Computer). Read the documents, and then choose Quit from the File menu (or press ⌘-Q).

3 To install Office 2001, drag the Microsoft Office 2001 folder from the CD onto the hard disk of your choice.

4 To install optional add-on software, assistants, templates, and fonts from the CD, double-click the Value Pack folder to open its window. (See Figure A-2.)

FIGURE A-2.

The Value Pack window

Double-click to install Value Pack items

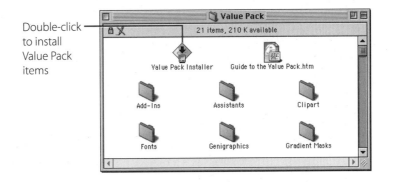

5 Double-click the Value Pack Installer. The Value Pack Installer dialog box appears, as shown in Figure A-3.

FIGURE A-3.

The Value Pack Installer dialog box

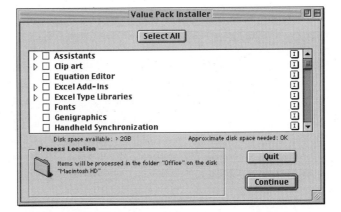

6 Select items to install by clicking their check boxes (or click Select All to select all items simultaneously). To view a brief description of an item, click the *I* (Information) box to the right of the item. You can click the triangle icons to expand the item categories, enabling you to view and install items selectively within a category.

7 Click the Continue button. After the selected items have been installed, a dialog box will appear. Depending on the options installed, you may be asked to restart your Mac by clicking the Restart button. Otherwise, click Quit.

8 To complete the installation, run any of the main Office 2001 programs: Word, Excel, or PowerPoint. Microsoft Office First Run automatically launches and copies essential Microsoft software into the System Folder.

Installing Microsoft Internet Explorer 5

Installing Office and the Value Pack does *not* install Internet Explorer 5. If you'd like to use Internet Explorer 5 as your Web browser, you can install it by copying the Internet Explorer 5 folder from the CD to your hard disk. (Refer to Figure A-1.) To complete the installation, launch Internet Explorer from your hard disk by double-clicking its icon. The first time you run Internet Explorer, Microsoft Internet First Run automatically copies a series of important files into your System Folder.

If you've already installed Internet Explorer 5—by downloading it from the Internet or obtaining a copy from your Internet service provider, for example—there is no reason for you to install this copy. The software hasn't changed.

Updating Office 2001

Periodically, Microsoft releases free updates to Microsoft Office. These updates may consist of useful add-on software or fixes for problems. To check for updates, launch your Web browser (Internet Explorer or another browser) and go to *www.microsoft.com/mac/products/office/2001/default.asp*, shown in Figure A-4. Any updates for Office applications will be listed on this page. Be sure to download only updates to *your* version of Microsoft Office 2001.

FIGURE A-4.

The Microsoft Macintosh Office home page

Index

About the Authors

Dr. Steven Schwartz is a psychologist and a veteran of the computer industry. He has written about end-user computing since the early days of the Apple II. In the past 22 years, Steven has written more than 40 books and hundreds of articles for popular computer magazines. His most recent Macintosh books include *Internet Explorer 5 for Macintosh: Visual QuickStart Guide* (Peachpit Press, 1999), *MacWorld AppleWorks 6 Bible* (IDG Books, 2000), and *FileMaker Pro 5 Bible* (IDG Books, 1999). Formerly, he was the methodologist and Editor-in-Chief of *Software Digest* and the technical services director for Funk Software. He currently writes articles for *MacWorld* and *PCWorld.com* and is the business applications editor for *The Macintosh Bible* (Peachpit Press).

Bob Correll and his wife, Anne, live in rural Indiana. Bob received a B.S. in History from the U.S. Air Force Academy. After serving for seven years as an Air Force Intelligence Officer, Bob worked for Macmillan Computer Publishing as a software development specialist and later as a development editor. He then joined the technology staff of an Indiana school district, where he provided Macintosh training and technical support. He now writes full-time and has contributed to several titles, including the *Microsoft Windows 2000 Professional Bible* (IDG Books, 2000). He is the author of *CliffsNotes: Creating Your First Web Site with Microsoft FrontPage 2000* (Cliffs Notes, 2000).

Colophon

The manuscript for this book was prepared and submitted to Microsoft Press in electronic form. Text files were prepared using Microsoft Word 2000. Pages were composed using Adobe PageMaker 6.52 for Windows, with text in Garamond and display type in Myriad. Composed pages were sent to the printer as electronic prepress files.

Cover Designer

Patrick Lanfear

Principal Electronic Artist

Joel Panchot

Principal Compositors

Carl Diltz, Barb Levy

Principal Copy Editor

Holly M. Viola

Indexer

Shane-Armstrong Information Systems

OWNER REGISTRATION CARD

Register Today!

0-7356-0971-3

Return the bottom portion of this card to register today.

Running Microsoft® Office 2001 for Mac®

FIRST NAME   MIDDLE INITIAL   LAST NAME

INSTITUTION OR COMPANY NAME

ADDRESS

CITY   STATE   ZIP

(   )

E-MAIL ADDRESS   PHONE NUMBER

U.S. and Canada addresses only. Fill in information above and mail postage-free.
Please mail only the bottom half of this page.

For information about Microsoft Press®

products, visit our Web site at

mspress.microsoft.com